THE MARKET RESEARCH TOOLBOX

FOURTH EDITION

SAGE was founded in 1965 by Sara Miller McCune to support the dissemination of usable knowledge by publishing innovative and high-quality research and teaching content. Today, we publish more than 750 journals, including those of more than 300 learned societies, more than 800 new books per year, and a growing range of library products including archives, data, case studies, reports, conference highlights, and video. SAGE remains majority-owned by our founder, and after Sara's lifetime will become owned by a charitable trust that secures our continued independence.

Los Angeles | London | Washington DC | New Delhi | Singapore | Boston

THE MARKET RESEARCH TOOLBOX

A Concise Guide for Beginners

FOURTH EDITION

Edward F. McQuarrie
Santa Clara University

Los Angeles | London | New Delhi
Singapore | Washington DC | Boston

Los Angeles | London | New Delhi
Singapore | Washington DC | Boston

FOR INFORMATION:

SAGE Publications, Inc.
2455 Teller Road
Thousand Oaks, California 91320
E-mail: order@sagepub.com

SAGE Publications Ltd.
1 Oliver's Yard
55 City Road
London EC1Y 1SP
United Kingdom

SAGE Publications India Pvt. Ltd.
B 1/I 1 Mohan Cooperative Industrial Area
Mathura Road, New Delhi 110 044
India

SAGE Publications Asia-Pacific Pte. Ltd.
3 Church Street
#10-04 Samsung Hub
Singapore 049483

Copyright © 2016 by SAGE Publications, Inc.

Printed in the United States of America.

A catalog record of this book is available from the Library of Congress.

ISBN 978-1-4522-9158-1

This book is printed on acid-free paper.

Acquisitions Editor: Maggie Stanley
Supervising eLearning Editor: Katie Bierach
Editorial Assistant: Nicole Mangona
Production Editor: Bennie Clark Allen
Copy Editor: Terri Lee Paulsen
Typesetter: C&M Digitals (P) Ltd.
Proofreader: Susan Schon
Indexer: Wendy Allex
Cover Designer: Scott Van Atta
Marketing Manager: Liz Thornton

SFI label applies to text stock

15 16 17 18 19 10 9 8 7 6 5 4 3 2 1

BRIEF CONTENTS

CONTENTS

———•••••———

PREFACE

———•◦•◦•———

This book is aimed at managers and business people. I assume that
however accomplished in your own field—computer engineering,
perhaps—and however experienced in business, you approach the topic of
market research as a beginner. The aim, then, is an initial orientation, a guided
tour of the topic—an overview.

Until this book came along, the manager seeking such a briefing had few
good options: (1) purchase a bona fide market research textbook, up to 1,000
pages in length, and try to extract what you need; (2) purchase a series of
small volumes on specific market research techniques, aimed at specialists
and often written at an advanced level, and try to integrate these accounts on
your own; (3) put your faith in a consultant and their research technique of
choice; or (4) wing it.

The goal, then, is a *thin* volume intended to provide an *overview* to the
interested reader seeking a place to *begin*. My assumption is that you need to
get your bearings (What is conjoint analysis anyway?), or maybe to conduct
some market research (Would a focus group make sense here?), or perhaps to
interpret a market research effort that someone else has championed (Can I
trust the results of this survey?).

I want to emphasize that this book is written primarily for *decision makers*. In tone, manner, and approach, the envisioned reader is a manager who
has to decide whether to do market research, what objectives to pursue, and
what specific kind of research to implement. This is not a standard textbook,
as a glance through the pages will make clear: it lacks the boxed inserts, the
snazzy graphics, and the chunking of text into bite-size morsels expected in
that marketplace. And as will soon be apparent, it doesn't read like a textbook:
the tone is direct and the style more oral than written.

Instead, the treatment strives to be concrete and specific: Do this. Don't do that. Watch out for this problem. Try this solution. The guiding idea is that managers are impatient people subject to conflicting demands who must act now. This book offers a practical approach addressed to their needs.

On the other hand, the book has been used successfully for many years at diverse educational levels, often as a supplemental reading, and this fourth edition includes a number of adaptations to address its use in a classroom (see "Note on Pedagogy," below). In my view, because of its intended focus on adult learners, it is best adapted to an MBA course aimed at working professionals, or to similarly targeted Executive Education offerings. The instructional materials that accompany the book assume an MBA class setting and further assume that the book will be combined with other readings and with Harvard-style cases. The book has also been used at the undergraduate level, but here the instructor should have a definite reason for not adopting a conventional market research textbook (i.e., distaste for that style or the typical topic coverage), and a plan to supplement this book with other material. Whatever the level, the more the class consists of adult learners with some business experience the more successful this book is likely to be.

In this fourth edition I have tried to keep these two audiences clearly in mind, labeling certain content as aimed at the one or the other, and incorporating some pedagogical material into the text, so that the nonstudent reader can grapple with it if he or she chooses to do so.

* * *

This book is distinctive in one other way: It focuses on business-to-business and technology examples. Modern market research as we know it was pioneered in the early middle of the 20th century to meet the needs of companies like Procter & Gamble, Quaker Oats, and Ralston Purina. Soap, cereal, pet food, and the like continue to be prominent among the examples and illustrations used to teach market research in the typical university course. This is entirely appropriate for textbooks aimed at a broad audience because consumer packaged-goods companies continue to spend large sums on market research and to provide many of the career opportunities in market research. However, living in California's Silicon Valley, my experience base is different. The research problems with which I am familiar preoccupy companies like Hewlett-Packard, Apple Computer, Cisco, and Oracle. Markets may be small and concentrated, products are often complex and expensive, customer expenditures are driven by the need to solve real business problems, and technologies are dynamic and rapidly chang-ing. Although much of the accumulated wisdom of market research is just as relevant to Hewlett-Packard as to Procter & Gamble, I have found it has to be taught differently. The readers I have in mind are impatient with examples based on the marketing of soap. They don't want to have to make the translation from mass markets, simple products, and stable technologies to their own rather dif-ferent situation.

If you fall within the core audience for this book, then you are a beginner and not a specialist. One of the important contributions of the book is to direct you to further reading. There exists an enormous amount of specialized mate-rial on market research. Part of my job is to help you sort through it so you can find the next book you need to read. If you intend to execute a particular market research project yourself, you certainly will need to read more than this book—for the sake of brevity, this book won't go into a great deal of depth on any single technique but will merely open the toolbox and explain its contents and application. This book *will* tell you what a hammer is, what it does to a nail, when it is useful to drive nails, and when you might be better off using a bolt and wrench, but it won't train you to do carpentry. The assumption throughout is that "carpenters" (experts) are available to you. Thus, the focus can be on the background context and the questions that need to be asked *before* you hire a carpenter (or embark on your self-taught career as a carpenter).

In summary, the target audience for the book is a person who has estab-lished him- or herself in business but who has never had occasion to take a course on market research—or, perhaps, any business course. Now in your new position the buzzwords come flying, budgets are under review, and the question presses: "What the heck is market research, anyway?"

PLAN OF THE BOOK

Part I describes how to think about market research in the context of business decisions. Market research is only a *means to the end* of business success. It aids in but can never guarantee the achievement of profit. Market research almost always costs money—hard, assignable dollars that come out of an individual manager's budget. Therefore, like any investment, market research has to be justified in terms of an expected return. Part I answers questions about what market research is, what kinds of market research techniques exist, what objectives can be met by market research, and what payoff to expect from market research. The purpose of Part I is to equip you with the necessary vocabulary and organizing concepts to think intelligently about how market research might assist you in your own situation.

Part II describes two archival research techniques: use of secondary data, and application of what is typically called "Big Data." The latter chapter is new to this fourth edition. The unifying theme of Part II is that here you do not need to collect data—it has already been compiled. The task is to figure out what to do with this data, and more particularly to examine whether it could save you the time and expense of collecting data yourself. All of the chapters in Parts III and IV, by contrast, presume that you have taken archival data as far as it can go, and that wasn't far enough, forcing you to go out and collect new data.

Part III introduces the two major qualitative research techniques in use today: customer visits and focus groups. The overview puts these two techniques in the context of other qualitative research techniques. Subsequent chapters discuss interview design and sampling issues that are common across all qualitative research techniques.

Part IV presents the major quantitative research techniques in use today, beginning with the technique most familiar to beginners to market research: the survey. Separate chapters discuss issues of questionnaire design, sampling, and data analysis. This part also includes two chapters on experimental methods in common use in commercial market research.

The departure from the conventional textbook approach is most stark in the case of Part IV. The typical market research textbook, whether undergraduate or graduate, devotes hundreds of pages to sampling theory and to the statistical analysis of data. The goal in this book is more limited: to provide the briefest possible introduction to these foundational skills consistent with providing useful insights for the managerial reader. The fact of the matter is that most managers will outsource to specialists the tasks of drawing a sample and analyzing the data. Nonetheless, managers are responsible for selecting these specialists and vetting the results of their efforts. The chapters on sampling and data analysis aim only to give a manager in that situation a leg up.

In Part V the first chapter describes how market research techniques can be combined to address a major business decision, and then steps back to assess the boundary conditions on market research. The goal of the first chapter in this section is twofold: first, to link individual research techniques to the business problems for which they are best suited; and second, to show how multiple research techniques can be combined over time to address large-scale business problems. That is, execution of a single market research technique may be sufficient to answer some specific question or to close some narrowly defined knowledge gap. However, most substantial business challenges, such as selecting a new market to enter or deciding where new product development efforts should be focused, require the application of multiple research techniques in sequence over time. Thus, the initial chapter in Part V gives examples of how techniques can be combined and sequenced. The final chapter wraps up the book by considering some particular cases, representative of a large number of business situations, where market research may be neither possible nor pertinent. It circles back to the basic theme of the book: Managers are people who have to make decisions under conditions of uncertainty. Sometimes market research can reduce uncertainty to a manageable level; sometimes it cannot. The manager still has to decide, research or no.

WHO SHOULD READ THIS BOOK?

Product Manager–Marketing

You may already have a business education, perhaps an MBA, and may even have one or more market research courses under your belt. If so, this book provides a refresher course, reinforcing your grasp of basic principles now that your schooling lies years in the past. Perhaps more important, it provides a resource that you can give to members of your work group in order to bring them up to speed on the contribution of market research generally and the rationale for individual research techniques. Especially in technology firms, market research won't get done—or worse, won't get used—unless multiple constituencies outside the product management function accept the need for and value delivered by market research. Thus, this book can help to elevate the discussion of research issues in your work group. Finally, if you are in a business-to-business (B2B) or technology firm, you may also find this book helpful in linking your business education, which may have emphasized packaged-goods examples, to your current job, with its rather different imperatives.

R&D Project Manager

You have the responsibility to create and design what the firm offers, with development of a new product the clearest example. It is your job to marshal people and resources to achieve a project goal. Today, that includes doing market research. Although you can reasonably expect considerable assistance from marketing staff, the effectiveness of the market research done for you will often be a crucial determinant of the project's success; hence, there is a limit to how much you can delegate in this area. You will probably be among the most intent and focused readers of this book inasmuch as when you finish, you will have to *act:* to request a budget, spend money, commit employee time. This book tries to answer as many of your questions as possible.

Quality Professional

Your charge today is customer satisfaction, not defect minimization. Depending on the culture of your firm, you may have assumed responsibilities classically assigned to the marketing function, for instance, building a commitment to customer satisfaction on the part of employees throughout the firm. You have solid statistical training but have grown uneasy about the heavy reliance on surveys commonly found within the quality literature. This book helps you to grasp the possibilities inherent in the whole toolbox. It also helps you to think about statistics in the context of social science—that is, the behavior of humans—rather than the production context where your statistical education probably began.

Executive

You are at a level where business strategy is set. Like many contemporary executives, you are probably receptive to the idea that being market focused is important, but, also like many, you are not entirely sure how this laudable goal can be implemented in a timely and cost-effective manner. For you, this book serves two purposes. It provides a briefing and reminder of what market research can and cannot do (this is particularly helpful if your background is technical and not business based), and it provides a resource you can recommend to your people and to the training function within your firm.

Instructor

You may be considering this book for use as a supplement in courses on product planning, customer analysis, competitor analysis, B2B marketing, and the like. These are courses that often include a project or other activity where students must gather data or make recommendations about data gathering. You've often wished there was a book you could assign as supplemental reading that would help students think about how to gather market data (including where to find additional information on specific research techniques). Until finding this book, you faced the unpalatable alternatives of (1) expecting them to find on their own a comprehensive market research textbook and read the appropriate sections (because you can't assume that your students have necessarily taken a market research course); or (2) hoping they will find, assemble, and read specialist volumes on focus groups, surveys, and so forth, and then make an intelligent choice among them; or (3) scheduling enough office hours to help students work through the above issues.

Instructors who adopt this book can obtain a sample syllabus along with a guide to selecting and teaching cases to accompany the book by visiting **www .sagepub.com/mcquarrie**. If you do assign this book in your class, I'd be interested to hear about your experiences—e-mail me at emcquarrie@scu.edu.

A NOTE ON PEDAGOGY

Because the book has frequently been used in classroom settings, I've added some pedagogical elements to this fourth edition to facilitate that use. Even if you are reading this as an independent professional, you may be able to use this material to engage more actively the content of the book.

- Near the end of each chapter I've listed several discussion questions or exercises. These are meant to stimulate reflection, not foreclose it. For most of these questions, there is no short answer, and for many of them, there is no straightforward or obvious "right" answer. Their purpose is to deepen understanding. My metric in writing these was, Could I use this as an essay question on a final exam? Or, Could I use it to engage an MBA class of working professionals in an extended discussion?

- After over thirty years in the classroom, it is nearly impossible for me to teach a marketing class without placing heavy reliance on Harvard cases. Hence, at the end of each part you will find the cases that I use when teaching market research to MBA students at Santa Clara University. The purpose of these cases is to provide extended, vivid examples of the kind of market research planning decisions faced by actual managers.
- For each of these cases, I give a brief synopsis, generally with a different focus than what Harvard supplies on its website (http://hbsp.harvard .edu), where the complete case can be purchased. The goal is to show how this case can be used in a class that also uses *Toolbox*. Not all of these cases were originally designed to be "market research" cases, and my use of them may not reflect the intentions of their authors.
- After each case I supply questions to guide students' reading. These are also the kind of questions that I use to structure class discussion of the case.
- In a few instances, there will also be fictional cases that I wrote, and the full text of these is included.
- Finally, at the end of each chapter there are suggested readings. In most cases, these are more in-depth or specialized readings that can help you go beyond the introductory treatment provided in this book. Annotations explain what each suggested reading might accomplish for you.

ACKNOWLEDGMENTS

I received all of my training in market research "in the field," and I'd like to acknowledge some of the individuals and firms from whom I learned the most. Particular thanks go to Nick Calo, Mike Kuhn, Ron Tatham, and many others at Burke Marketing Research, where I got my start moderating focus groups and doing copy tests of advertisements; to Dave Stewart of the University of Southern California and Bill BonDurant of Hewlett-Packard's Market Research and Information Center, for introducing me to best practices in the planning of market research; to Lew Jamison and Karen Thomas at Sun Microsystems, for inviting me to design a course on market research, thus giving me the confidence to attempt this book; and to Klaus Hoffmann and Tomas Lang, of HP

Marketing Education in Europe, for the initial opportunity to teach marketing research to managers. In more recent years, I'd like to acknowledge Richard Mander and Sandra Lukey for opportunities to teach on these topics in New Zealand, Alex Cooper and Tracey Kimball of Management Roundtable for opportunities to reach a broader spectrum of professionals and managers, Chris Halliwell for insight into market research and new product development, and John Chisholm, formerly of CustomerSat, for stimulating discussions about survey research in the age of the Internet. I also want to thank the editor for the first edition, Marquita Flemming at Sage, for actually giving me the impetus; Al Bruckner at Sage, editor for the second edition, for encouraging a revision; Deya Jacobs, for believing enough in the merits of the book to encourage a third edition; and Pat Quinlan and Maggie Stanley for bringing this fourth edition to fruition. Over the years, I've benefitted from discussions with many of my colleagues in the marketing department at Santa Clara, beginning with Shelby McIntyre and continuing most recently with stimulating discussions of the limitations of market research with Kirthi Kalyanam and Kumar Sarangee. I would also like to thank the following individuals who assisted in the preparation of the manuscript through their careful and thoughtful reviews: Stacey Barlow Hills, Southern Vermont College–Bennington; Vaidas Lukosius, Tennessee State University–Nashville; Christopher P. Hogan, University of Chicago–Chicago; Dennis Devlin, University of Cincinnati–Cincinnati; Ronald E. Goldsmith, Florida State University–Tallahassee; and Michael A. Jones, University of Tennessee–Chattanooga. Finally, I'd like to acknowledge the contribution of the thousands of managers and professionals who've sat through one or another seminar of mine, where we strove together to differentiate qualitative and quantitative market research and come to some defensible conclusions about the comparative merits of each.

PART I

INTRODUCTION

＃ ONE ＃

NATURE AND CHARACTERISTICS
OF MARKET RESEARCH

T he activities that can be described as "market research" cover a vast
territory, and it would require a hefty volume to offer a comprehensive
overview of all the activities that might be labeled by this term. This book has
a much tighter focus. Here, market research means *techniques for gathering
information from and about customers to support a business decision*. The
starting point, then, is that you are a businessperson who faces a challenging,
important, and probably risky decision. The question is whether collecting
information from or about customers could lead to a better decision. If your
answer to this question is a tentative "yes," then you are considering whether
to do market research. You hope to address an information gap that prevents
you from making the best decision possible. And that's the purpose of market
research.

The answer will not always be yes, let's do market research. Managers are
faced with countless decisions. Not all of these decisions can be improved by
collecting data from or about customers. One reason is that many business
decisions aren't marketing decisions (for instance, What metrics should I
apply to determine this year's annual raise for my employees?). But not even
all marketing decisions benefit from market research. First of all, the decision
has to be big and important enough to justify the cost—as we'll see, market
research can be quite expensive. Second, the decision has to have a long

enough time frame to allow for data collection. And finally, the decision has to be such as to benefit from collecting data from or about customers. Suppose instead that your product development path depends on the decision of an international standards body that is currently riven by dissension. It's unlikely that time or money spent on getting information from customers can give you insight into how that standards body will rule.

Conversely, the answer will almost certainly be yes, do consider doing market research, if there is enough money at stake and any of the information gaps listed below stand between you and a good decision.

If you don't know . . .

- enough about what customers actually need;
- what's on their minds or how their situation is changing;
- how many customers of Type X versus Type Y are out there;
- what they are (un)happy about, or what's driving this (un)happiness;
- how customers select a vendor, search for information, decide where to shop, and so forth;
- what drives the choice of one product configuration over another;
- how much they'd be willing to pay; and
- how many would buy at this price.

In summary, you should consider doing market research whenever you feel unable to decide because you lack information from or about customers. If you're not faced with a decision, you can't really justify doing market research. (You may and should collect marketing intelligence on an ongoing basis, but that's not covered in this book.) If it isn't a marketing decision, or information from customers can't really help, then too you should not be doing market research.

The point here is that market research is not like controlling costs, making processes more efficient, eating right, getting exercise, or any of the many activities that have to be done day in, day out. The need for market research only arises at specific points in time. No decision looming, or no ability to identify the decision, and/or no information gap indicates no opportunity or need for market research. As a businessperson, you don't do market research because it's virtuous; you do it when and if it promises a payoff.

HOW MANY KINDS OF MARKET RESEARCH?

The two fundamental modes of doing market research are exploratory and confirmatory. You either have a discovery orientation—a goal of generating possibilities and new ideas—or you want to narrow things down and eliminate possibilities so as to select the one best option—the right answer. Most exploratory research uses *qualitative* techniques: You want a better grasp of the different qualities of customer response. Most confirmatory research uses *quantitative* techniques: You want to count the frequency of or measure the strength of the various qualities of response identified during the exploratory phases. The distinction between qualitative and quantitative techniques provides an organizing framework for the book.

Different techniques apply when you are exploring or confirming. For instance, a focus group can't confirm much of anything, but it can generate lots of new possibilities. A survey can give exact estimates, but only about the things you already know. If you can keep the distinction between qualitative and quantitative modes straight in your mind, you will avoid the worst mistakes. Most of the horror stories in market research involve trying to make a qualitative technique do confirmatory work or rushing ahead to perform a highly precise quantitative technique before doing the necessary exploration.

So one answer to "How many kinds of market research?" is: There are just two. There are two basic approaches to collecting data from or about customers, corresponding to two different purposes: exploratory investigations of the specific qualities that customer response can take on versus confirmatory investigations designed to count or quantify the qualities discovered earlier.

From a slightly different angle, if we focus on what the market researcher actually does in collecting customer data, we can also distinguish four fundamental activities:

- Search an archive.
- Ask customers questions.
- Observe what customers do.
- Arrange for customers to respond to structured stimuli.

Combining the two purposes and four actions produces a roadmap to the named market research techniques to which the bulk of the book is devoted, as laid out next.

		Purposes	
A		*Exploratory*	*Confirmatory*
C	Search:	Secondary research	
T	Ask:	Customer visits Focus groups	Surveys
I			
O	Observe:	Customer visits	Big Data
N	Arrange stimuli:	[null set]	Experiments Conjoint analysis
S			

Note that there's no such thing as an exploratory experiment. Experimentation is the epitome of confirmatory research; so is conjoint analysis, which is a kind of experiment, as described later. The table sketches out a point that will be crucial throughout: Some market research techniques, such as exploratory techniques, typically come into play early in the decision process, when discovery is a priority, and others not until much later. Experiments are necessarily a tool used late in the decision cycle; they are the confirmatory tools par excellence. Finally, secondary research can be pursued in either an exploratory or confirmatory mode, depending on what kind of information is being sought for what purpose.

RESEARCH TECHNIQUES

With these preliminaries out of the way, let me introduce to you the specific techniques to which this book provides a concise guide. The metaphor that guides the book is that a manager trying to build an understanding of customers has available a toolbox. Like a carpenter's toolbox, it contains the equivalent of a hammer, a screwdriver, a wrench, a saw, and so forth. Now think for a moment about how a carpenter uses that toolbox. Does he pick up a screwdriver when he has a nail to drive? Of course not; the screwdriver is the wrong tool for that purpose. Does he throw the screwdriver away because it's a failure in doing such a poor job of driving nails? Not at all; he knows it will come in handy later, when he has to set a screw (try setting a screw with a hammer). The carpenter seeks the right tool for the job. Since a lot of different jobs have to be done in the course of building a house, he lugs the whole toolbox to the job site. Imagine how strange it would be if instead he brought only a 9-inch socket wrench and proclaimed: "I am going to construct this entire house using only this one tool."

This book presumes that as a beginner in market research, you need to see the contents of the toolbox laid out one by one. You don't want to be like the little boy handed a hammer to whom the whole world looked like a nail—you want to use the right tool for the job. You don't reach for the hammer every time. You don't throw away the screwdriver because it bruised your thumb the first time you tried to drive a nail with it. In the next chapter, we'll distinguish specific "jobs" and match tools to jobs, as hammer to nails, wrench to bolts, and so on. Here, using Table 1.1, I want only to name the tools to be addressed and give you a taste of what each involves in concrete terms.

With the tools laid out, let me clarify how the content coverage in this not-a-market-research-textbook differs from that of a more conventional treatment.

Table 1.1   Contents of the Toolbox

Tool	What It Involves	Example Application
Secondary research	Search information already collected by you or by someone else for other purposes	Obtain a market share report for your firm relative to major competitors, broken out by geographical region, industry, etc.
Big Data	A kind of nontraditional secondary research, sometimes focused on web-based data	Crawl the web for mentions of your brand and score them for positive and negative sentiment, this time period versus last period.
Customer visits	With colleagues you visit 12 customers at their place of work to ask a set of exploratory questions	Discover customer needs not being met or adequately addressed by current product offerings.
Focus groups	You recruit three groups of 8–12 individuals to meet in a specialized facility with a one-way mirror for a group interview conducted by a professional moderator	Explore how mouthwash users respond to different advertising appeals, and how response varies according to purchase motive and occasion.

Tool	What It Involves	Example Application
Descriptive survey	Using an e-mail invitation to recruit respondents, you administer a questionnaire containing several dozen specific multiple-choice questions, including scales where respondents rate the brand or their own feelings	Survey customers to determine their level of satisfaction. There will be global measures of satisfaction, ratings of how well specific aspects of the product or service performed, and classification questions, so you can compare the satisfaction of larger firms versus small, novice versus expert users, men and women, etc.
Experiments	Two or more treatments are delivered to equivalent groups, and the response to the two treatments is compared. The treatments could be advertising appeals, price points, or simply the presence or absence of a particular product feature.	E-mail announcements of a sale using two different subject lines. Send each to half the test sample, and tabulate which subject line drew more people to your website.
Conjoint analysis	An experiment that takes place within an individual, as that person is exposed to multiple different treatments, each of which consists of a particular configuration of performance levels on some set of features	In designing a new tablet computer, the customer is exposed to various configurations, and indicates their preference for each one (this much weight, this screen size, this resolution, etc.). The analysis of these judgments estimates how important it is for, say, the tablet to be one inch larger, versus one ounce lighter.

First, Big Data is actually just a particular form of secondary research. However, enough people think of Big Data as something new and different to make it worthwhile to give it a chapter of its own. Note also that Big Data is a really huge topic in its own right, and consistent with the limited purposes of this book, I'll only be treating a small piece of it. My focus will be more particularly on Big Data concerning customer behaviors.

Second, the term "customer visit" rarely appears in a conventional market research textbook, and its absence reveals more than anything else the business-to-consumer (B2C) focus of most such books. In such textbook treatments this chapter would instead be labeled "interviews," "one-on-one interviews," or in older treatments "depth interviews." More commonly, individual interviews would be lumped together with focus groups, under headings like exploratory research, qualitative, or just "interviewing customers." Whether individual or group, the interviews would take place in a specialized facility and be conducted by a trained professional, and this context is assumed in most textbook discussions.

I learned decades ago that actual practice in B2B and technology firms is quite different. Interviews do play an important role in B2B research, but they almost never take place off site in specialized facilities, and they rarely involve an outside moderator. Rather, teams from the vendor visit customers at their place of work and interview them there. The reason is two-fold: (1) in B2B categories, there are often multiple individuals to be visited at each firm; and (2) because of the complexity of many B2B products, it is important to be able to observe the product in use.

Given my target audience, I only devote chapters to the customer visit and focus group techniques, as both of these are regularly used by B2B firms. The overview to Part II situates these two tools in the larger context of qualitative research techniques, including techniques more commonly seen in B2C contexts, like ethnography.

In the next chapter, each of the tools named in the table will be described in somewhat more detail, and with particular attention to where they fit in the overall decision cycle. The goal is to get across the distinctive competency of each tool, which is simultaneously to reveal the failing, shortcomings, and limits of each tool. The specifics of executing research using each technique are then covered in the following chapters.

DISCUSSION QUESTIONS

1. The chapter suggested that secondary versus primary research, and within primary research, qualitative versus quantitative, provided an exhaustive compartmentalization of the market research techniques

now available. Can you think of any market research procedure that doesn't fit into those compartments and went unmentioned in this chapter? How about a research technique that can't be easily classified into just one of those compartments?

2. Give examples of business decisions where it might be helpful to gather information, but where that data collection effort would not be termed "market research" under the criteria advanced in this chapter.

   a. *Extra Credit*: Give examples *in marketing*, rather than in other functional areas of business (giving a human resources example is almost too easy). Can there be information gathering, performed by a marketing manager in the ordinary course of his or her duties, that can't be described as some kind of "market research"?

3. This book confines itself to market research in the context of a for-profit firm competing in the sort of economic environment found in the United States around the turn of the 21st century. Obviously, there is no law that prevents a charity, a university, a government agency, or any other kind of organization from conducting focus groups, doing surveys, or even running a conjoint study.

   a. Select two specific "nonprofit" organizations from different sectors (for example, the American Red Cross versus the Pentagon, or your university versus the Salvation Army).

   b. Next, select a specific for-profit firm in an industry or product category you know well (think carefully about whether you want this to be a B2C or B2B firm).

   c. Finally, select two or three specific market research techniques. What will be similar, and what will be different, about the use of each technique by the nonprofits versus the profit-seeking firm you chose? Will there also be a difference between the two nonprofits?

   d. Here are some hints to get you started:

      i. Typically, a charity doesn't have a competitor in the sense that Coke has Pepsi as a competitor; but charities do "compete" for donations. What exactly is different about competition among the nonprofits that you chose, and what are the implications for doing "market research"?

ii. How is soliciting a charitable donation the same as, or different than, attempting to make a sale? In both cases, dollars flow from a dispersed population to an organization, and these dollars do not flow without effort; but it is not the same activity.

iii. In a capitalist society such as the United States in the 21st century, are all organizations subject to an economic logic, even nonprofits? What is that governing economic logic?

SUGGESTED READINGS

Aaker, D. (2014). *Strategic market management,* 10th ed. New York, NY: Wiley.	This short book provides a brief introduction to the range of marketing strategies and strategy frameworks taught to MBA students today. These strategies underlie most of the decisions that market research can support—in other words, the purpose of most market research is to help the manager execute against one of these strategies.
Marketing News (MN)	This is the newsletter of the American Marketing Association (AMA), the major organization of professional marketers, and it regularly publishes guides to market research software, focus group facilities, and so forth.
marketingpower.com	The website of the AMA provides access to conferences on market research topics and other relevant resources.
Marketing Insights (MI)	This magazine, also from the AMA, is addressed to practitioners and provides many detailed examples of the actual market research practices and policies of leading firms.

Journal of Marketing Research (JMR) *Marketing Science (MS)*	The leading academic journals in this area, *JMR* features highly technical articles that emphasize tests of theories and new analytic techniques, while *MS* emphasizes the development and testing of mathematical models of marketing phenomena such as price elasticity and the effects of promotional expenditure.
Journal of Advertising Research (JAR) *Journal of Product Innovation Management (JPIM)*	These are two leading practitioner-focused journals. *JAR* offers research on all aspects of advertising, and often reports studies based on real-world data. *JPIM* is a good source for current thinking on new product development.
Green Book (greenbook. org)	Use this volume to find specialists in one or another market research technique, and contact information for vendors of market research services.

TWO

PLANNING FOR MARKET RESEARCH

⸻•◦◆◦•⸻

T he first step in planning a market research study is to identify the underlying decision problem. The importance of this initial step cannot be overemphasized. The more secure the researcher's grasp of the decision problem, the greater the probability that the results of market research will make a difference to the firm. Conversely, when the decision problem is left tacit or never developed, the research effort may be misguided or may address only part of the problem or even the wrong problem altogether. This is to reiterate that good market research is conducted to serve the needs of business decision makers. If one loses sight of this imperative, then research activities may simply be an expensive way to satisfy idle curiosity, or an exercise in politics to justify decisions already made, or an excuse for dithering and failing to act.

This prescription to articulate the decision problem at the beginning may sound straightforward, but it is surprisingly difficult to implement in practice. One difficulty is that the person responsible for designing and implementing the market research study is generally not the same individual as the decision maker who must act on the research results. This separation of responsibilities makes communication failures all too likely. If the researcher does not spend enough time in dialogue with the decision maker, the full dimensions of the decision problem may not come into view. When this happens, the decision maker is likely to be disappointed with the results of the research, finding them to be either beside the point or only half an answer.

Even when the decision maker and researcher are the same individual, it is still important to spend some time articulating the decision problem prior to designing the market research study. The reason is that most decision makers do not face isolated, clearly defined problems. Instead, they face tangled messes. Thus, a decision maker may find him- or herself musing,

> Sales fell short last year. But sales would have approached the goal, except for six territories in two adjacent regions, where results were very poor. Of course, we implemented an across-the-board price increase last year, so our profit margin goals were just about met, even though sales revenue fell short, so maybe there's no reason to be concerned. Yet two of our competitors saw above-trend sales increases last year. Still, another competitor seems to be struggling, and word on the street is they have been slashing prices to close deals. Then again, the economy was pretty uneven across our geographies last year . . .

Simultaneously, our decision maker is grappling with the dissonant views and varying agendas of colleagues. One colleague takes the sales shortfall as an opportunity to push once more for an expansion of the product line; another reiterates that the alignment of sales incentives with sales performance goals has not been reviewed in years and that one of the regions in question saw considerable turnover in the sales force. Just then, our decision maker's own manager may pop in with a reminder that a revised sales forecast is due at the end of the quarter. What a mess!

In short, whether or not the researcher and decision maker are the same individual, an effort must be made to identify the focal decision problem. Once the decision problem has been stated, you can make an intelligent judgment about whether to do market research at all, and if so, which technique to use. If the decision problem is not articulated, then the organization either does not do any market research, blundering forward as best it can, or defaults to whatever research technique is either traditional within the firm ("Let's send customers a questionnaire") or the personal favorite approach of some key manager ("Focus groups would be good here"). I cannot emphasize this point strongly enough: It is impossible to make an intelligent selection from among the many market research techniques available, absent a clear and comprehensive formulation of the decision problem the research is supposed to address.

FROM DECISION PROBLEM TO INFORMATION GAP

Table 2.1 outlines a process for identifying decision problems and translating these into a research design. Returning to our "sales are down" example, a good first step is to generate alternative statements of the decision problem. Here are some examples:

A. We need to overhaul our sales compensation system. What changes should we make?

B. Our product line has to be broadened. What expansions would be best?

C. We have to improve the price–performance ratio of our offering to make it more effective. Should we adjust price, add functionality, or do both?

D. We need to identify corrective actions in the six lagging sales territories.

Each of these problem statements can be mapped onto the decision maker's musings reproduced earlier. However, each statement is going to take you in a very different direction as far as conducting any market research is concerned. In fact, at least one of these decision problems—the sales compensation issue—can't be addressed by market research as conventionally understood. True, some sort of investigation may be conducted in this instance, as when you gather information on the compensation practices of other firms in your industry for purposes of benchmarking), but market research, at least from the perspective of this book, should not be confused with the broader category of social science research or the even broader activity of fact gathering in general. *Market research*, as I shall use the term, refers to a specific set of information-gathering activities focused on customers. Thus, problem statements B, C, or D can be addressed through some kind of market research, as defined in this book, whereas problem statement A cannot. In other words, one of the first fruits of attempting to formulate alternative problem statements may be the realization that market research is beside the point. If decision makers have other information that suggests that the sales compensation system is out of whack and that this misalignment is beginning to hurt company performance, they may well choose to nominate that problem as *the* problem and attack it first, without getting involved in market research per se. A more general account of the limiting conditions on market research will be given in the final chapter.

Table 2.1 Planning Process for Marketing Research

Stage	Issues to Be Resolved
1. Identify and articulate the decision problem	• Who is the decision maker? • What are alternative ways to state the problem? • Do these statements get at the problem or are they only symptoms of some deeper problem? • Is this a decision that can be addressed through market research?
2. Pinpoint the information gap: key questions that must be answered before a decision can be made	• What specific questions are most pertinent? • Is there one question or many questions? • Can this question be answered with the time and money available?
3. Evaluate which research technique(s) would be most appropriate for answering these questions	• One research technique or several? • Techniques used in combination or in sequence?
4. Design the research study	• What specific objectives should guide the research? • Who should participate? (i.e., if primary research, how many of what kind of customers?; if secondary research, what data sources should be consulted?) • Estimate needed budget, time frame, and other resource requirements.

Is it possible now to choose which of the remaining formulations represents the *best* statement of the decision problem at hand? In the abstract, as an outside researcher having only the information reproduced in these pages, there really is no way to determine which of the remaining statements represents the best formulation—only the decision maker knows. That is, the decision maker possesses a great deal of other knowledge, both explicit and tacit, that is essential for selecting which of the remaining statements should be used to guide market research. Until the decision maker weighs all the information available and comes to a conclusion such as "I'm really worried that we're not price competitive," or "My hunch is that the sales problem is local to those half a dozen territories," the design of market research cannot proceed. In the abstract, any of the remaining statements could be *the* problem statement (and these are far from an exhaustive list). Each statement is capable of guiding subsequent market research, each captures at least some of the uncertainty facing the decision maker, and each is plausible as a response to the triggering complaint—sales are down.

Role of the Decision Maker

The discussion thus far suggests several practical insights into the conduct of market research. First, if the researcher and decision maker are not the same person, then it is imperative that the researcher have some kind of meaningful dialogue with the decision maker. The decision maker has to decide what the problem is, and in the real world, beset by complicated messes and the competing agendas of colleagues, this is no easy task. Hence, to be effective, market researchers cannot simply be order takers ("Three focus groups, coming right up"). Order takers fail their clients, because to be effective, good researchers have to help clients think through the problems at hand. Order takers also fail in their own business because the model is flawed—successful market researchers have to be consultants, not order takers. If the decision maker and researcher are one and the same person, then the decision maker must conduct this Socratic dialogue with him- or herself, first generating alternative problem statements and then selecting the best candidate among them.

Second, it should be apparent that each of the remaining problem statements leads to very different sorts of market research efforts. Thus, a focus on broadening the product line may not delve deeply into pricing issues or involve a comparison and contrast of specific sales territories. What may be less apparent is that every alternative problem statement foregrounds or privileges some possible answer to the triggering complaint and minimizes or excludes other potential answers or resolutions. If you choose to focus your research on the six lagging territories, you are implicitly rejecting the idea that there is anything wrong with your product line per se. In selecting a problem formulation, you may be mistaken (after all, you haven't conducted any research as yet!), and this mistake may not be recoverable in the time available. There is no way to escape this dilemma. It serves as a reminder that problem formulation has to be done carefully. If you get the problem right, then some kind of market research will probably be helpful. If you get the problem wrong, then it may not matter how good the research is.

To continue through the stages outlined in Table 2.1, let's suppose that the decision maker has a strong hunch that there really is a localized problem in the six territories—or at least, wants to rule this out before proceeding to any other investigations. Once you have settled on a decision problem, as captured in statement D, the next step is to brainstorm the kinds of questions that have to be answered before corrective actions can be undertaken. For example, are the six lagging territories distinctive in some other way, relative to the remaining territories, beyond the difference in sales growth? Do the six territories share any common factors that are uncommon among the remaining territories? If you could find other shared differences or commonalities, you can examine these as potential causes for the sales shortfall in these territories.

Each such question identifies an information gap that market research might be able to close. Given questions of this sort, you can ask whether they are answerable at a reasonable cost and begin to identify an appropriate research technique. Note again that once you accept a problem formulation that focuses on the six problematic sales territories, you cease to ask questions about differences that are general across the firm's markets, such as your price–performance ratio or problems with product line breadth.

As phrased, the question about factors shared by the six territories, that in turn distinguishes them from other sales territories, seems eminently answerable. Generally, the firm will maintain one or more databases containing descriptive data on each territory. External databases should also be available, allowing us to ask about the overall economic health or growth rate of each territory, population factors associated with each territory, and so on.

In this case, then, the initial selection of research technique will be to tap into existing archives of data—that is, conduct secondary research. You design a secondary research effort by specifying the kinds of archived data you wish to examine and the specific variables you will analyze, in this case, for the purpose of comparing the six territories with the remainder. Thus, you might look to internal databases for data on sales calls undertaken, the ratio of wins to losses, sales force turnover in each territory, and so forth. You could consult external databases for information on competitor presence and activity in each territory, economic conditions affecting each territory, and so forth.

From Research Design to Implementation

At this point, the research design is essentially complete. You have formulated the decision problem, generated specific research questions to be addressed, and selected an appropriate research technique capable of addressing these questions. What remains is to conduct the research, analyze and interpret the results, and formulate corrective actions (which, in some cases, may themselves need to be vetted by additional research). To complete the loop, one of two outcomes is likely in the case of the running example. On the one hand, analysis of secondary data may produce a "smoking gun." For instance, you may discover that the struggling competitor, who slashed prices last year, has a strong presence in each of the six lagging territories but has much less of a presence in most of the remaining territories. You now have a potential explanation for the overall sales shortfall, in terms of localized competitive price-cutting, and can begin to generate potential responses. These might include authorizing a higher level of discount when going head to head with this competitor or more heavily promoting those aspects of your product's functionality where this competitor's product is weakest, and so on. Specific actions will now be founded on data.

Alternatively, your search for shared commonalities and differences across problematic and unproblematic territories may come up empty. After all, in any given year, there will always be six territories at the bottom of the list, and your average sales performance will always look better if you exclude the worst six territories on the list. In other words, the decision maker's hunch may be wrong. Sales growth may have been lower across the board. Perhaps the strong territories were not as strong as they should have been, even as the weakest territories were particularly weak. This outcome will probably lead you to reformulate the decision problem in more general terms so as to identify corporate-wide factors that could explain the sales shortfall. New research will have to be designed, probably taking the form of some kind of exploratory research involving customers, to get at issues such as breadth of product line, price–performance ratio, brand image, and so forth.

Note that this second outcome, in which factors distinguishing the six territories failed to emerge, in no way constitutes a failure of research planning. Given the decision maker's mindset, industry knowledge, prior expectations, and so forth, it was imperative first to investigate the idea that the sales shortfall was fundamentally a local problem specific to certain territories. This is particularly the case inasmuch as a relatively quick and inexpensive research process was available to investigate this decision problem (secondary research is typically among the quickest and cheapest of research techniques). Only once the secondary research comes up empty can the decision maker proceed with confidence to address other formulations of the problem, which are likely to entail more difficult, prolonged, and expensive market research.

TYPES OF DECISION PROBLEMS: THE DECISION CYCLE

Formulating the decision problem is a task that has to be done anew each time that market research is contemplated. The range of researchable decision problems is as wide and varied as business itself. Nonetheless, it seems to me that the vast variety of potential decision problems can be clustered into a smaller number of fundamental types. The utility of such a typology of decision problems is that it will allow us to make generalizations about the applicability of specific market research tools. The typology may also be useful in guiding our initial efforts at formulating the decision problem in a specific case, insofar as it provides examples of typical decision problems.

Figure 2.1 presents a simple typology of decision problems organized as a cycle that unfolds over time. After this model has been discussed, we will examine the alignment between specific research techniques and specific stages in the decision cycle. The goal in that discussion is to show that once you have located your particular decision within the decision cycle, you will have simultaneously narrowed the range of appropriate research techniques to a small number.

The notion behind the decision cycle is that any major decision—developing a new product or entering a new market, for instance—proceeds through a series of smaller subdecisions. Alternatively, smaller and more localized decisions, such as the problem we worked through in the previous section ("Why are sales down?"), can be situated in the model and seen in context as representing one kind of a decision rather than another. As a general rule, major decisions such as the development of a new product may require research activities at each stage of the decision cycle (see chapter 15 for examples). In the case of more minor or localized problems, there may be a single set of research activities corresponding to a single stage of the decision cycle. The remainder of the decision cycle is then worked through informally without the aid of formal research. Thus, in the running example, if secondary research had shown there to be a specific problem with the six lagging territories, options for addressing the problem might have been generated by management discussion, the best option selected through further discussion, and the results monitored simply by reference to monthly sales figures routinely distributed. Nonetheless, the fundamental assumption underlying Figure 2.1 is that any researchable decision can be logically parsed into four steps, however truncated a particular step might be in practice. Every decision begins with a look at the surrounding context, proceeds to the generation of decision alternatives, and continues to the selection of one alternative, which then requires an

Figure 2.1   The Business Decision Cycle

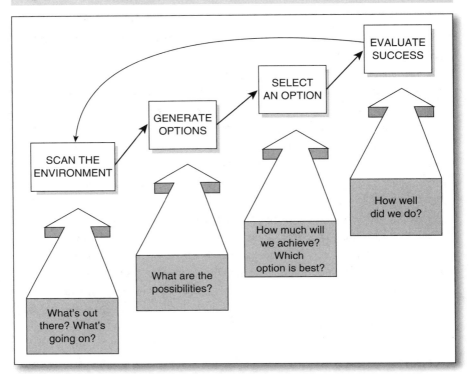

assessment of outcomes, which segues into a scanning of the environment in preparation for a subsequent decision. Finally, I will argue that the distinction of four stages within any decision is consequential for the kinds of research that need to be done at each stage. That is to say, the eligible research techniques are stage dependent.

The first stage in the cycle is to *scan the environment*. What's going on? What's out there? This activity of environmental scanning can be thought of as a sharpening and focusing of the activity of intelligence gathering, which, for any alert manager, should be ongoing. An example of scanning the environment would be to compile analysts' reports on the strategies, strengths, and weaknesses of your major competitors. In this early stage, you might also examine reports on how the market is segmented, who the biggest users of this product category are, what applications dominate, and so forth.

The second stage in the decision cycle is to *generate options*. What are the possibilities? What specific directions might be worth pursuing? What choices do you face? For example, if a product line has come to seem aged and tired, there is probably more than one possible approach to rejuvenating it, and all of these need to be identified and explored. If you are seeking to expand your market, you will want to identify all the possible groups that could be targeted for expansion. Likewise, before selecting a new theme for your ad campaign, you would want to examine a variety of candidate themes. Stage 2 can be thought of as the creative part of the decision cycle. The goal is to broaden your horizons so that you don't neglect opportunities or miss possibilities.

The third stage in the cycle is to critically examine and then *select an option* from among those generated in Stage 2. Which of these options is best? How much will this option achieve for us? It is at this stage that you must decide exactly what functionality a product will offer. This is where you determine which one among several markets is likely to be the largest, the most lucrative, or the best protected against competitive counterattack. Stage 3 is crucial because resources are always limited. This is a uniquely stressful stage because you have to commit to one option and abandon the remainder. You may have generated half a dozen attractive alternatives for market expansion, but the lack of money, people, or time will inevitably force you to select one or a few on which to concentrate your efforts.

The fourth and final stage is to *evaluate the success* of the decisions you made. How well did you do? Did you take market share away from the competitor you targeted? Did the new ad campaign change attitudes among the intended audience? How satisfied are customers who bought the new product? Results from the fourth stage are added to the stock of market intelligence possessed by the firm. These results also influence management's ongoing strategic review of business directions and set the stage for the next decision. For in business, decisions never stop.

MATCHING TOOLS TO DECISIONS

Research Objectives

A central purpose of this model of the decision cycle is to help you decide which market research tools might be useful at any given point. To do this requires a third concept that can bridge the gap between decision stages on the one hand and the market research toolbox on the other. Here the concept of a *research objective* is helpful. A research objective states, in a single sentence, what result you hope to achieve through the use of some particular research technique. An example might be, "Identify areas of satisfaction and dissatisfaction with our current product offering." Good research objectives always start with an action verb. If you leave out the verb, you end up with something vague and empty—a wish, hope, or yearning.

Articulating your objective in this concise and concrete way has two benefits. First, it forces you to stop and think: Really, what kind of information do I need given my formulation of the decision problem? This is a nontrivial benefit. Although a decision problem has been articulated, this problem was extracted from a mess, and that mess tends to reappear in the form of a wide range of poorly articulated issues and queries. Most managers are buffeted by numerous conflicting deadlines, interruptions, sudden changes of course, and the like. A requirement to spell out the specific information desired from this market research expenditure usefully concentrates the mind.

A second benefit of spelling out your objective is that you often discover that the objective you have just written out is insufficient—it reflects only part of what you are trying to accomplish. In conceptual terms, articulating research objectives represents a continuation and intensification of the initial attempt to formulate the decision problem. To continue the example given above, you may well realize that your actual objective is more comprehensive and better corresponds to this two-part statement: (1) identify areas of satisfaction and dissatisfaction and (2) prioritize areas of dissatisfaction according to degree of negative impact on revenue. Having reached this point, you may realize that the research procedures required to *identify* areas of dissatisfaction are not the same as those required to *prioritize* them. To identify requires an exploratory approach that can uncover what exists; to prioritize requires a precise and confirmatory approach that can take a set of existing things and order them from best to worst or most to least. With that realization, you are well on your way to articulating a research *strategy* encompassing multiple data collection activities that holds some promise of meeting all your information needs with respect to the decision problem at hand.

Table 2.2 lists a dozen verbs that often form the basis of research objectives along with some examples of typical objects for each verb. Thus, one can *identify* opportunities or problems or choice criteria, *select* markets or product concepts or ad themes, and so forth. Table 2.2 may not reflect *all* the verbs that provide a useful starting point for formulating market research objectives, but

Table 2.2   Examples of Research Objectives

Verb	Some Possible Objects
Identify:	Problems, opportunities, choice criteria . . .
Define:	Concept, design, potential . . .
Describe:	Decision process, usage, work environment . . .
Explore:	Perceptions, reactions, remedies . . .
Generate:	Hypotheses, alternatives, explanations . . .
Evaluate:	Feasibility, attractiveness, potential . . .
Select:	Product, concept, ad execution . . .
Test:	Preference, direction, profitability . . .
Measure:	Growth, size, frequency . . .
Prioritize:	Segments, needs, opportunities . . .
Monitor:	Trends, competition, events . . .
Track:	Spending, satisfaction, awareness . . .

it should cover most situations you will encounter. If you want to use a verb from outside this list, ask yourself whether it really adds anything and especially whether it is concrete and specific enough. For instance, in my experience, a favorite word of businesspeople in the context of market research is *validate*. But what does this mean? To validate is to confirm the correctness of some idea you hold—in other words, to test. Whereas *validate* is a long and somewhat unfamiliar word, thus vague in applicability and diffuse in meaning, *test* makes it clear that you are going to attempt to prove the truth of some proposition using fairly rigorous means. With *validate*, you could kid yourself that a dozen customer visits might be enough to validate your idea, whereas with *test* you are unlikely to convince yourself or anyone else that a dozen interviews is adequate. Hence, *test* is a more useful word because it gives more guidance as to what kind of market research might be able to fulfill your objective. *Validate* blurs the focus of your research planning; *test* sharpens it.

Decision Stages, Objectives, and Tools

Next, Table 2.3 integrates decision stages, research objectives, and individual research techniques. For each stage, certain research objectives are characteristic and customary. In turn, each research tool plays a primary role in achieving certain objectives and can contribute secondarily to the achievement of others. Table 2.3 is intended to serve several purposes. First, it provides the means to perform a quick check on a research proposal submitted by someone else in your organization. If someone wants to do focus groups in order to *select* which ad execution will have the strongest appeal, a warning light should go off in your mind: Focus groups are not listed among the tools used to select an option. Second, Table 2.3 provides a planning and scheduling tool for specifying needed market research over the life of a project. It affords you multiple opportunities to ask questions such as, What activities am I going to undertake so as to scan the environment? or, How will I go about identifying possible new applications for this instrument? A third benefit of Table 2.3 is that it provides three possible entry points to kick off your market research planning. Sometimes you will feel most confident about where you are in the decision cycle; sometimes a particular verb like *identify* or *explore* will be the hook; and sometimes you will be focused on a particular research tool. You can enter Table 2.3 from any of these points and build toward a complete research strategy from that point.

Table 2.4 provides an alternative viewpoint on the relationships mapped in Table 2.3. Now the individual research tools provide the rows and the individual research objectives the columns in a matrix. Where Table 2.3 was decision focused, Table 2.4 is tool focused. It facilitates correct use of each tool via the graphic symbols, which specify that the tool is a primary means of achieving an objective (double check), contributes secondarily to that objective (single check), or is generally misleading or dangerous in the context of a certain objective (X-mark). Blank cells indicate either that a tool bears little relationship to a certain objective, and hence, no warning is needed, or that it is meaningless to make any overall endorsement or prohibition, because so much depends on how the objective is interpreted in the specific case.

EFFECTIVE APPLICATION OF RESEARCH TOOLS

Parts II and III of this book discuss in considerable detail the strengths and weaknesses and best applications and misapplications of individual research

Table 2.3   Decision Stages, Research Objectives, and Research Tools

		Tools	
Stage	*Objectives*	*Primary*	*Supporting*
Scan environment – What's out there? – What's going on?	• Identify • Describe • Monitor	• Secondary research • Customer visits	• Focus groups • Surveys

Generate options
– What are the
  possibilities?
	• Generate
	• Define
	• Explore
		• Customer visits
		• Focus groups
			• Secondary
			  research

Select option
– How much will we
  achieve?
– Which one is best?
	• Evaluate
	• Test
	• Select
	• Prioritize
		• Experiments,
		  surveys
		• Conjoint
			• Secondary
			  research

Evaluate outcomes
– How well did we
  do?
	• Measure
	• Track
		• Surveys
		• Secondary
		  research
			• Customer
			  visits

tools. Here, in the course of elaborating on Tables 2.3 and 2.4, I will only attempt to flesh out the brief description of the tools given in Table 1.1. The focus here is primarily on the research objectives and how each tool relates to them; subsequent chapters focus on the tools and their execution.

To set the stage for this discussion, it helps to revisit the toolbox metaphor that underlies this book's treatment of market research. The toolbox has several compartments, corresponding, for instance, to the distinction between exploratory and confirmatory research. Within each compartment, there is the equivalent of a hammer, screwdriver, wrench, saw, and so on. It would be silly to always go to the same compartment to use the same tool as the last time you had an information gap. Yet it is not uncommon to encounter businesses that, faced with a need for market research, *only* conduct surveys or *only* do customer visits or *always* do focus groups. You will be much more effective if you can acquire a sense of the distinctive contribution of each tool together with an understanding of how the tools work together over the course of a project.

Every tool in the carpenter's toolbox is adapted to performing a specific task: hammers for driving nails, saws for making smaller pieces, wrenches for tightening bolts. It is the same with the market research toolbox: Each tool is effective in certain applications and ineffective in others. Just as market

Table 2.4 Research Tools Matched to Research Objectives

	Scan Environment			Generate Options			Test	Select Options			Evaluate Outcomes	
Tool	Identify	Describe	Monitor	Generate	Define	Explore	Test	Evaluate	Prioritize	Select	Measure	Track
Secondary research	✓✓	✓✓	✓✓	✓	✓	✓	✓	✓	✓	✓	✓✓	✓✓
Customer visits	✓✓	✓✓	✓✓	✓✓	✓✓	✓✓	X	X		X	X	
Focus groups	✓	✓		✓✓	✓✓	✓✓	X	X		X	X	
Survey research	✓	✓✓	✓✓	X	✓	X	✓✓	✓✓	✓✓	✓✓	✓✓	✓✓
Conjoint	X					X	✓✓	✓✓	✓✓	✓✓		
Experimentation	X	X		X	X	X	✓✓	✓✓	✓✓	✓✓	✓✓	✓

Stages/Objectives

Note: A double check indicates that a tool is a superior means of addressing the objective, a single check indicates it is appropriate for pursuing the objective, and an X indicates that the tool is *not* appropriate for this objective. Blanks indicate that the appropriateness or inappropriateness of the tool is uncertain, depending on exactly how the objective is interpreted in a particular context.

research should be done only when there is a payoff, each individual research technique should be used only where effective. There is no requirement to always visit customers or always field a survey or always use any one of these techniques.

Secondary Market Research

This research technique encompasses any data collected by someone else for some other purpose that also happens to be useful to you as you pursue your purposes. Common examples of external secondary research include data compiled by the Census Bureau and other government agencies, reports written by consulting firms and sold to interested parties (e.g., "Five-Year Projections for Mobile Advertising Revenue"), and publicly available information, such as articles in the trade press. Searching Google to understand what your competitors are doing would also be secondary research, as would almost any other Internet search intended to support a particular marketing decision. Common examples of internal secondary research would be sales records, customer databases, and past market research reports.

Secondary research has obvious relevance to the environmental scanning stage of the decision cycle. It is almost always quicker and cheaper to answer a question through secondary data than through conducting your own primary market research. In virtually every project, your first step should be to amass whatever secondary research is available and glean whatever insights you can. Secondary research can be used to identify market opportunities, describe market structure, and monitor competitive activity. For example, suppose you install and service video cameras used for security purposes. Using secondary research, you might discover that automated teller machines (ATMs) in non-bank locations offer a rapidly growing market for video security. You might encounter this fact in the trade press or perhaps in a syndicated report on market trends for small video cameras.

Because secondary research comprises so many diverse activities, one or another kind of secondary research may also play a supporting role in both generating *and* selecting options. Thus, a market opportunity identified at an earlier point may be further defined through secondary research. Continuing with our example, secondary research might help you formulate two market expansion options: (1) target large banks with extensive off-premises ATM networks or (2) target convenience store chains that have recently installed

ATMs in their stores. Information on market size or market structure gained through secondary research may also help you evaluate the relative profitability of two different strategic options. Thus, your own internal records may indicate to you that cameras mounted in very small stores require, on average, more servicing than cameras located in larger buildings, for which customers are billed per occurrence. This might be sufficient to cause you to select convenience stores as your initial target market, inasmuch as cameras associated with their new ATMs are likely to generate substantial service revenue.

A particular type of secondary research becomes of primary importance when you reach the fourth stage. Quite often you want to evaluate the outcome of a decision by measuring changes in market share for yourself and key competitors. Syndicated reports (regular studies, produced by independent consulting firms, to which you and other members of your industry subscribe) are often a source of market share data. Nielsen is a prominent example in the consumer sphere. Alternatively, your own review of secondary data may help you answer this question. Thus, if you can find information on how many ATMs were installed in a region last year, you can compute your share of these installations relative to your goals.

Big Data

Since Big Data, for purposes of this book, is secondary research writ large, with a particular focus on web behaviors and web-based databases, its profile in terms of the objectives served is very similar to that of secondary research overall. Here I'll simply give another example of its use. Suppose you are a service business of some kind—a vendor who offers training in some set of business skills, for instance. You will have a website, of course, and this site will serve multiple purposes: to promote individual training modules, to handle registration, and generally, to help people find you and assess whether they might benefit from what you offer. Since you are selling knowledge and skill, you will probably populate this site with more than promotional content: you may put up some teasers tied to particular workshops, maybe maintain a blog, include a reading or two, and so forth.

Where Big Data comes in is that if you are a business of any size, your website may record thousands of page views per day. Because the site consists of hundreds of pages, there are many possible routes through the site. The environmental scanning question here is not so much "What's going on?" as

"How are people using my website, and which elements are working well or poorly?" Software such as Google Analytics or Adobe Marketing Cloud can handle the staggering amounts of data thrown off by the day-to-day operation of a website of this kind. You can get counts of where the user came from (i.e., whether they came from a keyword search ad you placed on Google, or the one you placed on Bing; or from the user's own unsolicited search). You can get counts of where people go after landing on your home page, and which of these secondary and tertiary destinations are more likely to take the browser to a scheduling or registration page—that is, which content on the site is most effective in actually selling your training. You might find that a blog post written several months ago continues to attract more than its share of views, even though people have to search for it. That's a post that arguably should be turned into a piece of standalone, enduring content, and featured more prominently.

In sum, Big Data on the web offers a much more fine-grained and complete documentation of some types of customer behavior than had ever been available before, with highly actionable relevance to both environmental scanning and assessment of how well you are doing.

Customer Visits

Customer visits can be thought of as a combination of exploratory observation and face-to-face interviews. Hence, visits may be very helpful in the environmental scanning stage. Listening to customers describe problems can help to identify new product opportunities. Walking around the customer site facilitates rich descriptions of product applications. Regular contact with customers helps you to monitor emerging market trends and changes in the business environment.

Customer visits are also crucially important, along with focus groups, in the generation of options. This is because the loosely structured nature of these interviews allows for surprises. Similarly, extensive exposure to customers and their way of viewing the world often provides a fresh perspective. Moreover, the intensive dialogue that a two-hour face-to-face interview permits helps you to define issues and explore perceptions in depth.

Customer visits should almost never be used to test, evaluate, or select options. The small sample size and an unknown degree of interviewer bias make it impossible to trust the results of customer visits in this connection. As will be developed subsequently, these same shortcomings are less of an issue when customer visits are used appropriately to scan the environment and generate options. The lone exception is when you are planning to visit *all* your customers. This might be possible because these customers are all other divisions internal to your firm, or because the market for your product is very limited with only a few large buyers. If you can visit all your customers, then you have a census and not a sample, and the limitations cited above are less pressing. Even here, the portion of your visit devoted to testing and selecting among options will probably have a quite different feel relative to the rest of the visit and relative to more conventional applications of the visitation tool. To explore and to confirm are profoundly different activities.

Customer visits may sometimes play a minor supporting role in the evaluation of decision outcomes. Although in principle, customer visits are just as ill-suited to measuring and tracking as to testing and selecting, visits can potentially supplement more formal and confirmatory approaches such as survey research. Thus, although it is important to confirm whether your customer satisfaction numbers have gone up or down, it will not always be clear *why* the pattern of results takes the form it does. In this situation, a series of visits to customers whose satisfaction has increased and to customers whose satisfaction has not changed or has gotten worse is often illuminating. Such an application of customer visits serves as a reminder that the final stage of one decision cycle tends to merge with the first stage of the next decision cycle.

Focus Groups

In a focus group, 8 to 12 consumers meet in a special facility for approximately two hours. The facility enables you to view the group from behind a one-way mirror and to make audio and video recordings. The group discussion is moderated by a professional interviewer in accordance with objectives set by you. Focus groups are very similar to customer visits in being exploratory interviews, except that they lack an observational component. Hence, they are somewhat more narrow in their applicability. To a considerable degree, however, customer visits and focus groups are substitutes for one another, presenting the same opportunities and suffering from the same limitations. In the course of a given research project, most firms will do one or the other, but not both, if interviews are pertinent at all.

Same as any kind of interview, focus group studies can be useful in the initial exploratory stages of the decision cycle where you are scanning the environment and generating options. For instance, you might do some focus groups to identify emerging issues as viewed by customers within a particular segment of the market. At a later point, you might use focus groups to explore the pros and cons of several possible themes being considered for a new ad campaign. Part of generating options is defining these options in as much detail as possible, and the give-and-take of group interaction can be quite productive in this respect.

Focus groups are probably more effective at exploring, defining, and generating (Stage 2) than at identifying, describing, and monitoring (Stage 1); hence, their relegation to a contributing role during the environmental scanning stage. The power of focus groups comes from the interaction of customers within the group and whatever synergy results. The stimulus of group interaction is particularly useful when the goal is to generate fresh perspectives, define the differences among subgroups within the market, or explore consumer reactions. It is less useful when you want extensive descriptive data.

As with customer visits, generally speaking, focus groups should never be used to select among options. Again, the problem centers on the small samples of customers involved. Similarly, the skill brought by the outside interviewer to the conduct of focus groups may be more than outweighed by the distorting potential of group influence and dominant participants. Problems of group influence and conformity pressure, together with the fact that focus groups are a laboratory rather than field procedure, make it impossible to recommend their use for even a contributing role during Stage 4, evaluation of outcomes. In this sense, focus groups constitute a more specialized tool than either secondary research or customer visits.

Survey Research

A survey takes place when a fixed set of questions is asked of a large sample of customers. In many cases, the sample is carefully selected to represent the total population of interest. The questions are mostly descriptive and classificatory in nature: In a B2B context, questions asked of customers might include: "How big is your firm?" "When did you buy the product?" "How many other vendors did you consider?" and the like. Questions may also be structured as rating scales: for example, "on a 10-point scale where '10' is outstanding, how would you rate our performance on each of these aspects of service delivery . . ." What makes "asking customers questions" a survey rather than an interview is that the questions are fixed and asked the same way of every customer every time. Surveys provide a quantitative approach to asking questions of customers, interviews a qualitative approach.

Surveys can play a supporting role in environmental scanning. If you need a fairly exact factual description of the behaviors and simple perceptions of some customer group and if such data cannot be gleaned from existing secondary research, then it may make sense to execute a survey. If, however, good secondary data already exist, it is rarely cost-effective to do your own survey unless this takes the form of a small, fast, tailored survey directed at filling in a few gaps in the available secondary data. If the needed secondary data do not exist, and if you simply must have precise descriptive data on such matters as the frequency of certain applications among particular customer groups, or the average dollar amount of equipment purchases, or the average rating of your speed of service response relative to key competitors, then a survey may make sense.

You should ask yourself, however, whether you really need precise descriptive data at this early point in the decision cycle. Is it really that important to be able to state with precision that 54% of the time, this medical instrument will be used on auto accident victims, 24% on mothers undergoing childbirth, 18% on victims of gunshot wounds, and 4% with others? At this early point, what is the value added by these precise percentages as opposed to what you could gain from a program of customer visits? A couple of dozen visits would probably reveal that auto accidents, childbirth, and gunshot wounds were "major" applications, even though the exact percentages would be uncertain. In addition, and in contrast to the limited data supplied by a survey, the visits would provide opportunities to describe in depth how each of these applications place different demands on the instrument and on hospital staff, how this instrument interfaces with other equipment in the hospital, and so forth. Such rich descriptive data are often more useful, early in the decision cycle, than the thinner but more precise data yielded by surveys.

It is even more important to understand that surveys are far less useful in the generation of options than customer visits or focus groups. The relative weakness of surveys at this point in the decision cycle has several sources: (1) the fact that the questions to be asked are fixed in advance; (2) the reality that the phone interviewers who may implement the survey probably lack the ability, the motivation, or the opportunity to deeply probe customer answers, and that customers racing through a self-administered web survey will be similarly unmotivated; and (3) the unfortunate truth that the impersonal nature of the survey contact—the certain knowledge that one's responses are but grist for the statistical mill—will inhibit and limit the customer's investment of the energy required for discovery, exploration, and depth. Surveys are a confirmatory tool whose proper purpose is to limit, narrow, and specify; hence, this tool is largely incapable of expanding, broadening, and reconfiguring your understanding. Go easy on surveys early in the decision cycle.

Survey research comes into its own at the third stage of the decision cycle. All of the features that had been of dubious relevance or even liabilities at the earlier stages are here either neutralized or converted into strengths. In Stage 3, the time for discovery and in-depth insight is past; now it is time to make hard choices and allocate limited resources. Perhaps you only have the resources to write new software for one or at most two of your instrument's applications, and you must determine which application predominates. Large investments may follow from decisions of this type, and it makes sense to invest a sum of money in determining precisely which application is largest, is growing the fastest, or has the weakest competitive presence.

Survey research is also of primary importance in the evaluation of outcomes. The classic example is the customer satisfaction surveys now conducted by many firms. Whether administered through the web or by telephone, in such surveys, often conducted by a neutral outside firm, a standard series of questions is asked focusing on product and vendor performance. The surveys are often repeated on a quarterly basis so that changes in satisfaction can be tracked over time. Another example is the tracking studies conducted after initiating an advertising campaign. These telephone surveys track awareness, brand attitude, and perceptions in those areas addressed by the advertising campaign. Here again, descriptive precision is an absolute requirement; otherwise, comparison over time becomes impossible.

Experiments

The purpose of an experiment is to test which among a small number of treatments stimulates the greatest response. For example, you may be considering two different appeals for use in an e-mail promotion, and you want to know which appeal will be most successful in driving customers to your website. You could draw a sample of 1,200 e-mail addresses, randomly assign 600 each to receive alternative versions, and then count which appeal produced the largest number of hits to your website.

Experiments are highly specific in their contribution to decision making. Experimentation is *not* of much use in the initial stages of environmental scanning and option generation or in the final stage of outcome evaluation. Early in the decision cycle, you don't know enough to design a good experiment, whereas toward the end of the cycle, you want market data on what actually occurred, not experimental predictions of what is most likely to occur. Experiments are primarily intended for use in option selection. In fact, their design corresponds exactly to the crux of many business decisions: that is, which of these options is the best? Moreover, experiments can sometimes answer a related and very important question: How *much* will we achieve? For instance, the response rate for the winning headline in the direct mail example would allow us to estimate what the response rate will be for the mass mailing, and this in turn allows us to draw up a pro forma income statement showing the cost of the promotion and the anticipated revenue gain. Some kinds of conjoint analyses can generate such estimates as well, but arguably on a weaker empirical basis than in the case of field experiments.

Conjoint Analysis

In a conjoint study, consumers are presented with various product configurations consisting of a set of features each delivered at a specified level, and asked to indicate their preference. Thus, a computer monitor might be described in terms of resolution, price, screen size, contrast ratio, and so forth. Some subset of all the possible permutations is rated, and the mathematical analysis of consumer preferences gives insight into how consumers make trade-offs among different features and price points. Although there are many different ways to implement conjoint studies, regardless of format, the goal is always to build a model of how a customer makes a choice among the various product offerings available and, thus, to identify and quantify choice drivers (for example, how many dollars more, if any, will a consumer pay for a monitor with a resolution of 1080 × 1920?). The goal of conjoint analysis is thus to answer questions such as, "Which product attributes are most influential on the purchase decision?" and "How do customers make trade-offs between performance level and price?"

Conjoint analysis is again a valuable tool with strictly limited applicability. It makes little sense to use conjoint analysis during environmental scanning. Too little is known to justify use of a precise and narrowly focused tool of this kind. Conjoint analysis is not really appropriate for the generation of options, either. This is because to perform conjoint analysis, one must be able to say exactly what the key product attributes are, and part of the purpose of generating options is precisely to discover what product attributes might matter at all. Logically, environmental scanning and options generation precede and lay a foundation for more confirmatory techniques such as conjoint analysis.

The primary purpose of conjoint analysis is to assist in the selection of the best option in the specific sense of the optimal product configuration or price–performance point. When serious uncertainty remains about whether one bundle of features or another is the most attractive to consumers or about how to construct the optimal bundle of features, conjoint analysis is often a good choice. In turn, by the time one gets to the fourth and final stage of evaluating outcomes, as with experiments generally, the time for conjoint analysis has probably passed.

SUMMARY

Now that the contents of the market research toolbox have been spread out before you and each tool briefly situated within the decision cycle, a few summary statements are in order.

1. Secondary research is *the* all-purpose market research tool. Partly because of the great diversity of the types of information that can be obtained and partly because much secondary research is both cheap and quickly obtainable, your first impulse in planning any inquiry into customers and markets should be to ask, Has somebody else already gathered useful information on which I could build? The answer won't always be "yes," but the question should always be asked.

2. Interviews and surveys are probably the most heavily used techniques. The application of both these tools is a matter of asking questions and getting answers. If the issues with which you are concerned can be phrased as direct questions that customers are able to answer, then interviews or surveys will probably be rewarding.

3. Customer visits and focus groups anchor the exploratory end of the continuum. Here you may have some sense of what your key issues are or what some of your questions may be, but you are uncertain about what kinds of answers are even possible. By contrast, surveys anchor the confirmatory end if *descriptive* information is the goal. Here you know both the key questions and the range of possible answers, and your goal is to pin down the exact frequency of each possible answer.

4. The selection of options, unlike the other decision stages, tends to require highly specialized research tools such as conjoint analysis and experimentation. It is an error and a mark of ignorance if the management of a firm exclusively conducts customer visits, or surveys, or a review of secondary resources when the primary goal is to select an option. Selecting the best option—pricing is a good example—often requires you to go beyond asking questions of customers and to instead create environments in which customers act or choose so that you can analyze these behaviors to infer the answers you require. Both conjoint studies and experiments take this approach.

DOs AND DON'Ts

Do plan on using a variety of techniques over the course of a project. Make every effort to find the right tool for the job at hand. Every tool is specialized, and no tool is perfect.

Don't confuse exploratory and confirmatory techniques. Don't try to squeeze precision out of tools that can't provide it, and don't expect discoveries and new insights out of tools whose purpose is to narrow down the possibilities and eliminate options.

Don't fixate on specific research tools. Keep the focus on the decision to be made and what information would be most helpful. Let the tool follow from the research objective.

DISCUSSION QUESTIONS

1. Evaluate the claim that "every research technique has both special strengths and key limitations."

a.   Are there really no globally superior research techniques—no technique so robust, so scientifically sound, as to have wide applicability with few limitations?

b.   And are there really no globally inferior or weak market research techniques, with few strengths, that should generally be avoided, however familiar or customary?

c.   Focus your answer on the pragmatic circumstances of a manager with profit and loss responsibility, and an investment mindset, as described in the appendix to this chapter.

d.   Would your answer be different in the B2B versus the B2C sphere?

2. What should a manager do if market research is likely to be valuable, but no funds are available? To answer this question, be specific about the options you selected among. Doing absolutely nothing to gather information is certainly one option, but there are others as well. Which of these options is the most managerially sound way to proceed when market research really would have been helpful, but no funds are available?

a.   This question is best answered by anchoring yourself to a specific product category and a particular type of marketing decision (i.e., new product introduction, selection of customers to target).

Extra Credit: Select two different product categories, broadly defined, and answer for both. For example, discuss a B2B versus B2C case, or an intangible service versus a consumer packaged good.

b.   Now, to vary the question a bit: Suppose there are some funds available, but these are insufficient to do all the market research that would definitely be helpful. Perhaps there are enough funds to do an interview study but not follow it up with a survey; or enough to do a conjoint analysis but not lay the foundation with interviews. What's the best way to proceed, in general, when there are not enough funds to do everything that should be done?

This time, for extra credit, discuss B2B versus B2C cases specifically.

SUGGESTED READINGS

Churchill, G. A., & Iacobucci, D. (2009). *Marketing research: Methodological foundations,* 10th ed. Chicago, IL: Cengage. Malhotra, N. (2009). *Marketing research: An applied orientation,* 6th ed. Ontario, Canada: Pearson Education.	These are standard textbooks on marketing research that provide more detailed coverage of the specific tools discussed here and a thorough introduction to the statistical analysis of market research data.
Grover, R., & Vriens, M. (2006). *The handbook of marketing research: Uses, misuses, and future advances.* Thousand Oaks, CA: Sage.	If you are an established professional new to marketing research but with advanced training elsewhere in the social sciences, you may find this volume more palatable than the two student-focused textbooks listed above.

APPENDIX 2A: FINANCIAL PLANNING FOR MARKET RESEARCH

An important part of planning for market research is estimating the budget required to fund the desired project(s). In this appendix, I assume that some kind of market research seems to be indicated, so the financial question centers on how much to spend. The formula given also allows a determination that very little spending can be justified, in which case market research will probably not be done. However, a fuller account of the boundary conditions on market research, including potential payoff or lack thereof, is reserved for the final chapter.

This simple equation lays out the conceptual issues involved in developing a budget for market research:

$$\text{Market Research Budget} = K \times R \times 1/F$$

Let K be the amount at stake with respect to the decision the research is intended to support. This amount is the contribution to profit that could be lost or foregone if the wrong decision is made (let contribution equal revenue minus the cost of goods sold, including fixed costs directly attributable to the decision, e.g., new capital equipment required to launch a new product). For instance, if, upon introduction, crucial features in the product are lacking, what would that cost you? If you end up targeting the wrong application or the wrong group of customers, how expensive would this mistake be? If the product is a bust and withdrawn from the market, what would be the charge against profit?

In a corporate context, for most new product decisions, K may be an amount in the millions of dollars. If we drop down to the level of some particular marketing initiative—for example, reorganizing sales territories to align with customer segments—the amount at stake may drop to the hundreds of thousands of dollars. A simple rule of thumb is that as K begins to drop below $500,000, it becomes more and more difficult to cost-justify any kind of formal market research beyond secondary research. You can always go on Google for a few hours for nothing out of pocket, and in most cases you should; but as soon as you begin contemplating formal market research, the meter starts at about $10,000 and quickly ticks higher. And as developed next, that level of expenditure presupposes a K of $500,000 or more. One can of course do poorly conceived and ineffective market research for much less than $10,000; but why spend any money at all on faulty or imprecise data?

Second, let R be the reduction in the odds, expressed as a percentage, of making a wrong decision. This number is going to be quite a bit more fuzzy than the first number but can be estimated as follows. Suppose that 50% of new product introductions in your industry break even or turn a profit. The odds of failure, defined as incurring a loss, might then be estimated as 50%. You might then suppose that if effective market research were done, the odds of failure would decrease to 33%. R, the reduction in the odds of failure, is then estimated as 17%. Note that when the situation is either terminally confusing, or already quite clear, then R will be very small, maybe close to zero.

In fact, R will be large only when candidates for the "right" decision can at least be glimpsed, *and* when there are a manageable number of such candidates, *and* when there is little confidence or consensus among decision makers about which candidate decision is the best one to make. If decision makers are confident they know what to do, how is market research really going to improve the decision (or even alter it)? If the number of viable directions is large, will the cost of good market research exceed the payoff? If the path forward is terminally uncertain, is it believable that market research can improve the odds? Again, a more extended account of some of these limiting conditions will be given in the final chapter.

The underlying model here may be familiar to you from the decision-making and investment literatures. What the equation does is estimate an expected return by quantifying an outcome and then weighting this quantity by its probability of occurrence. The logic may become more clear if we let K and R be vectors rather than simple quantities. In that event, K^1 through K^5 might correspond to the financial impact of (1) a disastrous new product introduction, (2) a disappointing new product introduction, (3) a mediocre product introduction, (4) a good but not great product introduction, and (5) a blockbuster success. R^1 would then be the reduction in odds of a *disaster* to be expected from conducting market research, R^2 would be the reduction in the odds of a *disappointment*, R^3 would be the reduction (or increase) in the odds of a *mediocre* result, R^4 the increase in the odds of a *good* result, and R^5 the increase in the odds of achieving a *blockbuster*. Multiplying each element of K by the corresponding element of R and summing over the products would then yield the expected return from conducting market research.

F, the final element in the equation, can be defined as the desired return on investment (ROI) on the market research expenditure. It might also be thought of as a fudge factor. The result obtained from $K \times R$ reflects a chain of assumptions and guesses and will always be somewhat uncertain. It would be unfortunate if you invested \$250,000 in market research, based on an expected return ($K \times R$) of \$900,000, when in fact the possible return was only \$200,000 or so. Letting F be a number like 5, 10, or even 20 makes it much more likely that the market research investment will return a multiple of itself—as opposed to more or less netting out to no gain. In my opinion, F should never be less than 5, corresponding to an ROI of 500%. There are just too many other expenditures a manager could make to improve the odds of success, and market research is just too fallible an activity to justify any lower bar for target ROI.

The analogy here is to value-based pricing. In that approach to pricing, if your offering is estimated to save the customer \$200, you can't price it at \$200, or \$175, or even \$125—a customer will not feel motivated to spend a *certain* \$125 to *maybe* save \$200. Only if you set a price on the order of \$40 or even \$20 will the customer be motivated to pay that certain amount to achieve savings that are only promised and hypothetical. The fudge factor serves the same purpose in the context of setting a maximum market research budget. If F is set at 5, then the market research investment has the potential to pay for itself five times over. This is appropriate, because there are so many other investments you could make to improve the odds of new product success (additional research and development [R&D], larger advertising budget, etc.), and many of these alternatives will claim to pay back a multiple of themselves. The actual value of F in an individual case will vary with the conservatism of the firm and the perceived certainty of the estimate of $K \times R$. The more foreign market research is to the corporate culture (not uncommon in the case of technology companies in Silicon Valley) or the more skeptical the stance of management, the higher F should be.

The utility of the budget equation becomes apparent when it is combined with basic cost information concerning market research. These cost data will be discussed in more detail under the individual techniques, but some basic guidelines can be given. First, as mentioned earlier, $10,000 is about the floor for any execution of a particular market research technique (secondary data can of course cost much less, and I will return to this point). A more common level of expenditure for an individual technique would be $20,000 to $30,000, and most projects of any magnitude will want to combine multiple research techniques. As a rule of thumb, then, a meaningful market research effort over the life of, say, a new product development project is unlikely to cost less than $50,000, will often exceed the $100,000 range, and may require much, much more.

With this cost information in hand, the financial planning equation can be put to work. First, let the corporate contribution margin be 25%, let the reduction in the odds of failure attributable to good market research be 10%, and let the fudge factor be 20. Translated, assume a skeptical management, skimpy margins, and a lot of uncertainty. With these numbers, you can see that the new product has to have revenue potential of about $60,000,000 if one is to justify a market research budget on the order of $75,000. Specifically,

- If an important mistake in product design will cause the product to only break even rather than make a normal contribution to profit, the cost of a mistake (the amount at stake) is $15,000,000 (= 25% contribution × $60,000,000 in sales revenue).
- The maximum market research budget is then $1,500,000 (due to the expected 10% reduction in the odds of making a mistake).
- Applying the fudge factor of 20 yields the budget of $75,000.

By jiggering any of the assumptions just made, one can easily get the required revenue potential down to $20,000,000 or so. Thus, there exist software and other technology businesses with contribution margins well above 25% and even 50%. Alternatively, it may be more reasonable to assume that a mistaken product will produce an actual *loss* rather than break even. Moreover, the situation might be such that the reduction in the odds of error due to good market research will be more than 10% (but I discourage students from setting R much above 20% to 30%). Last, a more market-focused or more confident corporate culture might set a lower fudge factor. By a somewhat more heroic rearrangement of our assumptions, combining any two of the revisions just named, we could get the revenue level down under $10,000,000. Even by the most heroic assumptions, $2 million to $4 million, in terms of product revenue, is probably the lower limit for justifying a sophisticated market research effort that includes at least two distinct data-collection efforts and costs upward of $50,000.

Quite a number of useful conclusions emerge from this financial analysis. On the one hand, any Fortune 1000 corporation has many, many products with annual revenue potential in the tens of millions of dollars range, indicating again the pervasive opportunity for conducting market research. On the other hand, most small businesses and most technology startups will have to use ingenuity and rely heavily on secondary data and seat-of-the-pants reasoning rather than on market research studies per se (see the final chapter). In fact, it is probably fair to say that most mom-and-pop businesses cannot afford to purchase conventional market research. Much can be done on a shoestring, but it will mostly consist of secondary data along with an open, inquiring frame of mind.

Continuing along these lines, the higher the profit margin, the greater the opportunity to do market research, or make any other investment in long-term market success. Conversely, the lower the capital costs for introducing and then terminating a failed new product, the less the justifiable expenditure on market research. When I began consulting for insurance and financial services firms, I was quite struck by the contrast between their research budgeting and that of the equipment manufacturers with which I was then most familiar. To design and manufacture a new instrument or other electronic product inevitably entails a substantial R&D and capital expenditure. Introducing a new financial service or program often incurs modest costs that are several orders of magnitude less. In such cases, actual market introduction provides a relatively quick and inexpensive test of whether the program was or was not a good idea. Given this low cost of test-by-launch, upfront market research has to be inexpensive if it is to be done at all in the financial services sphere. Moral of the story: If it won't cost you much to be wrong, then you also should not spend very much on market research.

The logic of the equation has particularly troubling implications for program managers. This job category includes people who manage documentation, customer service, or lines of product accessories and the like. Program managers have no less need for market and customer information than project and product managers (these are parallel job titles in the engineering and marketing functions), but their efforts seldom have the kind of assignable revenue impact required to justify a substantial market research budget. Two solutions make sense for people in the program manager position. The first is to concentrate on secondary data, and the second is to find ways to piggyback on the market research efforts of project and product managers. If a program manager can add a question or two to a research study, this may have little effect on the cost of the study while yielding an invaluable supplement to his or her ongoing effort to stay on top of market developments. Program managers who regularly execute such piggyback strategies gain a constant stream of research data at little direct cost.

On a final note, a more subtle implication of the financial equation is that a short-term focus makes it difficult to adequately budget for market research. For technology companies in particular, substantial market research efforts may be best focused at the *product platform* level and not at the level of an individual product configuration. That is, just as smartphone manufacturers offer a variety of screen sizes, camera capacities and memory, at different quality levels, so also many technology products come in large and small, high-end and low-end versions, each aimed at a particular application or industry segment. Although each is a somewhat different product, all rest on the same basic assembly of technologies—the platform. Sales at the platform level, especially over the several years' life of the platform, will almost always be large enough to justify a substantial research budget, because although product life cycles have often shrunk to months, platform life cycles still last for years. Unfortunately, accounting systems and organizational groupings are often structured in terms of products. If the platform has no budget code, and if no team or individual has platform responsibility, then effective budgeting for market research becomes difficult.

Stepping back, the financial equation provides a way of acting on the truism that market research has to be considered an investment. It becomes clear that market research really *is* expensive and that the stakes have to be high to justify it. Conversely, the equation serves as a lever for use with those penny-wise, pound-foolish technical managers who choke at the idea of spending tens of thousands of dollars on something as intangible and squishy as market research. When a new product line is expected to generate revenue on the order of $100 million and there are some excruciating uncertainties concerning its design and intended audience, then a market research expenditure of $100,000 is a trivial price to pay if the odds of success can be materially improved. Note again that this kind of high-stakes situation is most likely to arise at the level of a product line or product platform and is much less common at the level of an individual product configuration or stock-keeping unit.

Note also that while the K component in the equation provides a bracing reminder that market research planning is basically about money payoffs, the R component provides an equally important reminder that market research itself boils down to uncertainty reduction. To the extent that you feel certain about what will happen or what will work, market research grows less necessary. For instance, if management has already made up its mind, for good or bad reasons, then market research can't reduce the odds of a wrong decision because it is not going to have *any* effect on the decision. Studies conducted under these circumstances are just politics and basically a waste of time and money. Conversely, when uncertainty is very high—your environment is essentially chaotic—market research may be beside the point. Since this situation is the more common one in technology firms, an example might help. Suppose that the success or failure of a given project hinges entirely on whether the technical standard to which it adheres does or does not end up dominating the market some years hence. Suppose further that the dominance or defeat of that technical standard is not within the control of company management or of any definable group of people, that it will, in fact, be a function of so many interlocking factors that it is impossible to grasp their interrelations. In that situation, the most that market research may be able to offer is an early warning of whether the technical standard is or is not moving toward dominance. If that early warning would not be helpful, then it may be best to spend nothing at all on market research in this connection and put the money to other uses, such as lobbying for the chosen standard at technical gatherings.

See again the final chapter for a more extended development of this kind of boundary condition on market research.

Perhaps you expected more than "uncertainty reduction" from market research. You hoped, in a nutshell, to achieve some kind of *guarantee* of making the right decision. Not to be too blunt, you were naive. Market research is a social science, not a physical science, and a young social science at that. It can reduce uncertainty but never eliminate it. On average, across a large business, over a period of years, this small reduction in uncertainty can be very lucrative and repay the cost of the research many times over. But all market research can ever do is reduce the odds of making a costly error and increase the odds of making a profitable decision. If instead it is certainty that you want, then may I suggest you go to a chapel.

CASES FOR PART I

NOTE TO NONSTUDENT READERS

This is the first of a number of suggested cases newly incorporated into the fourth edition. They are primarily intended to support use of the book in a classroom setting.

But what if you are not a student reader of this book, but a member of the original target audience consisting of professionals seeking a briefing? For you, the cases provide real-life examples of complex business situations where market research may play a role. (Anyone can purchase these cases from http://hbsp.harvard.edu.)

The questions following the synopsis are meant to focus your reading. Ideally, you'll be able to discuss the case and your answers with someone more senior or experienced.

SUGGESTED CASE: THE COOP (HARVARD, #9-599-113)

Synopsis

Mr. Buckmeister, an entrepreneur who built a chain of 76 fast-food chicken restaurants from scratch, has a problem: After many years of above-category growth in sales, something has changed for the worse, and sales in some previously strong stores have been noticeably weak in the current year. He faces conflicting advice from his team about how to proceed.

Discussion questions

1. State the decision problem Mr. Buckmeister is facing. (Hint: The decision problem is *not* whether to do market research, or what research to do; it is always a business problem involving revenue, growth, profitability, market share, and the like.)

2. Is there an opportunity to invest in market research? Make the case for an expenditure on market research. What should he do first? And what next? And what after that?

3. Evaluate the various research proposals on offer, including Mr. Buckmeister's own proposal for a simple comment card to be left by the cash register.

   (a) Can any of the suggested techniques be ruled out as obviously off point?

   (b) Which ones, if any, appear most relevant to the decision problem?

4. Formulate a complete research plan, indicating what research to do first, and what follow-up research might be in order.

5. There's obviously some tension between two of his VPs, the one representing the Quality perspective, the other the Marketing view. If you are in a marketing class, you can't just take the side of the Marketing VP—you need to make the case about what's wrong, if anything, with the recommendations coming from the Quality VP.

SUPPLEMENTAL CASE: DATA FARM

Synopsis

This is a fictitious case to be used immediately following the Coop. It won't make any sense if the Coop case is not fresh in your mind. I wrote it to parallel the Coop situation in every way except one: Data Farm is a B2B technology case. It provides an opportunity to discuss how the exact same decision problem has to be addressed somewhat differently when the firm manufactures a high-cost tool sold to businesses, as opposed to a discretionary consumer good, such as fast food.

Discussion Questions

1. What should Mr. Bilsurvant do first, and then what next, and then what? Is market research potentially relevant here?

2. Review your recommended set of research activities for the Coop case. Which research activities will be the same for Data Farm, and which ones, if any, will have to be adjusted or replaced by some other technique or procedure?

(Continued)

(Continued)

3. Overall, how different are the demands placed on market research by B2B technology firms, relative to firms selling a discretionary food purchase to consumers?

DATA FARM CASE

Data Farm is a manufacturer of rack servers. Its servers provide scalable processing capacity to a variety of customers, including:

(1) firms that provide outsourced data centers (i.e., take the day-to-day management of the corporate data center out of the hands of a corporation);

(2) website providers, who use the servers to support browsing of the website;

(3) corporate data centers that have not been outsourced; and

(4) laboratories and other specialized business operations that require a great deal of server capacity to support their day-to-day work. A portion of this business represents government entities.

The Data Farm product takes the form of server modules. Any number of modules can be combined. An individual module costs a few thousand dollars, but almost no customer buys just one, or even just 10; most purchase orders include dozens, hundreds, or thousands of modules. Because of the small size of the individual module, customers can buy precisely as much processing capacity as they need, and efficiently expand capacity when and as needed.

A dedicated sales force sells Data Farm products. Various service plans contribute substantially to overall revenue, as do supporting elements such as racks, inter-server and network connections, and management and monitoring software. Sales represent a mix of: (1) initial sales to new customers; (2) expanded capacity purchased by existing customers; and (3) upgrades to new versions of the server purchased to replace existing Data Farm servers.

Generally speaking, the rack server industry follows Moore's law: Processing power of a given size module doubles every 18 months. With changes in the supporting software, such as how the server interfaces with storage and/or with network routers, a rack server may be regarded as "old/out of date" after 24 to 40 months, and in most cases, will be obsolete after 36 to 48 months. Depending on customer operations, any time after 18 months of use, a business case can sometimes be made that it would be more effective to discard the still-functioning servers and replace them with the newest model.

CHALLENGE: SALES HAVE STALLED

In all other respects, Mr. Bilsurvant, the entrepreneur who heads up Data Farm, finds himself facing in 2010 exactly the same strategic challenge as Mr. Buckmeister of The Coop faced in 1995: After a long period of above-category growth, sales have stalled. Like The Coop, sales have been particularly problematic in about 20 sales territories.

Make these additional substitutions to see the parallels with The Coop in more detail:

For "76 restaurants"	Substitute "76 sales territories." All of Data Farm's servers are sold direct through its sales force, with a typical sale between $100K and $2M.
Instead of Anita McMichaels, VP of Quality, and her concern for quality and taste tests …	Make her VP of Sales, convinced that there is a problem with inadequate training and a need for systematic course development to improve selling skills. Or possibly, a need for a revamped sales compensation plan
Instead of Trevor Wallace, VP of Marketing …	Let him be VP of Business Development, arguing that the problem lies with the relative performance of the servers against competitors, and possibly their pricing, and not with any problem in sales training or sales force management.

(Continued)

(Continued)

For the income statement ...	Add a zero to every entry, so that Data Farm has about $500 million in sales.
Also in the income statement:	Make any other changes to convert this to a manufacturer's statement (substitute "manufacturing operations" for "store operations," etc.). In particular, substitute "sales force expense" for "advertising."

Keep everything else the same as The Coop.

PART II

ARCHIVAL RESEARCH

———•◦•———

OVERVIEW

The two chapters in this part share a focus on data that already exists, so that the primary tasks are to locate and analyze it. The chapters in Parts III and IV, by contrast, have to devote considerable space to data collection. Here in this part, the emphasis is on what data is likely to be available, how it can be used, and why it is valuable.

A second difference is that some kind of archival data will be almost universally relevant across marketing decisions. By contrast, the primary research techniques described in subsequent chapters are more specialized and may or may not be relevant to any specific decision.

The first chapter in this part, "Secondary Research," describes types of archival data that, with a few exceptions, are many decades old. The second chapter, "Big Data," describes kinds of data that are just now becoming available, as a result of advances in computer hardware and software. Accordingly, the managerial use of secondary data is well established, but potential managerial applications for Big Data are still being explored.

THREE

SECONDARY RESEARCH

———◆•◉•◆———

S econdary market research refers to any data gathered for one purpose by one party and then put to a second use by or made to serve the purpose of a second party. Secondary market research is thus the broadest and most diffuse tool within the toolbox, because it includes virtually any information that can be reused within a market research context. Secondary research is also the closest thing to an all-purpose market research tool, because virtually every project makes some use of secondary data and almost any decision stage may incorporate some kind of secondary research. As a general rule, relatively speaking, secondary research also is the cheapest and quickest form of market research. You ignore or skimp on it at your peril. Its range of application is limited only by your ingenuity.

By the way, most Big Data relevant to marketing research is secondary data. It is rare to see an enormous database compiled to support a particular decision (the definition of primary research). Most commonly, Big Data becomes available either as an off-shoot of some other activity, or because it was cheap and easy to compile, so that a manager at some point said, "Let's keep track of that stuff." Many gigabytes later, Big Data results. Although really only a novel form of secondary data, for this fourth edition I've devoted a separate chapter to it, immediately following this one.

Returning to more traditional forms of secondary research, it is helpful to distinguish between internal and external secondary data. Internal secondary data consist of information gathered elsewhere within your firm. The major categories include (1) sales reports and breakdowns, (2) customer databases, and (3) reports from past primary market research. Sales reports generally give data broken down by product category, region, and time period. More sophisticated systems may give breakdowns by distribution channel, level of price discount, customer type (large, medium, small), and similar categories. The most sophisticated set-ups deliver this data in almost real time in the form of a dashboard available on an executive's desktop. Dashboard software is an overlay on the underlying database. As sales and related data are entered or updated, the dashboard software produces updated totals and comparisons, often in visual terms. The goal is an up-to-the-minute understanding of how things are going, in an easily digestible form suitable for the busy but hands-on executive.

Customer databases might include a recording of brief descriptive data on all accounts (industry, contact person, phone number, purchase history), a log of tech support or response center calls, a record of specific products purchased, and the like. If your firm has a customer relationship management (CRM) system in place, this will often provide a rich source of data on existing customers. Finally, internal secondary data also include reports of past primary market research, such as results of surveys and focus groups conducted in prior years, accumulated customer visit trip reports, and so forth.

External secondary research includes (1) information gathered by government agencies such as the Census Bureau, (2) information compiled for sale by commercial vendors, and (3) various kinds of public and quasi-public information available from diverse sources. Government agencies such as the Census Bureau and the Department of Commerce collect an enormous amount of demographic and economic trend data. In recent years, the United States government has also done more to help companies seeking to export by providing information on overseas markets. Entire volumes are devoted to simply listing and cross-referencing various government reports.

An important kind of secondary data available from commercial vendors is known as the syndicated report. For a syndicated report, an analyst compiles a variety of data, using libraries, databases, phone calls, and even some primary market research such as interviews or surveys, in order to address a topic such as trends in social media participation, 2014 to 2018. The goal is to sell the report to as many interested parties as can be persuaded to buy. Syndicated reports may be one-time efforts or may appear periodically. Because the appetite for data is so huge, especially in technology markets, a whole industry of syndicated report vendors has grown up to satisfy this appetite

(Gartner, Inc. is an example). These commercial vendors function as one part librarian, one part statistician, one part detective, and one part proxy market researcher. They employ analysts who are in the business of being industry experts, and a certain number of hours of these analysts' time can be purchased along with the vendor's reports.

Public and quasi-public data sources include anything published in a magazine or newspaper, print or web based. Most industries have a few trade magazines devoted to coverage of companies, events, and trends. A few industries, like the computer and telecommunications industries, are the focus of a slew of publications. Similarly, most industries of note are, on occasion, the subject of a feature article in the *Wall Street Journal, New York Times, Los Angeles Times*, or other respected newspaper. Trade associations, university survey research centers, nonprofit agencies, and others publish data from time to time.

Today, most external secondary data will be located and obtained by using a search engine on the web. Anyone who is going to work with external secondary market research data on a regular basis needs to become adept at such searches. What you may not realize is that not everything is available on the public web for free. Duh—if there are people who will pay for this data, why put it on the web for free for anybody to see? In commercial contexts, market information may have a substantial dollar value. Hence, it gets locked up in specialized databases that will not be turned up by a simple web search. Learning about these hidden troves of information becomes part of establishing yourself in a given industry.

Finally, if you work for a large corporation, it will have some kind of library function in place, although this may no longer be a physical location with publications stacked on shelves. Whether physical or virtual, the economic logic of centralizing the acquisition of syndicated reports and other for-sale data is compelling. The "library" may even have a "reference librarian" who can assist you or may be charged with proactively gathering data and making it available to a distribution list of product managers and other interested parties. If you are a new corporate hire who is going to be charged with any kind of market research, then one of your first tasks after being processed through human resources is simply, Find the library!

If you don't work for a major corporation, then the equivalent of "find the library" is "fire up your web browser." Find some websites and blogs that seem consistently interesting and relevant, and visit them regularly. Get to know the respected publications and opinion leaders in the particular market with which you are concerned. You'll do better project-focused secondary market research if you don't come to it absolutely cold.

PROCEDURE

Let's assume that a decision is looming and you've been charged with gathering relevant secondary data. Maybe you are a product manager and gave yourself this charge; maybe you are an intern or new hire given this task by another. Step by step, here's how to proceed.

Identify Relevant Library Holdings (or Start Web Search)

Early in the environment scanning stage, you should budget some time for reading and browsing in the library. For example, you may try to construct graphs of trends in sales or market share by assembling a series of syndicated reports. For a second example, reading a set of reports interpreting industry events will help to constellate key issues in your mind. Again, if you don't have a corporate library, then the World Wide Web is your library, and that's where you start. Why not start with the web in all cases? Because the corporate library represents an edited source, prefiltered for relevance, and that can save you an incredible amount of time. The problem with the web is that it contains . . . so incredibly much: the gold and the dross, the expert and the crackpot, the leading edge and the long out of date. Search skills can help, but it's still generally a matter of too much information, too little time.

Assemble Relevant Internal Secondary Data

Using data from within your firm, you may be able to produce illuminating breakdowns of where sales performance has been strong or weak, profiles of typical customer applications, segmentation analyses of your customer base, tabulations of reported problems and complaints, and so forth. If you can assemble past primary market research reports that address, however tangentially, your area of concern, then you may gain perspective beyond anything you could obtain from reading outside analysts' discussions.

Decide How Much Is Enough

If the scope of your project justifies it, you may want to purchase some reports, buy access to a database, or sign up for a consultation with some market research analyst. You might go this route, for instance, if you were a product manager charged with preparing a backgrounder or white paper on whether the firm should expand into a particular market or pursue product development in a specific direction. In such instances, your responsibility is to pull together all the information available on this topic so that an expenditure of funds and a larger commitment of time can be justified.

In other situations, either most of the information that can be gotten from secondary data shows up early on or, conversely, after devoting the allotted time, you come up empty-handed. Both scenarios are common. The first is more likely in a large corporation and when the decision being researched concerns existing products and markets. The second is more likely when you are an intern, entrepreneur, or small-business person. Coming up empty is also more likely when researching new products and innovations. Sometimes you are asking a question no one has asked before, or you are asking a question so rarely pursued that no information provider has a service in place to address it. And sometimes you are asking questions so specific to the decision at hand that no one else has preceded you. It may then be time to conduct primary market research.

Decide Whether to Supplement the
Available Secondary Data With Primary Market Research

Sometimes you will learn everything you need to know from secondary data— or, more exactly, you will learn enough from secondary data that it would not be cost-effective to conduct additional primary market research (as discussed in Appendix 2A and the final chapter). In that case, the market research effort terminates with secondary research. It's very important to allow for this possibility. Again, there is no virtue associated with doing primary market research; there need only be a hard-headed calculation about whether additional information promises enough of a payoff to justify the time and expense.

Whether you proceed to conduct primary market research or not, it remains a smart move to have started with secondary research. Because secondary data are generally the quickest and cheapest to obtain, if the effort pans out, it was smart to start with it; if it doesn't pan out, it was still smart to establish that fact up front. Even in cases where secondary research produces little or nothing in the way of specific answers, once you do proceed to primary market research, your definition of the problem and your research objectives are likely to be much improved by your attempts at secondary research.

EXAMPLES

Because of the diversity of secondary research, a few typical applications showing how secondary data can help will be given in place of an extended example.

- *Sales and market share analysis.* Analysts compile data and do detective work to estimate market shares of key competitors, including breakdowns by application, by product subcategory, by region, by customer industry, and so forth. As part of this analysis, sales trends, including growth rates, are discussed.
- *Trend and scenario analysis.* Often, the goal of a report is to go beyond collecting and reporting specific numbers to encompass interpretation and analysis of underlying dynamics, critical success factors, implications of recent events and decisions, and the like.
- *Customer segmentation.* Reports may suggest a variety of schemas for distinguishing and grouping various types of customers and discuss the particular needs and requirements of each segment.
- *Competitor analysis.* Reports may dissect and critique business and marketing strategies of key competitors. Analyses will indicate strengths and weaknesses of products and describe markets where each competitor enjoys advantages or suffers disadvantages.

FUTURE DIRECTIONS

In the 20 years since the first edition of this book was prepared, the amount of secondary data has exploded. There is so much more of it than ever before, and it is more widely available and easier to access. Business students are trained to ask for it, American society continues its transition to a services and information society, competition continues to intensify, and all these factors support the growth and development of what might be called the market information industry. Undergirding the whole process is the spread of the World Wide Web, which makes it easier to find information, easier to aggregate it, and easier to disseminate it. Don't get me wrong: If you mastered the use of card catalogues and the Library of Congress classification system in a dusty library building decades ago, you are ideally suited to succeed in the Google era. It's the same basic skill. But the point is, today's information is neither limited to nor locked up in scattered library buildings under the Reference Collection sign. And because market information can be made readily available anywhere, 24/7, more of it gets produced. In terms of future directions, the initial transition of secondary research to a web-based, electronic interface appears more or less complete. But I would expect the trend toward compilation of more secondary data, at a more fine-grained level, and in something that more and more approaches real time, to continue.

The second change is that new kinds of market information have become available. Essentially the web is a self-documenting and self-archiving mechanism—it compiles data on itself at a furious pace. Thus, social media like Facebook and information feeds like Twitter spread like wildfire after about 2007. There is now an unprecedented amount of publicly available chatter; conversations that used to occur privately over the back fence and around the barbecue are now a matter of searchable record. Some of this chatter concerns brands, product recommendations, and other exceedingly relevant market talk. New services have sprung up to systematically search and quantify this "buzz." More informally, I know a manager who has a procedure for searching twitter.com whenever market news about her firm breaks. It gives her a quick read on how opinion leaders and customers are responding to the breaking news. Likewise, the spread of influential blogs in many technology markets has significantly broadened the sources of information and opinion. The old world, in which information was concentrated in the hands of a few trade publications and a small number of information compilers, has blown up—it's gone, and it's not coming back.

The third major trend is the development of entirely new categories of secondary data: information on web behavior, including tracking what consumers do on the web, how they navigate your website, where they came from, and where they go. Google Analytics is a leader here, but it is far from the only offering (see, e.g., http://www.adobe.com/solutions/digital-marketing.html). If you are marketing on the web, then you must come up to speed on these tools and the information they can provide. If your understanding of the technical aspects of browsers and websites is hazy, you could do worse than start with the 2010–11 series "What They Know," published in the *Wall Street Journal*. The next chapter goes into more depth about these new kinds of data.

What has not changed, and what I predict will only get worse, is the basic conundrum of modern professional life: too much information, too little of it relevant, too much of it unvetted. My advice to a young person entering market research or entering a job that's going to rely heavily on market research would be simply, You must have a learning strategy. How will you keep up, and how will you keep from floundering or drowning in the flood of information coming at you? Having a learning strategy, as an employed professional, is the 21st century equivalent of having good study habits as a student.

STRENGTHS AND WEAKNESSES

An important strength of secondary research is that it is generally quickly available for a modest cost. This is no small advantage in many business situations. Moreover, as discussed earlier, it is difficult to do any kind of primary market research for less than $10,000. If a few days in the library can remove most of the key uncertainties about market facts, albeit without giving exact answers to all one's questions, this may save you tens of thousands of dollars. A key strength of secondary research, then, is that it already exists and is readily available.

A particular advantage of *internal* secondary data is that it uses categories and breakdowns that reflect a corporation's preferred way of structuring the world. Outside analysts may use very different and not always comparable breakdowns. Internal databases often contain very specific and detailed information and very fine-grained breakdowns. Finally, one can generally get a fairly good idea of the validity of the data because one can discuss how they were gathered with the people responsible.

A particular strength of *external* secondary data is the objectivity of the outside perspective it provides. Reports are written by analysts with broad industry experience not beholden to any specific product vendor. Whereas product managers have many responsibilities and may be new to their positions, analysts spend all of their time focusing on market trends or industry analysis. Data are generally provided at the industry level so firm-specific results can be seen in context.

A final advantage in the case of some secondary data is that these may be the *only* available source of specific pieces of information. This is often true of government data, for instance. It would be impossible (and foolish) for any individual firm to attempt to match the efforts of the U.S. Census Bureau or Department of Commerce.

The most important weakness of secondary data stems from the fact that these data were gathered by other people for other purposes. Hence, they often do not exactly address your key question or concern. The answers, although not irrelevant, lack specificity, use breakdowns that are not comparable to other data, or don't address key issues in enough depth or from the desired perspective. Sometimes this potential limitation is not a factor, as in cases where the information you want is exactly the kind that secondary research is best suited to answer (e.g., aggregate market data). In other cases, particularly when customer requirements are a focal concern or when insight into the psychology and motivation of buying is crucial, secondary data may only scratch the surface.

Some external secondary data may be of suspect quality. One should never fall into the trap of assuming that a report, simply because it is well written and associated with a recognized consulting firm, offers some kind of window onto absolute truth. Quality varies—by analyst, by firm, by type of information, and by market category. Reports are prepared by people. These people may be very intelligent or less so, more meticulous or less so, thorough or slapdash, well informed or beset by unexamined assumptions. Most large buyers of secondary data develop a sense for which consulting firms are strong (or weak) in a particular area. This judgment may be explicit in documents prepared by corporate staff or implicit and locked in the heads of veteran employees who work with these vendors on a regular basis. It behooves you to tap into this collective wisdom before spending large amounts of money or basing crucial decisions on a single report from a firm you don't know well, however authoritative it may seem. In general, when reviewing a report you should carefully examine the appendix describing study methodology and come to your own judgment about study quality. If there is no methodology section to examine or if the sampling procedure is never explained, then beware!

A weakness characteristic of internal secondary data such as sales reports and customer databases is that they describe only your *existing* customers. Do not assume that these data can be extrapolated to describe the market as a whole. Rather, there is every reason to believe that your customers do *not* exactly reproduce the characteristics of the total market.

Be careful of data that may be dated or too old. Technology markets often change rapidly. Last, be aware that secondary data are less likely to exist outside the United States and the developed world. Particularly in poorer and less-developed nations, the secondary data that you'd like to have and could reasonably expect to find in the United States or Europe may simply not exist.

DOs AND DON'Ts

Do start every market research project with a search for relevant secondary data. You'll often be surprised by how much is available.

Do ask your colleagues' opinions of specific data vendors' performance.

Don't take numbers in syndicated reports at face value. Read the appendix and consider the methodology used. Pay particular attention to how samples were gathered and always maintain a healthy skepticism.

Do triangulate across vendors and sources. Compare numbers gathered from different sources by different methods. Often the truth lies somewhere in between.

Don't try to absorb a mass of secondary data all at once. Develop habits of regular reading; keep a notebook, electronic or paper, devoted to insights, reminders, and mental notes about possible models. Devise a system of folders on your computer and bookmarks in your web browser to make it easy to retrieve information at a later point.

DISCUSSION QUESTIONS

1. Evaluate the claim that "secondary research has to be the first step in almost any market research project."

   a. Is there any other activity that might precede it?

   b. Is the relative priority of secondary research a matter of logic, or of pragmatic good sense, or both, or neither?

2. Secondary data can be distinguished as internal or external to the firm, and both internal and external secondary data can be grouped into broad subcategories. For instance, one important subcategory of internal secondary data is financial accounting data: revenue and costs data broken out in various ways, such as by product, by region, by type of customer, and so forth.

   a. Devise a matrix as follows. Let the row headings be different types of secondary data, as you see it. Let the column headings be specific areas of market decision making—targeting consumers, setting prices, and so on. In the cells, indicate how this kind of secondary data can support that kind of decision. Pay special attention to the blank cells—justify.

SUGGESTED READINGS

Patzer, G. L. (1995). *Using secondary data in marketing research: United States and worldwide*. Westport, CT: Quorum Books.	Patzer provides a valuable international focus.
Poynter, R. (2010). *The handbook of online and social media research: Tools and techniques for market researchers*. New York, NY: Wiley.	Broad coverage of new as well as existing types of customer information that can be accessed online.

APPENDIX 3A: SEARCH TECHNIQUES FOR GATHERING MARKET INFORMATION

Today, no person can claim to be skilled in the conduct of secondary research if he or she is lacking in search skills. The proliferation of electronic databases of all kinds, the explosion of data on the web, and the availability of search engines such as Google make it imperative that you acquire good search skills. Search *is* a skill, and this section discusses just a few of the basics in the context of doing market research.

Principle 1: Not all data are electronic.

Corollary 1a: Electronic data available at your desktop are not always the most tractable source of the information you need.

I suppose there may come a time when all secondary data of any note will exist in sharable electronic form, but that time is not yet. The older the information, the less likely it is to be found in electronic form (and compiling trend data often requires older information). Even in 2014, paper still matters. The more voluminous and specialized the data, the less likely they are to exist outside their native paper format or be convenient to access in electronic form. Hence, it may be timely and cost-effective to search a library catalogue, if one is available to you, for physical resources early in your search.

The corollary is that even when all the information you seek is available in electronic form and accessible at your desktop, this may still not be the best way to access the data. Most electronic retrieval systems use the monitor screen (i.e., the amount of info that fits on a screen) as the unit of presentation, so they only show 10 links at a time, or one page of data, and so forth. Accessing the next page of links or the next page of data involves a delay that can be substantial. (Yes, broadband Internet access can be fast, but how often does *your* broadband connection live up to its maximum potential of near-instantaneous screen replacement? Mine continually disappoints.) The fact is, flipping paper pages can be much faster than refreshing page access on a computer screen. The advantage of perusing a paper volume, instead of searching an electronic version on screen, can be substantial, assuming it has a table of contents and an index and makes good use of headings and titles. The advantage of paper is greatest when you undertake a fuzzy search (i.e., when you can recognize useful data when you see it but can't necessarily formulate the object of your search in any precise way).

The first principle of search, then, is that paper can be "searched" too, and that searches of paper sources can sometimes be more effective than searches of electronic data. Don't fall prey to the silliness (a lingering vestige of the dot-com era) that treats information on paper as some kind of medieval entrapment to be avoided at all cost.

Principle 2: Not all electronic data are freely accessible via the web.

Corollary 2a: Search specialized sites, not just Google.

Although more and more data are stored in electronic form, the owner of the data does not always make them publicly available. A typical example is the archives of past issues that print publishers maintain. Here the data are stored in electronic form and are sometimes searchable, but these data may not be searchable from Google or any other search engine. These data can only be searched from within the publisher's site. The cover page or entry point to the private database may be located through a search engine, but the actual contents cannot be searched by means of the search engine—the spider or other program used by the search engine was never allowed to index the contents of the database. There are all kinds of reasons private databases will continue to exist walled off from web search engines. The owner may wish to charge a fee for access (as in the case of the print publication's archives), security considerations may make it undesirable to allow indexing of the database, data format issues may make this difficult, and so forth.

The practical implication is that when you are searching for a particular kind of specialized information, Google (or any other web search engine) may not be your best bet. Instead, you need to locate the appropriate specialized database that can then be searched. Sometimes Google can tip you off to the existence of a specialized database, sometimes you can ask a librarian, and sometimes this knowledge is just something you acquire by experience.

An example may be useful. Suppose you want to find the consumer magazines with the highest circulation among males. Put another way, you are looking for the most cost-effective way to reach millions of male magazine readers and want a list of likely magazines for further investigation into costs and so forth. If you had followed Principle 1, then your librarian might have directed you to one of the paper volumes published by *Adweek* or Standard Rate and Data Service (SRDS), which would contain such a list. If you were new to media planning and unaware that such compilations of circulation data have been published in print for many years, then you might attempt a Google search. Let's see how that might play out.

The first question is, What search string should you use? Some possibilities might include the following:

1. "Which magazines have the most male readers?"
2. "Magazine circulation male female"
3. "Magazine circulation data"
4. "Magazine circulation"

The first string might be characterized as a natural-language query—you phrase the search string just as you would ask the question of an expert if one were available. However, when first attempted on Google, this string failed to produce any useful links on the first page. Although search technology is moving toward being able to handle natural-language queries, in this case Google throws up sites that have one word ("magazine") or another ("male"), but there don't appear to be many sites that have all these words, and none of the top links was relevant.

Now consider the second search string. You might have said to yourself, what I'm really looking for is a table of some kind—let's search on the sort of headings that such a table would have. Unfortunately, what this string turns up is circulation data for individual magazines; the top links do not yield a site comparing multiple magazines (although the first page of links did turn up an interesting study on how news magazine circulation has evolved).

When you don't succeed with your first one or two attempts, it is generally a good idea to rephrase your query a couple of times using different rules. As an example of a rule, if you started with a long search string, simplify it; if you started with a simple string, add some more key words. Since we started with longer strings, the next attempt might be the third example: "magazine circulation data." Bingo! That proved to be an effective search string—one of the topmost links led to the website of *Advertising Age*, one of the leading publishers of data on magazines and other media. A quick navigation through the *Advertising Age* site takes one to the data center, where one of the tables lists the top consumer magazines with male and female readership data broken out. Other links introduce you to the Audit Bureau of Circulation, to sites offering trend analyses of magazine circulation over all. All in all, a terrific starting point for someone interested in learning more about magazine circulation data (the fourth search term is also pretty effective).

One caveat: I know *Advertising Age* and its position in the advertising industry. I also know of the Audit Bureau of Circulation, so I am less likely to dismiss the title of its link (ABC's . . .) as an attempt to game the search engine's listing order (like the AAAA Plumbing Service one can see at the head of some Yellow Pages listings). But it's easy to imagine a young person who had never heard of *Advertising Age,* much less the Audit Bureau of Circulation. Would this person recognize that he had just hit the jackpot and that one of these links should be clicked on immediately? Maybe not. My point here is that the greater your general knowledge of business, of marketing, and of your product category, the more effective your web searches for secondary data can be.

> Principle 3: Small changes in search string vocabulary can have a huge impact on which sites rise to the top of a search engine's rankings.

> Principle 4: The optimal search string—specific or general, long or short, natural-language or key words—is seldom a priori obvious. Be prepared to systematically vary the structure of your search string.

In the example, we looked only at the first page of links. Sometimes I look at second and third pages if I am enamored of my search string. Generally speaking, though, I would vary the search string a couple of times before delving too deeply into the second, third, or fourth page of links. If several search strings haven't produced the desired result, then I might repeat the most promising and look at a second, third, or fourth page of links. It rarely pays to go much further.

It didn't happen on this search, but sometimes a Google search will take you right to the desired site on the first try, whereupon you will discover that that site has the desired information—but you have to pay for it. In that event, might there be another site that has most of what you want for free? Sometimes there is, and sometimes there isn't. It is naive to expect that valuable information will always be free simply because you located it on the web.

Finally, sometimes the search process succeeds but is much more laborious than in the example. Thus, you try several search strings without much luck; go back to a string and review the second and third page of links; explore several of these links, each of which turns out to be a dead end; try another string, which does produce an interesting site that doesn't have what you want but gives you an idea for a different search string or a different source to consult, which finally yields the information you seek. That is the nature of the search game today. I don't expect that to change in my lifetime. Search engines will get better, but information will proliferate faster.

SUMMARY: SEARCH STRATEGY
FOR SECONDARY RESEARCH

1. Ask a librarian (or review your own experience) to see if an appropriate print reference exists. The quickest way to solve the example question would have been to open the *Marketer's Guide to Media*, consult the table of contents, and open the book to the desired table. If you routinely worked with media data, some such book would have been on your shelf.

2. If no printed reference work exists, inquire as to whether there are relevant trade magazines that might be expected to publish these data. If so, search first on their websites. (Again, information stored in a database may not be accessible from the public web—you only detect it if you get to the website and use that website's own search function.)

3. If Steps 1 and 2 fail, attempt a search of the web using Google or a similar engine. Here, type the first reasonable query that pops into your head. It is surprising how often this is successful. If at first you don't succeed, try the following strategies in roughly this order: (a) vary the search string; (b) look at second, third, and fourth pages of links; (c) take the best links and see where they lead; (d) try a meta-search engine or a directory like Yahoo; and last, (e) sleep on it. A different and better search string is most likely to occur to you if you step away from the problem for a while.

‖ FOUR ‖

BIG DATA

———◆———

Have old forms of internal secondary data really been sufficiently extended and transformed to justify the new term "Big Data"? My answer would be a cautious "yes": Big Data does represent something new and different in the world of marketing. What has changed can be summarized under the headings of: (1) scale, (2) detail, (3) automaticity, (4) timing, and (5) the character or type of data now archived. In unpacking these differences, it will be helpful to have a clear view of the older forms of internal secondary data clearly in mind, to serve as a reference point.

BEFORE BIG DATA

Traditionally, internal secondary data was primarily accounting data. To be very concrete, imagine the data record produced in the old days once a consumer had placed her groceries on the conveyor belt and the supermarket cashier had rung up her purchases. Place this vignette before 1980 so that there are no optical scanners, inasmuch as scanners were themselves an important impetus for the rise of Big Data. Focus now on the data record produced; even thirty years ago was decades after the advent of mainframe computers, so that cash register is going to yield some kind of data output, however rudimentary, that will be reported and aggregated. To manage cash as a merchant, one must have a record of transaction amounts, a requirement that hasn't changed since bookkeeping was invented during the Italian renaissance. Hence, back in the 1980s, at the store level, we will know that a transaction of $82.63 occurred at

10:05 a.m. on July 18. Store management will know by the end of the day that a total of 1,684 transactions occurred at that store, with total cash receipts of about $1.4 million. At the corporate level, that revenue will be recorded as coming from store #37 in the Northeast region, and there will be a corporate database that records other data about this store (square footage, number of employees, labor costs, etc.). Other databases will record the shipments of goods to stock the shelves and the costs to obtain and distribute those goods. All of this (and much more) is necessary to compute revenue, costs, and profit, as has been done since supermarket chains were introduced in the early part of the 20th century.

Please accept that quite a lot of interesting analyses can be done with this still very limited, 1980's era secondary data. Management can rank order and compare the firm's hundreds of individual stores on various metrics such as sales per square foot; can do analyses of sales trends over time, across regions, by season, and day part; can run straightforward promotions experiments; and much else. The firm may even be able to associate changes in its advertising and promotional expenditure with fluctuations in store sales, if its recordkeeping is good enough (see the Europet case at the end of Part II).

But there are two key limitations to what could be done in the old days. First, the consumer is invisible. Managers know that $82.63 was spent, but don't know by whom, and also don't know what specific goods were in their basket. Second, even back then the firm could extract a lot more information from these store encounters, *but only by engaging in effortful primary research*. The firm could station someone at the store entrance with a clipboard to tally how many men versus women shop there by time of day. The store manager could manually track the movement of goods displayed at the end of an aisle to confirm that end-of-aisle positioning provides a powerful boost to sales, and to quantify this boost (which lets the supermarket chain determine how much it should charge the manufacturer of those goods for the privilege). Because of these limitations, scale and detail are lacking, little is produced automatically and then only with a delay, and the firm has very little consumer data.

Now wind the clock forward to today and send that consumer (with a lot more gray hair) to that store (extensively remodeled) to place goods on the same conveyor belt (apparently unchanged—it's a mechanical device after all, not a piece of electronics). The "cash register" has changed most of all. It is hooked up to an optical scanner, and it can compile and record much more information than the transaction amount and time of day. The consumer has also changed in one other respect: he presented his loyalty card to be scanned as well as his credit card.

Consider the data string that can now be produced out of the same expenditure of $82.63. (Some of what follows is extrapolation and may not reflect what stores actually do with data collection today, but it is all in principle possible.) The optical scanner will capture information about each of the 34 items in the basket. It will record not only that this consumer bought yogurt, but that it was plain Greek yogurt in the large size container from a particular brand, not currently associated with any promotional offer, and the most expensive yogurt of its kind in terms of unit price. The scan record will note that blueberries and wheat germ were also bought with this yogurt, along with an organic juice, but no meat of any kind. (Are you getting a picture of this consumer yet?)

The loyalty card will at least identify the consumer by gender and ZIP code. By means of the card's identifying number, the store can if it wishes compile data on every purchase the consumer has made in the past N months, the frequency with which he came to the store, the things he buys every trip versus on many trips versus rarely, whether he uses coupons and from what source, and so forth. And it is potentially possible to link the data on the consumer recorded on the loyalty card to other databases; for instance, his credit card transaction set, which will give us a picture of this consumer's total annual spending, and from there, a good read on income (which we will already have gotten a sense of from his ZIP code).

At the corporate level of the supermarket chain, there are millions of loyalty card holders and millions of individual items scanned every day, chunked into sets of several dozen items per shopping basket. The transaction data accumulates in real time, although some of the aggregation operations performed on consumer data may only be run periodically.

With this contemporary example in hand, the meaning of scale, detail, automaticity, timing, and data type can be unpacked. Big Data is about scale and detail: millions of transactions at the item level, crossed with millions of individual consumers, with data strings on each consumer ballooning into the thousands of variables (yogurt yes or no, breakfast sausage yes or no, store brand yes or no, etc.). Big Data is about automaticity and right-now availability. Once there is an optical scanner hooked up to a competent database, all this detail on customer behavior is collected without human intervention and in real time. Once a program has been written to compile information by individual consumer, the program can perform these operations automatically and as frequently as management wishes. Finally, note that the character of the data that can be collected has fundamentally changed; it is no longer accounting data but data on *customer behavior*—who bought what. It is more particularly product constellation data, and knowing that the consumer bought yogurt, granola, fruit, and juice—and did not buy bacon, eggs, or Wonder Bread—tells us a great deal about lifestyle choices, and about other products the consumer might or might not be interested in.

In a moment I'll consider what Big Data might mean in a B2B rather than a consumer context, and examine other instances of Big Data apart from retail transaction data. First, here is an example of the power of learning about product constellations.

B2C Example

A store manager for a big-box discount chain[1] gets a call from an irate father: "I demand to know why you are sending coupons for a baby carriage and a cradle to my 16-year-old under-age, unmarried daughter. This is an outrage!" Store manager, exhibiting good customer focus skills, apologizes, promises to look into how that happened, and offers to redeem the coupon for cash if the father wishes, to be spent on a more appropriate product. "Yeah, I'll think about it," says the still-angry father. Next day, still feeling bad about the event, inasmuch as they attend the same rather strict church locally, the store manager calls the father back, to see if further mollification might be in order. Reached on the phone, the father hesitated a moment before replying, "I'm afraid there have been some things going on in my house that I wasn't aware of," and proceeds to explain that he had just learned his daughter *was* pregnant.

In this example we may presume that the store had implemented the kind of product constellation analysis described above for the supermarket. Analysis of the accumulated loyalty card data had perhaps determined that when product X and product Y are purchased together, then the probability is measurably higher that a baby carriage, baby furniture, and other paraphernalia associated with a new birth will be purchased within the next few months.

---

[1]This story is based on an incident reported at Target, described in the *New York Times Magazine* story by Charles Duhigg, "How Companies Learn Your Secrets," February 16, 2012. I've taken extensive liberties with the actual story to serve my purposes here.

The appropriate marketing response is to issue coupons for other members of the product constellation, in an attempt to corral for that store as much of the new mother's birth-related purchases as possible. A big-box retailer like Target or Walmart, with a very broad assortment of merchandise, is in a good position to implement this kind of strategy, sometimes referred to as "share of wallet" (winning as large as possible share of the consumer's purchases in some broad category).

The upshot is that the store knew the girl was pregnant before her family did. To say "knew" is a bit of a misnomer, of course. It's not a matter of a young staffer standing up in a cubicle at headquarters and yelling, "Jane Smith in Dayton is pregnant—get me a FedEx shipping label!" But in some meaningful sense, the store's loyalty card database "knew" about a particular product constellation, and knew that purchase of this constellation had just been initiated by customer #036-1264359-2 with a mailing address of Dayton, Ohio. Everything else happened automatically. Moreover, the response to the coupons will also be automatically tracked. The discount amounts will be refined, and the database will learn whether a baby carriage was the best member of the constellation to target with coupons, and whether product X was the best precursor for predicting launch of this constellation of purchases, and so forth. The system is self-improving in that sense; it "learns" and gets better as more data accumulates.

B2B Examples of Big Data

Can't think of any! More seriously, B2B markets are defined as those where there are a *small* number of customers making a few very large purchases on an infrequent basis—the 186 telecommunications customers worldwide who can spend $20 million on a central office switch, say, of whom 49 are your current customers. How do you get "big" data out of 49 customers and a product that is repurchased on a once every five- to seven-year basis? A great deal of internal and secondary data will be available in this category, of course, including logs of customer calls, sales projections for the industry, and so forth—but that was true decades before Big Data came on the scene, and involves something much smaller in scale.

A more helpful response might be that there are of course Big Data applications in the B2B technology space, but, only insofar as these are either: (1) not market research data per se; or (2) involve elements of business operations where B2B and B2C don't actually differ that much, either because the B2B market has tens of thousands of buying units rather than a hundred or two, and/or the Big Data in question involves an activity like maintaining a website, where the activities aren't so different across the B2B/B2C boundary.

As an example of the former, consider the "Internet of Things" (IoT). One of the major sources of Big Data going forward arises from the ever-increasing capacity to embed sensors in virtually anything, sensors that can communicate their data collection in real time. General Electric can embed sensors in its aircraft engines and monitor their functioning, for instance. But as this engine maintenance example makes clear, by and large, the IoT does not produce market research data, as defined in this book.

To give an example of a Big Data application that applies to B2B as well as B2C, what might be helpful is a nonretail example (there is no "retail" in B2B markets, making it one of the dividing lines that distinguish B2B from B2C). Branding issues, by contrast, are not so different across B2B and B2C, especially when the B2B product has tens of thousands or hundreds of thousands of buyers, as will be the case in professional services, office furniture, printers and other office equipment, some kinds of computers, and so forth. In these instances, a "business" is the customer, but counting departments in large firms, and small firms, and even individual professionals in some cases, the total number of customers is large, not small, and Big Data in the market research sense comes into play. In these cases, there is a proto-mass market—not the tens of millions of buyers seen in true B2C, but still, closer to that pole than to the telecommunications example where there were 186 buyers. Given a proto-mass market, mass communications and branding become a concern, and the issues aren't that different across B2B and B2C.

In the branding context, Big Data means the enormous amount of text produced on the web in which brands figure. Every day, countless tweets, Facebook posts, blogs, online reviews, Pinterest pins, and discussion board comments are produced that name a brand, a product category, or a consumer problem. It can all be aggregated using the same tools that allow you to search the web on Google or Bing. If you want to know what customers are saying about your brand and your product category, this information is now there for the scraping.

The challenge, of course, is what to do with it all. No individual or team could read even a fraction of what is produced concerning your brand. The reigning approach is to score it for sentiment using programs that contain a dictionary of positive and negative words. Various programs—or rather, the models underlying the program—will weight particular words differently. Should "stinks" receive a more or less negative rating than "awful"? Is "I am so angry" more negative than "this brand is so awful"? This kind of automated sentiment scoring is one of the frontiers of natural-language processing, and the underlying computer science continues to improve. With scoring of this type, you can take the pulse of your brand's sentiment on a very fine-grained basis, whether you are an old-line B2B manufacturer, or a new consumer service. In the old days, you were lucky if a brand awareness or brand attitude survey was taken once a quarter, and each of those measurements consisted of a stand-alone survey involving considerable time, effort, and expense (i.e., non-automatic and effortful primary research). Now, in the world of Big Data, you can measure it at least at the weekly level, or sometimes daily, and hourly may not be too far off, as the Twitterverse takes hold.

PROCEDURE

Big Data is so diverse that it is difficult to describe a single procedure that would apply to most instances. The steps below assume you are a forward-looking marketing executive who wants to explore what Big Data could do for your organization in the context of market research.

Step 1: What Do You Have?

Take stock of the customer data that you already have. If your firm is big enough, you may be surprised by the difficulty and effort required to accomplish this first step. And in a firm of almost any size, you should expect a mixture of pushback. ("What do you mean by Big Data?") and incomprehension ("Are you asking for fine-grained sales records?") You had better be prepared to give an example, perhaps using one of the stories supplied earlier in this chapter. For instance, "Where do we store data on loyalty card purchases—and what data do we have on each loyalty card holder?" Or, "Who monitors our website for usage and who keeps those statistics?" Or, "Do we use any services that crawl the web for mentions of our brand?"

Step 2: What Would You Like to Have?

Regardless of whether the yield from the first step is disappointing, as it will often be, early in the process you owe it to yourself to sit down with a blank sheet of paper, and set aside some time to think. What you need to get on the page is a list of possible data points you'd like to have. Start by envisioning a concrete customer—yourself, if you are a buyer in the category, or a named customer/firm that you know well. List each desired item of information as a variable with a self-explanatory name or label: for example, "purchase frequency" or "amount per transaction." In many cases, what you are looking for is not so much customer characteristics—age, income—as specific behaviors: what items were/were not bought, what service requests were made, and so forth. Those customer characteristics will be important down the road, but in many cases, this data is already in hand (especially in a B2B context) or already understood. It's the combination of customer characteristics, behaviors, and events that represent the future promise of Big Data; and to get to that combination, you have to envision the kinds of behaviors that could never before be easily tracked.

You will want to work on this effort over several different days—it's the kind of task that lends itself to unconscious processing offline, and you need to give it time. You will want a couple of white board sessions with colleagues as well. Throughout, you are looking for data points that could be automatically captured, or that could be constructed from automatically collected data (purchase frequency won't be in the raw data stream; you'll compute it from the string of dates on which purchases occurred). That is the promise of Big Data: behaviors that are tracked without special intervention or human decision, on an ongoing basis, in the course of accommodating the behavior itself (keep the supermarket optical scanner in mind).

Step 3: How, Who, Where, and When?

Next, how are you going to get this data (or how will it be stored, managed, and protected, if you already have it)? In terms of new data, this could be as simple as running an extraction program against existing scattered databases, or as complicated as setting up a loyalty card program. One way or another you have to end up with a database that allows you to view the data by customer, by web visit, or whatever viewpoint makes sense. However the data are actually stored, you need to be able to create a file for analysis in which customers are the row headings, variables are the column labels, and values are entered in the cells.

Finally, who is going to make sense of the data once you have it? At this juncture, finding a person who can make sense of the data—make it actionable in terms of marketing response—may be the greatest challenge of all. The Big Data skill set (itself only loosely defined) isn't central to most MBA programs. These particular data analytic skills also aren't part of the training of quantitative market researchers, at least as yet; that discipline was founded on knowledge of *sample* statistics, techniques appropriate for analysis of effortful, expensive, one-shot studies consisting of 1,500 customers or less. On the other hand, a typical marketing instance of Big Data is child's play for someone trained in computer science. The programming challenge is trivial—lots of people can write programs to be run against Big Data. The actual challenge, in terms of finding people with the necessary skills, lies deeper. To make this clear, I want to return to my earlier examples in this chapter.

What may have passed unnoticed on first reading is that each of the examples allowed for meaningful marketing action because there was an underlying *model* that could be applied to the raw data. Consider the example of sentiment scoring. The model here is literally one-dimensional: that there is a sentiment continuum with a positive pole and a negative pole, and many shadings in between. Consumers' positions with respect to a brand can be modeled on this one dimension: Each and every customer can be positioned in terms of how positive or negative they are toward the brand. The deep assumption is that a position toward the positive pole leads to approach actions, while a negative position leads to avoidance of the brand. This simple model allows the thousands of different words that might be used in connection with the brand to be organized into a single score.

The baby carriage example rests on a more sophisticated model, which I referred to in terms of a product constellation. This is the idea that consumers don't buy one product at a time in a compartmentalized fashion; rather, suites of products may be purchased, as occasioned by particular life events, of which having a baby is a prime example. Here the model is of a multidimensional space in which products cluster based on unobserved life events. As you might guess, the mathematics behind identifying a cluster are quite different than those required to place all adjectives on a single dimension of positivity and negativity.

The model behind the supermarket example was more sophisticated still: the idea that consumers do not buy individual food items, but rather, provision themselves for the meals they anticipate. In some deep sense it is wrong to model consumers as deciding whether or not to buy this brand of yogurt, or whether to buy yogurt or not. Those choices do get made, but fundamentally what the consumer is doing is deciding what kind of breakfast to have; and since few people want to face that choice afresh each and every morning, the decision is really about what kind of lifestyle to lead, and what types of breakfast follow from that lifestyle choice. The underlying model is sophisticated enough to know that for most meals and meal occasions, the consumer chooses from a small palette of culturally specified options; hence, meal choice, as gleaned from shopping basket data, is a window onto lifestyle choice, which in turn, is a powerful tool for segmenting consumers into different groups who may be more or less receptive to particular marketing offers. To whom would you send a coupon for a new organic entree: the yogurt and fruit consumer, or the bacon and eggs consumer?

The real problem with "who," then, is finding an individual with enough computer science chops to handle the programming of very large data sets, but enough business savvy to find the buyer behavior model that unlocks the marketing options latent in your newly assembled data set. You can't just bark at some programmer, "Find me the product constellation clusters." You don't know yet whether that's a useful model for your data. You need someone with a broad knowledge of the different models that have been applied to buyer behavior, who can reason creatively about what might be done with your data set. People with this particular combination of skills are still pretty rare as of 2015; but if you are a young person reading this book, who has both a taste for math and an interest in business, it is not a bad career path to consider.

FUTURE DIRECTIONS

In one sense, Big Data is itself one of the most important "future directions" in marketing research, making this section somewhat superfluous for this particular chapter. But within Big Data, I think I can point to one area that is not developing as quickly as some and whose potential still lies mostly in the future. Reviewing again the examples, two out of the three were not so far removed from older and more traditional forms of secondary data, which were focused on financial and accounting information. Both the supermarket and the baby carriage examples rested on purchase data—sales records—not different in kind from information that has been gathered for decades under the heading of internal secondary data. Only the third example, of sentiment scoring, used a kind of data not routinely compiled or even available in past years: large compilations of free-form text.

Hence, an important future direction within Big Data will be the development of more and more sophisticated models for *textual* analysis. I labeled automated sentiment scoring as a "one-dimensional" model with malice aforethought. Textual data is much richer in information than can be captured by collapsing it to a single dimension. Consider Yelp reviews, for example. To grasp the opportunity to go beyond sentiment scoring, I invite you to browse a dozen reviews each for two restaurants you have never visited but might be interested to patronize. Each Yelp review sums up its take on the restaurant with a simple sentiment rating on a 1 to 5 scale, as compared to the text of the reviews themselves, which for expensive restaurants, may run from 100 to 500 words in length. Try to formulate in your mind what is conveyed in the text of the reviews—what you *learned* about the restaurant—that isn't captured by the rating number at the top of the review. That, in a nutshell, is the challenge for Big Data moving forward: how to do more with free-form text than simply scoring it for sentiment.

A second future opportunity in Big Data lies in the automated analysis of pictures that relate to your brand or the product category in which your brand competes. After all, today there are not only countless text mentions of your brand on the web; with Pinterest, Tumblr, and Instagram, there are also countless images of your brand and category. Often these have a verbal tag and can be located as easily as a text comment. What can't easily be done today is to identify images relevant to your brand that are not verbally tagged. An even greater opportunity lies in analyzing the visual context in which your brand appears. Part of the challenge here is pure computer science; the piece that is of interest in the context of market research is procedures for making sense of image analyses once these improve. What should a clothing brand look for in pictures: Indoor versus outdoor settings? Daytime versus evening? Work or leisure? It may be marketed as a "business suit," but if large numbers of posted pictures show the wearer in a bar or nightclub after 10 p.m., clearly this is a product that serves more than one purpose. The march of technology will drive forward the needed computer science; the real challenge is deciding what to look for in images of your brand.

STRENGTHS AND WEAKNESSES

The key strength of Big Data is that it's, well, BIG! The data set examples in this chapter provide information on customer behavior that is orders of magnitude larger than could ever be gained from traditional market research. Because there are millions of records, rather than the hundreds produced by a survey, much, much more fine-grained breakdowns can be performed in identifying particular customer groups. To use a television analogy, Big Data compares to survey data the way an ultra-high-definition television compares to an Etch A Sketch: It has a much higher resolution, but that rather understates the difference.

A second strength of Big Data is that it is real: It consists of the purchases customers actually made, and the unsolicited comments customers actually made while going about their day-to-day lives. The bane of traditional market research, whether surveys or interviews, is that it often rests on self-report data; the customer tells you that he buys such-and-such a product "often" or "all the time." Nonbehavioral comments about unobservable mental states ("I think it is important to eat a healthy breakfast") occur in response to interview prompts given in a particular social setting that may elicit unnatural or calculated responses. Hence, self-report data is notorious for the biases that may infest it. Big Data is about the real world, a report of what was done and said out there.

A third strength is the automatic, ongoing, up-to-date character of Big Data. Traditional market research is delayed, effortful, and takes the form of a one-shot study. Even if repeated, the interval between surveys will often be substantial. The limitations of delayed data should be obvious: If a store can't tell that a woman is pregnant until after a birth record is purchased on a monthly sweep of county data, the store has no opportunity to market late-in-pregnancy products to her.

The primary weakness of Big Data, which I've ignored for the most part in the preceding examples, is that it provides data that are correlational but not causal. It shows that this purchase is associated with this other purchase, or that customers with these characteristics are more likely to buy this product. It does not show whether that characteristic caused the purchase; both the customer characteristic and the purchase might be a function of some third variable not in the data set. You can often infer cause from association—she bought this product because her pregnancy has advanced through the second trimester—but this remains an inference. Only when you target these individuals with a coupon for a baby carriage, and verify that we get much higher than baseline response to that coupon, do you have causal evidence. You can observe much with Big Data, but it is only when you act in response, and get a particular pattern of results, that you have strong evidence for the validity of the association as an index of some underlying cause, in this case, pregnancy. Big Data is initially passive data, weaker than what can be obtained from experiments.

A second key weakness of Big Data is that it tends to be mute and superficial. Big Data doesn't tell us what the consumer was thinking when they made that purchase, and it doesn't tell us what the consumer intended by that web post. This is the positive flip side of self-report data: The consumer has unique access to his state of mind and his own integrative calculus of sentiment. The strength of interviews in particular is the ability to understand the consumer on his or her own terms, to see the world from their standpoint. Interviews, as a form of human conversation, tap the human ability to understand another person by mutual dialogue. Big Data dispenses with this viewpoint, and tries to relate past behavior and future behavior directly.

This second weakness of Big Data has a long history in market research, dating back 50 years to the first eye-tracking studies of advertising response, and continuing through today's brain scanning methodologies. The promise has always been that the secrets of the human mind could be revealed without asking that mind what it thinks, but instead by observing some trace or track left by mental activity. I think of this quest in terms of fool's gold; on philosophical grounds, I don't think it is possible to tap into the inner workings of a mental system except through interacting with it as a fellow mental system— as in talking to the customer. But this continues to be a major debate within contemporary philosophy, which extends far beyond the narrow bounds of commercial market research.

A final weakness of Big Data, not intrinsic in the way of the first two but important to note, is its susceptibility, at least in the present era, to hype. A bonus of having lived in Silicon Valley for decades is that I've seen tech hype come and go; it's a staple of business here in the Valley. The plain fact is that multiple vendors stand ready to sell you expensive hardware and software to facilitate your Big Data setup. The more excited you are about the unbounded potential of Big Data, the more money they can earn as system providers. There's no money to be made by offering measured and judicious assessments like the one in this chapter.

DOs AND DON'Ts

Do have a plan with respect to identifying what Big Data you might have in-house, or could easily get, and how it could be put to work for you.

Don't assume that compiling Big Data is the same as getting answers from it. Data don't speak for themselves.

Do spend a fraction of each work week developing and assessing models of what drives your customer to do what they do. If you can come up with a model, you can probably find data with which to flesh it out for a test; but if all you have is data, it is unlikely that a good model will emerge spontaneously from that data.

Don't fall for the hype. Investments in Big Data should be subject to the same ROI analysis as any other market research expenditure.

DISCUSSION QUESTIONS

1. Consider the privacy implications of the Big Data examples (coupons for a baby carriage, loyalty card record of purchases for a supermarket). Will they vary by store type? How worried are you (or should you be) if there is a data string somewhere that records *everything* you bought over the past year (*every* legal purchase)? Remember that this data string will not sit quietly in a vault, but will be massaged for implications about what you might buy next—or even, whether you are likely to be an influenceable swing voter in the next election.

   a. If the data string was store-specific rather than universal across all your purchases, would it make a difference which type of store, in terms of how concerned you would be?

2. Two prominent examples of Big Data in the marketing domain are purchase transaction data (i.e., your complete shopping basket over time) and your browsing history (cookies indicate to a website what other websites you have visited and even what search terms you have entered; these can be used to select what banner ad to serve up).

    a. Compile a list of other examples of Big Data in marketing that are distinct from either purchase transactions or browsing history. You can point to data that may not be gathered yet, but that is likely to become available in the next few years.

    b. Across your list, explain which of these Big Data types are likely to have the greatest impact on marketing productivity, and which the least. Explain.

3. A skeptical take on Big Data is that it will provide a one-time boost to profitability that will soon peter out once the low-hanging fruit has been gathered. To use the Target example, there will be a boost to the effectiveness of promotion once the initial set of product constellations is identified. That will boost corporate results for a few fiscal quarters. But there will be no way to further refine the "baby products constellation" after that initial hit, and no possibility of identifying new product constellations after the first set of "obvious" ones.

    a. Take a position pro or con this skeptical view and defend it.

SUGGESTED READINGS

Trzesniewski, K. H., Donnellan, M. B., & Lucas, R. E. (2010). *Secondary data analysis: An introduction for psychologists.* Chicago, IL: American Psychological Association.	Not as economically focused as some treatments, hence helpful for Big Data approached in terms of consumer psychology.
Davenport, T. (2014). *Big data at work.* Cambridge, MA: Harvard Business Review Press.	Even in this business-focused treatment, note the number of applications that have nothing to do with marketing per se.

CASE FOR PART II

SUGGESTED CASE: EUROPET (HARVARD #KEL368)

Synopsis

The advertising manager for a multinational petroleum firm is challenged by a more senior executive to show that advertising for their service station/ convenience store combo has been effective. More particularly, she asks him to show that there is a positive return on investment for the television and radio advertising expenditure. The senior executive is clearly skeptical—she wants empirical evidence that there is a positive ROI. Otherwise, she seems likely to slash the ad budget.

Note: To answer the questions below, you will need to download the spreadsheet that accompanies this case on the Harvard site.

Your instructor may use this case to discuss the transition from traditional secondary research to the new world of Big Data. This case uses the traditional sampling approach: Sales and advertising data from one city and one time interval have been compiled, at the relatively coarse level of weekly data, along with half a dozen other variables potentially of interest. The 100 sales records that result suffice for a student to learn appropriate analytic techniques, or for a more old-fashioned executive to get a feel for the advertising–sales relationship in this particular line of business.

In the new world of Big Data, there would be no sampling: The advertising manager would use the *entire* sales database—thousands of service stations in dozens of regions worldwide, along with daily sales data, probably broken down into types of merchandise (no reason to expect ice cream novelties to have the same seasonality as hot coffee). The data string would also be much longer—not just the fewer than a dozen variables contained in the spreadsheet, but dozens more.

Nonetheless, most of the conceptual issues are similar, and also many of the analytic techniques are the same, regardless of whether one approaches the issue of advertising effectiveness in the spirit of old-style analysis of a sample of internal secondary data, or the new world of comprehensive Big Data.

Questions

1. Compute the ROI for television and for radio advertising separately, using the simplest possible linear regression containing just one predictor.

   (a) Hint: There are two steps to this problem. First you have to run the regression, and then you have to use the results to relate the cost of the advertising to the incremental profit (if any) produced by the advertising.

2. What's the best way to examine the joint effect of television and radio advertising? If the beta coefficients change when both types of advertising are included in the regression, what does that mean, and what are the implications for computing ROI on advertising?

3. Next, add one or more of the other predictors into the regression. Make an argument for whatever you include: Is it best to include all other available predictors, or only some? Which ones, if the latter?

   (a) If the beta coefficients for TV and radio advertising change after including other variables, what do these changes imply for the ROI analysis conducted initially?

   (b) How many possible regressions could be run against sales, if you were free to include any subset of predictor variables (e.g., temperature only, precipitation only, or both)?

      i. If there were exactly twice as many predictor variables, by how much would the total number of possible regressions increase?

      ii. In Big Data, there will always be at least two to four times as many variables as given here. How many regressions would be possible if there were four times as many predictor variables?

      iii. Extra credit: Discuss the implications of your calculations in i. and ii. for significance testing, and for extracting managerially useful findings in a world of Big Data.

PART III

QUALITATIVE RESEARCH

———◆———

OVERVIEW

This overview looks at the qualitative compartment in the toolbox and compares and contrasts individual qualitative tools primarily to one another, with an occasional nod to the fundamental factors that distinguish any qualitative tool from quantitative tools in general. I also give some space here to qualitative techniques that did not merit a chapter of their own, such as ethnography.

The element that unifies all qualitative research techniques is that a *human being* functions as the primary measurement instrument or tool for information acquisition. By contrast, in all quantitative techniques some artifact, like a questionnaire, intervenes to function as the primary instrument. Although human beings can acquire information about the world through any of their senses, in the context of market research the two primary senses are hearing and sight. Thus, in qualitative research you can listen to customers and you can watch what they do. Moreover, you can combine listening and watching in different proportions in any particular research endeavor, and the proportion of watching to listening is one of the key factors that distinguishes the different qualitative tools from one another.

A salient characteristic of human beings when asked to play the role of measuring instrument is that humans can be very acute but are seldom very precise. This contrast captures both the strength and the weakness of qualitative research techniques. You can obtain novel insights of great depth and richness by listening to customers and watching them interact with your product or service, but your results will seldom be very exact. The paradigmatic conclusion from qualitative research takes the form of a sentence such as "Some customers felt that _____, while many other customers felt differently that _____." There is, alas, seldom any prospect of being more exact than "some" or "many."

The value of qualitative research lies in the substance of what fills in those blanks, since qualitative will seldom yield any exactitude with respect to how many customers in the market feel the one way or the other, or what specific characteristics would help us to identify customers likely to feel one way or the other. If instead you want exact predictions or precise counts, the sort of thing that can be summed up in a single number ("This segment represents 37% of the market"), you have to do quantitative research, as discussed in Part IV. Put another way, if you can fill in the blanks above on your own—if you already know the feelings that matter in terms of dividing up the customer base—you can proceed directly to quantitative research to count how many people, of what kind, tend to feel the one way or the other. However, if you don't know what matters to customers or what divides them with respect to what's important—if the blanks are indeed blank—then you had better start with some kind of qualitative research.

Listening Versus Watching

The chart below provides a useful way of organizing the named qualitative techniques. It divvies these up according to whether the market is B2C versus B2B, and whether the particular technique is limited to listening or incorporates some degree of looking and watching as well.

	Listening only → → →		*Greater amounts of watching*
B2C	• One-on-one interviews • Focus groups		Ethnography
B2B	• Focus groups	Customer visits	

Interestingly, although pure cases are common on the listening side—qualitative research in which no visual observation of customers interacting with products occurs—it is rare in market research to see instances of pure qualitative observation, where the researcher takes a vow of silence and never converses with any of the customers involved in the research, but simply watches. This makes sense, if you accept that language is a key part of what makes us human, and that another key element that distinguishes human beings is our capacity to socially interact with other people using speech. If it is the human being that is the measurement instrument in qualitative research, why shut down the greater part of that instrument's capacity?

Conversely, language is so powerful, and our understanding of other people is so multilayered and intuitive, that it is easy to imagine qualitative research that skips observation altogether, relying on the consumers interviewed to tell us what we would observe if we did bother to watch them. And much of what we want to learn about by doing qualitative market research is unobservable in principle: It is virtually impossible to see satisfaction, or how satisfaction varies across elements of the service delivered, or how it connects to brand loyalty. But it is quite straightforward to converse about such matters.

Lab Versus Field

If the plan is only to listen to customers, then the interviews are likely to take place in a specialized facility, for convenience and for control of the environment, so as to prevent interruptions and other unwanted intrusions. These specialized facilities can be thought of as laboratories. Because of the logistics involved with focus groups, these almost always occur in such a laboratory setting. Once the choice is made to situate the research in a lab, it then becomes impossible to observe the customer using the product in situ. In my experience, such listening-focused, laboratory-situated kind of qualitative research predominates in the B2C context.

Far less common in B2C contexts, amounting to a specialized technique, is qualitative research that takes place in the field, or ethnography as this is termed. Ethnographic research is modelled on anthropological research with primitive tribes conducted by scholars like Margaret Mead, modified to fit the purposes of commercial market research.

To get a sense of the distinctive character and potential contribution of ethnographic B2C research, consider a manufacturer of barbecue grills used by suburban homeowners. This product category could easily be researched in a laboratory setting, probably via focus groups. A group interview, despite occurring in a laboratory, would allow any number of topics to be explored:

motivations for grilling, grilling occasions and the actions and preparations associated with each, roles of different family members in the overall undertaking, the meaning of grilling as a rite of masculinity, and on and on. But you would never see a grill in use with such laboratory research, nor would you see how the grill was set up relative to the kitchen and the back yard, nor would you have a chance to see who congregates around the grill when in use or how food is brought to, modified at, and delivered from the grill. And any part of these actions that is automatic or tacit is unlikely to be voiced by a customer in a laboratory.

An ethnographic approach would allow all these observations along with countless conversations. On this path, researchers engaged by the grill manufacturer would undertake to visit a number of suburban homes and spend a couple of hours at each on diverse eating occasions to observe the grilling process from start to finish. The researchers would also have many conversations of varying length with individual participants present at each barbecue. The researchers might not confine themselves to suburban homes but could structure the sample to include urban and rural settings as well. They might further visit stores that sell grills and hang around the sales floor for a few hours, observing and talking to a variety of people. They might visit grilling contests, or even shadow a professional barbecue outfit as it puts on a barbecue for a client. These outfits are common in California where I live, bringing their gear to parties, school events, fundraisers, and the like.

More subtly, the questions asked of customers by the ethnographic researchers will vary from what is seen in the laboratory setting as well. Rather than "How many burners do you require on your grill?" and "Why is that?" the researchers may ask questions like, "I was curious why you put that meat on your biggest and hottest burner but then insulated it with several layers of foil—what's going on there?" These will be questions triggered on the spot by observed actions of the customer. The important point again is that many such actions are so automatic, so tacit, that they might never be recalled or come up in a lab setting even if the question was, "Describe to me step by step how you grill _____." Part of the potential value of ethnographic research is that one can catch the customer "in the act," and ask a clarifying question on the spot. The more general promise is that with ethnographic research, the manufacturer can understand the entire social and cultural system in which their particular product plays a role, and also understand in depth tacit, un-vocalized elements of what the customer actually does with the product.

This promise is underwritten by the advantages of being on site, of combining observation with conversation, and of talking to multiple participants in diverse settings. Ethnographic research will always be about grilling, or perhaps even the suburban lifestyle, and never really about grill product features and functions. If the research is any good, it will inform the grill manufacturer's strategic marketing, but not in the narrow way of a finding such as "to satisfy experienced grillers, a gas grill has to have at least three separate burners with low medium and high BTU outputs."

Comparing Laboratory Versus Field

If I wrote the preceding section persuasively enough, you may be starting to feel that laboratory research—short one-on-one interviews taking place in a white-walled room on the third floor of a suburban office building—sounds pretty pallid, not to say insipid, and perhaps of no great value. Bracket that thought. It contains a germ of truth but also a good helping of ignorance. Since I am not going to discuss one-on-one interviews in a laboratory setting outside of this overview, I'll use it as my contrast case for developing the limits of ethnography. Essentially, all the canons and caveats concerning research planning laid out in Chapter 2 and applied to the overall market research toolbox apply equally well within the qualitative compartment of that toolbox. Here again, research planning means evaluating the suitability of a particular qualitative tool to the task at hand, and evaluating trade-offs in terms of cost, convenience, and payoff. Each qualitative tool, ethnography included, comes with its own package of distinct strengths and weaknesses.

For example, what would an ethnographic investigation of life insurance be like? Can you see life insurance being consumed? Where is life insurance consumed—at the kitchen table, or in the funeral home? On the other hand, it is easy to imagine an emotionally rich and intimate discussion of the motivations for purchase of life insurance occurring in a focus group or series of one-on-one interviews, with the depth of the discussion limited only by the professional interviewer's skill and empathy. To take a more mundane example, what would an ethnographic investigation of mouthwash look like? Shall we crowd the research team into the bathroom to watch people gargle?

It may have also struck you that although the field study of grilling would certainly produce a large volume of data, the task of translating those conversations and observations into actionable insights that can be used to market the grills of a particular manufacturer appears quite daunting. The skill required is likely to be rare. The ethnographic research described may also take a considerable amount of time, and it won't be cheap.

A tentative conclusion about ethnography, then, would be that it makes the most sense to the extent that one or more of the following elements is present.

1. The product category is visibly consumed over time and in space, the way durable products often are and services tend not to be. To be even more concrete, consumption of the product probably involves movement of the body within an everyday setting.

2. The product category is inherently rich in sociocultural meaning and is used in a social setting where there are multiple other constituents who, of course, would never be included in a laboratory-situated set of interviews.

3. The field in which the product is consumed is unfamiliar to the researcher or is novel within the society. The former may apply in the case of regional or subcultural consumption practices that fall outside the middle class in which most market researchers are rooted. How many Manhattan-based researchers really understand life in rural Mississippi? The latter applies in the case of new technologies.

4. The decision problem that motivated the research is long term and strategy-focused rather than centered on a particular product, and the research objectives are highly exploratory. Accordingly, the time frame is relaxed and the budget is loosely bounded.

5. The category is long-established, countless interviews have been done over the decades, and the firm seeks novel insights not obtainable through repeating the same sorts of interviews that have been done decade after decade. Put another the way, if the "green field, get new insights" criterion of #4 applies, ethnography is at least worth considering, even if it is ultimately not pursued due to criteria #1, #2, or #3.

When one or more of these criteria fail to be met, but there is still an impetus to do qualitative and exploratory research, then laboratory-situated interviews are likely to be conducted. Recall again the power of language and social interaction: For tens of thousands of years, until first literacy and then bureaucratic rationalization appeared, often the only way to learn anything was to ask questions of people who knew something about the topic. Asking questions to acquire information from others is part and parcel of what we do as humans. Lab-situated interviews are just a formalization of that intrinsically human practice.

Now back to the germ of truth in the perception that lab-situated interviews tend toward the pallid, as compared to listening and looking while out in the field. The truth of this perception has shaped qualitative research practice in several respects. The important thing to keep in mind is that much of what product managers might want to know about customers in order to improve corporate outcomes is, not to put too fine a point on it, mundane in the extreme, not to say excruciatingly tedious. The subject matter is fascinating to the product manager, because he or she lives and breathes these issues, and is highly motivated to advance his or her career by means of improved customer understanding. But to a neutral observer, and even to the consumers themselves, the product and its use often don't count for much. B-o-o-o-ring!

Accordingly, market research practice has responded to this uncomfortable truth as follows. First, in the B2C sphere, group interviews predominate over individual interviews. While products may be boring, other people are often interesting, and almost always stimulating. A group can spend two lively hours discussing a topic that would run dry with an individual in well under 30 minutes. The prevalence of group interviews, then, is one response to the mundane and unengaging issues that are nonetheless useful for marketers to understand. There are other factors that promote the use of group interviews, including the time efficiency of talking to multiple consumers at once, and social factors specific to group interaction, which I'll take up in the focus group chapter; but the need to make the topic engaging is not least among the reasons for doing group interviews.

Second, when individual interviews are done for whatever reason, they will almost always be instrumented—they won't consist merely of questions and answers in a conversational format. At the simplest extreme, the interviewee may review concept statements, examine packaging, or peruse past advertisements and rough ads for a future campaign. In more complex arrangements, the conversation may be structured by a procedure, such as laddering (a systematic attempt to expose the ultimate values driving a particular preference). The interviewer may provide structured stimuli, such as the set of competitive products, or may use projective stimuli, analogous to Rorschach inkblots, that have been designed to help consumers articulate tacit aspects of how they engage with a product category. All of these instruments, in addition to their knowledge contribution, help to keep the individual interview from sinking into tedium.

The third and final response to the pallid character of interviews conducted in white-walled rooms in a suburban office park is, Don't go there! Get out into the field, and look around as well as listen. This response is seen most often in B2B qualitative research.

Qualitative Research: B2B Versus B2C

Although there are enough applications for focus groups in technology and B2B contexts to justify a chapter in this book, I believe that the bulk of B2B qualitative research takes the form of some kind of customer visit activity. Customer visits are simply on-site interviews, and as long as they occur at the customer's place of business, there is an opportunity to look around as well as to listen. For this reason I stretched out the cell in the table above, to show customer visits as spanning a wide gamut of activities outside the laboratory. Very few B2B qualitative research studies go as far in the ethnographic direction as the grill example laid out earlier; but almost as few decide to remove customers from their work environment and talk to them one at a time in a white-walled room elsewhere. The typical B2B qualitative study will thus involve an extensive amount of time spent interviewing, but will also include a tour, a chance to walk around and get a feel for the customer's operation.

In short, B2B qualitative almost always includes an observational component—assuming the product is not like life insurance and *can* be observed in use—but seldom goes all the way to a full-dress ethnography. Listening is primary, but it is supplemented by looking around. This propensity to do qualitative in the field in part goes back to some of the fundamental distinctions between B2C and B2B. In B2B, the individual human customer is paid to work with the product being researched; it's part of his job. Why remove him from his place of work to talk about his work? The other B2B distinction that drives qualitative into the field is the fact that many B2B products are used by groups of people, and/or the purchase process involves multiple decision makers. What good would it do to haphazardly pluck one member of the buying center and take her to an off-site interview facility, separate from the other participants—how much understanding is that going to yield? And why try to convince all five members of the buying team to coordinate their schedules and travel off site to be interviewed, when it would be simpler to simply bring the interviewer on site while providing the visitor all the extra benefits of being there?

In summary, the key decisions in planning qualitative research are:

1. Field or laboratory setting?

   a. If field, what proportion of time will be spent on sustained conversation (interviews) versus observation?

   b. If laboratory, interview in groups or individually?

      i. If individual interviews, what sort of instrumentation will be used to supplement and support the conversation?

A caveat is that if you are in a B2B market, the first decision often defaults to "field."

In the remainder of Part III, customer visits and focus groups are each given a chapter, consistent with the B2B focus of the book. These are followed by a chapter on interview design, which covers issues common across interviews, including individual interviews in a B2C context, which are not otherwise addressed in this book. Part III concludes with a chapter on sampling for qualitative research, which again involves competencies that are general across customer visits, focus groups, and other kinds of qualitative research.

⊰ FIVE ⊱

CUSTOMER VISITS

———•◦•———

In a customer visit, one or more decision makers from a vendor directly interact with one or more customers or potential customers of that vendor. Of course, salespeople and customer support personnel have such contacts daily with customers. For our purposes, however, a customer visit, considered as a kind of market research, specifically occurs when a decision maker from outside these areas deliberately arranges to interact with customers to learn. For example, research and development would not normally be considered a customer-contact function. Hence, when an engineer travels to a customer site not to sell or to troubleshoot but to listen and learn, that is a customer visit. So it is also when a product marketer, as opposed to a member of the field sales organization, makes a visit, primarily to listen and learn, or when a member of general management or someone in manufacturing or someone in quality control travels to the customer site, again, with the goal of listening.

Note that the term *decision maker* is intended to be very general. It refers to anyone, not just upper management, who makes any kind of decision that affects customers. Thus, in new product development, design engineers are decision makers; in total quality efforts, manufacturing engineers and quality staff members are decision makers; in the design of marketing programs, marketing staff members are decision makers; and so forth. The term *customer* is intended to be similarly inclusive and encompasses present and potential customers, competitors' customers, internal-to-the-vendor customers, and key opinion leaders or influential persons who may shape customer buying decisions. Similarly, the individuals at customer firms who may participate in customer visits are not limited to purchasing agents, general management, or other traditional "vendor contact" positions but may include anyone who is involved in the consideration, buying, installation, maintenance, use, or disposal of the vendor's product.

Customer visits may be distinguished as *outbound*—where the vendor travels to the customer—or *inbound*—where the customer travels to the vendor site. Although I will focus on outbound visits to the customer work site, such contacts may also occur at neutral sites such as trade shows. Likewise, phone calls or video chats, if conducted in the same spirit of listening and learning and organized toward the same sort of objectives, may also be considered visits.

I further distinguish *ad hoc* from *programmatic* customer visits, and also an intermediate category that might be termed hybrid visits. An ad hoc visit is any contact where marketing research is *not* the primary agenda or driving force behind the visit but simply one of several motives. These generally occur one at a time, now and then, here and there, without any coordination. By contrast, a customer visit program consists of a series of visits that are conducted precisely to achieve some market research objective and for which market research is the primary and often the sole agenda. Be aware that while ad hoc visits provide an important opportunity for marketing intelligence gathering, only programmatic visits can be considered a market research technique akin to focus groups, surveys, and experiments. Hybrid visits may be more or less structured, and the more structured versions sometimes resemble B2C ethnographies as described in the overview to Part III.

Because I generally stay away from the gathering of market intelligence in this concise guide, concentrating instead on decision-focused market research, I won't have much to say about ad hoc or hybrid customer visits in this chapter. If interested, take a look at my book, *Customer Visits*, where several chapters are devoted to ad hoc and hybrid visits, and every aspect of this chapter is fleshed out in more detail.

PROGRAMMATIC CUSTOMER VISITS FOR MARKET RESEARCH

In the 1980s, or maybe even earlier, B2B technology firms such as Hewlett-Packard began to experiment with a more systematic approach to customer visits in which 12, 20, or even more visits might be executed in order to address some topic of interest. The most common applications for such customer visit programs are new product development, new market development (i.e., selling an existing product line to a new type of customer or for a new application), and customer satisfaction assessment. These programmatic visits are characterized by objectives set in advance, a carefully selected sample of customers, participation by cross-functional teams, a discussion guide used to direct the visit, an exploratory approach in asking questions, and a structured analysis and reporting process.

When I participated in my first customer visit program in 1985, just before I completed my PhD and took a job at Santa Clara, I was puzzled. Having managers gather information first hand from customers in an organized way seemed valuable and likely to be compelling. Why had I never seen the technique written up in a market research textbook? More to the point: Why, decades later, after publication of several editions of my *Customer Visits* book, along with books and articles by others (see Suggested Readings), will you *still* not see a chapter on customer visits in any textbook treatment of market research? The answer, I think, helps to illuminate some unacknowledged biases among textbook authors and the market research profession as a whole.

It remains a fact that the bulk of the money spent on commercial market research is spent in B2C categories. The products are often inexpensive, frequently purchased packaged goods bought by individuals. It's difficult to see how customer visits could make sense in this context. Not to put too fine a point on it, if someone from Procter & Gamble's (P&G's) detergent group called me up and asked, "Can we visit your home and watch you do a load of laundry and talk to you about it?" I'd either guffaw or hang up. No way am I going to disrupt my busy family routine to spend an hour or two with strangers camped in my laundry room. For that matter, it's not clear that my use of and satisfaction with laundry detergent is shaped by the fact that I have a generously sized laundry room, or by the nice cabinets I had installed over the washer and dryer, or anything else that P&G could observe by visiting me at home.

What companies like P&G learned to do instead, if they wanted to listen to customers, was to invite them to a focus group, where a financial incentive can be offered for attending and the power of group interaction can be harnessed (see next chapter). Or someone with a clipboard could be stationed in a mall to pull people aside and take them through a one-on-one interview. Or a consumer might be paid to go to a central site and invited to do an experimental load of laundry while talking out loud about it and being videotaped. Hence, what you will see in every other market research textbook is not customer visits but a discussion of one-on-one interviews and the sorts of exercises that can be incorporated into such interviews (laddering, projective tests, etc.). All textbooks allot some space to qualitative, exploratory research, but this will consist mostly of a discussion of B2C focus groups, with perhaps an aside on depth interviews. Focus groups are to B2C what customer visits are to B2B: the mainstream exploratory tool.

To see why B2B contexts instead favor customer visits, here's a different example. Suppose Cisco, which has primarily sold routers and switches to handle Internet traffic, were to consider expanding into the server market. Servers within corporate data centers are of course a primary source of Internet traffic. Cisco already sells routers to move data from these servers outside the corporate firewall and already sells network equipment to distribute data from servers inside the firewall. Why not sell the servers, too? In terms of strategic marketing, this strategy would be product development proper: selling an additional product to customers you already serve.

Under these circumstances, would customer visits make sense for Cisco? Probably—but it is important to lay out precisely why. First, the installation cost for a set of servers can total hundreds of thousands of dollars or more. Second, there will be IT staff whose business it is to stay on top of product development and who have a rational self-interest in and even a job responsibility for meeting with vendors to discuss unsolved problems and unmet needs. Cisco is much less likely to receive the brushoff from these IT professionals than P&G would have received from this homeowner. Third, because the server purchase is expensive and mission critical, it is probably a group decision. It makes no sense to pluck one data center employee out of the buying group and invite him to a focus group; too much of the decision process would remain invisible. Fourth, it really will help to physically visit the customer on site. Cisco can meet with multiple decision makers and observe existing server setups. These setups are likely to be heterogeneous across industries and corporate cultures in a way that laundry rooms may not be heterogeneous across family households.

To sum up, in B2B markets where products are expensive and complex, customer needs are heterogeneous, and multiple decision makers are involved, exploratory research should generally take the form of a program of on-site customer visits. Note that the words *technology*, *computer*, and *electronics* did not appear in the specification. To drive home the point, consider the Ditch Witch Company. They make a mechanical shovel, but this isn't a technology product, at least as we use that term here in Silicon Valley. It is a fairly complex piece of equipment used by commercial contractors, so it is assuredly B2B. Hence, I'd argue that Ditch Witch benefits from on-site customer visits just as much as Cisco. They, too, need the opportunity to talk to multiple decision makers and see the product in use under diverse conditions.

The reason most textbooks slight customer visits in favor of an extended treatment of focus groups is straightforward: The thought world of marketing academia and of the professional market research community is centered on what might be called the General Mills–Kraft–Procter & Gamble axis. On this axis, Cisco is not the first example that comes to mind when seeking illustrations of market research techniques, nor is Ditch Witch. And that's why a chapter on customer visits isn't found in other books: Customer visits only become important when B2B markets, not B2C, are the focus.

Within the B2B sphere, customer visits are simply the form that exploratory interviews tend to take. All the advantages and disadvantages of small sample qualitative research apply to customer visits same as they apply to focus groups or individual interviews in the B2C space. Hence, for this fourth edition I've created a separate chapter to cover the topic of interview questions and the management of customer interactions in the interview setting. This material is relevant to any interview technique, whether focus groups or customer visits (or to individual interviews of the kind that did not earn a chapter in this B2B-focused introduction to market research). The present chapter and the next one thus focus on the procedural details that are unique to customer visit programs on the one hand and focus groups on the other. Elements common across qualitative research techniques—interview skills and analysis techniques—are pulled out into separate chapters at the end of Part III.

What follows is an outline of the steps required to design and execute a program of customer visits. After that I give a couple of examples of programs, and then of hybrid and ad hoc visits.

Set Objectives

A program of visits tends to devolve into a series of ad hoc visits unless objectives are set in advance. Examples of feasible objectives would include the following:

- Identify user needs.
- Explore customer perceptions concerning market events or trends.
- Generate ideas for product enhancement.
- Describe how customers make their purchase decision.

In general, any of the objectives that were deemed appropriate for exploratory research in Chapter 2 are appropriate for customer visits. The specific objectives should be hammered out in advance and regularly revisited during the program. In my consulting experience, I was surprised how often the team of people who were to participate in the visits did *not* initially agree on what the visits were supposed to accomplish. This occurs partly because customer visits are a highly flexible tool that can handle a wide variety of issues and partly because it is often the only marketing research technique over which participants have any direct control. Hence, the visit program, unless checked, tends toward an "everything I wanted to know about customers but never had the chance to ask" orientation. For best results, remember that less is more: Fewer objectives more thoroughly addressed will generally be the best approach.

Select a Sample

Sample selection is a make-or-break phase of program design. It doesn't matter how incisive your interviewing or insightful your analysis if you visit the wrong customers—people who don't deal with the issues that concern you or are not part of the market you are trying to address. Garbage in–garbage out is the rule.

Begin by reviewing any segmentation scheme used by your business. This review of segments is important because you probably want to visit multiple instances of each important or relevant type of customer, *and* you want to avoid any kind of customer that is irrelevant to your objectives for the visit program at hand. For example, if your product is sold to four different industries, it may be important to visit customers from each; alternatively, if your product has half a dozen applications, and the changes you are contemplating only concern three of these applications, then you may want to include only customers with those applications in the sample. The result of this first stage of sample selection is typically a list of three to six types of customers yielding a tentative sample size of, in most cases, 12 to 36 visits (worldwide programs are generally somewhat larger, in the 30 to 60 range, but quite rare). In very concentrated markets, this list may name actual customer firms; in larger markets, it is only a statement of types, such as national distributors with mainframe computers and a wide-area network, batch manufacturers with local area networks, and so forth. See the latter part of the qualitative analysis chapter, Chapter 8, for another take on this issue of sample construction for customer visit programs.

The point of going through this exercise is to avoid, first, the pitfalls of excluding customer types that are important to understand; second, wasting your time on customers who can't really help you; and third (the most subtle trap), always returning to visit the same small group of comfortable, familiar customers. One firm that neglected this latter point watched its market share slowly shrink even as its customer satisfaction ratings continued to go up and up—because it was doing an ever-better job of satisfying an ever-smaller niche of the market. Often, the greatest discoveries and the most surprising insights come from visits made to less familiar customers, such as competitors' customers, or to customers who spend a lot on this product category but not very much on your product offering—which implies that from their perspective, something about your product is lacking.

The second phase of sample selection is specifying which job roles at the customer firm you want to visit. Most business-to-business products are bought and used by means of a group decision-making process that involves multiple individuals. If you only talk to one role—or worse, to different roles at different customers, thus confounding interrole differences and interfirm differences—you risk coming to a partial and misleading perspective on your market. An important part of the recruiting process is qualifying the persons you will be interviewing at the customer site. It is extremely disappointing to travel at great expense to a customer site and realize, in the first five minutes, that you are speaking to someone who has no involvement with your issues. Because customer visits are one of the very few market research techniques that allow you to understand multiple decision makers at a customer, and because group decision making is so characteristic of B2B markets, most customer visits should include multiple job roles at each customer. In many cases, this adds very little to the cost while substantially deepening the understanding gained. Recruiting itself can be handled by the program coordinator (common in concentrated markets with enduring vendor–customer relationships) or by an outside market research firm (common when customers are hard to find and also in close-to-mass-market situations with hundreds of thousands of buyers).

Select Teams

The best teams are cross-functional—for example, a team that includes some-one from marketing plus someone from engineering (in the case of new product development) or someone from quality control and someone from manufactur-ing engineering (in the case of customer satisfaction), and so forth. One reason for the superiority of teams is that a lot of work has to be done to make an interview effective, and one person can't do it all. A second reason is that cross-functional teams see with "stereo vision." Note that larger programs typically involve two or three teams to split up the work load so no one team has to visit more than 6 to 10 customers.

Devise a Discussion Guide

The guide is a two- to four-page document that functions as an agenda for the visit. In outline form, it lists the major topics to be covered and under each topic reminds you of key questions to ask and issues to watch for (see the chapter on Constructing Interview Questions for more on this issue). The top-ics are arranged in a sequence that develops naturally and is comfortable for the customer. A discussion guide performs three valuable functions: It keeps you on track during each visit, it ensures consistency across visits, and it coor-dinates the efforts of multiple teams in large visits.

Conduct the Interviews

You are *not* executing a survey in person; that is to say, you are not asking a fixed set of questions in a rigidly prescribed manner. Rather, you are engaged in a directed conversation with an expert informant—your customer. Explora-tion in depth is the focus.

Debrief the Teams

Immediately after concluding the visit, it is important that the team members debrief one another. In the beginning of the visit program, debriefing provides an opportunity to discuss improvements to the discussion guide and interview procedure. Toward the conclusion, debriefing gives you a head start on the analysis, as you ask how today's visit compares and contrasts with previous visits. Throughout, debriefing provides a cross-check on each team member's perceptions of what customers are saying.

Analyze and Report Results

Analysis typically proceeds via a review of visit notes to uncover themes, contrasts, discoveries, and enumerations (i.e., customer needs or requirements identified through the visits). A typical report structure will touch on the one or two most important discoveries up front and then organize the remainder of the material in terms of key themes. Each theme may be illustrated with a few verbatim quotes from customers; customers always speak more vividly and powerfully than any vendor employee would dare. As in the case of discussion guides, the report of a customer visit program will look very similar to the report of a focus group study. It is fair to say that the quality of the analysis of customer visit data depends quite heavily on the insight and industry experience of the person(s) analyzing the visit. Although no kind of market research ever eliminates the need for judgment and perspective, this need is particularly great in the case of customer visits. Routinized surveys may all but analyze themselves, but customer visits never do.

EXAMPLES OF VISIT PROGRAMS

Here are two examples of visit programs, one conducted by Sun Microsystems to better understand sources of customer satisfaction and dissatisfaction and the other conducted by Apple Computer Co. to explore the potential for a new product.

Sun Microsystems wanted to understand problems associated with a customer's first encounter with the company, specifically, from the point where the shipment of computers first arrived until the system was up and running. This effort was spearheaded by members of the company's quality function who perceived that the first encounter was sometimes more problematic than it had to be. Cross-functional teams conducted more than 50 visits worldwide, yielding a variety of insights that would be difficult or impossible to obtain in any other way. These ranged from the impact of the packaging used to international differences in desk layout and office configuration to subtle problems with the usability and installation of various pieces of equipment.

Because solutions to many of these problems cut across departments and functions, the cross-functional makeup of the visit teams proved crucial in addressing identified problems.

The Display Products Division of Apple wanted to explore the potential for an entirely new product category that would expand the division's offerings. The goal of the visit program was to discover unmet needs that the present products did not satisfy, to describe customer requirements that the new product would have to meet, and to explore the fit between Apple's core competency and these requirements.

The division conducted more than 30 visits in the United States and Europe. A product manager from the marketing function coordinated the visits, and a wide range of scientists and engineers participated, inasmuch as the new product solution was much more than an incremental change or twist on an existing offering. Marketing managers combined information gained from these visits with secondary and other market research to help division management understand the issues surrounding the decision whether to invest in the new solution.

The visits yielded a wealth of data, summarized in profiles, about applications for the new product, problems with existing solutions, and perceptions of Apple's ability to deliver a successful solution. Design engineers came away from the visits with a clear vision of what the product had to do in order to succeed.

HYBRID AND AD HOC EXAMPLES

In a hybrid customer visit setup, there are multiple visits, like in a program, and these visits take place in a compressed time period, like in a program. Unlike a program, the customer contacts undertaken vary in structure—they are not all driven off the same discussion guide and may not all use the same sit-down-for-an-hour-and-talk format. Here is an example: An overseas manufacturer of Braille keyboards and other assistive technologies for the blind sought market input in the United States to shape future product development. For this category, like many medical products, the sales channel was complex. Blind adults might purchase individually from local distributors, or K–12 schools might purchase in bulk for students. State government agencies were key specifiers of which technologies were eligible for welfare spending. There were scattered user groups of technology enthusiasts who met regularly.

The management team made two visits to the United States, one to California and one to Texas. They visited a school for the blind, and spent time interviewing the technology specialist at that school, several teachers, and even spent a few minutes with a class of elementary students tossing out questions about the keyboards. They visited distributors and attended a user group, and then met with some state agencies that funded purchases of this equipment. When they were finished, their count of full-dress, sit-down, one-hour interviews was fairly low, perhaps a dozen. But in total, they had meaningful interactions with perhaps 50 individuals, and some contact with 50 more, spread across their entire channel, and not consisting of just end users. In addition, the management team got valuable exposure to the "foreign" U.S. market, and in-depth understanding of how a technology product like this, aimed at a specialized and often needy population, got specified and funded in the United States.

Essentially, hybrid visits of this type move a long way toward the ethnographic pole, as in the research for a barbecue grill manufacturer described in the Overview to Part III. It is an appropriate procedure early in the development cycle, when management is looking for fresh insight—green field research, as it is sometimes described. I should note that there are several other kinds of hybrid visit setups, as described in my book *Customer Visits*. All of them rest on the insight that exploratory interactions with customers need not occur exclusively through sit-down interviews of a specified length, but can include a wandering around component, or multiple kinds of more piecemeal contacts.

Ad hoc visits are too various for a single example to be meaningful here; it might be more helpful to describe the major types and suggest a procedure for harvesting marketing intelligence from such visits. Most ad hoc visits occur under one of the following auspices: (1) sell, (2) tell, or (3) fix. A technology leader is called in to help the account team to close a key sale, a product manager goes on a roadshow to explain the firm's development path to key customers, or an engineer is called out to fix an equipment problem that defeated the local field engineer. As a general rule in American firms, these opportunities (or obligations) increase as an individual climbs the management food chain. In all these instances, there is very little time to listen and learn; the primary task is to sell, tell, or fix. But little time is not zero time. And in a firm of any size, the total number of ad hoc customer contacts, on an annual basis, can be quite large.

The key thing to do to get more marketing intelligence out of such visits is to have a plan. You don't know who will be doing visits, or when, or under what auspices, but you can be certain that such visits will occur over and over. Four steps are required to get more value from these visits. First, decide on what I call perennial questions: open-ended discussion starters that could be asked of almost any customer if you had five minutes to spare after the sell, tell, or fix was completed. Examples might be, "What business problems are keeping you awake these days?" or "What do you see as the strengths and weaknesses of competitor X?" Next, find a way to log the answers: a form on a shared drive, perhaps, or a wiki, or even a custom, private social media site. Then, develop the habit of sharing and circulating these logs among members of the management team. Once a quarter or so, sit down and put your heads together to discuss what it is that customers are trying to tell you.

The goal with managing ad hoc customer contacts for marketing intelligence is to keep your ear to the ground so that you hear early rumblings of change. It's to keep all members of the team, and not just the sales force, immersed in the world of the customer. These visits are virtually free in terms of incremental costs and the potential volume of information flow is quite high. All it takes is planning.

COST

A good estimating procedure is to tally up the direct travel costs incurred by a two-person team (airfare, hotel, car rental, meals). At most, two customers can be visited in one day; it is hard to schedule more than three days of visits in one week to get them all on one airfare. Run the math on airfare, hotel, car, and meals, and you will find it is difficult to spend less than $6,000 on even a small program consisting of a dozen visits. Programs with a substantial international component will cost rather more. Stepping back, $6,000 to $15,000 is a good estimate range for purely domestic programs, and expect to spend $12,000 to $30,000 for programs with a substantial international component. Of course, any experienced manager can bury these costs in assorted travel and lodging (T&L) budgets, but that doesn't make them go away. Likewise, programs in which all the visits are conducted locally by car will have negligible out-of-pocket costs. Purely local programs are generally not a good idea, however, because your mental models are probably already overly shaped by local customers and because there is often considerable geographical diversity in customer viewpoints, inasmuch as different industries are concentrated in different locales. One approach to controlling costs for out-of-town visits is to bunch several visits onto a single airfare, inasmuch as airfare is the major component of travel expense. Another is to piggyback research visits onto existing trips: if you are already scheduled to go to Atlanta for a conference, why not stay an extra day or two and conduct several visits as part of a program that will span a month or two?

Bottom line: A programmatic approach to customer visits is going to cost real money. The total cost is about the same as for a comparable focus group project. As developed earlier, market research isn't cheap. That's why you have to take a systematic approach to market research planning, including the planning of customer visits.

STRENGTHS AND WEAKNESSES

The customer visit technique has several key strengths that combine to position visits just behind secondary research as a general all-purpose market research tool within the B2B contexts where they are appropriate. First, visits are field research. They take you out of your world and put you into the customer's world. Second, visits take the form of face-to-face interaction. Research has shown that face to face is the richest of all communication modes, in the sense of being best able to handle complex, ambiguous, and novel information. Third, the combination of field study and face-to-face communication is ideal for entering into the customer's thought world—the customer's perspective and priorities. Being able to think like a customer is a core marketing competency that is too important to be confined to marketers, and customer visits provide one of the best means of helping nonmarketing functions such as engineering to envision their customers. Fourth, customer visits provide information that is gained first hand, directly. As someone remarked to me, "Everyone believes his or her own eyes and ears over others." Customer visits can sometimes be helpful in changing hearts and minds because the evidence of an unsatisfied need is so much more vivid and compelling when gathered this way. Overall, the distinctive strength of customer visits is depth of understanding. For instance, you can spend a whole hour nailing down exactly what goes on in a particular application or process. Sustained dialogue gives you the picture seen from multiple reinforcing angles in a way that a set of cross-tabulated survey responses never will.

The great weakness of customer visits is the potential for interviewer bias. If you have spent six months slaving over a design concept, will you really be able to listen to and explore the response of that customer whose initial reaction is something along the lines of "what a silly idea"? Historically, the consensus of academic opinion was that managers could not be trusted to conduct their own market research; rather, the combination of greater objectivity and expertise made outside professionals the superior choice. Perhaps a more balanced perspective would be that although bias is a constant danger, nonetheless, the advantages listed in the preceding paragraph compel the involvement of managers and other decision makers in customer visits, whatever the pitfalls. Given this realization, one can act to control bias in two ways: first, by the use of teams (although my bias is invisible to me, it is painfully apparent to you!), and second, by following up customer visits with other more confirmatory procedures, such as survey research, choice modeling, and experimentation.

The second abiding weakness of customer visits is the instability and imprecision consequent to small sample sizes. Often there is a great temptation to treat a customer visit program as a kind of survey and to report such findings as "75% of our customers had a positive reaction to adding this piece of functionality." Just a little statistical reflection reveals that in a random sample of 16 customers, the 95% confidence interval around an estimate of "75% agreement" extends from about 53% to 97%. If you want the kind of precision that percentages imply, you need a large sample survey. If you can rest content with "Many customers had positive reactions to this functionality" rather than holding out for "75%," then you can do quite well with small but carefully drawn qualitative samples, as discussed further in the chapter on qualitative data analysis at the end of this part. Nonetheless, where customer visits excel is in explaining *why* some customers had a favorable reaction to a piece of functionality and others did not. Visits aren't very useful for estimating the proportion of customers who have one or another reaction— visits offer the chance to discover that there really are customers who have an unsuspected but justified negative reaction to that same bit of functionality. If the time has passed for exploration and discovery, you should probably not be visiting customers, but using some other kind of market research technique instead.

FUTURE DIRECTIONS

In this chapter, I was tempted to answer "no changes." There is a tribal and viscerally human aspect of in-person customer visits: From the customer's perspective, this vendor employee, at some cost to him- or herself, took the time and trouble to come here and visit me in my place of business. An e-mail, a phone call, or a video chat doesn't signify the same level of commitment. From the vendor perspective, there is no substitute for being there and no new technological tool, other than one's total human sensorium, for taking advantage of the fact of being there. The tribal, visceral aspect of visiting customers is one reason this is a worldwide business practice, understood and accepted on every continent. It can't be improved upon any more than one's humanness can be improved.

Nonetheless, two relevant developments can be noted. First, video technology and web bandwidth have improved to the point that I can envision a day when certain kinds of customer visits will take place virtually rather than physically and be little the worse for it (pace the tribal comments just made). Simply google the word *telepresence* to see what is becoming technologically possible, albeit still too expensive for truly widespread use. Second, relative to when the first edition of this book was written, business travel has become an ever more dispiriting, joyless, discombobulating affair. This might be my advanced age talking, but I really don't think so. This makes customer visits more costly, in every sense of the word, for the employees who participate in this activity. After the Great Recession, these same employees, if they still have a job, are ever more burdened and less capable of putting aside their other responsibilities to go on the road.

The upshot of these two developments is that customer visits that do not require or take advantage of an on-site observational component or a relationship-building component will increasingly be done virtually rather than physically. If you don't have to be there physically—if there isn't a significant ethnographic component to the research—you won't go there. You'll walk down the hall to your videoconference room. Visits that are actually only interviews, purely conversational, won't be able to justify the costs of business travel. This trend is still nascent, but the combination of the advances in technology and the increased financial and personal costs of business travel makes it ineluctable. The number of conversations with customers isn't going to stop growing, but the number of in-person visits that require the apparatus of airfare, hotels, and rental cars may well plateau.

DOs AND DON'Ts

Do get engineers and other nonmarketers involved in customer visits.

Don't confine yourself to a conference room. Walk around and observe. Soak up the total picture of this customer's operation.

Do enlist the support and cooperation of the local field sales organization. They can do much to frustrate or assist your purpose. They know these customers well and can add perspective to what you hear.

Don't ask customers for solutions—ask them to identify problems that need solving. The customer is the authority on what the real problems are, but the vendor is the authority on what a profitable solution to those problems might be.

Don't talk too much. You are there to listen. The more you talk, the more you shape customer responses and the less the chances of making a discovery or being surprised.

Do use visual aids. Diagrams, short lists, and the like help the customer to focus on the total idea to which you want reactions.

Do use verbatim quotes from customers in reports. Customers often express themselves more vividly and with less inhibition than you would allow yourself.

DISCUSSION QUESTIONS

1. One way to think of surveys is as an instrumented interview. Just as a telescope "instruments" the effort to observe stars, and a microscope instruments the effort to observe germs, a questionnaire instruments the attempt to learn about customers.

   a. Is the metaphor apt? The telescope and microscope analogues argue that a questionnaire is a more powerful device for learning about customers than questioning them out loud, as in a customer visit. Take a position on this argument.

   b. Is it a matter of the questionnaire being a more powerful instrument for some purposes, and an interview for others? Be specific. Can an un-instrumented option—the ordinary interview or visit—ever be superior to an instrumented option, for *any* market research purpose?

    i. This question will work best if students have some familiarity with the history of the scientific revolution and the role played by instrumentation in it.

    ii. Alternatively, if Max Weber's term *verstehen* is familiar to the class, the discussion can proceed from that basis.

2. A counter-argument to the above question might be that whatever its strengths, a written questionnaire is a highly constrained communication channel, relative to what can occur in an on-site in-person customer visit.

    a. Be specific about how the on-site in-person interview, considered as a communication channel, is less constrained—i.e., allows for transmission of a greater variety of information—relative to the written web questionnaire. What types of information can be conveyed in an interview that cannot easily be conveyed on a questionnaire?

    b. Is the constraint two-way or one-way—does the questionnaire constrain information coming from the participant, communication to the participant, or both?

3. Keeping the focus on the on-site, in-person interview: To what extent are its strengths, relative to a survey questionnaire, a function of taking place *in-person*—as a live interactive dialogue—and to what extent are these strengths a function of being *on site*—a field rather than a lab study?

4. Historically, market research books discouraged managers from conducting their own interviews, warning of potential bias, and encouraged the use of professional interviewers, for both their objectivity and superior skill.

    a. In the spirit that every concrete instance of market research planning involves trade-offs, is there anything gained by having managers do their own customer interviews, which might offset the risk of bias and the likely lower level of skill?

    i. Be specific about what is gained, and about any additional risks.

    ii. Does your assessment change if the interviews occur in a B2B versus B2C space? Does the technical complexity of the product category matter?

        1. *Extra Credit*: Would your assessment differ if the interviews the manager proposes to conduct were on-site in-person visits, semi-structured phone interviews, group interviews at the customer site, or a conventional focus group?

b. Assume one manager has a degree in marketing, has been successful in marketing, and has the sort of personality stereotypically associated with successful marketers. Assume another manager started as an engineer, was successful in engineering, and has the personality stereotypically associated with successful engineers.

    i. Does your recommendation about the advisability of a manager conducting his own interviews change across these two examples? Why, or why not?

    ii. How much "skill" is required to be an effective market research interviewer? Is this something like driving a car, which most people manage; or like running the mile in high school, which many but far from all teenagers can do at a reasonably fast pace; or is it something like making a living trading stocks, where very few people succeed?

5. *Exercise.* Design a customer visit program for a company or product category that you know well. Your write-up needs to include: (1) statement of the decision problem, with background information as necessary; (2) specific research objectives; (3) research design, including the number of customers, the sample grid from which customers will be selected, and the job roles to be included on both the customer and the vendor side; and (4) the discussion guide that will be used to moderate the groups.

SUGGESTED READINGS

McQuarrie, E. F. (2008). *Customer visits: Building a better market focus* (3rd ed.). Armonk, NY: M. E. Sharpe.	Offers a complete step-by-step guide to designing, conducting, and analyzing a program of visits.
Guillart, F. J., & Sturdivant, F. D. (1994). Spend a day in the life of your customer. *Harvard Business Review* (January/February): 116–125.	Describes some uses of inbound customer visits and clarifies the kind of perspective customers are uniquely qualified to give.
Shapiro, B. (1988). What the hell is "market-oriented"? *Harvard Business Review,* 66 (November–December): 119–125.	Shows how customer visits can be used to turn around a stagnant organization and make it more market focused.

SIX

THE FOCUS GROUP

———◆———

T he term *focus group* is sometimes used loosely to cover any group interview. Strictly speaking, however, within the world of market research, a
focus group is a particular kind of group interview supported by a specialized
infrastructure. This infrastructure includes (1) the facility, (2) the market
research vendor, and (3) the moderator.

The facility is typically an independent small business that has at least one
specialized meeting room. This room has a table large enough to seat a dozen
consumers, a one-way mirror from behind which observers can view the pro-
ceedings, and the capacity to record audio and video of the group. The facility
typically is located in a shopping mall or office building.

The market research vendor is generally a separate business entity responsible for coordinating the entire focus group research project. The three specific responsibilities of the vendor are to find a facility, supply a moderator
who will lead the groups, and arrange for consumers to be recruited to attend.
Sometimes, both the moderator and the recruiter may be separate business
entities; alternatively, the facility may handle recruiting in addition to hosting
the group, and the moderator may be an employee or contractor of the vendor.
The value added by the vendor is fundamentally that provided by any middle-
man or broker: The vendor consults with you to design an appropriate research
strategy, brings together all the external resources required to implement the
study, and then drives the process to its conclusion.

The moderator is an individual with general skills in conducting interviews and specific skills in managing group interaction. Virtually all focus

group moderators also conduct one-on-one interviews, but not all people who conduct one-on-one interviews are capable of running a focus group. Interviewing a group is more demanding. In addition to leading the group, the moderator also works with the client before the group to refine the objectives for the discussion and is typically, but not always, the analyst who writes the report on the groups. If the infrastructure just described is not present, it is probably best to refer to your research study as simply a group interview in order to avoid confusion.

APPLICATIONS

Focus groups have essentially the same applications as customer visits. All the topics that may be explored in customer visits can be explored in focus groups as well, and all the objectives that are suitable for customer visits are suitable for focus groups, too. The goal in most focus group projects, as in all qualitative research, is some combination of discovery and insight. Any exploratory technique allows for surprise; and every exploratory face-to-face technique makes customers more visible and real. When an experienced, thoughtful marketer has vivid encounters with real, live customers, insights occur, patterns are glimpsed, and understandings jell. Note the caveat: These favorable outcomes of qualitative research are specific to *experienced, thoughtful* marketers. Hasty and unreflective marketers are easily misled by the vivid but partial nature of focus group discussions. Fundamentally, qualitative research produces not findings but education; not facts but perspective. The more thoughtful and experienced the manager, the greater the gain from focus groups.

COMPARISON TO CUSTOMER VISITS

Generally speaking, everything customer visits can't do, focus groups can't do either; and everything focus groups can do, customer visits can also do. Nonetheless, there are shades of difference and a few exceptions where one technique is preferable to the other. First, I look at some trivial cases where focus groups aren't possible or advisable for some external or superficial reason. Then I'll turn to the more interesting cases, where some intrinsic property of focus groups makes them more or less apropos than customer visits.

Among the superficial cases, a conventional focus group simply isn't possible in the B2B case where the number of eligible customers is small and geographically dispersed. Likewise, a focus group probably isn't advisable if it means getting direct competitors into the room and expecting them to talk about how they compete with one another. A focus group is also contraindicated once the desired respondents pass above some threshold in terms of title and responsibilities. You aren't going to be able to schedule eight VPs from Fortune 1000 firms on a given evening or be able to incentivize them to attend. But you might be able to visit each of them in their offices if you are persistent and can accommodate their schedules. Finally, a focus group may not make sense if the subject matter is too technical or esoteric. Professional moderators are by nature quick studies and skilled in conveying an impression of incomplete understanding in order to get customers talking. But there are limits, and it is, in the end, difficult to lead an insightful discussion on a topic that the moderator really does not comprehend. This is not such a big problem in a customer visit; you simply make one of your technical experts a member of the visiting team.

Turning next to superficial cases that cut in the other direction, to favor focus groups: A focus group project will generally place a much smaller personal burden on vendor personnel. Rather than schlepping yourself all around the country to 12 different customer sites, with all the background logistical support that implies, you simply outsource the whole thing to an independent market research firm. All you have to do is show up in a couple of cities and watch; or, with today's technology, kick back in your office and watch the webcast of the group. As a bonus, you get the objectivity and interview skills of a professional moderator. This logic of outsourcing is most compelling when the people at the vendor who need to vividly experience customers are at a higher management level, where the odds of getting free of other obligations to go on a program of customer visits are vanishingly small.

The more interesting cases stem from the intrinsic differences between a *group* interview conducted *off site* versus *individual* interviews conducted *on site*. Groupness is the key advantage (and disadvantage) of focus groups, and situatedness is the key advantage (and disadvantage) of customer visits. I touched on these differences earlier in the Overview to this part under the heading of Lab Versus Field. Taking the latter first, the fundamental problem with focus groups is that they represent a laboratory technique: an artificial situation hosted in a specialized facility in which customers are removed from their day-to-day environment. There is no opportunity for field observation; what you can learn is limited to what can be described in the conversation of participants. Conversely, the disadvantage of situatedness is that the customer knows that Symantec is visiting today; the vendor in a program of customer visits can't hide the corporate identity. Because focus groups are observed from behind a one-way mirror in an anonymous office complex, the vendor's identity can be hidden or withheld until a crucial point and deliberately released. This makes focus groups a better means of studying the brand image of one's own firm and of competitors.

Turning now to identifying the advantages of groupness, theory and research in social psychology and on the diffusion of innovations suggest several possibilities. Innovation involves social communication, and focus groups provide an opportunity to *observe* such communication as one respondent tries to explain something to another. Second, a group of strangers brought together and asked to interact moves through two phases, termed *unification* and *polarization*. As strangers brought together, first we seek out what we all have in common, and once that's established, we proceed to differentiate ourselves.

These two group phenomena have important implications in the context of exploratory market research. The unification dynamic suggests that where focus groups are logistically feasible, they should be preferred at the very earliest stage of attempting to enter a new market of customers never served before. Suppose a manufacturer of computer equipment used in offices proposes to expand into the hospital environment where nurses rather than clerks will be the primary users. If focus groups of nurses are convened, they will recreate what might be called "nurse world": the tacit assumptions about computing generally shared by nurses. One could, instead, laboriously visit hospital after hospital and interview nurse after nurse and probably eventually be able to identify lowest common denominator sentiments among nurses concerning computerization; but a focus group makes this easy and more likely.

The utility of the polarization dynamic is that it can help you discover unsuspected segments and also new ways of segmenting your customers. Via the polarization dynamic, customers etch out the differences that separate them in front of your eyes. The polarization dynamic is particularly useful when customer individuals are very powerful. An example would be cardiac surgeons: lord-princes within their own domain and powerful barons within the typical hospital. What are the odds that a lowly product manager, hastening down the corridor alongside, can challenge such an individual or get him to entertain alternative points of view? Inconceivable! Ah, but put a group of cardiac surgeons together, and now you can sit back and watch them tear into one another. They will challenge each other and define themselves as proponents of different positions vis à vis treatment regimes and the like. In observing these cycles of challenge and response, you may well glimpse an explanation of why your product sells very well in some hospitals and markets and not so well in others.

The disadvantages of groupness are well known: conformity pressure, bandwagon effects, confusion and tumult, competition for air time, compulsive monopolizers, and so on. True, much of what one pays a professional moderator for is his or her skill in riding herd on these group pathologies. But really, how easy is it to control groups of human beings who are not beholden to you? On substantive grounds, customer visits are going to be preferable whenever you want to go into considerable detail and technical depth with each customer interviewed. And of course, customer visits will also be preferable when the "group" of interest is the intact buying unit at each customer site.

In a B2B technology market, net of all the factors covered above, in many cases, customer visit programs will be the preferred choice over focus groups. The preference will be stronger the more the market corresponds to the classic B2B criteria: small and concentrated, with long-cycle expensive purchases made by a group. But there will remain numerous circumstances where focus groups will edge out customer visits as the better choice, whether for superficial logistical reasons or more fundamental properties. Hence, they earn a place alongside customer visits in this concise guide for beginners.

PROCEDURE

1. You send out a request for proposals (RFP) to several market research vendors outlining the kind of customers you want recruited, the number of groups you expect to be held (three or four is typical), and the issues and topics to be explored in the group.

2. One or more vendors respond with a proposal describing what they will do and how much they will charge. Stronger proposals will summarize the problem as stated by the client and offer some insight into why specific recommendations were made.

3. The selected vendor retains and schedules a facility (often groups are held in two or more cities to encompass regional differences in consumer response), puts you in touch with a moderator, and prepares for your review the screener that will be used by phone recruiters.

4. You edit the screener, which consists of four to five questions designed to make sure that the consumers who are recruited are, in fact, the right kind of people for your purposes. For example, if you are a tablet manufacturer exploring the needs of users who work at home, the screener will be designed to ensure that each participant (a) does work at home for some minimum number of hours; (b) does have a tablet; and (c) does use that tablet as part of working at home. The screener might also ensure that one or more applications are present—for example, that a spreadsheet is used. Finally, the screener might be used to sample from defined subpopulations: to recruit users of Apple, users of Windows, and Android users, perhaps. See the latter part of the qualitative data analysis chapter (Chapter 8) for additional perspectives on screening.

5. Phone recruiting commences. Many calls have to be made to get a person on the line. Some of these people prove to be ineligible, and some of the remaining are not interested. As recruiting proceeds, you review the completed screeners to make sure the right kinds of people are being recruited.

6. Meanwhile, you meet with the moderator to develop the discussion guide. Typically, you have written a memo describing the topics and issues to be raised in the group discussion and some specific questions to be asked. The moderator transforms this into a discussion guide that functions as an agenda for the group. The discussion guide indicates how topics are sequenced and how questions are worded. See Chapter 7 on constructing interview questions for more information on discussion guides.

7. You and any of your colleagues who will be attending the focus group meet with the moderator at the facility an hour before the group is scheduled to begin. As consumers arrive, you stay in touch with the facility host/hostess to double-check eligibility and to make snap decisions about whom to include if a surplus of people actually show up. Consumers are generally served food while they wait.

8. The group session lasts 1½ to 2 hours. You have the opportunity to send in one or two notes and to briefly huddle with the moderator before the wrap-up. After each group (two are generally held in an evening), alterations can be made to the discussion guide.

9. After the last group, the moderator or analyst spends one to three weeks preparing a report that varies in length according to what you're willing to pay. Longer reports contain verbatim quotes drawn from the tapes. You may also choose to have a summary video recording made that contains 10 to 15 minutes of selected, particularly insightful discussions.

COST FACTORS

For business-to-business groups, budget for $5,000 to $12,000 per group and a three-group minimum. It is somewhat rare to see a project that includes more than six groups, so you can assume that most focus group projects will cost between $15,000 and $72,000. Costs go up with the difficulty of locating respondents and with the dollar amount required to incentivize them to participate. Hence, groups conducted with a specialized population of affluent individuals can cost four to five times as much as groups conducted with ordinary consumers.

EXAMPLES

The first example is a business that made small, handheld testing equipment used by customers whose factories manufactured a variety of electrical systems. The product in question was one among many made by the division, which in turn was part of a large, well-known multinational firm. Although the product had been offered for decades in one form or another, it had never been the leading brand in its market.

A strategic review indicated it was time to develop a new generation of the product to reflect advances in technology. Product marketing staff argued for focus groups as an initial stage of market research. Staff members pointed out that objective measures of product performance and business strength did not square with the product's weak market position. Something else must be going on, and if the next generation of the product was to succeed, this "something else" had to be understood.

Four focus groups were conducted with technicians and engineers who used this product in the course of their work. The screeners used in recruitment ensured that users of several brands, including the company's own, were present. Given the firm's weak position in the market, however, a majority of those who attended were users of other brands. The use of an outside research vendor ensured that the sponsoring firm remained anonymous. This contributed to a frank and candid atmosphere in the groups.

The group discussions, which were viewed by marketing staff and engineering management, were like a bucket of cold water. Some quite harsh and belittling comments were made about the sponsor and its product. Comments such as "Overengineered and overpriced" and "Way too delicate for use on the factory floor" give some indication of the tone. Intriguingly, the charge of fragility had no basis in objective fact. Engineering analyses had shown the product to be no less sturdy or durable than its competitors. Rather, fragility was an inference made by potential customers based on how the product's casing looked and felt, in conjunction with images of this brand compared with other brands they had experienced.

The focus groups had a salutary effect on management—a "wake-up call," as one put it. A 15-minute video containing highlights was widely shown and had a galvanizing effect. Follow-up research was conducted to extend and confirm the results of the focus group. The new product designed in light of this research was extremely successful in the marketplace, with the result that the leading competitive brand lost a substantial chunk of its market share.

The second example comes from a large computer manufacturer that undertook research to better understand the issue of software quality. Although the firm had always had a commitment to making high-quality products, the growing importance of software to its revenue stream, in combination with an emerging emphasis on total quality, suggested a need for exploratory market research. In particular, corporate quality-control staff had the uneasy sense that quality had come to be too narrowly defined as errors per million lines of code and was seeking to understand the customer's perspective on the meaning of quality.

Eight focus groups were conducted as part of what was intended to be a two-stage research project, where the second stage would be a large-scale conjoint study designed to identify the importance of each of the quality attributes identified in the focus groups and to assess the perceived quality delivered by each major competitor. Although some members of the corporate market research staff had wanted to move immediately to the conjoint study, quality-control staff insisted on doing focus groups first out of a sense that too many issues remained undefined.

Two groups each were conducted in Boston, New York, Atlanta, and San Francisco. Four groups concerned engineering or technical software applications (e.g., computer-aided design), and four groups concerned general commercial applications (e.g., word processing, accounting). For both the commercial and engineering software sets, two groups consisted of ordinary software users, one group consisted of management information system (MIS) directors responsible for supporting such users, and one group consisted of independent software consultants and software suppliers. Screening during recruitment ensured that users of large and small computers, users of the firm's own software and other brands, and employees of large and small businesses would be included.

The groups proved valuable in several respects. First, the customer perspective on quality became much more richly articulated. Diverse attributes of quality, such as "robust" and "intuitive," which had been little more than catchphrases before, were elaborated with examples, clarifications, and contrasts. Second, the term *software quality* proved to hold virtually no meaning for the typical user. Blank stares were a typical reaction when the moderator introduced this term in the early groups. Components of the software product, such as manuals or help screens, sometimes elicited energetic discussion of good or bad, but software quality per se was not a concept that users could easily define. Third, likes and dislikes proved very heterogeneous across users—whatever software quality was, it was not one unvarying thing. Fourth and most important, most users were familiar with only one brand of software—the one they used. Competitive products had essentially no visibility in most cases.

As a result of the groups, the anticipated large-scale conjoint study was canceled. The particular study under consideration required ratings of competitor software products—a task that would clearly be impossible for users in light of the focus group discussions. Hence, the focus group project yielded two benefits. The corporate quality staff's understanding of software quality from the customer's perspective was greatly enriched, and an expensive and ill-advised quantitative market research study, costing many tens of thousands of dollars more than the focus group study, was avoided.

FUTURE DIRECTIONS

For some years now, suppliers of market research services have experimented with technologically enhanced alternatives to the traditional in-person focus group procedure described in this chapter. Audio conferences were attempted early on; online chat room discussions have also been tried. The economic logic that drives these attempts is inescapable. It's ever harder to get people on the phone to recruit their participation, harder and more expensive to get people to show up, expensive to maintain a specialized facility, and so forth. Nonetheless, my personal opinion is that **as yet**, none of these technological alternatives really serves to re-create the effect of or successfully accomplish what a traditional focus group does. The traditional approach makes customers visible to management just short of face-to-face interaction, and creates a bona fide, albeit temporary, human group in which people react to other humans who are fully present to them as social beings. By contrast, on the Internet, as the joke runs, "no one knows you're a dog."

But this unduplicated and unmatched "in-person" character of the traditional focus group is going to succumb to technological advance eventually. As webcams spread and online meeting technologies get better, virtual groups, in which everyone is visible to everyone else, will begin to rival the capabilities of in-person groups at a far lower cost. Likewise, as telepresence technology diffuses, the same sort of virtual group can be recreated by sending recruited customers down to the local copy shop, ushering them into the videoconference room, and voila, they are on screen, and all but there, with nine other customers and the moderator. Cisco and other Internet suppliers have the same economic interest in making this happen as pickax and shovel manufacturers in 19th century California had in broadcasting every new gold find back East.

In the meantime, rather than trying to create a poor imitation of a real focus group in an online chat session, the opportunity online lies elsewhere: not in attempting a simulacrum of a focus group but in coming up with entirely new kinds of qualitative research techniques that take advantage of web technology to do new things. Two examples will suffice. First, courtesy of Facebook, blogs, user forums, and other kinds of social media, the equivalent of a vast focus group discussion concerning your brand, your product category, your industry, and your competitors is going on right now, 24/7. You should be thinking about how to mine and harvest data from this free, unprompted, unsponsored never-ending focus group discussion. Services are springing up to address this need; simply google a search string like "track online buzz and chatter" to get a sense of the players.

The second opportunity lies in what might be called "managed social media." Here you create a mini-Facebook or custom social media site that is available by invitation to customers (note how the nature of B2B markets makes this believable in a way that a social network of "Crest toothpaste users" might not be). Someone in your organization then regularly blogs for the site: he or she supplies news, tips, insight into developments in the product category, and so on. Users have the opportunity to maintain a page, dialogue with one another, comment on the blog, make posts, and so forth. Now to this point in the description, we have only a virtual user group. The crucial final step is the weekly discussion question. This is a post by the marketing group that sounds exactly like the kind of question asked in focus groups. Customers sound off in response, and in response to each other—exactly like a focus group. Result: a finger on the pulse of customer sentiment, and the same kind of input into subsequent, more formal research as focus groups have been historically tasked with supplying. (See the Communispace case at the end of this part for an example of how the essence of this example might even be outsourced.)

STRENGTHS AND WEAKNESSES

The great strength of the focus group technique is its capacity to produce surprise and a fresh perspective. Because the interview is minimally structured, because participants react to and provoke one another, and because the moderator drives the group to reflect and explore, there is a high probability that management will hear something new and unexpected. Hence, focus groups make a great deal of sense *early* in a market research project.

The unique strength of the focus group is that it brings multiple customers into direct interaction with one another. It is customary to extol the *synergy* that results. However, this rather vague term can be given a much more precise definition drawing on theories from social psychology, as discussed earlier in the comparison of focus groups to customer visits: It is the twin dynamics of unification and polarization that make focus group discussions so fruitful. Finally, focus groups have a number of minor advantages that can be useful in certain circumstances. In the United States, at least, the identity of the sponsor need not be revealed to participants; but this is not always the case overseas. This can be most useful when you want to hear frank and candid assessments of your brand as compared with others. Another useful feature is that focus groups occur in a concentrated time interval. Busy high-level managers are much more likely to show up for two evenings, and thus view four focus groups, than they are to accompany you on the week of travel required to make six customer visits. Because the focus group can be unobtrusively recorded, you can, by creating and circulating an edited "highlights" video recording, expose a large number of employees to almost direct customer input.

The most important weakness of the focus group technique is one that it shares with customer visits and other exploratory tools: the reliance on small samples and the potential for idiosyncratic developments. Because the sample is small and may or may not reflect the larger population of consumers in the market, the kinds of conclusions you can draw from focus group research are limited. You can *never* extrapolate a percentage or frequency from a group with any precision. Thus, it is never appropriate to conclude from groups that "consumers preferred concept A to concept B by a two-to-one margin." Looser and less precise directional judgments may be supportable, as developed in Chapter 8 on qualitative data analysis, but, as with customer visits, the concern should be with discovering what responses actually exist among customers, not with estimating the frequency of any given response.

It might be objected, "Well, how useful are focus groups, really?" To refer to the first example application given above, the focus group revealed the fact that one or more real customers believed that the product was overengineered and overpriced and the fact that some customers viewed it to be fragile. Ensuing discussion also revealed possible sources for such beliefs and their position within the network of other beliefs. However, were these beliefs held by a *few* idiosyncratic customers, by *a certain subgroup* of customers, or by *many* customers? There was no way to know until follow-up research was conducted. All management could know based on groups alone was the nature and character of those beliefs, together with the fact that at least *some* customers held them. If those beliefs and their exact nature came as a surprise, then the groups paid for themselves. If managers had already known (and taken seriously) all these things, then the groups might have been a waste of time.

Focus groups suffer from a number of other weaknesses that are distinctive and not shared with other kinds of exploratory research. Most of these stem from the very fact that a group is involved. Specifically, focus groups are quite vulnerable to logistical foul-ups. Traffic jams, random events, customers' busy schedules, and so forth may produce a higher-than-expected number of no-shows. It is hard to do a focus group when only three people actually show up. Worse, most of the money spent to that point is irretrievably lost.

More generally, focus groups are vulnerable to dominant individuals who monopolize the conversation, to shy individuals who withdraw, and to bandwagon effects, where group members simply acquiesce with an initial vehemently stated position. A good moderator can control many of these effects, but they remain liabilities.

The group synergy characteristic of focus groups also has a downside: limits on airtime. In a two-hour group with eight people, an average of 15 minutes of airtime is available to each person. Can you learn everything you need to know from an individual customer in 15 minutes? For many relatively simple consumer products, the answer may well be yes; but for business-to-business and technology products, the answer may be no, in which case, customer visits should be examined as an alternative. Also because of airtime restrictions, focus groups are an inferior idea-generation technique. Research has shown that interviews with 32 individuals yield more and better ideas than four focus groups with eight people each. Of course, focus groups may be a *satisfactory* idea-generation technique, even though not a superior one, especially given the time savings associated with conducting four groups versus 32 individual interviews. But focus groups are probably better suited to examining a few key topics in depth than to generating a wide variety of ideas.

Last, the use of a professional moderator is both a strength and a weakness. The moderator contributes interviewing skills plus detachment and objectivity. The downside, for many technology and business-to-business marketers, concerns the moderator's ability to quickly assimilate the essentials of your business situation and the technical specifics of your product. Absent that understanding, the moderator is not going to be able to effectively probe topics raised in the groups. The complexity of some technology products is such that I have encountered businesses that have soured on focus groups precisely because of their experiences with moderators who could not effectively probe key issues. If your product fits this profile, it is crucial that you be comfortable that the moderator you intend to use has the requisite understanding. Otherwise, consider doing customer visits instead.

DOs AND DON'Ts

Do invite key players in different functional areas to view the groups. Much important thinking and discussion occurs behind the one-way mirror.

Do monitor the telephone screening of potential participants. Look at the completed screeners and ask yourself if this is, in fact, the kind of person you intended to recruit.

Do vet the moderator—much depends on this person's skill.

Don't take votes seriously. Votes are okay as a springboard for further discussion: It is when you draw precise inferences about the population of customers based on the vote taken in the group that the trouble begins.

Don't distribute and analyze questionnaires. It is okay to get additional background information to help interpret the responses of participants, but it is not okay to treat the people who happen to attend the groups as grist for an almost-free survey. It will be among the worst surveys you have ever done.

Don't stop with one group or two. If focus groups are worth doing at all, you should do three or more.

Don't make the recruiting parameters too ambitious. This drives up the cost and may cause recruiting to fail altogether. It also suggests that you are seeking a precision that focus groups can't give. A desire for detailed breakdowns by type of customer suggests the need to do a survey instead.

DISCUSSION QUESTIONS

1. Identify three or four product categories in the B2C sphere where either focus groups or individual interviews would be feasible (i.e., avoid the easy cases where logistic difficulties or convenience would drive the choice of one or the other). Assume that the research objective is to explore consumer perceptions of brands, motivations for purchase, and response to different appeals. For each category, make a recommendation whether it would *generally* or *typically* be best to do group or individual interviews, and explain why.

   a. This exercise will be most successful if you can identify at least one category where you can support a recommendation to do individual interviews, and another where you can strongly recommend groups instead.

2. I can envision situations where *both* focus groups and field interviews (ethnographic in the B2C case, customer visits in the B2B case) might be conducted as part of a project.

   a. Think of one or two specific examples where this might occur. (Hint: This is easier to do in the B2B sphere.)

   b. In the context of your examples, what would be the specific function of the focus groups, and what would be the function of the field interviews?

   c. Which would you do first, and which second?

3. Most veteran research practitioners would say there's nothing magical about a focus group; it's simply a group interview, with the strengths and weaknesses of any interview, plus the strengths (and weaknesses) of doing the interview in a group setting.

   a. What is the "group effect," exactly? What additional advantages does a group setting contribute, and at what cost, relative to interviewing individual customers concerning the same topics and questions?

   b. An observer, less favorably disposed to focus groups than the author of this book, asserts: "Whatever its merits in B2C, there are very few applications for focus groups in a B2B setting; and the more the B2B setting is distinctively B2B (e.g., concentrated market, rational purchase process), the less pertinent the focus group technique."

      i. Do you agree or disagree? Either way, justify your stance.

   c. An even less favorably disposed observer renders the following negative judgment: "Focus groups are a holdover from an earlier age in marketing, when the emerging post–WWII market was new and firms were scrambling to get in touch with the newly affluent post-war consumer. Decades on, most large B2C firms have done hundreds and hundreds of focus group projects, and have squeezed every possible drop from that stone. Time to retire the focus group technique, in favor of ethnographical research on the one hand, or intensively instrumented individual interviews on the other, plus buzz harvesting and managed social media."

      i. Take a stance on this assertion and defend it.

4. *Exercise.* Design a focus group study for a company or product category that you know well. Your write-up needs to include: (1) statement of the decision problem, with background information as necessary; (2) specific research objectives; (3) research design, including the number of groups, the number of customers in each group, and whether the groups will be replicates (e.g., four groups of the same type of customer) or a structured sample (e.g., two groups with men and two groups with women); (4) the phone screener that will be used to recruit the groups (this also provides a statement of the kind of people you want to study); and (5) the discussion guide that will be used to moderate the groups.

SUGGESTED READINGS

Fern, E. F. (2002). *Advanced focus group research.* Thousand Oaks, CA: Sage.	This book has no parallel in the extensive literature on focus groups. It is the first attempt to provide a comprehensive conceptual and theoretical account of what can be learned from the focus group considered as a social science methodology. Although addressed primarily to the academic reader, it is accessible to thoughtful practitioners as well.
Bystedt, J., Lynn, S., Potts, D., & Fraley, G. (2010). *Moderating to the max: A full tilt guide to creative, insightful focus groups and depth interviews.* Ithaca, NY: Paramount Publishing. Goldman, A. E., & McDonald, S. S. (1987). *The group depth interview: Principles and practice.* New York, NY: Prentice Hall. Langer, S. (2001). *The mirrored window: Focus groups from a moderator's point of view.* New York, NY: PMP.	These books are for moderators who want to improve their skills. If you are a person who will have occasion to conduct group interviews from time to time, you also will find useful advice. Goldman and McDonald are particularly strong on the psychological aspects of group interviews.

SEVEN

INTERVIEW DESIGN

———————◆•◆•◆———————

A s noted in the Overview to this part, all qualitative research techniques, whether lab or field, group or individual, rely on interviews. These interviews have to be designed, same as the questionnaires used in survey research. The major elements of interview design are selecting the questions to be asked, arranging these questions into an effective sequence, and deciding what if any supplements should be added. Interviews use a style of questioning appropriate for face-to-face interactive conversation, and this style is quite distinct from that seen in questionnaires and other quantitative research techniques. The purpose of this chapter is to flesh out that distinction with specific examples of the kinds of questions that make best use of the opportunity presented by an interview. Subsequently, Chapter 10 will similarly treat the very different style of questioning appropriate to a survey questionnaire.

In addition to constructing specific questions, the design of interviews also includes the assembly of these questions into a workable ensemble. This entails decisions about sequencing topics, and about including and excluding topics and questions. Beyond devising and arranging questions, this chapter also covers issues associated with what might be called the stance, attitude, or mental set of the interviewer. There is an irreducible element of spontaneity in qualitative interviews. To be effective, a qualitative researcher has to be prepared to exploit unexpected avenues that open up and respond to disconcerting replies that may be made. How could it be otherwise, when the purpose of interviews is to explore and discover?

STYLE OF QUESTIONING

In terms of question style, the key distinction lies between what are called "open-ended" versus "close-ended" questions. An open-ended question sounds like this: "What would you like your next smartphone to do that your present smartphone cannot?" Compare a close-ended approximation: "Do you want your next smartphone to run more than one app at a time?" or the even more close-ended, "How many phone apps do you need to have running at the same time—one, two, three, or more?" In any open-ended question, the possible answers are left unspecified and "open": In the example, the respondent is left free to formulate the gap between present and future performance in terms of his or her choosing. The customer might even answer in terms of support or surrounding infrastructure, rather than capabilities of the smartphone itself. In a close-ended question, by contrast, the possible answers are pre-supposed: either "yes" or "no," as in the second instance, or specific multiple choices, as in the third instance.

Thus, the first and most important guideline for constructing good interview questions is: *emphasize open-ended questions and minimize the use of close-ended questions.* Minimize is not the same as eliminate; close-ended questions do have a role to play in interviews. So the sense of the rule is to lead with open-ended questions, and allocate the bulk of the time available to open-ended questions, while confining close-ended questions to a supporting role, as when these are used to "close" an extended discussion triggered by an open-ended question.

A second important distinction regarding the style of questioning proper to a qualitative interview lies in the nature of how the interviewer treats the answers to whatever questions get asked. In quantitative research answers are taken at face value, left alone as it were, so that these can be counted and tabulated. Their surface is opaque. "Yes" means yes, "no" means no, and the point of the research is to determine the precise proportion of "yes" answers, and to discover if this position represents the majority view, a strong minority, a niche sentiment, or a rare outlier.

Interviews are different; since we are generally not asking yes or no questions, the answers will be quite a bit more complex and fuzzy than "no," and ought not to be recorded verbatim and then let be. The purpose of an interview question is not so much to be answered as to initiate a conversation. Answers, in an interview, are simply the launch platform for additional discussion.

Interviewers aren't seeking an answer to be tabulated so much as an entry point into the world as it appears from the customer's point of view. In quantitative research, proper phrasing of the question stem, and careful specification of the answer set, is crucial to getting value out of the research. In qualitative interviewing, the attitude of the interviewer counts for more than the words used to ask the question, because the question itself is just a pretext to get the customer talking. The value of the research lies in what the interviewer takes away from the resulting dialogue, and not in the spoken answers per se.

A final point of distinction is that interviews require a blend of spontaneity and preparation. By contrast, the questionnaires used in surveys are all preparation, zero spontaneity. You cannot get the desired precision from a survey unless the exact same questions are asked the exact same way in the exact same sequence, in every single administration. Conversely, interviews won't be successful unless the interviewer permits him or herself to vary the question phrasing and sequence to suit the particular needs of the human being participating in today's interview, who may be quite different from both the customer interviewed yesterday and from your mental image of the prototypical customer. The need for spontaneity and flexibility follows directly from the previous distinction: Since the goal is to spark a discussion on the topics of concern, you needn't be too particular about whether you use a wooden match, a butane lighter, or a magnifying glass held up to the sun to deliver that spark. Furthermore, because the aim is to spark a discussion, which may then take an unexpected path, a good interviewer has to have the flexibility, and the fluency, to come up with good questions on the spot.

At the same time, there must be enough preparation for the interviews to consist of more than "management by wandering around." It won't do to approach the interview with a few jotted notes and a vague sense of what topics might be interesting; this would be like trying to run a meeting without an agenda. But indeed, what you need is more analogous to an agenda than a questionnaire—you need a guide, not a script.

A key part of preparation is scrutinizing potential questions for their fitness and probable information yield. Any number of questions may occur to you when the purpose of the interview is truly exploratory; but there is time to ask only a small subset of these. In terms of fitness, there are a variety of question phrasings that have proved useful over the years across different contexts. And there are definitely some phrasings that should generally be avoided during an interview. There are also some questioning gambits that have limited applicability but can be productive in specific situations. And there is a further set of what might better be termed devices rather than questions per se, that still fulfill the basic purpose of any qualitative interview question, which is to get the customer talking. All of these will be laid out in a subsequent section; but I think it might be helpful to begin with a description of the procedure by which interview questions come into being and get assembled into a workable set. The desired output from this procedure is termed a "discussion guide," and these are reasonably similar in structure across virtually any kind of interview.

PROCEDURE FOR QUESTION SELECTION

1. Start by revisiting your research objectives. This should give you insight into the major topics that will have to be covered in the interview.

2. Get a sheaf of blank paper, if working alone, or a white board, if performing this step as a team; either is feasible.

3. Depending on personal or group cognitive style, either list at a high level the 6 to 10 major topics to be covered (topics correspond to areas where you'd like to have a discussion), or start brainstorming specific open-ended questions. Either approach will work, but most people gravitate toward the one or the other entry point—general topics or specific questions—as most natural.

4. [This next step is best done by an individual.] Take the raw output of the initial session and organize it into a discussion guide, using the template in Exhibit 7.1. At this point you begin to "freeze" on what the key discussion areas will be, and you should have at least some good discussion launch questions. All of this material needs to be gathered together into a workable sequence that you believe will flow well. Your output is a draft discussion guide suitable for circulating among team members and other constituents.

5. Next, if at all possible, circulate the draft to team members, to managers who have funding authority, and to any constituent you expect to have to act based on the research results (you want early buy-in from these people). Ask for a detailed markup: missing topics or questions,

superfluous topics, alternative ways to broach a topic, alternative sequences. If you are working alone, sleep on the draft for a few days, and then undertake this markup yourself. Two spaced iterations are best; it's tough for an individual to duplicate the panoramic perspective of a team.

    a. *Focus group note*: If there is an outside moderator who will actually conduct the interviews, as will typically be the case with focus groups, the team leader's role more or less stops here. The remaining steps will be undertaken by the professional moderator in consultation with the team.

6. Prepare the final version of the discussion guide for use in the interviews. In my own work, I print the guide as an outline following the template in Exhibit 7.1, using two to three pages, and allowing for lots of white space on which to scribble notes.

7. If the project is important enough, conduct one or two pilot interviews, to give the discussion guide a test run, as it were. You can use a colleague who used to be on the customer side, or even a well-known and friendly local customer. Sometimes you'll discover that your one-hour discussion guide is really a two-hour guide, or vice versa, or that a much better sequence of topics is possible.

    a. By the way, this step only applies to customer visits and individual interviews. Part of the logistical challenge of doing focus groups is that there are no dry runs.

8. Last but not least: Allow the discussion guide to evolve as the interviews proceed. Again, this is not a questionnaire that has to be executed the same way every time if it is to have any precision, but a kind of agenda, which can be modified as needed to optimize interview outcomes. In most cases, you can't really anticipate the very best way to guide an interview until you're already half way through the project.

The result of this procedure will be something that follows the template in the exhibit. The task in a discussion guide is first, to map out a sequence of discussion; second, to indicate the major discussion topics; third, to state key questions that will open each major discussion topic; and fourth, to provide reminders to the interviewer to probe for specific issues if these are not volunteered. A further note on sequencing topics: It is generally best to proceed from the general to the specific, and from issues likely to be familiar to the customer (past, present) to those more remote (i.e., the future). A final tip is that if you are going to expose the interviewee to stimuli, such as a concept statement for a new product, or drafts of advertisements, these properly come in the late middle of the interview. To introduce them earlier is to poison the well, to bias what was supposed to be the interviewee's unprompted response to your initial open-ended questions.

Exhibit 7.1

Template for a Discussion Guide

  I. Opening
     A. Introductions, purpose
     B. Key orienting questions (job role, applications of the product)
  II. Current situation/issues
     A. Changes in environment
     B. Likes and dislikes regarding existing products
     C. Problems and hassles
  III. Desired future (enhancements, corrections, replacements)
     A. Specific needs and desires
     B. Underlying motivations
  IV. Reaction to concepts [if any]
  V. Miscellaneous issues (e.g., vendor selection process)
  VI. Closing

Note: The template assumes a customer visit within a B2B market and that the customer visited is an existing account. See the Suggested Readings at the end of the focus group chapter for examples of discussion guides appropriate to B2C markets and focus groups.

SOME GOOD (AND BAD) QUESTIONS

A good question is one that opens up the customer and triggers an on-topic discussion that taps into the customer's honest or native worldview. A bad question is one that shuts down discussion or produces a response that reflects something other than the customer's true, natural perspective on these matters. Good questions are most likely to flow from a proper stance or attitude on the part of the interviewer, so a subsequent section goes into some detail on good and bad interviewer behaviors. Interviewer mindset is crucial, since so many questions have to be devised on the spot, without preparation. Here I focus on helpful versus problematic question phrasing, in the case of questions that can be prepared in advance.

Workhorse Questions

The paradigmatic interview question is one that launches a discussion some minutes in length. Therefore, the most common "good" interview question is the follow-up question that keeps the discussion going, helps steer it in a desired direction, or takes it deeper. These are generic, in the sense of applying across B2B and B2C interviews, individual and group interviews, and so on. Examples of such workhorse questions include "What else?"; "Any other [problems, issues, etc.]?"; "Could you give me an example?"; "What specifically was the [problem, outcome, etc.]?"; "What happened after that?"; and "How did you respond?" These workhorse questions get asked over and over, as needed, in a good interview.

The next category of workhorse questions concerns the customer and his or her actions. Not every draft discussion guide recognizes this imperative. An old joke runs, "That was no customer visit—it was nothing but a *product* visit!" Sad to say, all too many interviews are structured so as not to be about the customer, but about the product, which, after all, is often what is front and center for the interviewer. It's as if a chatty partygoer turned to you after a long monologue and said, "Well, enough about me—what do *you* think of me?" Me, me, me is the bane of interviews. The point is to learn about the customer. Your product will come into the discussion, but it should be neither central nor foundational.

Examples of customer-centric questions in a B2B context would include questions about task demands ("What does this product accomplish for you?" or "What job did you 'hire' this product to do?"), context ("What other devices supply this instrument with input, and where does its output go?"), and supporting infrastructure ("Who uses this product—who's responsible for its output?"). The animating idea behind these questions is that no one really cares about products per se; the driving force, and the unit of analysis, is the task the product performs for the B2B customer. Products are just one of many resources that a business brings together to accomplish its goals, and the key to understanding how a product could be improved or made more competitive is to understand what the customer does with it.

In B2C contexts, the same principle holds, but it is expressed differently. Not all B2C products are utilitarian, so the language of task demands fails. Instead, you ask about motivations, specific uses, and/or occasions for use. Whereas firms are organized to accomplish tasks, consumers pursue life projects: finding a mate, staying fit, being a good parent, and so on. The point again is that consumers are not single-purpose product choice engines floating in the ether. People make life choices and gather the products and brands that can assist them in acting on those life plans. Therefore, in B2C contexts customer-centric questions seek to situate the product or service within the life world of the consumer.

A very powerful instance of a customer-centric question is to ask about problems, hassles, and gaps ("Is there anything you need to do with this product that the present model can't do?"; "Where does this product fall short—what can't it do?"; "Is there an application where this product has failed, or not been very successful?"; or "What's the worst part of using this product?"). To ask explicitly about "your unmet needs" is often much less successful. Only product marketers walk around with needs lists in their heads. Customers spend their time worrying about problems, and the way to get at unmet needs is to perform a gap analysis. Unmet needs, therefore, are best gleaned by identifying the set of unsolved problems.

Yet another category of workhorse questions provides a bridge between the customer and the product. In almost every case where the person interviewed currently owns the product of interest, it will be appropriate as the interview progresses to ask "What do you like, and what don't you like, about [product]?" With a firm understanding of task and context laid, asking about likes/dislikes will help you understand how the present product fulfills (or doesn't) the customer's expectations. The important thing is to get all the likes and dislikes out on the table, and to follow up on each one. You don't want to move on until you understand why *this* customer likes or dislikes *this* aspect of the product. That understanding requires tying that liking back to the task demand or life choice that drove the purchase in the first place.

A similar bridging role, also appropriate to the middle of the interview, is played by questions about the decision process for B2B customers, or purchase occasion and process for B2C customers. How formalized is this B2B customer's buying process? Who gets involved in what role? How are vendors vetted and qualified? How do purchase criteria get identified? A perfectly functional B2B product may fall short of its potential if the vendor doesn't understand how its products are purchased differently in different segments or submarkets.

Specialized Questions

A good open-ended question, properly followed up, may produce a dozen or more answers—specific problems, sets of likes, and so on. When the customer has run dry, it is appropriate to step back and get some sense of the priority among answers. Typical focusing questions include "Of all those you mentioned, what are the top three?" or "If you had $100 to spend to solve all these problems, how would you allocate those dollars?" The important thing is not to just tabulate the answers, as when doing a survey ("The average rank importance of X across the 15 customers interviewed was …"), but to use the customer's stated priority as a device to probe further ("Why did you place half your budget on solving this one problem?"). You can't learn the true rank order in the market from a small number of interviews; but you can gain further insight into a particular customer's worldview from this follow-up.

A related gambit is to push customers to make trade-offs. Quite often customers will express potentially contradictory desires: They want the process to be faster, and they want fewer errors. The industry knowledge of the interviewer may suggest that either goal is feasible, but that it will be very expensive, or even technically impossible, to achieve them both. It is quite appropriate at that point to confront the customer with the trade-off, and ask which goal they'd pick if they could only afford to realize one. Here again, the goal is not to count how many customers make which trade-off, but to set up the opportunity for further probing into the customer's reasons.

Another specialized question of note is to focus *your* customer on the issue of who is *their* customer, and what does it take to satisfy that downstream customer. Most B2B customers are part of a value chain, and asking about the next "customer" downstream can be helpful in breaking out of a narrow product focus to get at the fundamental task your customer is trying to accomplish.

A final example of a specialized question comes into play when you must question customers about a certain kind of event that is reasonably rare, so that the last occurrence may have been months ago, with other occurrences strung out over the preceding years. To ask about that type of event in the abstract may well draw a blank. It is more effective to use the question stem, "Think back to the last time you [installed a new operating system, had to qualify a vendor, etc.]." This stem is designed to surface the most recent concrete instance of that type of event, which you can then probe with open-ended questions in the standard way. It's much easier to get a rich discussion going in the case of a specific event. Later you can ask "How about the time before that?" to get additional examples of the event in question. Once you've surfaced and probed several concrete instances, you can go deeper into the nature of the customer's response to that type of event.

Interview Devices

A device is anything that isn't a question per se, but that serves the same goal of stimulating discussion. The major categories are: (1) concept statements, 2) advertisements, (3) physical products, and (4) projective stimuli. A concept statement presents a new product idea in terms of half a dozen bullet points, or even, in some B2B markets, as a small PowerPoint presentation conveying key elements of product design. Ads can be roughs of future ads or actual ads, your own or competitors'. Products can be actual products obtained from the factory or purchased from the store, and also prototypes or mock-ups. Projective stimuli run the gamut from comic strip panels showing a customer situation with a blank word balloon, to little stories, to prompts like "If each of these brands were an animal, which animal comes to mind for each?"

The goal of any device is to give the customer something concrete to grapple with, and thereby make the discussion richer and more meaningful. With all the devices mentioned, the key again is not to tabulate responses, or take votes, but to use the responses as opportunities for further probing. You don't care whether the customer in front of you today likes the new product idea or not; your task is to understand *why* they like or dislike each element and why they are or are not favorably inclined toward the overall concept. Particularly with the presentation of new product ideas in a self-managed customer visit, the temptation can be very strong to go into sell mode ("Don't you see, this feature would be great for you because …"). Your goal is to learn enough now that you won't have to sell so hard later, because the product is designed to be just right for its intended segment.

Bad Questions

A bad question, again, is any gambit that shuts down discussion or produces an artificial or slanted take on the customer's actual position. One of the arguments for the use of professional moderators, as in focus groups, is precisely the expectation that outside professionals will bring a higher degree of interview skill, with minimal risk that bad questions will be asked. Conversely, a major risk factor in self-managed customer visits is the danger that the people doing the visits haven't a clue about what makes a particular question worthwhile or a waste of time. Historically, the conventional academic view was that managers couldn't be trusted to be either skilled or objective in self-conducted interviews with customers, so that research had to be outsourced to independent professionals. I prefer to think of the danger of bias as a risk to be managed, rather than as a knock-out argument against managers interviewing their customers. In the end, an interview is simply one human being conversing with another, seeking information in a goal-oriented way. There are varying levels of skill, but a basic capacity to interview is widespread.

The goal of this small section, then, is to alert you concerning a few of the more common types of bad questions. These include: (1) unclear questions, (2) unproductive questions, and (3) inappropriate questions. Unclear questions include those that are too long (shorter is better), those whose syntax is too complicated (a question that contains a semicolon is likely to be unclear), and those that use jargon (such as too many TLAs).[1] In terms of avoiding unclear questions, let the KISS (keep it short and simple) principle be your guide. The ear is much more limited than the eye when it comes to processing long or complex material. When complex issues must be broached, it is imperative to build up the complexity in a series of simple steps, rather than trying to get there all at once.

An unproductive question is one that is either too hard or too easy, too vague or too narrow. Open-ended questions that are too open are one example; imagine starting an interview with "What's going on?" It's certainly short and it's very simple, but the customer can't break into such a vague and sweeping offer. Productive questions give the customer something to grab hold of: "What challenges have you faced in moving functions to the cloud?" This question identifies "challenges" as the focus and names a specific sphere of

[1]Three-letter acronyms (TLAs) are the bane of most technical fields.

operations (it does presume that earlier conversation has established that the customer *has* moved some functions to the cloud; otherwise it prejudges the issue). Overly technical and specific questions, especially early in the interview, may strike the customer as too hard and hence unrewarding to pursue. There is likewise a problem with asking too many close-ended questions early in the interview; these are too simple and unrewarding.

Inappropriate questions are those that impose the interviewer's preconceptions or worldview on the customer, obscuring what might have been learned if the customer had been allowed to speak for him or herself. More specifically, inappropriate questions typically take the form of either leading or biased questions. Like most practicing researchers, I've encountered a few hilarious instances over the years ("Wouldn't you agree that our Model TJ-X55 offers the highest level of performance in the industry?" or "We know that ads from competitor X irritate our customers—what do you dislike about them?"). A good rule is to avoid questions that begin with a negative contraction (e.g., "Don't you think that ..." or "Isn't it the case that ..."). These lead the witness. Also helpful is to avoid any question that begins with an assertion about what you know or what "everybody knows," or that in any way reveals your position—no matter how certain you may feel that this customer shares your view. Any such tipping of the hand may bias the customer's reply.

GOOD (AND BAD) INTERVIEWER BEHAVIORS

Because the human being is the primary measuring instrument in interview research, and because so many interview questions have to be devised on the spot as the conversation moves in unexpected directions, the success of an interview depends much more on the mindset and stance of the researcher than in the case of most other forms of market research. In terms of mindset, a suggestion I have found helpful in training interviewers is that you should treat each customer as an "expert informant." This puts the customer in the role of knowledge-holder, and the interviewer in the role of apt pupil. Imagine how you would behave around somebody that you regarded as a distinguished expert in an area that you badly wanted to learn more about. This attitude or mental stance will serve you well in market research interviews. It encourages a respectful focus on what the customer knows that you do not, and it will go far to shape questions that occur spontaneously to you in a helpful direction.

Another behavior that must be cultivated by good interviewers is to probe. Customers are just human—even a terrific open-ended question will sometimes elicit only a vague reply or gobs of word salad. At other times, customers will respond beautifully to a question with a thoughtful answer, but the thing to remember is that there may still be more answers there. If they identify one challenge, there is probably another; if they identified two challenges, there is often a third, and if there were three, there may be more. The proper response to both the word salad and the articulate answer is to probe further. Good interviewers are constantly asking "What else?" or "Anything else?" Much of the real labor of interviewing is performed by such follow-up questions. With practice, you will also develop an ear for when the customer has given a partial, vague, or wandering answer, and will almost automatically ask "Can you give me an example?" or "What specifically was the problem?"

Conversely, most bad interviewer behaviors stem from taking a self-centered or egotistical approach to this human interaction. Bad interviewers spend time asserting their own viewpoints, knowledge, or expertise; the interview becomes a monologue by and about the interviewer rather than a dialogue with the customer. The customer is either put off, or shrugs and thinks "okay, let's take the free education on offer from this apparently quite knowledgeable visitor, and forget about conveying my own views." Either way, you are sunk. Adopting the attitude that the customer is an expert informant is a helpful corrective.

Alternatively, bad interviewers badly want the research to produce a specific finding, and labor mightily to shape the interview so as to produce exactly that finding. This produces leading and biased questions, or even arguments with the customer to convince them that they think a certain way. These can be seriously off-putting to customers, who then tend to withdraw from the interview and terminate early.

The bad interviewer behaviors described are obviously much more of a risk in self-conducted customer visits than in interviews outsourced to a professional moderator. The task of the outside professional is much easier: it's not his product, it's not her career path, and outsiders literally don't care whether the product succeeds. Their commitment is to professionalism: performing well in the interview and earning their fee. And the outside professional's experience base is much greater. What drives self-conducted visits is the need for technical and industry knowledge of the sort that can only be possessed by a product manager immersed in the issues. Plus, it is vendor firm management that must ultimately gain a clear vision of the customer, and it is not clear that achieving that vision can benefit from outsourcing.

To sum up, a research interview is a human interaction. Human beings, by and large, speak most freely and most informatively when they feel well-treated by, and favorably disposed toward, the fellow human being who is asking them questions. The technical term for this tenor of relationship is rapport. Successful interviewers know how to establish rapport with a complete stranger within a few minutes. The purpose of regarding the customer as an expert informant is precisely to instill an attitude of respect and rapt listening, calculated to foster such rapport. It is not the only way to bring about rapport, but whatever stance the interviewer adopts, rapport must be created if an interview is to be the site of productive discussions.

DOs AND DON'Ts

Do focus on the customer. Make each customer central to the interview. Take a respectful stance that leaves you and your own views in the background.

Don't talk too much. The customer should be speaking about three fourths of the time.

Do ask lots of questions, but keep each question short.

Don't ask too many close-ended questions, however pleasingly specific these might seem back at your desk.

Do follow up on customer answers. Your job is not to record what they say but to understand how they think.

Do prepare for the interview by organizing your questions into a sequence that will flow for the customer, and do work on the best way to phrase key questions.

Don't try to control too tightly the course of the interview, and don't worry if every interview covers the same broad territory using a different path.

DISCUSSION QUESTIONS

1. Both interviews and surveys consist of questions devised by the researcher along with the customer's attempt to answer these questions. In terms of distinctions between the two, in the one, the questions are spoken, without too much "version control" (i.e., many differences in wording across interviews), while in the other, question wording is fixed. Another difference is that interviews are generally few in number, surveys many.

   a. What else is similar across interviews and surveys, and what else is different?

      i. In your answer, please assume a self-administered web survey, and an in-person interview.

   b. Is there a kind of question that can *only* work in surveys, or can anything that can be asked in a questionnaire also be asked out loud in an interview?

   c. Same question in reverse: Are there questions that "work" in an interview, but would not work when written down in a questionnaire?

2. One of the ways to conceptualize a process that takes place in time, such as an interview, is to divvy it up into a beginning, a middle, and an end. The middle occupies the bulk of the time and, of course, fulfills multiple purposes; but beginnings and endings may have a more specialized function. Assuming this to be a useful conceptualization, answer the following questions:

   a. What is the primary function of the beginning of the interview? What actions or types of questions have to be avoided at the outset of an interview, if that function is to be fulfilled? What particular actions and questions would be notably helpful and useful?

   b. What function(s) have to be performed at the conclusion of an interview? What actions or types of question should be avoided here? What particular actions and questions would be notably helpful and useful at the end of the interview?

3. Although risky, it is possible to present a product concept or other stimulus to customers in an interview and have a dialogue about their response.

   a. How would you word the first question to the interviewee after presenting the concept?

   b. Assuming the product concept can be decomposed into particular elements, would it be best to present the complete concept, and follow up with a discussion of individual elements? Or, better to present the elements one at a time, discuss each, and then step back and discuss the ensemble? Explain your answer.

   c. What exactly are the risks when a product concept is floated during an interview? Who is subject to these risks?

      i. Many observers would argue that the risks are greatest when, as in a customer visit, the person who presents the concept is part of the management team, and not, as in a focus group, an outside moderator. What risk, exactly, is feared here? Are there any compensating advantages to having an insider rather than an outsider present the concept?

4. Studies of when market research is likely to get used and when it is likely to be ignored suggest that surprising and unexpected results were particularly likely to be ignored by executives who commissioned the market research.

   a. What are the implications for qualitative research, which is often pitched as a discovery tool for exploring unfamiliar aspects of the customer experience?

5. An old joke defines a consultant as "someone who borrows your watch to tell you what time it is, charges you a fee for so doing, and then walks away with your watch when done." Assume and research that the joke holds a grain of truth about the perils and opportunities of outsourcing market research. Now relate the joke to the risks and benefits of self-conducted customer interviews in a highly technical B2B product category.

6. *Exercise.* Assume that you work for an architectural design firm. You have received the contract to design a new building for the business school at a leading university. The new building will primarily contain faculty offices and meeting spaces. You are preparing to interview 16 members of the faculty to get a sense of their needs and requirements relative to the building design. Your team has brainstormed a motley mix of topics and questions to make up the discussion guide for these interviews, as listed below.

   a. First, there are likely to be one to three "duds" in the list—questions that are either inappropriate for a qualitative interview, or not helpful or relevant to the task of designing this building. Cross these out.

   b. Next, rearrange the remaining questions into a sequence that would flow well and be effective. What's the best beginning or opener from this list, and what questions need to be postponed until late in the interview?

   c. *Extra Credit*: Flesh out your sequence in (b) into a complete discussion guide, adding any questions or topics that appear to be missing. Reword or rephrase any of the starting questions as appropriate

Brainstormed topics and questions:

- Which building(s) on campus work particularly well/poorly?
- What are your likes and dislikes concerning the present business school building?
- State three features that the new building must have to be a success in your eyes.
- Would you like the new building to contain a cafeteria?
- Where on campus should the new building be located?
- What kind of features would you like to see in the new building?
- How many square feet should a professor's office have?
- Should the windows in the new building be capable of opening, or be fixed in their frames?
- What features should be omitted/avoided in the new building?

SUGGESTED READINGS

See the Suggested Readings sections in the chapters on customer visits and focus groups.	The books listed there have chapters that focus on interview design and the kinds of questioning strategies that work well in qualitative research.
Payne, S. L. (1951). *The art of asking questions.* Princeton, NJ: Princeton University Press.	A classic, timeless book on effective and ineffective ways to word questions.

⊰ EIGHT ⊱

QUALITATIVE SAMPLING AND DATA ANALYSIS[1]

————— ◦•◦•◦ —————

This chapter is the first of two discussions of sampling; the second, in Chapter 13, will consider sampling issues that come up in *quantitative* market research, especially survey research. Here I focus on sampling issues associated with *qualitative* research such as customer visits and focus groups. Since it comes first in the sequence, this chapter will also cover some basics common to sampling across qualitative and quantitative research. Conversely, while this chapter combines the topics of sampling and data analysis in the qualitative case, the topic of quantitative data analysis is so large that it gets its own separate chapter.

Just as a heads up, the treatment in Chapter 13 is fairly conventional and includes topics that appear in virtually every market research textbook. The present chapter, by contrast, is unique to this book. No other market research textbook that I have seen has a chapter on sampling for *qualitative* research. The failure to treat explicitly issues in qualitative sampling causes many problems in conventional accounts, to the point of making it inexplicable why a manager would ever bother spending money on small-sample qualitative market research at all.

---

[1]A shortened version of portions of this chapter was published as McQuarrie, E. F., & S. H. McIntyre, "What Can You Project From Small Sample Qualitative Research," *Marketing Insights,* March/April, 2014.

WHY SAMPLING?

It's not always necessary to take a sample to conduct market research. There are B2B markets where the total number of buying firms, worldwide, your accounts, and all your competitors put together may only amount to 12. You could talk to every single one if you wished. At the extreme, suppose you sell a nuclear bomb component to the Air Force; in this case, the size of your market is equal to one, where it will always remain, since expanding your market by adding new customers might get you charged with treason.

In most cases, however, the number of customers is larger than you can feasibly or cost-effectively visit. Hence, it is necessary to draw a sample, that is, select that small fraction of customers you will visit or assemble into a focus group. In discussions of sampling, the total market, however defined and circumscribed, is referred to as the population. The goal in sampling is to talk to a small number of customers that effectively represents the larger population of which they are part. The word *represent* in the preceding sentence means that you believe you can generalize findings obtained from the small sample to the total population. If a representative sample by and large likes the new product idea, then you infer that the population will by and large like the product, too. If the sample discerns three applications for the new technology, then you infer that the market will accommodate those same three applications. If the CIOs in your sample show little enthusiasm for the solution, while data center managers, typically two levels below the CIO in the organization, rave about it, then you infer that out in the market, the solution is best targeted at data center managers, not CIOs. These are all examples of generalizations or inferences from sample to population.

So far, so good: Most managers intuitively understand that the goal of working with a sample is to look through the sample to get a glimpse of the population. The population means the market, and the market is where you make (or lose) money. Here's the rub: Only certain kinds of samples are representative. If the sampling procedure is handled badly or approached in ignorance, it is unlikely to be representative—and you may have just wasted some tens of thousands of dollars.

As an example of an unrepresentative sample, suppose your boss's boss stops by your office and says, "I played golf with Joe Dutton yesterday, we went to college together. He's a big buyer of our widgets and he suggested we need to configure the new product this way." In this example, the representativeness of the "Joe" sample is simply unknown. The real problem here is not that the sample size is $N = 1$. Suppose your boss's boss is an avid golfer, and, after playing with Harry, Sue, and Tom, with each of whom he has a long history, he notes that two of them also voiced a preference for this configuration. The representativeness of this sample of $N = 3$ also remains unknown. There's no reason to suppose that a few personal connections of some executives provide a representative subset of your customer base.

I can easily imagine small customer visit programs whose sampling procedure is no better than that just described. One customer enters the set because he's been bugging the sales rep, another because her office is next to the same airport, a third because he impressed your boss at the trade show, and so on. Ten visits assembled this way are of doubtful value. Not only is the representativeness of this sample in doubt, but there also can be no assurance that we are even sampling from the population of interest—the target market relevant to the decision at hand.

Again, so far so good: I've never met a manager who didn't have an intuitive sense that some approaches to sampling were inferior to others, that is, less likely to be representative. But right about here is where conventional textbook treatments of the representativeness of *qualitative* samples go badly awry. Consider this quote from a leading textbook concerning focus groups:

> "The results are not 'representative' of what would be found in the general population, and thus are not projectable."

> (Churchill & Iacobucci, 2009, p. 85; see also
> Chapter 2, Suggested Readings)

Taken literally, this statement rejects the value of all qualitative samples and, by extension, of qualitative research itself. For if a sample is not representative—it gives us no reliable projection to the population—why bother with it? In the conventional textbook treatment, then, all qualitative samples are equivalent to your boss's boss's golfing buddies, and no qualitative sample is representative.

Obviously, we are not intended to take the quoted statement literally. Conventional textbooks continue to devote many pages to discussions of focus groups and other qualitative market research techniques, implying that these are effective market research tools—which they could not be, if their samples allowed no projection to the population of interest. How to explain this puzzle?

I think what happened is that a laudable motive—to caution managers against attributing to qualitative research more precision than it can muster—got mixed up with a misunderstanding of what, in fact, can be generalized from the very small samples typically seen in qualitative research. Had the quoted statement said something like, "a dozen or two customer visits can't give you the kind of detailed percentage splits you can get from a large sample survey," it would have been unexceptional. Precision—whether the population is going to split 61–39 in favor of the new product, or 48–52 against—is always less in small samples (see Chapter 13). It's unlikely that 20 customer visits could reliably discriminate between these two alternative population states, no matter how representative the sampling, whereas a survey completed by a representative sample of several hundred customers most definitely could.

What got mixed up was that the limited precision of qualitative samples, which everyone acknowledges, somehow morphed into no precision whatsoever, that is, into a fundamental lack of representativeness; hence, an inability to project anything at all. The remainder of this chapter attempts to disentangle these confusions. Practically speaking, qualitative research can be valuable and effective. This could not be true if it was not possible to project anything from small qualitative samples. The question is, what, exactly? I begin with the limiting case: What can be projected or inferred when you sample exactly one customer from a large population of interest?

PROJECTION FROM $N = 1$

Suppose one has an enormous urn filled with a large number of beads. A draw is made from the urn and the bead turns out to be iridescent in color. What inferences about the color of the beads remaining in the urn can be supported, and with what degree of confidence, based on this single draw?

1. It is 100 percent certain that before the draw, the urn contained at least one iridescent bead.

2. If the urn contains many beads, it is very likely that there are additional iridescent beads remaining. If there were an infinite number of beads, the odds are infinitesimal that you drew the only iridescent bead in the urn. If the urn contained 100 million beads to start, the odds against drawing the only iridescent bead in the urn are about 100 million to one.

Translating back to market research: Every research result in a qualitative study is projectable in the specific sense that every viewpoint expressed in an interview is highly likely to be a viewpoint held by some number of other customers who are part of the market but are not present in the research sample. This holds true as long as the qualitative research participants are, in fact, drawn from the population of customers you wish to understand. To return to the example, only if you had drawn the bead not from the urn but from underneath the cushions on the couch where you sat would you be unable to make and justify a projection about the color of other beads remaining in the urn. The bead plucked from underneath the cushion would be a "Martian" with respect to the beads in the urn; results from it are not projectable to the urn.

Note that with $N = 1$, you don't have to make any assumption about the nature of the sampling process used, random or otherwise. If the bead is drawn from the urn, it permits some inference about the other beads in the urn, no matter how limited or constrained. Even Joe, your boss's boss's golf buddy, if he is a member of the population of interest, establishes that at least some customers feel that way.

On the other hand, as is obvious when $N = 1$, the fact that the bead drawn was "not black" tells you very little about either the existence or the possible incidence of black beads remaining in the urn. You learn only that not 100 percent of the beads were black. And since in the behavioral sciences, very few responses are given by 100 percent of the population, this means you learn very little indeed from the absence, in the smallest possible sample, of some particular occurrence.

In summary, some degree of projection is possible from even the smallest qualitative sample. The crucial stipulation is that the sample must come from the population of interest; it must not be a Martian. What this means in practical terms is that a substantial fraction of the effort invested in qualitative sampling takes the form of defining the population and making sure that the obtained sample comes from the defined population. In many B2B cases, "population" is almost a misnomer: The target market is often something very specific, like "current users of the NX-700A router in the financial industry with a title of manager or director who must deal with data flows across the corporate firewall." There may still be hundreds or thousands of individuals in this "population," so sampling is imperative; but the crucial first step in developing a representative sample for a customer visit program aimed at these individuals is to define the population with something like the exactitude given and then to ensure that everyone visited is, in fact, a member of that population.

This account of what can be inferred from samples of $N = 1$ also serves to flesh out the meaning of certain pleasant-sounding adjectives that crop up in discussions of the value or benefit of focus groups, customer visits, and other qualitative research. When qualitative research is said to be "exploratory," this means that it allows for discovery: Imagine the intense scrutiny if one had never before seen an iridescent bead prior to the draw. When qualitative research is said to provide "insight," what this means formally is that one has a chance to observe and examine iridescence: to see how the bead shimmers when held in sunlight, how rapidly the colors shift when the bead is turned, and so forth. In other words, once an iridescent bead is in hand, one has a chance to inspect its particular *qualities*. Qualitative research is useful for discovering the existence of a consumer phenomenon and learning its exact nature—its qualities.

Conversely, if one already knew about iridescent beads and had had plenty of opportunity to examine their qualities, then qualitative research might be a waste of time or money. For as I shall show next, there are strict limits on how much can be projected from a small-sample qualitative study, beyond the fact that a certain quality of consumer response does exist and has a particular nature. It is these true limits that are the proximal source for the broad and unsupportable claim that "results . . . cannot be projected."

Finally, I made the bead iridescent to highlight a disjuncture between academic and practitioner mindsets that goes far toward explaining why academic treatments of qualitative research are so often unsatisfactory. Doubtless the reader has encountered other discussions where beads were drawn from urns to make a point about sampling theory. In academic accounts, the beads are always white or black, or red, blue, and green, and so forth. That is, bead *qualities* are already known and exhaustively specified. The task of estimation is to determine the incidence of each known quality in the urn—its quantity. Actual business practice is fundamentally different. The pressing question early in the decision cycle, when qualitative research will be considered, is simply, What color beads may be found? Or put another way, Are there any colors in the urn not already known and fully described? Exploration and discovery are profoundly important in applied, practical research. As a businessperson, you are motivated to do qualitative research because you simply don't know what might be found in the urn.

The next question becomes, Is that all there is? Can qualitative research do any more than reveal the existence of a customer response and allow us to examine the nature and qualities of that response up close? A case in point: As noted earlier, most qualitative samples can't distinguish between population splits of 61–39 versus 48–52; in other words, they can't distinguish a firm majority from a toss-up. So how about population values of 80–20 versus 50–50, or even 20–80—is it reasonable to expect that a dozen or two interviews can reliably distinguish between a new product idea that is going to meet an overwhelmingly positive reception in the market, versus one that is going to meet with an ambivalent reception, or appeal only to a niche? As it turns out, you *can* project rather more than the fact of existence from small qualitative samples—as long as you carefully sample from the population of interest and not some other or unknown population.

PROJECTIONS FROM QUALITATIVE SAMPLES OF $N \leq 32$

When I say "can project," I mean that certain inferences are warranted; and by "warrant" I specifically mean "the probability of this inference being mistaken is less than 5 percent, or 1 in 20 occasions, were the sample to be drawn an infinite number of times." This is how conventional statistical inference proceeds (see Chapters 13 and 14). Thus, if the odds that two mean values come from the same population are less than 1 in 20 based on an appropriate test statistic, it is customary to conclude that the means are different, "$p \leq .05$." By the prevailing social science convention, if a conclusion would be wrong in less than 1 in 20 iterations, I accept that conclusion as warranted by the data. I don't know beyond a shadow of a doubt that the conclusion is correct; I am simply confident that the odds of being wrong are acceptably low. If a 90 percent presence of some consumer response ("I like it") in a small qualitative sample would correspond to a population incidence of less than 50 percent on fewer than 1 occasion in 20, then the qualitative researcher has warrant to project from overwhelming presence in the sample to the claim that "a majority" of the much larger population will also approve.

In short, the name of the game here is the extent to which I can project some proportion occurring in the qualitative sample to the population at large. It might be the proportion that approve of some idea, the fraction that have had a certain experience ("the screen went blank and the keyboard froze"), the

prevalence of some particular reason to buy ("once the sales guy demonstrated we could reduce our headcount, it was a done deal"), or any customer
response that can be present or absent, so that a sample produces a proportion
or percentage split.

This issue of the projectability of a proportion can be approached from
various angles. A decision maker may wish to know how likely a majority
position found in a sample of 30—say, a 60–40 split—would be to occur when
the true population split is something else—either split evenly, split in the
reverse direction, or split any other way. This is the simple case of Type I error,
where the fear is that the qualitative result indicating a modest majority is flat-
out wrong. Or a decision maker may want to know how likely a qualitative
sample is to overlook—to never gather any instance of—a consumer response
that is present in the population at any given rate, say, 20 percent. This is a
somewhat more complex kind of error, analogous to Type II error, in which I
falsely project, based on a qualitative study, that few or no customers in the
market hold a certain view, seek a particular benefit, engage in some behavior,
and so forth, when in fact the population contains some reasonable incidence
of these individuals, that is, 20 percent.

Any probability of this type can be easily estimated if a Bernoulli process
is assumed in which each research participant is independently and randomly
sampled from the population. Although qualitative samples are not always
drawn in this fashion, there seems no intrinsic reason why they could not
be—especially if you have a good list to work with. As I shall show, when it
comes to projecting proportions from small qualitative samples, matters may
be worse than most practitioners' intuition might suspect but rather better than
the reflexive response of academics who toss off statements such as
"results . . . cannot be projected."

Now as a practical matter, no experienced qualitative researcher would
write up a small interview study using statements like "60 percent of participants agreed . . ." or "less than 10 percent reported the problem . . ." Every
veteran knows to avoid that kind of specific quantity in a qualitative report.
Instead, fuzzier language would be used, such as "a majority agreed" or "hardly
anyone mentioned." To keep the following treatment both practical and formally correct, it is necessary to translate this sort of locution back into specific
quantities using some kind of rubric. Only then can the binomial theorem be
used to calculate the probability that a particular sort of result in a qualitative
sample can support a specific projection to the population. Here is the rubric:

Circumlocution Used in Qualitative Report	Split Perceived in Qualitative Sample
"virtually everyone"	All but one or two participants, or 90–10
"most consumers"	80–20 split
"a majority"	60–40 split
"opinion was mixed"	50–50 split
"a minority"	40–60 split
"few consumers"	20–80 split
"hardly anyone"	Only one or two participants, or 10–90

The notion, then, is that qualitative researchers pretend to be cautious by reporting results using fuzzy phrases such as are found in the left column but surreptitiously intend their audience to project the corresponding expectation about population values given in the right column. The task is to assign a precise probability to the prospect of any given population value producing a particular observed split in a small sample.

BINOMIAL INFERENCES

Table 8.1 reports the probability that a given discrete distribution of a binomial outcome would occur in a small qualitative sample of the stated size if the incidence in the population is set at various values ranging from 90–10 to 10–90. To translate, typical examples of a "binomial outcome" in a set of interviews might include (1) agreement (disagreement) with a point of view; (2) presence (absence) of an event, problem, or application; (3) mention (no mention) of a particular attribute, benefit, or desired feature; and so forth. The table entries represent the probability that an attribute would be mentioned by m out of n interviewees, where m is the row label indicating the count of occurrences in the sample, while the column label specifies a given level of incidence of this attribute in the population. Cells with probabilities less than .001 are blanked out; at the top and bottom of each column, as appropriate, cells greater than .001 that cumulate to a probability less than .05 are shaded.

In keeping with qualitative practice, each locution in Table 8.1 is assigned a range of values. The table entries cumulate the probabilities associated with each specific split assigned to a locution. The specific cumulations imposed reflect my judgment about the range of perceived sample splits that would guide a veteran qualitative practitioner toward a particular locution. The assignment is not always symmetrical about the midpoint or consistent across sample sizes, because practitioners would not treat "1 or 2 exceptions" the same way in a sample of 32 as in a sample of 12; nor would "all but a few" represent the exact reciprocal of "only one or two." The table organization reflects these realities of human judgment in the day-to-day practice of qualitative research.

Consider first the table entry for a sample of $n = 6$. Here, every possible value of m is listed without the cumulations applied to the larger samples to give a clear indication of how the table values are calculated. Starting at the upper left corner, you would expect that when a problem or event is present for 9 out of 10 consumers in the population, then were you to draw an infinite number of samples of $n = 6$, in 53.1 percent of these samples, six out of six interviewees would report that they had experienced that problem. More to the point, in only 2 percent of those samples would all six interviewees report a problem that in fact was experienced by only 50 percent or less of the population (reading row-wise). Reading column-wise, if a problem was characteristic of 90 percent of a population and you interviewed six customers independently and randomly sampled from that population, you would expect that 98.4 percent of the time a majority of these interviewees would report they had experienced that problem.

Even samples of $n = 6$, if they were to be randomly and independently drawn, allow you both to support and also to rule out a reasonable number of population projections at $p \leq .05$. If this seems surprising, remember that sample size serves as an exponent or factorial in the binomial calculations. Thus, 53.1 percent in the upper left cell is simply the population incidence of .90, raised to the sixth power. Because sample size serves as an exponent in binomial calculations, probabilities can quickly become very small. This is the unguessed power of small-sample research and the key fact that underwrites the ability to project *some* results, and not just existence, from qualitative research.

Type I Errors

As sample size gets larger, even within the very small range of sizes characteristic of qualitative research, the likelihood of making a Type I error declines.

Table 8.1 Binomial Probabilities of Obtaining Selected Sample Splits for a Range of Population Values

Qualitative Locution	Perceived Sample Split	Incidence of the Response in the Population						
		90%	*80%*	*60%*	*50%*	*40%*	*20%*	*10%*
Sample size = 6								
N/A— exact counts	6	53.1%	26.2%	4.7%	1.6%	0.4%		
	5	35.4%	39.3%	18.7%	9.4%	3.7%	0.2%	
	4	9.8%	24.6%	31.1%	23.4%	13.8%	1.5%	0.1%
	3	1.5%	8.2%	27.6%	31.3%	27.6%	8.2%	1.5%
	2	0.1%	1.5%	13.8%	23.4%	31.1%	24.6%	9.8%
	1		0.2%	3.7%	9.4%	18.7%	39.3%	35.4%
	0			0.4%	1.6%	4.7%	26.2%	53.1%
Sample size = 12								
All	12	28.2%	6.9%	0.2%				
Almost everyone	10, 11	60.7%	49.0%	8.1%	1.9%	0.2%		
A majority	7, 8, 9	11.0%	42.2%	58.2%	36.8%	15.5%	0.4%	
A minority	4, 5, 6		1.9%	32.0%	54.0%	61.6%	20.2%	2.5%
A few	1, 2, 3			1.5%	7.3%	22.3%	72.6%	69.2%
No one	0					0.2%	6.9%	28.2%
Sample size = 16								
All	16	18.5%	2.8%					
Almost everyone	13, 14, 15	74.6%	57.0%	6.5%	1.0%	0.1%		
A majority	9 to 12	6.8%	39.5%	65.1%	39.1%	14.1%	0.1%	
A minority	4 to 8			28.3%	58.8%	79.3%	40.0%	6.8%
A few	1, 2, 3				1.0%	6.5%	57.0%	74.6%
No one	0						2.8%	18.5%

(Continued)

Table 8.1 (Continued)

Qualitative Locution	Perceived Sample Split	Incidence of the Response in the Population						
		90%	80%	60%	50%	40%	20%	10%
Sample size = 24								
All	24	8.0%	0.5%					
Almost everyone	19 to 23	89.3%	65.1%	4.0%	0.3%			
A majority	14 to 18		34.0%	61.0%	26.7%	5.3%		
Views were mixed	11, 12, 13		0.4%	29.6%	45.9%	29.6%	0.4%	
A minority	6 to 10			5.3%	26.7%	61.0%	34.0%	2.7%
A few	1 to 5				0.3%	4.0%	65.1%	89.3%
No one	0						0.5%	8.0%
Sample size = 32								
All	32	3.4%	0.1%					
Almost everyone	26 to 31	93.0%	53.5%	0.9%				
A majority	19 to 25	3.6%	46.3%	59.5%	18.8%	2.1%		
Views were mixed	14 to 18		0.1%	37.5%	62.3%	37.5%	0.1%	
A minority	7 to 13			2.1%	18.8%	59.5%	46.3%	3.6%
A few	1 to 6					0.9%	53.5%	93.0%
No one	0						0.1%	3.4%

An example of a Type I error would be projecting that a majority of the population agrees with some position based on lopsided results in the sample when, in fact, this is a minority view in the population. In samples of 12, to see a view advocated by 10 or 11 interviewees when this view is held by less than half the population would occur less often than 1 in 1,000 occasions. Similar results hold in reverse: in a sample of 16, a view held by 80 percent of the population will be espoused by a majority of interviewees 999 times out of 1,000.

On the other hand, it remains true that samples of this size lack precision compared to the sample sizes routinely used in survey research. In a survey of

100 people, the 95 percent confidence interval on an estimate of 61 percent will not include 50 percent, allowing one to project from that 60 percent estimate the assertion that "a majority" of the population holds this view. Likewise, a sample of 400 people would allow projection of 55 percent agreement in the sample as indicative of a "majority view" in the population (see Chapter 13 for the formulae used). No such precision is available from qualitative samples. Even in the best case of 32, a split result in the sample, where from 14 to 18 people take a position, is compatible with both a 60–40 and a 40–60 split in the population. It is only in the case of lopsided results in the sample or the population that small qualitative samples provide acceptable protection against Type I error.

Type II Errors

As discussed earlier, the driving goal for much qualitative research is discovery. It is true that qualitative researchers do want to get some sense of which customer responses are common and which rare per the discussion just given; but often, what drives the funding of the research is the hope of turning up an iridescent bead for the very first time and getting a chance to examine it in some detail. In probability terms, this can be formulated in terms of the likelihood that a customer response, having some stated incidence in the population, will make zero appearances in the sample of interviews and, hence, not be discovered. A response that exists at some reasonable frequency in the marketplace but never makes an appearance in the qualitative research represents a Type II error.

Returning to Table 8.1 and attending to the bottom right corner of each panel in the table, it takes a sample of 16 before the probability of completely missing a particular viewpoint held by 20 percent of the population drops below .05. Likewise, only with a sample of 32 can you have that degree of confidence that a low-incidence view held by 10 percent of the population will make at least one appearance in the qualitative sample. It's somewhat unusual for qualitative research to include much more than 30 participants, so it makes sense to set the threshold on the "resolution" of qualitative research in terms of customer responses that have an incidence of 10 percent or greater in the population, with the proviso that for smaller samples on the order of a dozen, resolution is blurred further, able to pick up only responses having a population incidence of 20 or 25 percent. Responses less frequent than this can't be picked up with adequate confidence.

As a practical matter, few businesses are concerned with low-incidence segments or opportunities. Were a niche marketing strategy at issue, you probably would have recruited the qualitative sample mostly from that niche and, again, not be very interested in a view held by less than 10 percent of the niche group itself. The upshot is that Type II error appears to be low enough in modest-sized qualitative samples that assertions about whether a particular consumer response exists, based on which responses appear in the qualitative sample, may indeed be projected to the population.

It should be no surprise that the math works out this way. One of the classic, conservative uses of qualitative research is to generate content for a subsequent survey questionnaire—specifically, to get a sense of the language that customers use and the particular response options that need to be supplied for the multiple-choice questions to be used in the survey. In other words, the questionnaire designer uses the qualitative sample to make an exhaustive projection as to the answer categories that need to appear in the survey—the number and identities of the qualities whose incidence is to be quantified. The binomial mathematics just reviewed underwrites this practice and again gives the lie to the canard that "results . . . cannot be projected."

A more complete account also has to consider the multinomial case. That is, the actual question faced by a business is not so much a matter of "Will I see any iridescent beads in the sample, given that the incidence of this specific color is 10 percent?" but rather one of "When I'm done, I want to be confident that the urn contains these seven colors of beads and that I didn't miss any eighth or ninth color." Here the math gets a little more complicated.

MULTINOMIAL INFERENCES

In many instances a more complex model of customer behavior is at issue than "does she or doesn't she?" One expects to see either multiple benefit segments, or multiple applications, or several different choice criteria, or numerous distinct customer problems, and so forth. Technically, the probability to be estimated is not the probability of overlooking a particular benefit or application, but the probability of missing *any* of k benefits, problems, or other consumer responses. In terms of dice, it's not the likelihood of never throwing a "6" (the binomial case), but of failing to throw any particular one of the six die faces, after N trials (the multinomial case).

This again is analogous to Type II error: erroneously concluding one has a die with k -1 faces, when in fact it has k faces. A kind of Type I error can also be discerned in the multinomial case. In consumer contexts, some benefits, choice criteria, problems, and so forth may be relatively common, and others less so. If qualitative research estimates the incidence of four benefit segments as in the ratio of 3:1:1:1, how likely is this to occur, when in the marketplace, the segments are actually equal in size? This is Type I error, in that one draws a mistaken inference that one customer segment is bigger, or one choice criterion is more common, or one customer problem looms larger, relative to others.

To estimate the probability of missing any one face of a six-sided die in 12 throws requires, in addition to the straightforward calculation of multinomial probability for any specific result, an application of combinatorics along with the integer partition function (for a worked-out example, interested readers may consult the Web Appendix to the McQuarrie and McIntyre paper in the Suggested Readings). Hence, only a small number of values of N and k for Type II error estimation are tabled (Table 8.2). For Type I error, see again the McQuarrie and McIntyre paper.

Type II Error in the Multinomial Case

Beginning at the top right corner of Table 8.2, there is clearly some vulnerability to Type II error even in a relatively large qualitative sample of 32, where there remains an almost 10 percent chance of missing—failing to discover—any one of eight distinct customer responses. In a smaller sample of 12, it is highly likely—over 90 percent—that one (or more) of the responses with an incidence of 1/8 will be missed. Conversely, as the number of responses to be identified decreases toward four, modest-sized samples of 16 or 24 do become able to meet the standard of $\alpha \le .05$, with respect to discovering all members of a set of four or five equally possible customer responses. The practical import is that if the goal of the qualitative research is to exhaustively specify all k attributes considered by customers, or benefits sought, or problems experienced, and so forth, and k is half a dozen or more, then it is imperative to use a larger qualitative sample on the order of 32. In addition, the resolution of even this large a sample tops out at about $k = 8$. If there are 10 distinct answers possible to an interview question, all equally probable, then there is a real possibility that qualitative research, given the sample sizes typically used, is going to miss one of those answers. Table 8.2 thus places a limit on the discovery potential of small qualitative samples.

Table 8.2 Probability Any of k Customer Responses Will Fail to Appear in a Sample of Size N

$k =$	4	5	6	7	8
Miss 1+ of k with $N = 12$	12.5%	32.2%	56.2%	77.1%	91.7%
16	4.0%	13.8%	30.2%	50.2%	69.3%
24	0.2%	2.4%	7.6%	16.4%	29.7%
32	***	0.4%	1.7%	5.0%	10.7%
Miss 2+ of k with $N = 12$	0.1%	2.1%	10.6%	29.0%	53.9%
16	***	0.3%	2.2%	8.8%	22.3%
24	***	***	0.1%	0.6%	2.7%
32	***	***	***	***	0.1%
Miss 3+ of k with $N = 12$			0.5%	3.8%	15.1%
16			***	0.4%	2.7%
24			***	***	0.1%
32			***	***	***
Miss 4+ of k with $N = 12$				0.1%	1.6%
16				***	0.1%
24				***	***
32				***	***

Note: Table entries are to be read as follows, beginning with the first entry in the upper left cell, and reading down within that cell: "Given a set of four equally probable and mutually exclusive customer responses, the likelihood that any one or more of them will fail to appear in a probability sample of 12 interviews is 12.5 percent. This drops to 4.0 percent in a sample of size 16, to 0.2 percent in a sample of 24, and to less than 0.1 percent in a sample of 32 interviews." See appendix for a worked-out example of how these probabilities were calculated. To calculate the probability of missing exactly k responses, simply subtract the parallel entry in the row below. For the appendix case with $N = 12$ and $k = 6$, the probability of missing exactly one response is 56.2 percent − 10.6 percent, or about 45.6 percent.

Combinations that are not meaningful (miss 4 of 4) are left blank. Entries with probability < .001 are marked by asterisks (***). If all entries in a cell are < .001, the cell is also left blank.

MEASURES OF ASSOCIATION

A third type of projection that qualitative researchers might want to make is to assert an association between membership in some consumer group and a particular response. At the simplest level this might take the form of "men were interested in the service, while the reaction of women was mixed." The inference to be projected, then, is that there is an association between gender and purchase interest. A somewhat more complex association might be "First-time buyers relied primarily on information from friends and family, while repeat buyers more often made use of public information sources." In any such instance, the observations made during the interviews can be reproduced in the form of a contingency table:

	Used public information	Used private information
Trial purchase	2	6
Repeat purchase	6	2

The question of interest is how lopsided the association would have to be in a small sample, such as $N = 16$, to be projectable, again with an alpha less than .05. Two cases are of interest. In the repeat purchase example, the row pattern of the one is the reverse of the other. This provides a strong indication of association and is liable to require smaller sample sizes and/or less lopsided results to achieve the desired alpha level. In the gender example, one group was evenly split and the other tilted in one direction. This is a weaker indication of association, but quite likely to occur in practice, hence important to assess.

Fisher's exact test was used to generate Table 8.3. Notably, when two groups split in a reverse direction, even the smaller samples of 12 or 16 allow inferences at $\alpha \le .05$ that the two groups are not both split evenly on this issue out in the market. It is not even necessary to obtain the most extreme split (all vs. none). At the larger sample sizes, one needs only about a 70–30 and 30–70 split to meet the standard. The standard is rather more difficult to meet, however, if one group is held to a 50–50 split. In a sample of 12, even the all/none split fails to satisfy the test; and at the large sample sizes, the split needs to be all/none, or all but one, to meet the test of $\alpha \le .05$.

The practical import is that in most small qualitative samples, two groups have to split in the reverse direction, and the split has to be lopsided, before the researcher can confidently project that the two groups are different. If one group splits evenly, only an extremely lopsided split in the other, along with a larger sample size, can give confidence. Put another way, reverse splits exceeding a 2:1 ratio will generally be required to support a projection that two groups or situations are "different." This hurdle is much higher than that

Table 8.3   Observed Disproportion Required to Infer a Significant
Difference Between Two Groups for Selected Small-Sample
Sizes

Sample Size	Required Split(s)	Cumulative Probability[a]
Case 1: Reverse splits		
12	5:1	.040
16	6:2	.066
20	8:2	.011
	7:3	.089
24	9:3	.020
	8:4	.110
32	10:4	.028
	9:5	.128
Case 2: One split constrained to be 50–50		
12	6:0	.091
16	8:0	.038
20	10:0	.016
	9:1	.081
24	11:1	.039
32	13:1	.018
	12:2	.064

Note: Table was calculated using Fisher's exact test. Table is to be read as follows, beginning with the first row of entries: "In a sample of 12, if one group splits 5:1 and the other 1:5 on an issue, there is only a 4 percent probability of observing that split or a more extreme split (e.g., 6:0) if, in the population, both groups are split 50–50 on the issue in question." In the bottom panel, the calculations show the lopsidedness of the required split in one group if the other group is split 50–50 on the issue.

[a] When no split is within +/- .02 of an alpha of .05, the two splits yielding alphas bracketing .05 are listed (exception: case 2, sample of 12). All values are cumulative; the stated probability is that of observing the stated split and all those more extreme in the same direction.

required of a survey sample of some hundreds, where splits of 57–43, or a ratio of 4:3, might support such inferences. Qualitative samples really do lack the degree of precision that surveys typically provide.

SUMMARY: RULES OF THUMB

The rules laid out below assume that each member of the sample was independently and randomly selected. Subsequently, I take up the special case of focus groups, where participant responses are not independent.

> *RULE #1*: Lopsided splits in a small qualitative sample are always directionally interpretable, even in very small samples of a half-dozen. The 80–20 rule applies: If 80 percent or more of the sample splits in one direction, you can be confident (at the 95% level) that a majority of consumers in the market (> 50%) are split in that same direction.

> *RULE #2*: If you are serious about discovery—if you want to come out of the qualitative research with an exhaustive specification of the 8 benefits customers seek, or the 10 possible answers to "what problems have you experienced?" or the 9 points of difference perceived between you and competitor X—then you need a large sample on the order of 30, or even a little more. Only if the elements to be discovered are as few as 4 can you be confident in using a sample as small as 16. Interviewing 10 or 12 customers is not enough when discovery of emergent customer needs is the goal. Finally, you cannot be confident that any normal-sized qualitative sample will pick up a response that characterizes less than 1 customer in 10.

> *RULE #3*: Lopsided group differences that are the reverse of one another—for example, where men split 70–30 and women 30–70—are likely to hold true in the market, provided the sample size is 24 or larger. But if one group is mixed, then the other group has to be split at 90–10 or better, *and* the sample size needs to be at the limit of those used in qualitative research, to be confident that the group difference will hold true.

The Special Case of Focus Groups

A typical focus group project will include 3–4 sessions with 8–10 participants, yielding what might be considered a fairly large qualitative sample of two to three dozen consumers. But that is the wrong sample size to use with respect to the tables included with this chapter, for the obvious reason that responses given during the focus group session are not independent.

Most accounts of what can be projected from focus groups stop right there: Due to non-independence of responses, "results ... cannot be projected." But this is too harsh. To grasp the conditions that make some degree of projection possible, suppose during a focus group that one participant states loudly "that policy is an outrage!" Murmurs of assent and vigorous nods spread around the table. Obviously, you cannot enter the result as "all 10 participants were opposed," and tabulate those 10 on the negative side of the final project tally. All that can be projected is that consumers do exist who feel strongly negative about this policy, and that there exist other consumers who will echo the sentiment when it is expressed in public. The sample size after a single group is $N = 1$.

Now suppose the study is larger than most, with 6 groups. Suppose also that in 5 of the 6 groups, the same sort of negativity occurs, with the same drumbeat of support. Only in one group did a second participant counter with "no, that policy is not an issue that concerns me," with a vigorous back-and-forth ensuing. Now the tables in this chapter are pertinent, and consulting Table 8.1 for $N = 6$, we can be confident in projecting that the negative sentiment expressed is common in the marketplace, and perhaps more important, that this sentiment is a potentially contagious idea, the kind that is likely to command assent when vigorously asserted. In short, if one is willing to invest in larger focus group projects, Rule #1 applies, with the proviso that what counts is whether the lopsided split was obtained across groups, not within a group. With this caution, and provided a probability sample was recruited, focus groups results *can* be projected.

Conclusion

Results from small qualitative samples can be projected. Interviews can do more than just examine in depth the qualities of some customer response. Exploration and discovery are not the only rationales for doing small-sample qualitative research.

On a more nuanced level, the binomial and multinomial calculations laid out indicate that lopsided results are more forgiving, with respect to sample size, than might have been expected: Not even a dozen interviews may be required to confirm that a particular customer need is common in the marketplace. Conversely, discovery is more demanding of sample size than might have been guessed: A dozen interviews will often not suffice to uncover all the important customer needs in a segment. Likewise, group differences have to be stark, and samples must exceed two dozen, before qualitative research can give confidence that men and women, novices and experts, or any two groups out in the market really will respond differently.

Small samples, whether using interviews or other techniques, have their place in market research. But even here, size matters: A sample of 30 interviews has considerably more power than a sample of 12.

IMPLEMENTING QUALITATIVE SAMPLES

Implementation proceeds rather differently in the case of focus groups versus customer visits, so I'll discuss these techniques separately. As developed in Chapter 6, focus groups are recruited by means of a screener administered by telephone. From the perspective of this chapter, the screener questions define the population of interest; an example is given below. In the case of customer visits, the more common procedure is to lay out the relevant segmentation or submarket structure in grid form—that is, define the strata of the population of interest. In both cases, *population* rarely means "all warm breathing bodies over age 18," but something much more narrow and focused, more akin to what managers have in mind when they say the "target" or "target market" for the product. Always keep in mind that any inferences from the qualitative sample only apply to the defined population from which it was drawn.

Sampling for Focus Groups

The key thing to remember in assembling the screener is that it will be executed by a relatively low-paid and uneducated staff on customers who have been interrupted by the phone call and are all too ready to hang up on the recruiter. Hence, the KISS principle applies in spades: Keep it short and simple (or however you spell out that acronym). You are limited to, at most, five questions to determine whether the customer at the other end of the phone line is a member of the population of interest, to be coaxed into attending the focus group. These questions have to be very straightforward. "Have you purchased a widget in the past 90 days?" will work; "Do you consider yourself to have a high Need for Cognition, or would you say you are more of a cognitive miser?" will *not* work.

Essentially, you are limited to asking whether a particular event or behavior occurred (e.g., purchase, usage, visit to a store), whether the customer is a member of some conventionally defined group ("Do you manage other employees?" or "Do you have budget authority?"), and asking questions that can be answered yes or no ("Please tell me if you recognize any of these brands of widget."). It's difficult to ask anything complex, difficult, sensitive, or potentially embarrassing. As a general rule, then, you can't use any kind of psychographic or lifestyle segmentation as part of the population definition that makes up the screener (any of these can be allowed to emerge in the group discussions, of course). For the most part, you are limited to determining whether the potential recruitee is in the market (has purchased or is considering purchasing), identifying his or her familiarity with major brands, and taking simple demographic measures.

Sampling for Customer Visits

Sampling for customer visits proceeds rather differently, consistent with the differences between B2B and B2C markets. Most notably, there will typically be a database of customers, which can provide the sample frame. Likewise, most B2B markets will be approached as prestructured: divided into strata or segments. Thus, many business markets are divided into "industry verticals"; the idea is that the computing needs of banks, aerospace manufacturers, and retailers may be fundamentally different. Hence, it would be folly to sample from "customers"; this would be to mix together separate populations. It's more appropriate to sample from the population of banking customers, the population of manufacturer customers, and so forth.

The first step in sampling for customer visits, then, is to lay out the relevant subpopulations and strata. This will often take the form of a grid or cube diagram or possibly a tree diagram (see worked-out examples in my book *Customer Visits*). The goal is, first, to effectively represent the diverse populations in the market of interest, and then, second, to select which subpopulations need to be sampled for the particular research project at hand. As part of this process, certain qualification criteria may be applied. Just as a focus group may be screened to include only individuals who have brought a broadband connection to their living room TV, a B2B sample may be screened to include only customers who have adopted "LINUX networking protocol 3.13.1."

Once the screening criteria have been applied, the subpopulations laid out, and the few maximally relevant segments specified, the actual sample can be assembled by drawing half a dozen instances of each. This yields a total sample of one or two dozen, the sweet spot for most customer visit programs in my experience. Note that with respect to Table 8.1 and the kinds of inferences that can be made, the sample size here will generally be six—the number drawn from a given subpopulation. Note finally that if names are selected from subpopulations using judgment ("He's always friendly and interested when he visits our booth at the trade show") rather than randomly or systematically, then Table 8.1 no longer applies.

Finally, the grid, the screening criteria, and everything else used to devise the sample should be retained and included as part of the methodology of the customer visit program. These materials define the population to which the visits pertain. Inferences from the visits apply to this particular population, not to vague generalities such as "customers" or "the widget market."

QUALITATIVE VS. QUANTITATIVE SAMPLING—AN INTEGRATION

Anyone with a college education in business or engineering has a rough and ready understanding of the probability mathematics that underlies quantitative sampling, because statistical inference has been part of those curricula for decades. Qualitative sampling and the underlying rationale remain much less familiar. Hence, it seemed best to present the integration of the two here, in the chapter on qualitative sampling, as one final attempt to clarify what sampling for qualitative research is all about.

Essentially, a decision maker can make one of two kinds of generalization from a response noted in a sample: to the *incidence* of that response in the population at large or to *identification* of it as a bona fide element of that population—that is, discovering that it exists. Figure 8.1 gives a graphical representation of these two axes of generalization. The first axis, incidence, is the one to which every market research textbook devotes copious attention. It dominates the mindset of most market researchers other than qualitative specialists. There are all kinds of business situations in which it makes a great deal of difference whether 61 percent of the target market is likely to approve of the new product or only 48 percent. To get that level of precision from an incidence generalization requires a sample size in the hundreds (see Chapter 13 for more on these sample size calculations).

Figure 8.1   Two Axes of Generalization From Sample Data

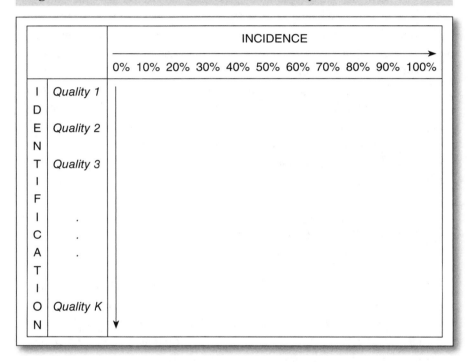

However, there are a host of other business contexts in which the crucial requirement is to identify whether any iridescent beads exist and to have the opportunity to carefully scrutinize the qualities of any iridescent beads that do exist. What you are after in this kind of research is an exhaustive specification of the set A . . . K—the set of all reasons to buy a product held by 15 percent or more of the market, the set of applications for the technology, the set of problems experienced in upgrading an operating system, and so forth. This axis of generalization rarely appears in academic discussions, because in academic contexts, discovery is rarely the objective of research—rather, precise estimation of incidence is the goal. To return to the metaphor of colored beads in an urn, in standard quantitative market research such as a survey, you have already identified all the colors of bead that exist; you simply need to determine their relative incidence.

In real-life business, especially in fast-moving technology markets or new product development generally, often you don't know what colors of bead may exist in the urn—the whole goal of the research is to discover those colors and get a good look at them. Figure 8.1, along with Table 8.1, spells out in formal terms what is meant by research objectives such as "discover," "explore," or "gain insight into" and their implications with respect to drawing a sample of customers for qualitative market research. The gist is that samples of a few dozen are more than adequate for the typical qualitative research effort, whereas samples in the hundreds, up to a thousand or more, are required if a quantitative research study is to estimate the incidence of some response with the desired precision.

In summary, any good qualitative sample of modest size (good because drawn from the defined population of interest) can support inferences about what customer responses do or do not exist and identify their qualities. If the sample was drawn as a probability sample (see Chapter 13), then very rough projections of incidence can also be made within the limits shown in Table 8.1.

QUALITATIVE DATA ANALYSIS

You will typically find even less information in a conventional textbook about how to analyze qualitative data than you will find concerning qualitative sampling. At least, you will find cautions about projecting from qualitative samples, but there may be no structured account at all of what to do with that mass of interview data once you have it in hand. Here I can only hit a few highlights; see the Suggested Readings for more advanced treatments, and for a worked-out example, see Chapter 13 of my book, *Customer Visits*.

Two key things to keep in mind about the analysis of customer visit and focus group data are:

First, in a very fundamental way, success in qualitative data analysis is a function of the insight, the industry experience, and the strategic ability of the analyst.

An experienced product marketer with good marketing knowledge, some years spent in the industry or category, and familiarity with the decisions facing management is going to be able to extract a great deal of useful knowledge from a set of interviews. By contrast an inexperienced newcomer, or a plodder who isn't privy to management's thinking, is liable to drown in too much information.

Second, theThe output of the analysis is the identification and enumeration of the *qualities* of customer response, along with a rich description of each.

To return to the metaphor guiding this chapter, you may have heard about iridescent beads but never had a chance to study one up close. In a nutshell, that's what qualitative data analysis produces: a richly detailed description of particular types of customers—why they buy; what's important to them and what's not; how their preference for X drives related behaviors A, B, and C; what they perceive to be competitor strengths and weaknesses; and so forth. Because of this richness, experience has shown that one of the best ways to convey insights from qualitative research is to find visual arrangements of information. An early example was the House of Quality that formed part of QFD efforts (quality function deployment, an awful bit of jargon best translated as "a commitment to design processes that satisfy specified customer requirements;" see Hauser & Clausing, 1988). Many more examples of visual arrangements for qualitative data can be found in Miles and Huberman (1994).

Perhaps I can best conclude by highlighting the differences between the analysis of qualitative data and the much more familiar analysis of quantitative market research data.

1. Qualitative analysis concerns the words spoken by customers, while quantitative analysis concerns the numerical representation of responses obtained from customers. Qualitative develops meanings; quantitative compares magnitudes.

2. Most qualitative analyses depend heavily on analyst skill, and each qualitative analysis has to be built up from scratch. By contrast, in many commercial contexts, quantitative analyses can be routinized and prepackaged: Satisfaction ratings are up since the last survey, or not, and a report template can be created in advance and the latest numbers dumped in. Feature A has the highest utility weight in the conjoint analysis, or it does not, and a bar chart template can be created

and the results of the current study dumped in. Software does most of the actual "analysis."[2]

3. Qualitative analysis, if successful, yields discoveries and new insights. Quantitative analysis, when successful, yields projectable comparisons of numbers showing which is the greater or lesser. Qualitative reveals what new applications and requirements are just now emerging in this market; quantitative pinpoints which segment is larger, which benefit is more important, which application is most common.

4. Qualitative research yields patterns; quantitative yields precision.

In summary, if you commission qualitative research and you will be involved in the analysis of the results then you should plan on being a pioneer. There's not yet much in the way of settled wisdom or established training regimes.

DISCUSSION QUESTIONS

1. A journal reviewer rejected an earlier version of this chapter on the theory that "qualitative research is never about counting"; hence, it was inappropriate to talk about the inferences that could be drawn from small *qualitative* samples. Discuss.

   a. Hint: Is "1" a counting number? Is the determination of presence or absence "counting"?

   b. Can there be scientific knowledge without measurement?

2. What is lost and what is gained when a qualitative interview sample uses a judgment sample rather than a probability sample? Focus your answer on a prototypical B2B market of your acquaintance: concentrated, expensive, with a long purchase cycle.

---

[2]I hasten to add that this routinization only applies to commercial statistical analyses. In academia, enormous amounts of one-off ingenuity and creativity are applied in constructing the statistical analyses that underlie published journal articles.

3. You read a focus group study in which there were six groups containing eight customers each. Recruiting was carried out through random digit dialing (the product is consumed by almost everyone). At the appropriate point in the late middle of each group, customers silently and individually noted their preference for one of two ad executions on first encounter; these ads were then extensively discussed. The report notes the percentage of participants who preferred execution A prior to discussion.

   a. What is the sample size for applying Table 8.1? Defend your answer.

   b. A separate validation study conducted that same week randomly sampled 48 customers as they entered a local shopping mall in the same ZIP code as the groups were held. Ads were individually exposed and preference noted prior to discussion.

      i. How close would you expect the split in preference across the two ad executions to be, across the focus group versus the validation sample?

      ii. Note: The very inexpensive product in question is distributed through grocery stores, not shopping malls. If this matters to your answer, explain.

   c. The focus group report notes that there was a notable shift in preference between the two ad executions after discussion, a shift that occurred in four of the six groups.

      i. As a manager, which distribution of preferences would you put the most weight on: (1) the pre-discussion split in the focus groups, (2) the post-discussion split in the groups, or (3) the split in the validation sample conducted at the mall.

      ii. A colleague states: "I wouldn't put much weight on any of the splits. These were rough ad executions and I don't care which execution 'won'—that wasn't the purpose of the research."

         1. Is this a defensible position? Explain.

SUGGESTED READINGS

Griffin, A., & Hauser, J. (1993). The voice of the customer. *Marketing Science, 12*(1), 1–27.	Provides an alternative derivation of the sample size needed to draw inferences from qualitative samples.
Hauser, J. R., & Clausing, D. P. (1988). The house of quality. *Harvard Business Review, 66,* 63–73.	Provides a good introduction to QFD (few workshop attendees recognize this acronym anymore) and thus to early attempts to represent qualitative data visually.
Lewin, A., & Silver, C. (2007). *Using software in qualitative research: A step-by-step guide.* Thousand Oaks, CA: Sage.	Advances are continually being made in the analysis of verbal text by software. This volume provides a good introduction to what's possible.
Miles, M. B., & Huberman, M. A. (1994). *Qualitative data analysis: A sourcebook of new methods* (2nd ed.). Thousand Oaks, CA: Sage.	The leading reference work on spotting patterns in qualitative data, and the visual representation of same, but requires some translation by the business reader (the authors were education researchers). If you intend to become an expert on qualitative data analysis, a search of Amazon.com using that phrase will reveal a number of more recent titles, but these tend to be tightly focused on the needs of academic social scientists rather than business practitioners.

CASES FOR PART III

SUGGESTED CASE: SCOPE MOUTHWASH (HARVARD IVEY #98A030)

Synopsis

The brand team for Scope mouthwash in Canada believes that the brand might benefit from a fresh approach in its advertising—either a new message, or a new and distinctive execution of the existing message. The situation is complicated by fluctuating trends in market share, the penetration of private-label mouthwashes, competitor product introductions, and so forth. The team believes that some kind of market research would be helpful, and the initial proposal is to run two focus group sessions.

Questions

1. Can market research help in this kind of situation? Explain why or why not. If some kind of market research would be appropriate, what is the argument for *qualitative* research here? If there is an argument for qualitative research, are focus groups the best choice, or would it be better to do one-on-one interviews?

[These next questions assume only that yes, an argument can be made for doing some kind of qualitative research; answers will be mostly the same regardless of the whether group or individual interviews are recommended.]

1. Develop the screener for these interviews. Begin with a rough statement of the kind of people you would want to include (only current mouthwash users? Only Scope users?). Then, write out the questions as they would be spoken by the telephone recruiter.

   Remember, you are allowed five questions max, and these have to be questions that could be delivered by a recruitment company employee paid the minimum wage—and understood by an ordinary citizen. No marketing jargon allowed!

2. Draft a discussion guide for use in the interviews. Pay attention to such issues as: (a) what would be a good ice-breaker or initial question?; (b) what would the major topic areas be, and what would a key open-ended question be for each?; and (c) would you show any stimuli (past ads, projective stimuli, etc.)?

3. Flesh out the remainder of the study design: how many groups of what size, if focus groups, or how many individuals, if one-on-one? If groups, would you mix different kinds of customers (e.g., men and women), or keep them in separate groups? Would you invite anyone from the ad agency to view the interviews, and if so, what job roles?

SUGGESTED CASE: COMMUNISPACE (HARVARD #9-510-018)

Synopsis

Communispace sets up Web communities for clients and poses questions to consumer participants recruited to join these communities. This creates an ongoing flow of qualitative research findings, enhanced by reports written by Communispace moderators and analysts. It provides an example of emerging kinds of market research that take advantage of Web-based social media capabilities.

The particular issue that vexes Communispace management is whether the firm's market research capabilities can be leveraged to provide a sales and marketing service to interested clients—that is, whether the brand communities can be used to sell to consumers as well as learn about them.

Questions

1. Take the role of a brand manager at a B2C firm—someone who may have an annual budget for market research in the hundreds of thousands of dollars. Assess the advantages and disadvantages of hiring Communispace to do ongoing qualitative research online, relative to the old-fashioned approach, in which interviews and focus groups would be conducted offline on a project-specific, as-needed basis.

2. Now take the role of a product line manager at a B2B technology firm, and assess the advantages and disadvantages of using Communispace from

this perspective. Here the old-fashioned or traditional approach might have been to set up user groups that meet regularly offline, and are not directly controlled by the vendor, supplemented by ad hoc customer visits.

(a) Typically, market research will be a less well-funded operation at a B2B firm, and the alternative to Communispace would not be focus groups or other formalized, conventional market research. Hence, cost will be a bigger hump to get over for a potential B2B client, but the incremental gain in consumer insight might be much greater, due to the paucity of existing market research. Please factor both considerations into your answer.

3. Are there any limits in terms of the type of product categories where these brand communities might be more or less feasible? Define these limits.

4. What decision would you recommend, in terms of the client request to leverage Communispace's existing competencies to sell as well as learn?

(a) New revenue sources are almost always good, but dilution of strategic focus is almost always bad. Please factor these considerations into your answer.

SUPPLEMENTAL CASE: OFFICE SYSTEMS

Synopsis

A manufacturer of cubicle furniture systems seeks new product development opportunities in the form of improved versions of the office furniture it currently offers. One product design has coalesced, and the firm is ready to seek customer input on that design, and on new product opportunities generally.

Questions

1. Is qualitative research in fact appropriate at this juncture, or should the firm use some other kind of research procedure? If qualitative research is in order, is there a good argument to do customer visits instead of focus groups, or vice versa? Explain.

2. Either design the sample for the customer visit program (i.e., lay out a sampling grid), or work out the screener questions, if focus groups are recommended.

3. Work up a discussion guide for use in the visits or groups. Identify the major topics to be covered, and indicate a good open-ended question to launch the discussion of each topic.

    (a) Pay particular attention to how the new product concept should be handled: when should it be introduced, how should it be introduced (i.e., what should be said about it), and how should discussion of it be handled?

OFFICE SYSTEMS (A)

In October 1997, Bob Mullins was the director of Business Development for Office Systems (OSYS), a firm that supplies turnkey office furniture solutions. OSYS sells panels and furniture that can be flexibly combined to create cubicle spaces. The panels come in 4-foot and 8-foot widths; most clients specify cubicles that are $8' \times 8'$, $8' \times 12'$, or $12' \times 12'$. The standard height for panels was 5 feet (although some lines allowed for variation). Clients could outfit an individual cubicle with several types of desk surfaces, a selection of storage units for holding books or files, several types of chairs, and with miscellaneous accessory furniture, such as a small table for meetings.

OSYS PRODUCT LINES

By 1997, OSYS had developed three lines of cubicle furniture positioned at three price points. Within each cubicle line, all the components use a consistent design so that they look right together. Clients customize their cubicle purchases by selecting a color scheme from among those offered, and by specifying the configuration of an individual cubicle (how many desk surfaces, in what kind of arrangement; horizontal and vertical cubicle dimensions; inclusion of accessory furniture; and so forth).

(Continued)

(Continued)

The lowest-priced line was typically purchased by clients who employed clerical workers performing similar, routinized tasks. A state Department of Motor Vehicles unit, or the credit card billing operation of a bank, would be examples. The typical buyer of this line tended to specify cubicles of a smaller size, purchased less-expensive chairs, and bought fewer accessories (except in the case of those cubicles intended for supervisors). OSYS was able to offer a lower price on this line by limiting the number of color schemes offered, restricting the number of available options, and by requiring clients to design their own layouts and assemble the cubicles using their own maintenance staff.

The mid-price line was typically purchased by white collar and professional workers who perform a wider variety of less routinized tasks. An example might be the tech support unit of an equipment manufacturer, or the sales force for a large distributor. A larger number of color schemes was offered, and a wide variety of all the other options were available. For this line, OSYS offered optional layout design services and turnkey installation. Layout services added value by allowing clients to fit the maximum number of cubicles of a given dimension into an existing space, while meeting all code requirements and avoiding a crowded or unaesthetic appearance. Turnkey installation was valuable because OSYS installers were less likely to damage parts, likely to complete the installation in markedly less time, and likely to produce a more shipshape appearance (true 90-degree corners, all vertical surfaces plumb, etc.).

Because of the great variety of options available, actual selling prices for the middle line varied over a wide range. A client purchasing a minimal setup without services might pay not much more than a client purchasing from the lower line. Conversely, a client purchasing an elaborate setup with all services might pay not much less than a client buying from the high-end line.

The high-end line was sold to clients who intended to house a more highly paid employee, and/or clients who anticipated a reasonable flow of customers or other valued constituents through the office setup. The emphasis in the high-end line was on aesthetics and on appearance more generally. Thus, panels and other furniture might have polished wood trim; panel fabrics were more luxurious; and color schemes were less pedestrian or ordinary, and included colors not available elsewhere in the line. Taller panels (5' 6" and 6') were an option, for privacy, and to give the illusion of an individual-walled office. Overall, the number of options was actually less than in the middle line, because lower cost options and less aesthetic options were not offered at all. Conversely, the very best chairs (ergonomic, high back, leather surface) were designed specifically for the high end. Similarly, certain types of credenzas were only available here, and this was the only line to make use of polished wood accessories. Almost all high-end purchases included value-added services, as these were included in the base price.

In recent years OSYS's sales revenue was split between the three lines in approximate proportions of 25 percent, 50 percent, and 25 percent. Gross profit from the lines, however, broke down as 19 percent, 47 percent, and 34 percent. OSYS used a direct sales force plus a small number of large distributors to sell the lines.

OFFICE FURNITURE MARKET

The OSYS company was one of a half dozen firms that dominated the cubicle furniture market, and was estimated to have a market share of approximately 23 percent. Its share of the total office furniture market was smaller, perhaps 12 percent. The difference was due to the fact that much office furniture was sold to clients who either had true walled offices or who housed employees in large spaces haphazardly divided by structural walls ("bullpens"). OSYS sold only cubicle furniture systems; it did not sell standalone desks, for instance.

Cubicle systems had come to be installed in a larger and larger share of offices in the United States, ever since they were introduced in the early 1970s. Both bullpens and individual offices were becoming less common. Most new buildings put up after about 1990 were not designed for individual offices divided by permanent walls—this arrangement was increasingly seen as too expensive on the one hand, and too inflexible on the other. Rather, the building would contain a

(Continued)

(Continued)

large floor(s) and each tenant would configure that space as they saw fit, using a cubicle system, or less commonly, a bullpen of some kind.

Despite these trends, the individual-walled office retained its place as the most esteemed sort of office space; cubicles continued to come in for derision, both in conversation and in portrayals in popular culture. Nonetheless, the trend toward cubicle designs was regarded as irresistible. In 1996, approximately 70 percent of new buildings were designed to accommodate cubicles; projections suggested the trend would not top out until 90 percent was reached. Similar percentages applied to the conversion or refurbishing of existing buildings; about 7 percent of class A and B office buildings in the United States underwent a major refurbishment or conversion in any given year. Legacy space (buildings designed before the 1970s and not yet converted) meant that perhaps 15 percent of office workers continued to work in individual-walled offices, and another 30 percent continued to work in larger or smaller bullpen spaces. If sufficiently large, a bullpen space could be converted to cubicles apart from any conversion or refurbishment of the building infrastructure, and this was another source of cubicle sales.

SOURCES OF REVENUE

Sales of cubicle systems typically followed one of four patterns. The bulk of OSYS and industry revenue came about when a department, division, or firm moved into a new space (either a new building or a newly refurbished one). Typically, the old furniture was left behind and the destination office had to be completely outfitted with new furniture, down to the last chair. These moves occurred either because of a change of location (e.g., merger), a consolidation of physically dispersed workers, or a company expansion. For some workers in some of these cases, the new move would be their first experience of cubicle furniture (they would have occupied either bullpens or individual offices before). These sales typically consisted of 100-plus cubicles.

Another kind of sale happened when an existing cubicle setup was judged outdated or worn out, and was replaced with a new system. Replacement sales of this kind were also a major source of revenue. On balance, the expected life of a cubicle system was 10 years. The actual furniture might remain usable for 20 years or more; hence, it was worn appearance (scuffed and torn panels, scratched furniture) that drove most replacement sales. Because the furniture was still functional, replacement sales were discretionary to some degree. These sales typically consisted of 50 to 100 or more cubicle systems, but could be as large as a new building sale. The average sale was smaller because firms tended to remodel a department, or building floor, rather than an entire division or building, mostly because of budget reasons.

A third and more minor source of revenue came about through piecemeal expansion. A business unit might have added employees, gained floor space, done a small conversion, and so on, and would have a need for 10, 20, or even more cubicles. Clients in this situation almost always purchased cubicles from the same system and manufacturer that had provided the bulk of their existing furniture (unless this was judged too old or itself due for replacement). If the piecemeal expansion was not automatically routed to the existing furniture supplier, it provided an opportunity to compete for new business. Winning the bid for the piecemeal expansion put the new manufacturer in a favorable position to bid for either the next wholesale replacement of furniture, or the next piecemeal expansion. A growing firm might offer a steady flow of such piecemeal business, and become a relatively large customer in short order.

The final source of revenue consisted of replacements and upgrades. Thus, a piece of furniture might have been damaged, or a worker might require an upgrade to a U-shaped desk arrangement from an existing single desk surface. These purchases almost always went to the existing supplier, either because of proprietary interlock systems or a desire for aesthetic consistency.

Because of trends in population and economic growth, the majority of existing cubicle systems was installed in Southern, Southwestern, and Western states. These areas also had the largest share of new building construction in the late 1990s. In the

(Continued)

(Continued)

Northeast and Midwest, a higher proportion of buildings were older and less likely to have cubicle systems. By the same token, conversions to cubicle systems were concentrated somewhat in the Northeast and Midwest, and small or partial conversions were most likely to occur here, as were installations of cubicles in existing, unconverted buildings.

THE NEW PRODUCT

One of Bob's teams has been exploring the potential for a new product that could serve as an expansion of one or more of the existing lines. Alternatively, its key features could be added as options to an existing line(s). Some people even thought it could become a fourth standalone line—this decision had not been made. The new product was targeted at those offices that either made unusually intense use of computers or had major computer networking needs. One example would be software development firms where individuals might have multiple computers on their desk and might be connected to more than one type of network. Beyond such obvious examples, it was believed that there might be a much larger segment of office workers whose work was becoming either computer centered or computer intensive.

OSYS and other cubicle firms had benefited from an increased pace of cubicle system upgrades in the late 1980s and 1990s when the personal computer had first begun to be widely diffused in offices. At this time, OSYS and most other manufacturers had added options to their lines to accommodate PCs. Thus, most desk surfaces now allowed the user to specify a keyboard tray as an added option. Similarly, some desk surfaces offered a place to put the system box underneath the desk in a convenient location. The customization potential of cubicle systems in general was perceived by clients as better able to accommodate a PC than traditional office furniture, so that to some extent, the spread of PCs had become a driver of the purchase of cubicle systems.

Nonetheless, in Bob's view the typical manufacturer, OSYS included, had made only grudging accommodations to the growth of computers in the office. Cubicle systems were still designed from the standpoint that the user might need or want a PC—or might not. Hence, the accommodations to PCs tended to options at best, afterthoughts at worst. No one had designed a system that was optimized from the ground up to meet the needs of the worker whose office time was centered on or dominated by PC usage. According to secondary research Bob had pursued, the diffusion of office PCs to the desks of white collar workers would reach well over 90 percent by early in the next century. Moreover, the number of workers who would have multiple computers in their workspace (including laptops) was expected to climb to 30 percent or more. Similarly, the number who would have more than one peripheral (e.g., scanner as well as printer) in their personal space was also expected to climb drastically. Last, individual computers were more and more likely to be networked, and in many cases, this implied installation of new cables into a space not originally designed to accommodate them.

To address this market, Bob had set in motion internal development work to identify possible enhancements to the product line. Among the ideas brainstormed thus far:

- Panels with channels to hide cabling
- Panels with extra acoustic technology to better hide equipment noise
- Panels 6' in height, to better limit the spread of equipment noise throughout a space
- Panels 4' in height, to reduce the social isolation sometimes associated with intensive computer work
- Sturdierpanelsthatallowedbookshelvestobeplacedanywhere (so that computer manuals could be placed within reach of any part of the office)
- Desk surfaces that varied in height to accommodate a keyboard, a writing surface, and a monitor—all at ideal heights for usability
- Desks predesigned with different surfaces or areas to accommodate different kinds of work, such as writing, desktop

(Continued)

(Continued)

> computing, or laptop computing, and the types of equipment needed to support that work

- Desks that provided storage for various computer supplies in a handy location
- A super ergonomic chair
- A chair with three preset modes—at a push of a button, it would configure seat height and angle for computing vs. conversing vs. writing
- A quick easy-lock system that would allow cubicle panels and furniture to be easily and quickly reconfigured
- A fixed interlock system for panels and furniture, much less flexible, but better able to accommodate a great deal of weighty computer equipment and to hide cabling
- Integrated electric wiring (in the panels) and lighting to provide task lighting suitable for computing and other work

THE CONCEPT

Several of these ideas had coalesced into a product concept that went by the name of the Integrated Design (ID). The ID enabled the client, for each employee, to check off from a sheet the kinds of computer equipment they would have, the other furniture options needed, and the size of cubicle required. OSYS design services would then compute the optimal location for each piece of equipment within a worker's cubicle, and specify a set of desk surface heights and an arrangement of same. (Present layout services left the inside of the cubicle blank or unspecified, and concentrated on the arrangement of cubicles and corridors.) The resulting cubicle would use the fixed interlock system for better stability. Design services would also lay out the total set of cubicles to make the best use of the available space. The panels marking out the cubicles would have channels for cabling, and design services would also optimize the cable runs as part of the total layout. Panels would be uniformly specified as 6' in height.

NEXT STEPS

At this time the new ID product was in the advanced conceptual stage—little actual money has been spent thus far on product design, but the idea has been around long enough to acquire some momentum internally, with several champions emerging. If Bob and the rest of the management team give the go ahead, a substantial investment in product and process redesign would have to be made to actually produce the new product extension. If successful, the new line could add millions of dollars to OSYS's contribution margin.

Not everyone was enamored of ID. Some were unsure that the features included were the most marketable from among those brainstormed. Others were unsure if the optimal bundle of features had been found. Still others felt that too little was known about the emerging "computer centric" worker to design an optimal system.

To gain more insight into this market, and further advance the product definition work, Bob was receptive to the idea of conducting some kind of market research. He charged Sally Dutful with developing a proposal for some customer visits to explore these issues.

Bob's words echoed in Sally's mind: "It seems clear that we could learn something from a systematic attempt to talk to customers. But how many customers should we visit? What kinds of customers do we need to see, and what topics should we cover during the visits?"

PART IV

QUANTITATIVE RESEARCH

———◆◆◆◆———

OVERVIEW

Unlike qualitative research, in which the human being of the researcher is the means to immediate knowledge of customers, all quantitative research produces *mediated* knowledge of customers. The mediation is provided by some kind of instrument, and what distinguishes different quantitative techniques from one another is the difference in the instruments used.

Although many different kinds of instruments are in use, these fall into two broad categories: passive and active. Passive instruments are primarily designed to measure the customer, as a tailor measures a body in order to sew a suit that will fit it well. The aim is a set of numerical relationships—more versus less, larger versus smaller, stronger versus weaker—that reflects the properties of the consumer population being studied. Accurate numerical *description* is the goal in this kind of quantitative research. The survey questionnaire is probably the most familiar example of such a passive instrument.

Active instruments first manipulate the consumer and then measure the consumer's response. Yes, manipulation is a harsh word—but it is exactly the right word. That is why academic psychologists used to call the students who signed up for their experiments "subjects," before political correctness set in[1];

---

[1] The current preference for referring to experimental "participants" has the same Orwellian flair as when prison wardens refer to the inmates as "clients." If individuals actually participated in constructing the meaning of the experimental treatment, rather than simply being subjected to it, the experiment would be ruined.

these students were subjected to a manipulation. This is what an experiment consists of: manipulating the circumstances to which subjects are exposed, and then studying how they react. The experimental design—the contrasts built in to the set of conditions created—together with the outcomes measured constitute the instrument. Market experiments are perhaps the most familiar kind of active instrumentation; conjoint analysis can be thought of as a specific family of experimental designs.

Lest you recoil in horror from the idea of subjecting consumers to a manipulation, keep in mind that once you have learned the strengths of experimentation, it will become difficult for you not to insert the word "mere" in front of "measurement." To merely measure consumers is to obtain a much weaker kind of knowledge than to subject them to a carefully designed manipulation and observe their response. The slightly pejorative tone of the contrast between passive and active instrumentation is intentional. In fact, by the time you finish this part of the book, I hope to have made you less interested in surveying customers and more interested in running them through experiments.

The trait that all quantitative research techniques share is the representation of customers as numbers, or more precisely as sets of numerical relationships. To do quantitative market research is to make measurements. These can be measurements of what already exists—the customer as you find him—or measurement within an artificial situation that you construct for customers, circumstances that do not exist outside of the research endeavor. As a consequence, something like the field versus laboratory distinction introduced in the overview of qualitative research applies here as well.

Although surveys, because of their passivity and necessary artificiality, don't fit very well into this distinction, experiments can occur in the field or in the laboratory. As with the contrast between ethnography and interviews, there are trade-offs that must be understood in deciding whether to do experiments in the field or in the laboratory. Field experiments, sometimes called "market tests" or "in-market research," may have the capacity to produce more reliable results. Field tests may be reliable in the specific sense that results of a small test taking place in one city or with a small sample of customers are expected to carry over when the test is repeated in the total market. But field tests (excepting tests of websites) are almost always slower and sometimes vastly more expensive than laboratory tests. Conversely, with lab tests you always worry about whether the customer will respond the same way back out there in the market as he or she did within the narrow confines of the artificial laboratory test; but lab tests are both quick and cheap, and often better designed, because more carefully controlled, allowing more precise measurement of the effects of the manipulation. A knowledgeable manager may make a different trade-off between field and laboratory on one occasion versus another, but he or she can't escape the need to weigh the trade-offs involved.

In these few introductory paragraphs I am skating over the surface of a vast literature on measurement, because I can't do it justice in the available space, and because I don't think it is appropriate in a concise guide for beginners. If market research becomes your full-time career, you will likely become ever more interested in theories of measurement, and regard the topic as more and more important. For purposes of this introductory treatment, it suffices to point out that in commercial market research, measures are only means to an end. You are interested in cost-effective measurements that can guide the way to profitable decisions. To be cost-effective, you will almost always have to work with a small sample from the much larger market where the profitability of your decisions will be determined. Because quantitative research almost always uses samples[2], the question of generalizability from sample to market is pressing.

What you hope to generalize is the numerical relationships found in the sample, at a particular point in time, to larger populations, over some surrounding time period. If 62 percent of the survey sample of 400 reports experiencing a particular problem with their smartphone's Internet connection, then the expectation is that 62 percent, more or less, of the 20 million owners of that brand of smartphone, or 13.4 million individuals, have experienced that same problem. Likewise, suppose a conjoint study with 200 data center managers indicates that the inclusion of some new feature in a computer server justifies paying $1,850 more than if the server lacked that feature. The expectation is that within the total market consisting of approximately 15,000 data center managers with purchase authority for such servers, a new model introduced with that feature can be priced up to $1,850 higher, more or less.

---

[2]For the most part, only in extremely concentrated B2B markets will this assertion fail to hold. There, it may be possible to take a census.

Now please re-read the preceding paragraph, paying careful attention to the two generalizations offered as examples. Both instances are clearly extrapolations from numbers produced in the research to numerical relationships in the world outside; but they are not the same kind of extrapolation. And in fact these are just two instances from among the great variety of kinds of generalizations that might be made from particular quantitative research studies. The common properties are one, that it is numerical relations that are generalized, and two, that the generalization is always made with a caveat that the key numbers will obtain, *more or less*, in the larger population and at other times. A third and more subtle property is that the generalization only holds for the population from which the sample was drawn, and that the time period for which it will hold is finite. You can't expect a survey of smartphone users in 2012 to give good generalizations in 2015; and you can't expect results from a survey of Android phone users to apply equally well to owners of Apple phones.

Accordingly, the key capacities that a practitioner of quantitative market research has to cultivate are: (1) the ability to translate decision uncertainty—which action to take—into an uncertainty about the magnitude of particular numbers, and to come up with a research design that once implemented will resolve that numerical uncertainty—that is, estimate those numbers in the market of interest; (2) the skill to come up with a sample of the right provenance and size to estimate those numbers with enough accuracy and precision; and, again more subtly (3) a habit of caution with respect to how accurate and precise the numbers coming out of the quantitative research really are. The first capacity concerns research design: the ability to come up with questions and answer categories for the survey, or to construct a particular experimental design. The second capacity is competence in sampling. The third capacity is a mental stance that respects the inherent imprecision or noisiness of research done with human beings, however quantitative in intent.

The remainder of Part IV goes into specifics with respect to the design of surveys and experiments, followed by chapters on sampling and data analysis for quantitative research.

⊰ NINE ⊱

SURVEY RESEARCH

———•◆•———

I n survey research, a particular kind of questionnaire is completed by a large sample of respondents. Now most quantitative market research uses large samples, and similarly, questionnaires may play a role as delivery vehicles outside of a survey context or in very small samples. It is thus the conjunction of a certain kind of questionnaire with a particular approach to sampling that constitutes survey research as a distinct market research tool. The survey sample generally has to be large—in the hundreds—because the intent is to project the questionnaire results with precision to the entire population of customers that is of interest to the researcher, a population that may be in the millions. In turn, the questionnaires used in survey research are distinguished by their style and by the use of rating scales of various types.

As an example, suppose Verizon is interested in understanding parents' decisions to buy or not to buy a smartphone for a preteen child. The population might be as broad as current Verizon landline households, or the more narrowly specified group of current Verizon Wireless customers who have a multiline cell phone plan, or the even more narrow group where each parent already has a smartphone on the multiline plan. There may be no archival way to identify in advance parents with preteen children from within any of these groups, in which case the questionnaire itself will have to identify this subset (nonparents or parents with older or younger children can be asked a few other questions of general interest so that time to reach them is not wasted). Note that *population* here doesn't refer to the citizens of the United States or to inhabitants of planet Earth; it refers to current Verizon customers who are parents of preteen children, or an even smaller subgroup. The point is, one of the very first steps in survey design has to be to define the population. You can't draw the sample or judge whether a particular sample would be appropriate until that step is taken.

Given a sample, Verizon can deliver the questionnaire in a couple of ways. In the old days of 10 or 15 years ago, it would almost certainly have been administered by means of a telephone call, and that may still be the preferred approach in this instance. Alternatively, customers could be invited to a website and the survey administered there. In either case, the questionnaire will contain lots of questions that are primarily descriptive in intent and designed to differentiate the sample into subgroups that can be compared. In this case, we'd want to know the number and ages of children, whether any of them have a cell phone now, and at what age they got their first cell phone. We'd probably want to distinguish the only-child case from the multiple-sibling case. We'd also need to know a few things about the parent's own cell phone possession and usage. In addition to these descriptive questions, we'd also ask the parents to react to or evaluate various statements. We might list a number of benefits that giving a preteen a smartphone might foster and also list a number of potential negative outcomes. Some kind of scale would be supplied so that parents could calibrate their reaction to these benefits and costs, perhaps from "not at all a concern" to "very much a concern for me." The scale itself might offer 5, 7, or 10 gradations. Other scales might be used to rate perceptions of the Verizon Wireless brand as compared to other cell phone brands.

The description just given of the kinds of questions used in survey questionnaires should feel very different from the descriptions given in the chapter on interview questions. The level of detail is much greater, the specificity is greater, and there are few parallels in interviews for the rating scales routinely used in surveys. Conversely, none of the survey questions would be very useful for starting a discussion in an interview. Survey questions have a different purpose: not to explore and discover, as in interviews, but to describe exactly, to pin down precisely, and to set up multi-way contrasts.

If the sample is of adequate size, as described in Chapter 13, and a probability sample, then an analysis of the results will allow Verizon to draw conclusions such as the following:

- In the only-child case, parents are twice as likely to buy a smartphone for a child under 10.
- About 78 percent of preteens that already had a cell phone received it after their ninth birthday.
- The most frequent reason cited for not giving a preteen a smartphone was fear of inappropriate behavior such a sexting.
- The two factors that best distinguished the Verizon brand from competitors were signal quality and the variety of phones offered.

Given results of this type, the expectation would be that promotional efforts might be better designed. For instance, the child portrayed in ads must not appear too young. Likewise, the information could be used to improve product and service plans, such as by incorporating greater parental control over content received.

This first example highlights two distinguishing features of asking customers questions in the context of a survey as opposed to asking customers questions in the context of a customer visit or focus group. First is the amount and level of detail of the questions themselves: Virtually any survey will provide detailed breakdowns, counts, and scaled answers that can be expressed as means. Second is the opportunity for and precision of comparisons across subgroups of customers. By contrast, in results from customer visits and focus groups, everything is approximate, imprecise, suggestive, and tentative. Later we'll consider the downside of asking questions in a survey context, but the upside is clearly a matter of both the quantity and the precision of the information acquired.

Here is another example. Suppose Bank of America is interested in assessing the satisfaction of small-business owners with the business checking services provided by Bank of America. Here there will be descriptive questions, but they will concern characteristics of the business rather than of the individual respondent: perhaps annual revenue, number of employees, number of checks written per month, how many other banking services are also used, and so forth. The scaled questions in this case will include some measure of global or overall satisfaction and then measures of specific components of satisfaction, such as satisfaction with the courtesy of bank employees, the breadth of checking services offered, and so forth. Results of such a survey might be used to assess whether customer satisfaction is above some threshold (e.g., 8.5 on a

10-point scale) and whether it has increased or decreased since the last time it was measured. The results might also be analyzed to see whether some types of businesses are more satisfied than others or to determine whether specific patterns of checking account usage are associated with higher and lower levels of satisfaction. Finally, the internal relations among results can be analyzed— that is, which component of satisfaction best predicts overall satisfaction?

Stepping back from the two examples, it is clear that survey research offers the manager masses of numbers reflecting factual details, plentiful opportunities to compare and contrast subgroups of customers, and an occasion to apply any number of statistical analyses. And the underlying premise is that all these results are projectable to the market at large. So if 10 percent of respondents expect to buy their preteen a smartphone, and there are 22 million preteens between 9 and 12 years of age in the United States who don't have a smartphone, and parents expect to spend an average of $62 on this phone purchase, then preteen smartphones represent an approximately $136.4 million market opportunity ($.10 \times 22M \times \$62$). That's what precise projection from the sample to the population entails.

Survey research, as narrowly specified in this chapter, provides descriptive and evaluative information. The typical result takes the form of a percentage figure (e.g., "35 percent of home computer users are dissatisfied with their current broadband service"), a frequency count (e.g., "on average, C++ programmers make two calls per month to software vendors' technical support lines"), a mean or average ("satisfaction averaged 7.5 this quarter, a significant drop from last quarter's 8.2"), or a cross-tabulation comparing groups (e.g., "47 percent of MIS directors with exclusively IBM mainframes reacted favorably to this proposal, as compared to 28 percent of MIS directors having both IBM and non-IBM mainframes in their shops"). The managerial use of such descriptive and evaluative information is further elaborated in Chapter 14.

Surveys can be administered in person (very rare today, except for mall intercepts, where a shopper is stopped by a clipboard-toting interviewer), by telephone (still a common method in commercial market research, although Internet surveys are coming up fast), by mail (increasingly less common because of low response rates), and by electronic means (typically taking the form of an e-mail invitation or pop-up that leads the willing respondent to a website where the survey resides). Each method of survey administration has its own body of craft knowledge associated with it. Thus, design and execution of a computer-assisted telephone interview will draw on a different skill set than design and execution of a web-based survey. In keeping with this book's pledge to provide a concise introduction, this chapter steers clear of concepts specific to one or another method of survey administration and concentrates on generally applicable procedures. Note that I didn't specify the mode of administration in the Bank of America example, and I doubt you noticed that absence. The fundamental properties of surveys, in terms of the kinds of questions asked and the nature of the results generated, are relatively constant across most modes of administration.

The survey is probably the most familiar of all market research methodologies. Virtually every adult reading this book will have been on the receiving end of some kind of survey: a phone call at home, a letter in the mail, a person with a clipboard in a mall, a website popup, an e-mail invitation. Moreover, it is a rare business student today who completes an undergraduate or graduate degree in business without having occasion to design, conduct, or analyze at least one survey. This familiarity, combined with the incredible ease with which a web survey can be initiated and completed, and in conjunction with the comfort that comes from obtaining seemingly precise numerical data, creates a problem: *There are almost certainly too many surveys being done in market research today!* By this, I mean that some substantial portion of the effort firms currently put into surveys would be more productive if invested instead in either conjoint studies and controlled experiments, on the one hand, or customer visits and focus groups on the other. In fact, for the managerial reader of this chapter, I would be quite happy if it served as a bucket of cold water. Surveys can be enormously time-consuming, with burdensome data analysis possibilities and an uncertain relationship to pressing decisions. If this chapter causes you to question whether your current level of investment in surveys is ill considered, then it has partly served its purpose.

The number of cases in business in which it is worthwhile to take the time or spend the money in order to estimate precisely some percentage or frequency for primarily *descriptive* purposes is limited. If such descriptive precision is really your goal, then of course the survey is the tool of choice; when it is not, then the survey may be a poor use of resources indeed. Conversely, evaluative surveys have a greater claim on your research dollar. If customer satisfaction is dropping or dissatisfaction is keyed to a particular action (or inaction) on your part, that's actionable information and probably important to know. If your brand is fading in customer perceptions or a competitor brand is gaining strength, that too is important to know. The question with respect to a proposed survey effort is the same as with any contemplated market research study: What is the value of the information it will provide? What will it enable me to do or to change, and how important is that deed or change?

The final thing to remember about survey research is that everything depends on the quality of the questionnaire and the effectiveness of the sampling procedure. Surveys, like the other quantitative techniques discussed in subsequent chapters, are in some meaningful sense less robust than the qualitative techniques (customer visits, focus groups). Thus, if the initial set of questions prepared for a customer visit study has flaws, new questions and good follow-up questions can be devised in real time as the interviews proceed—interviews are robust against that initial error. With a survey, questions cannot be changed in midsurvey, and we often cannot interact with the respondents to clarify their answers. Similarly, although better and worse sampling strategies can be devised for any qualitative research study, the kinds of generalization undertaken with qualitative data (see Chapter 8) are more forgiving of limitations of the sample. By contrast, with a survey, I am trying to say that the proportion of (dis-)satisfied customers in this market segment is precisely 35 percent, with only a small allowance for error. Unless your sample is very good, the number 35 percent obtained from the statistical output may really only mean something as vague as "at least 10 percent, and probably not more than 60 percent of customers." If accurate description is the goal, such imprecision renders the survey useless.

To conclude on this same pessimistic note, I would argue that the proportion of surveys conducted by businesspeople that are useless or misleading is much higher than the proportion of customer visits, focus groups, conjoint analyses, and experiments that are bad in that same sense. More often than not, the problem lies with sampling (arguably, good questionnaire design is not as difficult as executing an effective sampling plan). And more often than not, the sampling problem does not lie with the sample that was asked to complete the questionnaire but with the sample of respondents that actually did complete the questionnaire. If the response rate is 10 percent, or even 5 percent, as became the case with commercially fielded mail questionnaires, and now occurs with broadly distributed web surveys, it seems unlikely that one has in fact obtained a good sample with respect to precisely describing the population of interest. You may have started with a great list, but most of those people aren't in the obtained sample. So how good are the obtained sample and the numbers derived from it?

Bad surveys not attributable to flaws in the questionnaire or the sample generally result from a failure on the part of the decision maker to justify the need for precise *descriptive* data. As we will see in Chapters 11 and 12, using other tools, it is often possible, for an equal or smaller expenditure, to obtain powerful *predictive* data. Decision makers often prefer good prediction over an accurate description, because such data are more actionable. The prediction is also generally more relevant to deciding among options. If an individual is in learning mode, that is, new to the category or industry, then descriptive data might be quite interesting (and prediction premature). But if one is in learning mode, will you learn most by gathering precise descriptive data or by exploring in depth via qualitative research, after reviewing available secondary data?

In short, it can be difficult and costly to obtain high-quality descriptive data via a survey, and even when you succeed, the accurate descriptions so obtained may not be worth much. Conversely, if the survey was cheap and easy, then its data probably aren't very accurate. Keep this perspective in mind next time someone in your group casually suggests, "Let's send them a survey." You need to start asking, "Why? Why bother? What will that survey help us to *do*?"

PROCEDURE

It is quite possible, although not necessarily advisable, to design, conduct, and analyze a survey yourself, and today this will almost always take the form of a web survey, as discussed subsequently. Alternatively, you can hire a vendor to do it for you. Survey research is a mainstay of many market research firms, and there is no shortage of assistance available. Whereas focus groups are something of a specialty item and conjoint analysis even more so, virtually every market research vendor, large or small, is in the business of conducting surveys for clients. There is enough expertise involved in conducting surveys and enough economies of scale that the classic outsourcing argument applies: An outside vendor can often do this better and faster than you. So as a businessperson, your choice is to spend your money or spend your time—with the risk that quality will be sacrificed—or do the reverse. Your call.

In what follows, the procedure for conducting a survey with a vendor's help is described. Issues involved in conducting your own survey are summarized in the next section.

1. You prepare a request for proposals (RFP) that outlines the characteristics of the population you want to survey (e.g., female heads of household who own cellular phones), the kinds of information you want to obtain, and the purpose of gathering this information (e.g., to describe current patterns of usage of smartphones so as to prepare for the design of new calling plans targeted at this population). In the RFP, you should also give some indication of the desired sample size and the source of the sample (a list provided by you, a list bought by the vendor, a random calling procedure, etc.), as these are important cost factors. Alternatively, as part of their proposal, vendors may propose solutions to these issues based on their expertise.

You will also have to indicate in the RFP your expectation as to how the survey is to be administered. Things are changing so fast today, and the best mode is so dependent on the particular population to be reached, that I'd solicit vendor recommendations rather than precommitting to a particular mode.

2. The selected vendor will work with you to hammer out the text of the questions and the answer categories to be used in the survey. See the next chapter for detailed advice on this step.

3. You and the vendor decide upon the size and the source of the sample. As we will see in Chapter 13, there is no mystery to setting sample size; well-accepted statistical formulas exist. However, these formulas work best when you can provide some prior information to the vendor, such as the expected frequency of different answers. Your vendor will also probably have rules of thumb about sample size based on experience with surveys of this type. Remember that it is your prerogative as the paying customer to ask for an explanation of how sample size was determined. If you get an evasive answer or you can't understand the answer, that's a bad sign. The mathematics of sample size selection is straightforward and should be well within your vendor's competence.

The source of the sample is generally a list that you provide, a list that the vendor buys, or some kind of random sampling process, such as random-digit dialing. In random-digit dialing, phone numbers to be called are generated by a computer. The process of number generation anticipates and allows for a fair number of dud calls (businesses, numbers not in service, etc.). The rationale for random-digit dialing is that many people have unlisted phone numbers, and people with unlisted numbers may differ in significant ways from those with listed numbers. Plus, an existing list cannot always be found. Unfortunately, as more and more people have cell phones only, random-digit dialing doesn't hold quite the promise it had some years ago (see Chapter 13).

In any case, the audience for this book—business-to-business and technology firms—is less likely to use random-digit dialing, which is primarily important in mass consumer markets. Instead, you will almost always be working from some kind of list. If you can supply the list, and if it is a good list in the sense of having few duds (i.e., names of people who have moved, changed jobs, don't fit the population), then the cost of your survey research will be substantially less. If the vendor has to buy multiple lists, or if there are no good lists available, then the cost goes up accordingly. The list industry is huge and growing, and some kind of list can generally be obtained, but cost goes up with the rarity and inaccessibility of the sample sought.

The most important thing to remember is that your entire survey research project is only as good as the sample and that sample is only as good as the source from which it was drawn. If the list is biased—not representative of the population of interest—then your results will be biased as well. For example, suppose you use warranty cards to compile a list. Unfortunately, return rates for warranty cards are notoriously low—5 to 10 percent or less in many cases. Who knows how different the nonreturnees may be? Similarly, you may have a list of names of people who attended an industry conference. Some possible problems here include a geographical bias (depending on conference location), an employer success bias (only companies healthy enough to have adequate travel funds sent people to the conference), and so forth. "Know your list" is the rule, and be sure to keep its limits and shortcomings in mind as you analyze results.

4. Next, you pretest the survey. I cannot overemphasize the importance of this step. In any substantial effort, you should plan on a small-scale administration to a dozen or two members of the target population. After each person completes the survey, he or she is interviewed about possible misunderstandings, the meaning of answers, and sources of confusion. A survey that may seem perfectly clear to a 26-year-old MBA-educated project manager immersed in the product category may be regarded very differently by a 43-year-old engineer who only uses the product on an occasional basis.

In real-world situations, you will often be tempted to skip the pretest because of time pressures. This is yet another example of how much easier it is to do a bad survey than a good one. But remember: If the questions on the survey are confusing, if the list of answer categories is incomplete, or if the language is wrong, then it doesn't matter that you have a large, representative sample— your results are still all too likely to approximate garbage. At the very least, ask your spouse and the spouses of teammates to look it over. Get *some* outside minds involved, even if it's only a half dozen.

5. The survey is administered. This can be a very short and quick process if a web survey tool is used. Other techniques take longer.

6. Next, the survey results are analyzed and reported. Typically, the basic form of the analysis will be a comprehensive breakout of the frequency of the answers to each question on the survey. A web survey tool will dump this out into a spreadsheet for you, and programming logic will ensure that surveys with contradictory or too many omitted answers are dropped. I'm old enough to remember when data cleaning, from paper forms or telephone reports, was a major concern in both textbooks and practice. But in the Internet era, simple tabulations from clean data just appear by download, without any additional effort. Miraculous! The software tool still can't select which cross-tabulations to perform, or decide what means to submit to a comparison, what rating scales to correlate, or what should be regressed on what; but the simple percentages just pop right out.

For instance, if the question was, "Do you use your smartphone for any of the following applications?" the report might then include a table showing that:

83% send text messages

52% browse the web

51% access social media

45% send or receive pictures

39% post pictures online

33% listen to music

30% check e-mail

37% other

If the question had been, "How satisfied are you with each aspect of your laptop computer, using a scale where 10 equals 'completely satisfied' and 1 equals 'not satisfied at all'?" the tabulation might look like this:

7.5 speed

8.2 color graphics capability

6.0 expandability

5.7 preloaded software

7.9 reliability

Most reports conducted by outside vendors also include a number of cross-tabulations that combine answers to two or more questions. (If you don't know how to set up a cross-tabulation in Excel or a specialized statistical software program, or how to test tabulated differences for statistical significance, are you sure you want to do the survey by yourself?) For instance, you might want to compare the applications typically used by owners of Windows PCs to those typically used by owners of Apple Macintoshes. Then you would see a chart something like this:

	PC Owners (n = 893)	*Macintosh Owners (n = 102)*
Word processing	80%	48%
Spreadsheets	49%	22%
Data collection and analysis	27%	18%
Photo processing	12%	58%
Games	45%	31%

Cross-tabulations are where survey results start to get interesting, and that's why a lack of knowledge on your part of how to easily set up and test cross-tabs is a contra-indication for doing the survey yourself. Consider again the breakdown of cell phone activities given above. Do you think the percentages would change if you broke out the sample by age groups? Hint: What do you know about young people and social media? Would it change if you broke out months since phone purchase? Probably; newer phones are likely to have more capabilities, users with newer phones may be heavier users of certain cell phone features, and the ease of doing some of these activities goes way up if you've got a newer phone. Any cross-tabulation of this sort may substantially increase the utility of the survey data for decision making or just for understanding what actually is going on in the data. But the only thing automatically produced by most web survey packages is the simple tabulation given earlier. You won't even come close to tapping the potential of survey data if you can't manipulate the data in this and similar ways.

A good report includes a variety of additional data. In an appendix or elsewhere, look for information on confidence intervals (i.e., the precision of the numbers contained in the report). You need to know how many percentage points have to separate two estimates before you can trust that there is a real difference. Thus, in the first example above, with any decent-sized sample, you can probably conclude that sending text messages is more common than sending pictures; but is sending pictures really any more common than storing and sharing them? There's no easy way to know unless the vendor has included the necessary information on confidence intervals. You must recognize that a survey only gives estimates of the true values in the total population, and any estimate is only that—a probable value. Do not fall into the trap of treating the numbers in a survey as an oracular pronouncement or a relatively exact physical measurement like height or temperature.

Other data whose presence should add to your comfort with the vendor and the survey include information on response rate along with comparisons, to the extent possible, of how respondents differ from nonrespondents. If the response rate is low, your confidence in the results has to be lowered accordingly. For instance, you may have started out with a large, representative sample of technical support employees; but if only 10 percent of these people returned your survey, then your obtained sample is probably both small in number (making the results less precise) and systematically different from the population of interest—the total population of all technical support personnel in the market you serve. However, if the list you used to obtain the sample contained some additional information beyond name and phone number—for instance, each support person's years of experience and whether he or she works in hardware or software support—and if you compared people who responded to the survey with people who did not, then you may be able to establish whether the obtained sample is biased on these two counts. If, in fact, the obtained sample of support personnel is similar to the initial sample in terms of years of experience and the hardware/software split, then your confidence that the sample is representative goes back up despite the low response rate.

On the other hand, if there is no information that allows a comparison between respondents and nonrespondents, then, as a rule of thumb, the lower the response rate, the less confidence you should have in the results. Large percentage differences in the case of high response rates (i.e., a 62 percent to 38 percent split on an agree–disagree question where the response rate is 80 percent) are unlikely to vanish altogether even if there were substantial response bias. The same majority of 62 percent agreement, but with a response rate of only 20 percent, will disappear if the nonrespondents happen to split 53 percent to 47 percent in the reverse direction. As a general rule of thumb, a small percentage difference (say, 55 percent/45 percent) on an agree–disagree question will be virtually uninterpretable in the case of a low response rate. The survey could easily produce the opposite of the true breakdown of responses in the population at large.

CONDUCTING THE SURVEY YOURSELF

If you have another department within your firm conduct the survey (your in-house market research staff, for instance), then this section does not apply—that's not much different than retaining an outside specialist. In this section, I am concerned with you—the generalist—doing the survey yourself. From one angle, it's not going to be that hard to do if you have a good list and use a web survey tool. On the other hand, you have to ask yourself why the outsourcing argument does not apply in your situation. Parts of survey research, especially designing the questions and analyzing the replies, can be very labor intensive and time-consuming. Is it that you or your direct reports have idle time that you want to put to good use? (Hah!) Moreover, writing a good questionnaire and usefully and correctly analyzing the results are all specialized technical skills unlikely to be possessed by the typical product, project, or program manager.

Nonetheless, it may make sense to conduct your own survey under the following circumstances:

1. The decision, while not unimportant, cannot justify a substantial expenditure.

2. You have a few straightforward questions and a couple of issues that you want clarified (perhaps you are doing a follow-up to a set of interviews).

3. You would be content so long as the sample is not awful, or you have a captive sample, or you can take a virtual census of the relevant population.

4. The goal of your analysis is to identify lopsided majorities or split opinions via simple tabulations.

These circumstances are not uncommon. Maybe you want to ask a few questions of your field sales force, and their management has agreed to assist you. Maybe you have customers attending an event and you are curious about a couple of things. Of course you should have some kind of warranty card included with your product and of course this card should include a couple of questions. If you don't take any one instance of this kind of survey too seriously, and if you keep each such survey short and simple, and if you do these surveys as only one part of your information gathering, then yes, it may make sense to do these surveys, and yes, you can do them yourself.

You should ask yourself several questions, however. First, will the survey really make any difference? What will you do with the data that you couldn't do without it? Any survey requires a chunk of your time—precious time of which you have too little. Second, how would your time be better spent: searching for high-quality secondary research or conducting a not-great, not-awful survey yourself? This has to be answered on a case-by-case basis. If no relevant or useful secondary data exist, then of course you may have no choice but to do your own survey. But it would be a shame if you labored mightily to produce an okay survey when there already existed some outstanding secondary research that you could have found if only you had gone to the trouble. Third, are you seeking a *description*, or some *understanding*? If the latter, why not make a series of semistructured phone calls (a kind of customer visit) as opposed to firing off a written survey? A semistructured phone interview really isn't a survey because it has so much flexibility. You're not calling to take a count but to get inside people's heads and gain a perspective. That's an interview, not a survey. In which case, you want a few starter questions, but you want the emphasis in the phone call to be on the follow-up questions that you formulate on the spot in response to what the person said. As noted in Chapter 5, and in contrast to survey research, you are probably better placed than an outside vendor to conduct an effective interview. So why not do what you do best?

COST FACTORS

Sample Size

The cost of web surveys is not heavily affected by the sample size; most of the fee will be for design and analysis. A web panel can be tapped to yield a sample of about 500 for a few thousand dollars; if you will do the design and analysis, that's the total cost. If you blast out e-mails using your own list, and do the design and analysis, then there is essentially no out-of-pocket cost. If you resort to an outside firm to perform a more traditional phone survey, larger samples of 1,000 or more can drive the cost to well over $100,000.

Sample Accessibility

If lists of these people are expensive, or if the lists are bad so that many calls are wasted, or e-mail is returned as undeliverable, or if these people are hard to reach on the phone, or if many refuse to participate, or if many terminate the interview prior to completion, then the cost goes up accordingly. Hard-to-find specialized populations are always more expensive than samples of the general consumer population.

Survey Length

The longer the survey, the more it costs, either in dollar terms or the way in which it erodes sample quality (longer surveys produce more partial completions and early terminations, which depresses the effective response rate). Length has no effect on web survey dollar costs, but what kind of nerd of a customer will spend 37 minutes working through 62 screens' worth of questions? Someone who represents the central tendency in the population of interest, or a very unusual individual with way too much time on his hands? Maybe a student intern assigned to the task, rather than the executive you thought you were sampling?

Keep it short and simple. Shorter is always better, up until the point where no relevant information is gained.

Analysis

If you want many cross-tabulations, more sophisticated statistical analyses, or more elaborate reporting, then the cost increases. However, analysis costs are generally modest relative to the three factors named above, unless the survey was done on the web, in which case design and analysis may be the only costs.

APPLICATIONS

Because surveys are such a familiar kind of research, this section describes a range of applications rather than giving one or two specific case studies. Although the survey is an enormously flexible tool, the eight applications described below probably account for the bulk of the market research surveys conducted in a given year.

Customer Satisfaction

In a customer satisfaction survey, a large and representative sample of a firm's customers will be contacted and asked to rate the firm's performance in a variety of areas. These may include relatively specific actions (e.g., "timely response to inquiries") and more general and intangible aspects (e.g., "offers solutions that are at the cutting edge of the industry"). Customers may also be asked to indicate whether certain problems have occurred (e.g., "Has your system required a service call?"). Customers give the satisfaction ratings on 10-point scales or similar measures. The primary output of this survey will be numerical indices that report, in both global and specific terms, how well the firm is doing. These satisfaction surveys will typically be repeated on a quarterly, semiannual, or annual basis so that trends can be discerned.

The most powerful and useful efforts will include customers of competitors as well; the meaning of a finding that 88 percent of your customers are satisfied changes a great deal, depending on whether the corresponding number for a leading competitor is 83 percent (you are doing rather well) or 93 percent (you are falling behind). Since satisfaction numbers generally skew high, it is difficult to interpret scores unless you have competitor scores against which to benchmark.

Segmentation Studies

In a segmentation survey, a large and inclusive sample of customers for some product or service will be asked a wide variety of questions. For example, some years ago, Levi Strauss conducted a survey to segment the market for men's clothing. Attitude questions (e.g., "Dressing right is a complete mystery to me"), shopping behaviors (e.g., "Do you prefer to shop on your own or with someone else?"), and usage data (e.g., "How many suits do you own?") were included. The goal in a segmentation survey is to gather enough data that well-defined clusters of consumers with distinct buying preferences can be identified. In the Levi Strauss study, the "classic independent" segment emerged as the best target market for wool-blend clothing as compared with some of the other segments (e.g., "mainstream traditionalists"), for whom a different product (polyester suits) was more attractive. The primary goal of a segmentation survey is to provide a rich description of the differences among groups of consumers along with linkages between these differences and behaviors of interest (heavy usage, brand preference, media use, etc.). A wide variety of multivariate statistical analyses can be performed to uncover and represent segment differences and preferences.

Product Usage and Ownership

In the case of innovative product categories, it is often of interest to know what kinds of people have adopted a product early in its life cycle, what they use it for, and what other products are used with it. For instance, what kinds of people have bought a Roku, Apple TV, or Slingbox device to make Internet-based video available on a living room television? How many of these early adopters have a computer, engineering, or other technical background? How often do they get video content this way? Did they cancel or downgrade their cable or satellite television service? Even mundane and noninnovative products may benefit from a usage survey if years have passed since the last survey. A bank might survey its customers on which bank products are used (checking, savings, certificates of deposit, etc.), by whom, how heavily, and for what purpose. The primary goal in any product usage survey is to get more complete and detailed information on product users and nonusers (or heavy versus light users) so as to facilitate subsequent marketing, advertising, and product development efforts.

Purchase Intentions

A purchase intentions survey examines how many of which kind of people intend to buy some product or service within the next 6 to 12 months. Sometimes these questions are combined with a product usage survey. The primary goal in a product intentions survey is to get data useful for forecasting future sales. These efforts make the most sense for expensive durables; I believe they were pioneered in the automobile industry.

Brand Image and Perceptions

In a brand image survey, you try to understand how your brand is regarded in the marketplace, generally in comparison with other brands. Most often, questions will take the form of rating scales ("On a scale of 1 to 5, how prestigious is this brand?"), and the factors rated can range from very tangible to very intangible ("provides good value" versus "daring" or "mainstream"). Whereas a satisfaction survey is primarily evaluative—a kind of report card—a brand image survey is primarily descriptive—a profile or portrait. The goal in a brand image survey is typically either to more broadly diagnose problems, as in the case of a brand that has lost ground in a market, or to diagnose strengths and weaknesses, as when preparing for a new advertising campaign.

Tracking Studies

Advertisers use tracking studies to determine whether an ad campaign is having the desired effect. The typical procedure is to conduct a baseline survey prior to the launch of the campaign (continuous tracking may also be obtained). The survey may measure brand awareness, brand image, knowledge of a brand's features and capabilities, usage type or frequency, or anything else that the advertising campaign is aimed at changing. At regular intervals following the launch of the campaign, this survey will be readministered to a new sample drawn so as to be comparable to the baseline sample. The primary goal of a tracking study is to determine whether and how well the ad campaign is working. If a tracking study is conducted apart from any ad campaign, then its purpose is probably trend monitoring: for instance, how many people are considering purchase of a tablet, current beliefs about the utility of a tablet versus a laptop for performing work, and so forth. Some of the major advertising agencies conduct such surveys to monitor changes in lifestyles and values.

Media Usage

A media usage survey asks about magazines read, television programs watched, preferences in radio format, and the like for some specified group of people (e.g., buyers of a certain product category, such as mutual funds). Today it might take the form of which Internet sites are visited, what is the home page on your browser, how much time do you spend on browsing websites versus social media, and the like. A media usage study will probably be conducted by the vendor firm or its ad agency in order to guide the allocation of ad spending toward the most efficient media vehicles. Thus, you may discover that a large number of networking engineers happen to read *Scientific American* magazine and that the ad rates in this magazine compare favorably with those of more obvious choices such as *PC Magazine*. Media spending is so substantial (Intel has spent hundreds of millions of dollars promoting its brand of processor chips, and Procter & Gamble spends over a billion dollars per year) that even a quite expensive media survey may quickly pay for itself if it leads to a marginally better allocation of media dollars.

Readership Studies

A readership survey will be conducted by a magazine or other media vehicle in order to develop a profile of the people who read the magazine. Readers are the "product" that magazines sell to advertisers, who are their true customers (advertising dollars account for the bulk of most magazine revenues). The readership questionnaire asks demographic (age, occupation, income, etc.), psychographic (attitudes, opinions, interests, hobbies, lifestyle), and product usage questions. The primary goal is to describe the readership so as to facilitate efforts to market the magazine to advertisers. If you are a provider of instructional software aimed at children and I am a magazine publisher, if I can show you that my readers are very interested in education and child development and have substantial discretionary spending power, then I can hope to win some of your advertising dollars.

FUTURE DIRECTIONS

The major change in survey research in the past 10 years has been the rise of web survey tools. Perhaps no other market research technique has been more altered by the spread of the web than survey research. Two factors drove this change. From the survey researcher's standpoint, especially for the beginner or nonprofessional researcher, conducting a survey on the web is overwhelmingly quicker, easier, more convenient, and more cost-effective than via any other mode of administration. From the standpoint of convenience and cost, web surveys are decisively superior. The second factor derives from the Achilles heel of all survey research: Participation is intrinsically dysphoric. The request is an intrusion and participation a Procrustean experience, as the respondent is forced to fit his lived experience into the little boxes provided by the survey. In other words, one reason for the spread of web surveys is the increasing difficulty of getting people to participate in any of the more traditional modes of administration. There was even a brief period where the novelty of web surveys compelled a somewhat more enthusiastic participation. That period has passed; but it remains quicker and cheaper to get 250 responses to 8,000 e-mail invitations than to get 250 completed phone interviews out of 1,100 attempts.

Whether the rise of web survey tools is a good thing is a separate question. As any economist will tell you, free and nearly free goods tend to promote excessive use and waste. If there were too many ill-advised surveys before the web, as has long been my view, then the problem has only been exacerbated in recent years. A more subtle problem is that the ease and cheapness of getting a big enough sample using the web tends to obscure the importance of sample provenance. The goal with almost any survey is to project results to a larger population, and this can only be done if the sample is representative of that population. Hyper-low response rates consequent to the cheapness of web surveys call into question the representativeness of web samples, which was fraught to begin with, inasmuch as even today, web access doesn't have the penetration that phones achieved decades ago.

A complementary trend is the slow death of phone surveys—the gold standard of commercial survey research not too long ago (like, when the first edition of this book was published). Speaking personally, years ago I used to respond to those calls I found halfway interesting, if only in guilt at having inflicted a survey on hundreds of people as part of my dissertation research; but now I scarcely respond to any. The phenomenon is general: Citizens feel more and more badgered, guard their time and privacy more and more jealously, and more and more often make a rational calculation that participating in a phone survey is not a good use of their time. An entire era may be coming to an end; I can imagine my grandchildren regarding the idea of strangers calling on a landline phone and asking interminable questions with the same quizzical expression as my children regard the idea of a vinyl "record" as the best way to listen to music. What's new, then, is the prospect of the slow death and eventual disappearance of high-quality phone sampling for commercial market research.

There has been one other important change in survey research that has nothing to do with mode of administration. This is the switch from sampling *people* to sampling *events*. This nascent tendency has profound implications for the impact and actionability of survey research. It can best be illustrated by returning to the Bank of America example given at the beginning of the chapter. Recall that here, the satisfaction of small-business owners was the overall concern. As part of assessing the components of satisfaction, there would probably have been questions about the quality of service received, how complaints were handled, courtesy of tellers and branch managers, and so forth. As described in the example, this survey sampled people: The population was defined as small-business customers, and this population was sampled periodically, probably in the middle of each calendar quarter.

In the new approach of event-based sampling, the bank would instead have defined a population of *events*: loan requests, checks received by the small business from its customers that bounced when presented to the bank, meetings with a branch manager, complaints, and so forth. To understand service delivery, there would be ongoing sampling of these events: every nth customer filing a loan request would be contacted and given a brief survey about that specific, recent event. Continuously updated numbers on service quality can then be delivered to the desktop of the executive responsible; desperately unhappy customers can be flagged for immediate remedial action. What had been a relatively passive, diffusely focused, good/bad news scorecard, delivered at intervals, becomes instead an ongoing, targeted radar sweep. The event-based survey is more meaningful to the customer because it asks about a recent, concrete experience, and it is more useful to the bank because it is more actionable.

STRENGTHS AND WEAKNESSES

The great strength of survey research is its ability to deliver precise numerical estimates of the frequency and magnitude of some consumer response. Survey research tells us not that "many" customers are seeking some benefit but that 39 percent desire it; not that satisfaction has "decreased" but that satisfaction has dropped from 8.6 to 7.8 on a 10-point scale; not that new smartphone owners "regularly" purchase apps but that owners spend an average of $76 on apps in the year following purchase. This strength is valuable because ultimately, most businesses have to measure their success in precise numerical terms: profit dollars, unit sales, market share percentage. In turn, survey research is most useful to businesses in situations where precision matters a great deal, that is, where small differences can be consequential. Thus, any percentage that ultimately concerns the potential size or growth of your multibillion-dollar market ought to be precise. A few percentage points may translate to tens of millions of dollars and may mean the difference between a market big enough to be worth pursuing or too small to consider entering. Similarly, precision is valuable when a high level of uncertainty would be intolerable. Thus, you could conduct lengthy visits with dozens of customers, hear all kinds of stories about your product, and still have no clear sense of whether the overall satisfaction of your customer base is increasing, staying level, or dropping. In any application that requires or resembles a scorecard, a forecast, or a comparison to determine big versus small, the precision of survey research will be valuable.

A second strength of survey research lies in its superior objectivity—its capacity to break you free of biases. Managers are continually creating and revising a mental map that describes their customers, competition, and markets, and have all kinds of daily experiences that feed into that map. Unfortunately, because virtually all businesses have to deal with markets that range in size from large to huge to gigantic to vast, the personal experience of each businessperson is necessarily limited and partial and, thus, biased to some unknown degree. Just as an automobile extends the legs and a telescope the eyes, a good survey extends personal inquiry. Your questions are put to a much larger number of people than you could personally interview, and this large number represents that still larger population of customers that constitutes your market. Thus, the survey can be thought of as a "question machine" that, like all machines, functions to expand unaided human capacity.

The amplification capacity of the survey, its ability to extend your individual effort, actually functions to correct two kinds of biases: those due to personal *prejudice* and those due to personal *limitations*. That is, as individuals, we all have personal viewpoints that shape our perceptions. These viewpoints accommodate our individual experience—most notably, the angry customer we spoke to yesterday, the sales pitch that works for us, the friendly customer who always takes our phone calls, and so forth. But in addition, no individual is "large" enough to directly encounter all the diverse components of an entire market. Of course, objectivity, like precision, matters most when you face a close call and some evidence exists in favor of both options. Here the survey functions as the equivalent of a microscope, clarifying a difference too small to be reliably discriminated based on the personal experiences of you and your debating partners.

A third strength of survey research is that it allows you to apply a wealth of statistical techniques that can enhance the rigor and add to the depth of your knowledge. An enormous amount of academic research, developed over a period of 70 years or more, has been directed at developing tools for analyzing the kind of data that surveys produce. Although such narrowly focused and arcane academic research is sometimes the butt of jokes in practical business circles, let me suggest that statistical analysis is like the police—it's easy to have a dismissive attitude until the day your need becomes acute. How big is "big"? How precise is "precise"? How different is "different"? It is the purpose of statistical analysis to answer such questions, and when millions of dollars hang on getting the right answer, you may come to appreciate the many ways in which survey research lends itself to analysis in statistical terms.

Another strength of surveys is their capacity for illuminating and pinning down differences between groups. A large sample and a precise estimate enable you to do two things: first, to determine whether a difference between groups really exists, and second, to more accurately describe the nature of any difference that does exist. Intergroup comparisons are typically important in segmentation analysis and in the assessment of strengths and weaknesses relative to the competition. For instance, suppose you find that your customers are, on average, working in larger facilities and concentrated in Sunbelt states, as compared with your competition. That knowledge will make your marketing efforts more effective. For another example, exactly how do people who prefer to put their savings in certificates of deposit differ from those who prefer to put their savings in money market mutual funds—in terms of education, income, source of savings, and geographical region? That knowledge can make your advertising appeals stronger. Again, small differences may have a major dollar impact in terms of the efficiency of marketing and advertising efforts, and an effective survey research procedure may be the only way to uncover such differences.

Last, surveys become especially powerful when they are repeated over time. There are a couple of reasons why repeating a survey at intervals is often money well spent. First, most markets are dynamic rather than static. Repeated surveys thus yield data on trends. Furthermore, actually possessing data from multiple past points in time probably provides a more accurate picture of the evolution of a market than asking customers to give a retrospective account of how things have changed over the past few years. Similarly, for forecasting purposes, you are better off projecting a trend from several data points than trying to take a single data point (i.e., the customer's self-forecast) and extrapolate it.

From another angle, when a survey is repeated, many small biases that may bedevil a single administration cancel out. Thus, the estimate of brand awareness you took today may be off the mark because your sample is a biased subset of the population. But if you use the same questions and sampling procedure three or four times and the data show an upward trend, that trend is probably more reliable than the absolute value (i.e., 20 percent or 24 percent) that you estimated in any single administration.

On the other hand, perhaps the most significant weakness of descriptive survey research is that it tends to tell you *what* but not *why*. You learn that customer satisfaction is down but you don't know why. You find out that a substantial percentage of your customers are interested in a piece of functionality but you don't learn what is driving that interest. Of course, this is not a problem if you combine the survey with more exploratory techniques such as focus groups or customer visits. It is a big problem if you were expecting to do only survey research for your market research effort.

A related but more subtle weakness is that typically, a survey cannot reveal what you didn't know you didn't know. If you *do* know what it is that you don't know ("known unknowns," as the phrase has it), then you can devise the questions and the answer categories needed to resolve that uncertainty. Thus, surveys can readily answer a question such as "Which of these problems is most commonly experienced by our customers?" However, surveys aren't very good at answering questions such as, "What new and unsuspected problems have recently begun to bother our customers?" This is because surveys emphasize closed-ended questions in which the answer categories are specified rather than open-ended questions. In a word, surveys are a precision tool, not a discovery tool.

Another weakness of surveys is that they rely on self-report data. If the customer does not know something, cannot or will not verbalize that something, or cannot accurately recall that something, then a survey will not reveal it. Some examples of information you might like to gain but that customers may be unable to self-report include (a) what they will do in the future, (b) what the most important factor is in their purchase decision (they can tell you what they think is important, but will this be reflected in their actual behavior?), (c) what other people in their organization think or do, (d) exactly how much time or money they spent on something, (e) which parts of the user interface cause them to make errors, and so forth. Just as the weaknesses of surveys with respect to explanation and discovery drive you to supplement surveys with focus groups and customer visits, so also the weaknesses associated with self-report data should drive you to supplement descriptive surveys with experimentation. In experiments, people *act* and *choose* rather than or in addition to *speaking and reporting*, and analyses of these actions and choices can reveal matters of which the customer is unaware or that the customer is incapable of verbalizing.

A more subtle weakness of survey research is that most of the time, for most people, participation in a survey is intrinsically unrewarding. This is one reason why phone surveys in commercial market research rather quickly drove out most mail surveys: It was harder to ignore or dismiss a phone call as opposed to a letter. Surveys are just not fun. People participate out of inertia, out of a sense of obligation (recognizing that their information is probably useful), or to give voice (more likely in the case of aggrieved customers, which of course introduces a bias). In comparison to an interview, which is a person-to-person encounter and which offers potential rewards such as feeling understood, getting through to someone else, learning something, being stimulated to think, enjoying company, and so forth, ultimately, participating in a survey means being mechanically processed as grist for a statistical mill—an opportunity to be a generic instance of a population rather than a unique individual. How does that make you feel?

Two implications follow from this weakness. First, surveys tend to be most useful for getting broad but shallow data. You can't ask hard, provocative, challenging questions because respondents won't play. You can't do extensive follow-up on answers because you are not employing phone interviewers with that level of skill (and a web survey cannot have too many branching paths). Second, surveys have to be designed to minimize the costs of responding and to maximize the rewards (Dillman, Smyth, & Christian, 1999). In designing a survey, you have to drive toward brevity and ease of responding. Otherwise, the cost goes way up and the quality goes down. If the survey is too taxing, so many people will discontinue taking it that the representativeness of your obtained sample will be called into question.

Yet another weakness, implicit in much of what has been said earlier, is that surveys are only as good as the sample and the questions used. It would be fascinating to study how American society developed to the point where ordinary college-educated people became prone to assume that surveys are clear glass windows onto the truth. The source of this delusion might be the respect paid to quantification or perhaps the rhetorical power of anything that sounds scientific. Howsoever, from my perspective as someone holding a PhD in social psychology and having a smattering of philosophy of science, it is nothing short of appalling how credulous the average businessperson becomes when confronted with a survey. DON'T FALL INTO THIS TRAP! Gazing at a four-color pie chart, the tendency is to say "Wow—63 percent of the market wants the product to do this—let's build that functionality in!" A more accurate statement would often be,

> Sixty-three percent of the people we managed to get on the phone, whose names happened to be on the only list we could afford, and who stuck with us to this point in the survey, answered the only question we knew to ask with an indifferent "sure, why not?"

Don't kid yourself that a survey yields truth. Think instead of surveys as yielding one more fallible data point, to be combined with other data that are fallible for different reasons, as input to a decision that ultimately remains your own but that is more likely to be successful because you gathered and integrated diverse kinds of data.

A final weakness of survey research applies mostly to business-to-business markets in which the characteristic purchase decision is made by a group rather than an individual. A survey of individuals is unlikely to address the group decision-making process effectively. Even if the total survey includes people holding various job roles, it probably was not designed to include the full set of job roles from each company included in the sample. This is one of the great advantages of on-site customer visits: You can meet with several decision makers at each firm you visit, alone or in groups.

DOs AND DON'Ts

Don't fall into the trap of assuming that a large sample size can overcome sample bias. True, small samples give unstable results, independent of whether there is systematic bias; but once the sample size is adequate, further doubling or tripling its size does not in any way reduce whatever systematic bias may be present. If your list contains an unusual percentage of chemists with PhDs relative to the total population of chemists, then your obtained sample is going to be biased by this high education level, regardless of how big the sample is or how high the response rate might be. Hence, there is no substitute for a good list or sampling procedure.

Do look at confidence intervals on all means and percentages contained in survey reports. Be sure to find out how big the difference between two numbers has to be before you can be confident that that difference is real.

Do conduct focus groups or customer visits in preparation for surveys. Look to these exploratory procedures for information on what topics to include in the surveys, what language to use, what questions to ask, and what answer categories to use.

Do prepare rough tables and table headings for all frequency counts and cross-tabulations you expect to produce in the analysis of the survey. The point of doing this is to see whether you actually have a use for or need of certain questions. The tendency in survey design is to ask lots of questions in the hope that something interesting will emerge. This is a bad idea. When you are forced to rough out table headings in advance, you will find yourself asking, in certain cases, "What's the point? What good will this do me?" Whenever you ask that, your next question should be, "Should I even bother with this particular item on the survey?" Often the answer is no.

Don't indulge idle curiosity. The longer the survey, the more it will cost and the more likely the obtained sample will prove to be unrepresentative because of excessive attrition. Every question in the survey should do a job that needs doing. If you can't meet this standard—if your basic feeling is one of overwhelming ignorance or uncertainty, and this is the factor driving you toward the kitchen-sink approach to survey design—then you probably are not ready to conduct a survey. You need to do more secondary research, customer visits, or focus groups.

Do ask managers to predict the results of key questions. Ask them what the major points of difference will be between two groups. Ask them to predict the approximate percentage of agreement and disagreement with certain opinion statements. Get them on the record. The point of doing this is to make it impossible to say, after a survey has been done, "We already knew that," when in fact the results are a surprise. Documenting the fact that survey research yielded a fresh perspective and corrected some misunderstandings is one of the ways that you establish the value of market research to your organization.

Do think of the survey in terms of a social exchange between sponsor and respondent. Exchanges are facilitated when you find ways to minimize the perceived cost of the exchange and maximize the perceived benefits. In the case of surveys, you minimize the cost by keeping them short and making the questions as clear and easy to answer as possible. You maximize the benefits by making the questions relevant and of obvious importance—things a customer would want a vendor to know about or understand.

DISCUSSION QUESTIONS

1. The claim was made that event sampling may be more useful and actionable than the traditional approach of sampling people, especially in the context of assessing customer satisfaction with a service.

    a. Evaluate this claim. Be specific about the circumstances where it will hold and the boundaries past which event sampling either isn't pertinent or isn't superior to people sampling.

2. It was asserted that evaluative surveys, which describe a customer's stance toward the brand or positive and negative experiences with product ownership, might by and large be more valuable than surveys that simply describe customer characteristics and behaviors. Why is that?

3. The author clearly believes that too many surveys of indifferent quality are conducted, at least in the context of commercial market research in the United States around the turn of the 21st century.

   a. Do you agree? If so, what is the explanation? Is it a function of organizational realities, the personal proclivities of the kind of people who become marketing managers, the cultural Zeitgeist, or something else?

   b. You may choose to disagree. Support your position by locating examples of past surveys and explaining their probable value to the sponsor. Restriction: The survey must be primarily descriptive.

4. Exercise. Design a survey for a company or product category that you know well. Your write-up needs to include: (1) statement of the decision problem, with background information as necessary; (2) specific research objectives; (3) research design, including the population from which you will sample, the sampling procedure, and the size of the initial and obtained samples (read the quantitative sampling chapter first); (4) the questionnaire to be used for the survey (read next chapter first); (5) mock-ups of two or three of the key tables that you expect to include in the report; and (6) a brief discussion of how management might respond, depending on how the results, for the tables just mocked up, play out.

SUGGESTED READINGS

Alreck, P., & Settle, R. (2003). *Survey research handbook* (3rd ed.). New York, NY: McGraw-Hill.	There is a vast amount of material on conducting surveys, and many technical issues that occupy experts. This handbook provides a window into that specialized literature.
Dillman, D. A., Smyth, J. D., & Christian, L. M. (1999). *Internet, mail and mixed-mode surveys: The tailored design method* (3rd ed.). New York, NY: Wiley.	This is a how-to-do-it reference, guided by a coherent philosophy of what a survey must be like if it is to get a decent response rate.

Cooper, B., & Phillips, M. (2010). *Custom surveys within your budget: Maximizing profits through effective online research design.* Ithaca, NY: Paramount Publishing.	Helpful if you intend to go the do-it-yourself route using a web survey.
www.qualtrics.com	A good example of software for constructing web surveys. If you are a student, your institution may have a license, allowing you to use the site for free to conduct surveys. The search term "free web survey software" will direct you to other such sites.

TEN

QUESTIONNAIRE DESIGN

-----◆•◆-----

A s we saw in the introduction to Chapter 9, *questionnaire* is a broader and more inclusive term than *survey*. A questionnaire may be defined as any fixed set of questions intended to be completed by some group of respondents. The key point is that the set of questions to be asked and the arrangement of those questions are fixed in advance. This is why it is bad form to refer to the discussion guides used in qualitative research as questionnaires; with discussion guides, anything can vary from interview to interview, including the questions that actually get asked, their sequence, their phrasing, and so forth. Also central to the idea of a questionnaire is the expectation that these fixed questions will be administered to a large number of respondents so that the distribution of answers to any given question is the focus of interest. With a questionnaire, you are generally uninterested in the fact that John Smith gave a "no" answer to question 17. This is because you aren't interested in learning about John Smith the individual; rather, you want to understand the population of which he is a member. You want to know what percentage of the total sample gave a "no" answer to question 17. If you are developing fixed sets of questions to be completed by individual customers with the goal of better understanding each individual who answers, it is probably better to refer to these questions as a form, an instrument, documentation, or just paperwork. Job applications, registration forms, and standardized achievement tests all contain fixed sets of questions but are not typically referred to as questionnaires.

The advice in this chapter concerns only questionnaires as defined earlier. Unless otherwise noted, I have in mind a questionnaire designed as part of a survey research project. However, much of the advice also applies to other kinds of questionnaires. Nonsurvey applications of the questionnaire would include those used in concept tests (to be discussed in Chapter 11), the evaluation forms often completed by customers after a training session or other event, warranty cards, and so forth. The assumption that guides the treatment in this chapter is that the customer's completion of the questionnaire is to some degree elective or optional—in other words, a survey questionnaire is typically a document that the customer is quite free to toss in the wastebasket, close, or delete. Hence, the need to motivate the customer to participate and to complete the questionnaire once begun becomes an important design criterion.

PROCEDURE

The procedure for devising a questionnaire is similar in outline to the procedure for designing an interview discussed in Chapter 7. Both tasks have a creative component and an iterative aspect.

1. Generate a list of potential topics to be covered and the kind of information to be collected. A group session with a white board may be helpful. This session will work best, however, if the team leader brings a short list to serve as a seed. (More information on generating the content for a questionnaire can be found in the next section.)

2. Construct a first draft of the questionnaire. This draft should consist of actual questions and answer categories in the expected sequence. Lists of topics and categories of information only take you so far; at a relatively early point in the design process, it is important to draft something that looks like a questionnaire, not a bulleted list. Many problems only become evident when one attempts to take the vague "information on applications for the product" and translate it into a specific question with answer categories. Generally speaking, the project leader undertakes this draft. If there are problems with the scope or thrust of the desired information, these generally become apparent when the initial draft is attempted. Thus, the number of questions required to come even close to covering a topic may prove unacceptably large (this may happen when the topic is better suited to a customer visit or other exploratory

techniques). Or a seemingly simple topic might have so many contingencies associated with it as to be unwieldy. What makes questionnaire design difficult is that the questions have to stand on their own; there is little opportunity, even if administered by an interviewer, for someone to assist the customer in grappling with difficult questions (either the phone staff is not sufficiently knowledgeable or too many heterogeneous, improvised clarifications to the questionnaire make it unlikely that answers can be meaningfully aggregated). The process of drafting actual questions brings such issues to the fore.

3. As with any creative task, one of the best things for the leader to do, following completion of the first draft, is to put it aside for a few days—at least overnight and preferably until later in the week or over the weekend. Then, take another look at the draft. You'll be surprised how many changes often get made on your second attempt at a first draft. The worst thing to do is to complete the first draft and then immediately attach it to a broadcast e-mail requesting comments from the team. The most likely outcome of such speedy action is that several of your teammates will decide that you are perhaps not so capable a questionnaire designer as they had hoped.

4. Let me acknowledge that this advice is much easier for a professor to follow than for the typical overburdened manager. However, the poor working conditions that many managers must endure—for that is what they are—don't change this fundamental fact of human cognitive processing: There is a digestion component in any design activity. When you put aside the questionnaire draft, at least overnight, your total intelligence, of which the processes immediately available to the conscious mind are only a part, has the opportunity to go to work on the problem and uncover new perspectives or alternative avenues of attack. In short, the construction of questionnaires, unlike memos, status reports, and similar appurtenances to bureaucratic life, represents a design process that benefits from being broken up into iterations over time.

5. Once the team leader is satisfied that the best possible draft has been created, it is now useful to circulate that draft more widely for comments and critique. A meeting may be useful to incorporate or address the comments made by various parties. A reason that group input to the draft questionnaire is so helpful at this point is that any one person designing a questionnaire will have a particular cognitive style and probably some quirks in terms of chosen mode of expression. However, the questionnaire has to succeed in being clear and understandable across a wide range of respondents with

diverse cognitive styles. Having the questionnaire vetted by a group typically uncovers idiosyncratic turns of phrase or approaches to the subject matter that would fail to be clear to respondents not having the same cognitive style as the questionnaire drafter. In sum, revisions suggested by the team, all other things being equal, serve to make the questionnaire more robust against misunderstanding. Of course, if the team consists exclusively of graduates of a particular MIT engineering program, this robustness is unlikely to be achieved; but most teams incorporate some diversity.

Another benefit of having a wider group vet the draft is that key omissions are likely to be uncovered—topics at least as pertinent to the research objective as those included but that for some reason fell within the team leader's blind spot. Similarly, the draft questionnaire will almost always be excessively long. It is useful for the team as a whole to discuss which topics and questions have the lowest priority to facilitate subsequent editing and shortening.

6. The team leader, or whoever is ultimately responsible for devising the questionnaire, should then retire and produce another draft. If the project is complex, there is a lot at stake, or the principal parties are relatively new to questionnaire design, then this draft again should be circulated for comments. Most of the major problems will have been resolved by this point, but there may still be many opportunities to improve the phrasing of question stems and answer categories. Plus, there are probably one or two topics where the best approach remains uncertain or controversial.

7. After incorporating feedback on this draft, the questionnaire designer should attempt a penultimate draft. This draft should observe all length constraints, phrasing and sequencing should be in their proposed final form, and interviewer instructions (if it is to be administered by phone or in person) or preparatory material (if it is to be self-administered in print, by mail, or over the web) should be drafted.

8. In any project where the stakes are substantial, a pretest should now be conducted. A small sample of people from the respondent pool should be enlisted to complete the questionnaire and then discuss their experiences in so doing. Such a pretest serves as a final disaster check and almost always introduces additional clarity at the margin.

9. The final version of the questionnaire is then ready to be administered.

GENERATING CONTENT FOR QUESTIONNAIRES

The preceding section described a collaborative process for moving from the blank page to a completed questionnaire. Here I take a closer look at possible sources for the specific questions and answer categories that will make up the questionnaire. Most survey questionnaires contain three types of content: (1) questions that allow you to categorize the respondents into subgroups; (2) questions that solicit the specifics of and maybe the frequency of events, behaviors, or responses; and (3) rating scales. Hence, one way to rough out a questionnaire is to simply list these headings at the top of three blank sheets of paper.

The easiest piece is the categorization set, because these questions will often be standard, or copied from a previous effort. In a consumer context, you typically want to know age and gender, maybe income and education, perhaps family size. These variables are referred to as demographics (characteristics of people). More subtly, you may want to know what brand(s) have been purchased and whether respondents are loyal to a particular brand. In a B2B context, you often want to know number of employees and revenue so you can categorize respondents as enterprise versus small or medium customers. You probably want to know job title and the respondent's role in the purchase or use process. Whether B2C or B2B, any such question is going to allow you to break out and compare responses of younger and older consumers, larger and smaller businesses, managers versus individual contributors, and so forth. The important thing to understand about categorization questions is that while every questionnaire needs a few, they are exceedingly boring and unrewarding for respondents. Hence, in almost all cases, categorization questions should be placed at the end so as not to be off-putting. This advice is so often ignored by beginners in questionnaire design that I'm going to repeat it later in this chapter.

The second type of content is extremely diverse and varies a great deal across questionnaires. In a B2B context, this might include questions about applications, processes, or responses. Maybe you want to know how they go about upgrading a piece of software and the incidence of particular problems. Or maybe you want to know how they go about issuing a request for proposals. Or perhaps you want to count outages or work stoppages or quantify the time a particular process takes. The list is endless because this is the section that most differentiates any one questionnaire from another. This variability makes it the toughest section to get right or to generate in the first place. Questions in this section are going to be used to profile the respondents ("The average IT manager has to conduct 2.6 software upgrades per month") or will be cross-tabulated with categorization questions ("Twice as many enterprise customers reported this problem") or with rating scales ("Satisfaction was greater among small distributors as compared to large").

The third type of content is diverse in terms of the question stems for rating scales used but standardized in terms of the form or format of these scales. For instance, if you are going to measure the components of satisfaction, the individual components named in the stem will be very different for a bank versus a network switch; but the scale used will probably range from "Not at all satisfied" to "Completely satisfied" in each case. You can fiddle with the endpoints ("very dissatisfied" vs. "very satisfied"), but there are only a couple of feasible alternatives if your goal is to have customers rate satisfaction on some kind of a scale. Visually, this type of content takes the form of a block, with the item text or question stem in a column on the left and the scales laid out horizontally beside them. Later, I'll introduce a few other types of rating scales other than satisfaction; there are half a dozen scale types that appear regularly.

Now that you know the basic types of content to be generated, start the drafting process by revisiting your research objectives. Try to translate these in a direct way into topics to be covered in the questionnaire. Thus, if the objective is to describe the process used to qualify new vendors, possible topics include (1) Who plays a role in vendor selection? (2) How is vendor qualification triggered? and (3) How often is the preferred vendor list revised or updated? Similarly, if the objective is to prioritize customer requirements, then the first step is to list the known requirements, and the second step is to decide whether customers will rate the importance of each one, rank order the list from most to least important, and so forth. The point is that if the research objectives have been well chosen, then they should map fairly directly onto the content of the final questionnaire, with topics or categories of information serving as the bridging terms.

Next, review past questionnaires from within and without your organization. The first reason to do this is that there is no point in reinventing the wheel. Many of the questions that appear in any one market research questionnaire will also appear in other market research questionnaires produced in that firm. This is particularly true for categorization questions and rating scales; countless firms across the whole spectrum of industries and technologies ask some version of these questions over and over. If someone else has already hammered out a serviceable phrasing, customized to fit your industry, then there is no point in starting from scratch. You are still responsible for making an independent judgment as to whether the phrasing and answer categories are suitable (existing questionnaires may be of poor quality), but there is no need to shut yourself away from existing precedents when generating items for a questionnaire. (If you wanted to devise completely novel kinds of questions, you should have gone into academia, not industry.)

The second reason for reviewing prior questionnaires is to ensure that both your questions and your answer categories are consistent with prior data. Given this consistency, many interesting and fruitful comparisons can potentially be drawn between your new data and other existing data. This point is obvious in the case of satisfaction data—one is almost always interested in comparing present satisfaction levels to past levels and this group's satisfaction level to some other group's level—but it applies to all kinds of questionnaire content. In a sense, you multiply the analytic power and potential of your results whenever you include questions and answer categories that have been used in other past questionnaires.

The point applies most strongly to the answer categories. There may be a dozen different ways to phrase a question about global satisfaction with a purchase, all roughly equivalent in meaning and equally suited to this purpose. The important thing is whether, for the answer categories, both present and prior questionnaires used a five-point scale labeled only at the extremes with "very satisfied" and "very dissatisfied" or whether one questionnaire instead used a four-point scale with each step labeled respectively as "completely satisfied," "satisfied," "partially satisfied," and "not satisfied." There is no exact way to equate the distribution of answers to the five-point and four-point scales just described and, hence, no way to say whether the satisfaction of the one group of customers measured the one way is greater or lesser than the satisfaction of another group measured the other way. It behooves you to avoid this trap by standardizing on a particular set of answer categories for questions of this sort. Get it right and stick to it.

As an aside, there do not seem to be any copyright issues when one copies a single item or set of answer categories from an existing instrument. Even if copyright pertains, it would generally apply to the questionnaire in its entirety and only with respect to exact duplications of it. Moreover, the owner of the prior questionnaire would have difficulty showing that no one else had ever asked the question that way. (Imagine attempting to assert a copyright on either of the satisfaction answer scales just described.) Of course, I am not qualified to give legal advice, and if you are duplicating a substantial proportion of what is clearly someone else's unique effort, then you may wish to consult an attorney knowledgeable in matters of intellectual property.

The next step is to consult textbooks on market research, survey research, and questionnaire design. Most such sources contain many examples of different approaches to asking and answering the basic questions that appear over and over in market research. As mentioned under the Suggested Readings section for the survey chapter, some purveyors of web survey tools maintain sets of questionnaire templates, which may provide a useful starting point.

Last, the ultimate source of questionnaire content is, of course, your own background knowledge and ingenuity. The more time you have spent within an industry, the more copious your knowledge of product applications, key classifications that distinguish different segments of customers, and so forth. In terms of ingenuity, it helps to envision yourself having a conversation with an articulate customer within the target population. Simply write down what you would need to ask this person conversationally to determine whether she was, for instance, satisfied or dissatisfied and in what customer grouping she could best be placed. Ultimately, a questionnaire is still just one person asking another person a series of questions, albeit in a highly formalized and mechanized way.

BEST PRACTICES AND RULES TO OBSERVE

The advice in this section is organized under three headings with respect to the questionnaire as a whole, the phrasing of individual questions, and the selection and calibration of answer categories. The greater the likelihood that respondents will refuse to participate or fail to complete the questionnaire, the more important these rules will be. In that sense, many of these suggestions deal with how to motivate people to participate and how to keep them motivated through completion of the questionnaire. Most of the remainder concern ways to maximize the accuracy, meaningfulness, and utility of the information obtained via the questionnaire.

The Questionnaire as a Whole

1. Maximize the perceived rewards of responding and minimize the perceived costs.

This general piece of advice is developed at length by Dillman, Smyth, and Christian (1999). The next few rules give some specific examples of how to do this. Reward maximization combined with cost minimization represents the fundamental formula for motivating respondents. As mentioned in Chapter 9, in the case of most questionnaires prepared for use in commercial market research, there really aren't very many rewards for the respondent, and the costs of participation, in terms of lost time and frustration, are immediate and very real. Hence, most questionnaires require an introduction that stresses the importance and value of the respondent's participation. It is more rewarding to participate in an important enterprise as opposed to a trivial one. If you can't write such an introduction with a straight face or really don't believe what you've written, then I suggest you either ramp up the financial incentives for participating or consider whether the questionnaire is worth doing at all. How helpful will it be to analyze responses given by a few obstinate and opinionated respondents who persevered through to completion despite being bored to tears?

2. Shorter is better.

Every factor internal to your own corporate processes will tend to drive up questionnaire length. Everyone on the team has a pet topic, important bosses must be placated, the issues are complicated, the segmentation scheme is elaborate, there are numerous past studies with which you wish to be comparable, and so forth. To fight back, keep in mind that (a) survey costs are a power function of survey length—costs go up faster than the unit change in length, and beyond a certain length, costs skyrocket; (b) response rate and completion rate both drop rapidly as length increases—and the lower these rates, the less reliable the information gained; and (c) the incidence of unthinking or essentially random responses increases rapidly once the survey comes to seem long in the respondent's eyes. In short, failure to trim back the questionnaire may ruin the entire study so that little useful information is gained on even the most central and important issues.

As a rule of thumb, in print terms, the questionnaire should be four pages or less. One page is a wonderful target but often not feasible. For phone questionnaires, 15 minutes is a useful target, and five minutes, like the one-page questionnaire, is a wonderful target. It is certainly true that length restrictions can be relaxed when participation is to some degree compelled, either because of financial incentives or because the audience is to some degree captive. However, there remains a threshold beyond which the randomness of response increases rapidly.

3. Cluster the related content and seek a natural flow.

This is one of those small steps that can have a marked effect on the perceived cost and hassle factor of participation. If instead topics are addressed in essentially random order and the questionnaire jumps back and forth between topics, the effect is wearisome.

4. Place demographic and other classification questions last.

However crucial to the analyses, these are the most boring questions imaginable from the standpoint of the typical respondent and, hence, must be placed last so as not to poison the well.

5. Lead with questions that are clearly relevant, interesting, and nonthreatening.

If the initial questions stimulate thought (unlike a query about one's gender or age) and appear clearly important for a vendor to understand, then the perceived rewards of participation in the survey are enhanced. It comes to seem interesting and engaging rather than tedious and off-putting.

6. Use plenty of white space and seek the most professional appearance possible consistent with time and budget.

White space makes the questionnaire seem easy to complete (i.e., minimizes the costs of participation). In web surveys, this translates to chunking content such that no one screen seems too cluttered or too long. Rigorous proofing, clear language, and useful answer categories are imperative. Anyone today can fire up a word processor, invoke a numbered and bulleted template, and obtain something that looks like a bona fide questionnaire as fast as one can type. And anyone can pull down a few web survey templates, jam together content, and tap the *send* button. But when the construction of the survey betrays carelessness and haste, inevitably the message sent is, I didn't spend much time on this. What effect do you suppose that message has on the respondent?

Question Phrasing

1. Keep it simple.

Other things being equal, the shorter the question, the better. Plan on using simple language; targeting an eighth-grade reading level is about right. It is true that in technical industries it may be necessary to use technical vocabulary, but that is no excuse for complicating the syntax. Even in the best of cases, the respondent is probably reading rapidly with less than full attention. You want to be understood despite these constraints.

Sometimes there is no choice but to depart from the ideal of simplicity. For instance, your questionnaire may need to include a branch (i.e., "If your answer is no, skip to Question X.") One branch will work if carefully handled, and maybe two. If you have more than two branches, nested branches, and so on, respondents will start dropping like flies. Remember, the easiest response when frustration or confusion occurs is to simply chuck the questionnaire. Hence, complexity is like length—it has to be fought every step of the way.

Now the good news is that web surveys make branching invisible to the respondent—the software takes the respondent down one branch or the other and then returns them to the main stem, skipping anything irrelevant. In this instance, the limit on branching becomes your own limit in terms of handling complexity. Too many branches suggests to me that you really wanted to interview individuals, not survey a mass.

2. Be specific.

At the level of the individual question, this rule sometimes conflicts with the previous one. Consider, for instance, a simple approach to asking about income:

"How much do you make?"

It is hard to ask this question in fewer words! (Maybe, "What do you earn?") The problem is the vast range of possible answers, depending on how a given respondent interprets either question: Should I give my hourly rate? My annual salary? Should I include my bonus? What about dividends? We're a two-income household; does he want both? To eliminate such ambiguity, which would render the average answer meaningless, since, in essence, respondents were answering different questions, you may be forced into a lengthier phrasing that is less subject to ambiguity:

> What was your total household income last year, including salaries, bonuses, dividends, and other income?

Although longer, the question is still clear and is more likely to produce usable information (allowing for the fact that no matter how you ask a question about income, some proportion of respondents will refuse to answer).

3a. Ask mostly closed-ended questions.

A closed-ended question supplies specific answer categories that the respondent need only check off ("Which of the following kinds of documents have you created on your tablet?"). An open-ended question requires the respondent to generate and then to write in all the answers that pertain (i.e., "What documents have you created on your home PC?" followed by a series of blank lines). Open-ended questions, while ideal for qualitative research, are problematic in questionnaires because they require so much more effort to respond to and are so subject to forgetting and to salience biases, making responses less comparable across respondents.

3b. Always ask a couple of open-ended questions.

Conversely, especially in the context of satisfaction surveys or other questionnaires where there is a crucial, central question that divides respondents into groups (e.g., happy or unhappy customers), always follow the key question with an open-ended comment box that allows customers to elaborate upon why they checked "would not recommend to a friend" or something similar. Reading through these verbatims, as they are called, can be enormously helpful in understanding why people are dissatisfied, not planning to repurchase, negatively disposed toward a brand, and so forth.

4. Minimize demands on memory.

If most respondents would have to consult some paper record to give a truly accurate answer, then the question needs to be rephrased. (Respondents won't consult a record, resulting in guesses of widely varying accuracy.)

An example would be the question, "How many times did you eat out at a restaurant in the past six months?" Better would be to ask, "How many times did you eat dinner at a restaurant in the last month?" with answer categories of zero, once, twice, more often. Taking the immediate past as representative and using this latter phrasing likely offers all the accuracy you can hope to obtain.

5. Match questions to how the market works.

Suppose you ask a question like, "How many brands of turkey stuffing can you recall?" Many consumers, even avid homemakers, are likely to report "none." Does that mean that all the brand advertising in this category has been wasted? More likely, this is a product category where purchases are made by recognition rather than recall—when there is a need for stuffing, the shopper seeks out the aisle where this product is shelved, encounters the available packages, and only at that point retrieves from memory any relevant brand information. It is pointless in such a category to ask about recall; better to reproduce the packages or the brand names, complete with logo, and ask respondents to check any brands they recognize and any they have purchased during some past time interval.

To give another example, in a technology context, one may be interested in perceptions of the brand relative to its competitors to the extent of wanting to ask detailed comparative questions about strengths and weaknesses of each brand. If the questionnaire goes to a manager or to a member of a buying group that has recently had occasion to solicit bids from different vendors, then these questions may work just fine. If, instead, the questionnaire goes to individual users of the same vendors' products, in many cases, these users will have experience of *only one vendor* and may never have used any other vendor's product in this category. Nonetheless, many respondents will do their best to answer the questions about all the other vendors despite near total ignorance. The result? Garbage.

6. Avoided loaded questions.

Loaded questions contain "angel" or "devil" words. For example:

Do you think the power of big union bosses needs to be curbed?

Or, for those of you of an alternative political persuasion:

Do you think fat cat executives should be allowed to ship American jobs overseas?

The best tone to strike is mild mannered and matter of fact. Keep question phrasing as neutral as possible. If the topic is controversial, give respondents a way to express their position, whether pro or con. The questionnaire should equally accommodate respondents who naturally think in terms of "worker's rights" versus "union bosses," or "free enterprise" versus "fat cat executives."

Answer Categories

1. Use the right number of answer categories, no more and no fewer than necessary.

For any given question, there is an optimum number of answer categories. Some factual questions, such as whether an event has occurred or something is present in the home, really are yes–no questions and benefit from having exactly two answer categories. Other factual questions, such as education level, may require four or more answer categories (did not finish high school, high school grad, some college, college grad, master's, doctorate). When a question has four or more possible answers, it is almost always worth asking whether it would be better to collapse some of these categories. With respect to the education example, one can imagine many contexts in technology industries or, in the case of products targeted at affluent people, where a high portion of the respondents will have a college degree and many will have diverse graduate degrees, so that the only useful distinction is no college degree, college degree, graduate degree. In my experience, beginning questionnaire designers are excessively enamored with precision and with attempting to capture all possible categories of response, as in the education example. A helpful discipline is to look ahead to the ultimate analysis and make several mock-up tables involving the question. It is rare that very many 5 × 5 cross-tabulations appear in commercial survey reports (or are interpretable when they do). Often, the first thing that happens as analysis proceeds is that categories get collapsed in order to make important findings more salient. Thus the analyst, looking at the distribution of replies and finding many almost empty cells (i.e., less than high school education + income over $250,000 annually) or finding a breakpoint where results shift, quickly recodes the education variable as college degree: yes–no. All further tables involving this variable are then presented in that two-column format to highlight the fact that those without a college degree have very different responses. If this kind of outcome can be anticipated, then you might as well reduce the number of answer categories on the questionnaire itself.

As a general rule, if categories are likely to be collapsed in the analysis, they might as well be collapsed in questionnaire design so as to simplify the respondent's task. Of course, this rule can be broken from time to time. Thus, one might distinguish college grads with and without graduate degrees, just in case having even more education accentuates the effect of interest, even as one is prepared to collapse these categories after the initial examination of the data. But if a designer makes this same choice every time, always proliferating categories "just in case," the questionnaire becomes longer and more unwieldy than necessary, with a lower response rate and more respondent fatigue, adding more random noise to the answers. Hence, the thrust of this piece of advice remains: Fewer categories are better.

There is one other occasion where answer categories may be proliferated, and that is when this proliferation increases respondent comfort and ease. An important instance of this phenomenon occurs when you wish customers to react to various statements of opinion by agreeing or disagreeing. Technically speaking, there may be only three distinct responses to a statement such as "Windows software seems vulnerable to viruses"—agree, neither agree nor disagree, disagree.

However, when responding to a series of such items, respondents may start thinking, "I guess that's right, but I don't feel nearly as strongly as I did on the previous one, so maybe I should check 'neither'!" This obscures what you are trying to learn, which is this person's initial lean toward or away from the opinion proffered. Hence, when using agree–disagree items, it is standard practice to differentiate "strongly agree" from "agree" and "strongly disagree" from "disagree." This allows respondents to feel that their answers reflect distinctions in how strongly they feel about one opinion versus another and increases their comfort that the survey is going to yield meaningful results and hence is worth completing. However, pursuing this logic one more step and using a seven-point scale for agree–disagree items is generally a mistake. There isn't any consensus as to whether the responses in the seven-point case should be labeled "strongly agree," "quite agree," and "sort of agree" (or by some other set of qualifiers) or any stability in how these labels are interpreted by ordinary people. ("Quite" is a word that is quite a bit more common on campus than off.) The "fewer is better" rule applies again; stick to five categories (or sometimes four; see the following) when using agree–disagree items.

2. Distinguish between bipolar and unipolar response types and match answer categories to response type.

Every beginner knows about the agree–disagree answer format. Based on the questionnaires that cross my desk, especially from students, this is also the only scaled answer format most beginners ever use. Stop it already! There are a couple of other scaled answer formats that are more robust and have wider utility than the agree–disagree format, which, when properly used, has a very narrow application. Good questionnaire design distinguishes between issues that have a natural pro or con element (for which the bipolar agree–disagree response is appropriate) and other issues where the underlying response continuum is unipolar, ranging from zero to a lot. Consider the difference between these question prompts:

"Baseball is a wholesome sport."

"The Cubs will lose the World Series."

"I enjoy watching baseball on TV."

Arguably, only the first statement is well suited to an agree–disagree format. It is a classic statement of an opinion that concerns an intangible predicate. The second statement is really a request for an assessment of probability, itself a unipolar judgment. One is asking for the respondent's subjective probability that the event will occur, and the logical response categories would be anchored by something such as "0 percent probability" and "100 percent probability." The third statement is really seeking to discover how well this description fits the respondent. The logical response scale is again unipolar, anchored by "Does not describe me at all" and "Describes me very well." The point of these examples is that some questions admit of opposite responses, whereas in other cases, responses vary only in terms of the degree to which they deviate from some zero point. The first may be appropriate for agree–disagree items; the second is not. Failure to attend to this difference undercuts the quality of the data collected.

3. Attend to the integration of the set of answer categories used for a question.

By *integration*, I mean that the answer categories collectively have to be mutually exclusive, have to exhaust the possibilities for responding to the

question, and must also not contain any superfluous or heterogeneous categories. The easiest way to convey this point is to illustrate typical violations.
Consider the question ",What is your age?"

Answer Set A	Answer Set B
< 18	< 18
19–25	18–25
25–34	26–35
35–44	36–45
45–54	46–55
> 54	56–65
	Retired

With answer set A, there is no category for a person who is exactly 18, and
a person who is 25 has a choice of two categories. With answer set B, the very
different category of retirement status is mixed in with categories that distinguish
age. Errors of this sort are common in first drafts of questionnaires; it is one of
the reasons why having other team members scrutinize a draft is so powerful.

*4. Think carefully about whether to include a "don't know," "no
opinion," or similar "not applicable" response category.*

There are no simple hard-and-fast rules about when to include an "opt-
out" response category. If I am asking respondents to rate their satisfaction
with aspects of a service, not all of which may have been personally experienced by all respondents, I think it is good practice to include an opt-out
response. Basically, if a respondent has never called tech support, he can't be
either satisfied or dissatisfied with its responsiveness. If you omit the opt-out
category and include a neutral or mixed category (reasonable when measuring
satisfaction), some proportion of the "neutral" responses will represent people
with no experience of the service who settled on the neutral category as the
closest to "not applicable." The result is to muddy the data, especially when
comparing service aspects that vary widely in the number of customers who
have any experience of the aspect. There might be an aspect experienced by
few but very satisfying to those with experience that comes across in the
results as a weak or problematic aspect because of the number of people who

wanted to check "not applicable" but settled on the middle category instead, resulting in a lower average score for that aspect.

Conversely, if I am seeking to discover whether customers lean one way or another with respect to some subjective evaluation where there is no factual right or wrong and where anyone can have a viewpoint without needing to have some specific kind of experience, I may choose to omit both the opt-out response and the neutral response and use a four-point scale with two levels of agree and disagree. This is particularly true when seeking top-of-mind initial impressions about intangibles. For instance, when measuring brand percep-tions, you might want to present a series of statements such as, "Apple is a fun brand," "Apple attracts people who think differently," and so forth. If given the neutral option, the more stolid respondents may well choose it at different levels of frequency across different questions, saying to themselves something like "darned if I know." In fact, a great deal of brand knowledge is tacit but sufficient for people to have a leaning one way or the other if forced. The intent of the question is precisely to tap into this tacit knowledge and to do so uniformly across items and respondent temperaments, hence, the utility of forcing respondents to lean one way or the other.

On the other hand, I can envision questions where many respondents genuinely have no opinion because it is clearly an issue requiring some reflec-tion, which they haven't had the opportunity for. Here, an opt-out response makes sense because you may not be interested in the snap judgments of people who haven't really formed an opinion. Thus, a brokerage firm might present investors with a statement such as, "Do you favor having option prices quoted in minimum increments of one cent, as opposed to 5 cents and 10 cents, as is done currently?" An opt-out response will be gratefully accepted by many respondents in such an instance, and the proportion of investors who don't have an opinion on this score may be of interest in its own right.

I hope these three examples give some taste of the complexity involved in deciding whether to include an opt-out option. Most experienced practitioners are able to make a judgment in a specific case about whether an opt-out response seems appropriate, but it is difficult to abstract a simple set of rules underlying these judgments.

5. Use ratings rather than rankings.

In ranking, say, the importance of each of a set of things, the respondent has to indicate which is most important, which is second most important, and so forth. If the number of items is greater than three, the task quickly grows demanding and wearisome. There is also little reason to believe that, say, the fifth-ranked item will reliably be placed above the-sixth ranked item by this respondent, if the survey were to be repeated; hence, lower ranks tend to be "noisy," with a strong random component. It is far easier for a respondent to apply a rating scale where $0 =$ no importance and $6 =$ extremely important to a dozen statements than it would be to rank that same dozen from 1 to 12 or even to select the three most important items from the set of 12.

Ranking is one of those spuriously precise measurement approaches of which beginning questionnaire designers become enamored. It is not at all clear that most consumers in most circumstances natively use more than the first three ranks. Plus, from the standpoint of statistical analysis, rank data are peculiarly gnarly. Hence, most of the time, it is better to use a rating scale and examine the ordering of average ratings across the sample to determine the rank order of individual items. The exceptions are when the number of things to be ranked is small (< 4) or when you have reason to believe that many items will be uniformly rated as "very important." However, in the latter case, perhaps a survey is just the wrong tool. Conjoint analysis is superior in such instances because it forces customers to make trade-offs. The nature of the conjoint task makes it impossible for the customer to rate everything as equally important.

DOs AND DON'Ts

Do take your time in the design phase. Questionnaires, like most significant design tasks, benefit from periods of digestion and time away from the task.

Don't let a desire for precision breed unnecessary complexity. Keep it simple.

Don't give in to a desire for comprehensive coverage. Keep it short.

Do ask yourself what is the single most important question in the questionnaire. Arrange things so that this question is likely to receive the full attention of respondents.

Don't proliferate grouping variables needlessly. If there is no reason to suppose that gender influences the responses of these industrial buyers and no intention of implementing a different marketing mix for men and women, don't include the question. It's not relevant.

Do make mock-up tables showing which items will be used to break out responses on other items. If an item doesn't enter into any such breakout, is it necessary to include it?

DISCUSSION QUESTIONS

1. The chapter asserted that demographic questions should be left to the end of the questionnaire. Any exceptions? Explain why.

2. Pick a B2C and a B2B product category (see guidance in the sub-bullets). Assume the goal of the questionnaire and survey is to describe the brand perceptions of your own and competitors' customers, and how these differ across customer segments. Devise a couple of questions that would be suitable to *begin* the questionnaire.

   a. Let the B2C product be an inexpensive packaged snack food.

   b. Let the B2B product be some kind of computer technology, with not too concentrated a market, say 20,000 +/- buying units, mostly IT managers, and a price point in the hundreds of thousands of dollars per sale.

   c. Discuss the differences in these opening questions. Can you formulate any rules about how questionnaire openings will differ across B2B and B2C packaged goods?

3. Using the B2B and B2C products in #2, come up with a minimum set of demographic variables for inclusion at the end of the questionnaire. Be specific about the answer categories for each question, and keep the number of questions in each case at six or fewer.

   a. Discuss the differences in these demographic question sets. Can you formulate any rules about how needed demographic information will differ across B2B computer technology versus B2C packaged goods?

      i. Hint: Stay focused on what you know about mass market snack foods on the one hand, and computer technology sold to IT managers on the other.

b. For these demographic questions, change the product category as noted below, and indicate which, if any, of the demographic questions from the first set above you would remove, and what new questions, if any, you would add. Keep the same purpose for the questionnaire (understanding brand perceptions across different segments of customers).

   i. Change the B2C product category to a piece of personal electronic technology costing some hundreds of dollars—a tablet, music player, piece of audio equipment, etc.

   ii. Change the B2B category to a banking or other financial service sold to corporate finance departments of nonfinance firms (software for managing accounts receivable, for instance, or health insurance for employees).

   iii. Discuss how the demographic variables changed. What's the fundamental factor guiding the selection of demographic information?

4. *Exercise.* Go to Qualtrics.com or any other free web software tool site and construct a complete questionnaire for the brand perceptions survey for which you have already constructed opening and closing questions as part of #2 and #3 above.

a. How long did that take? Would you describe the level of effort required as very easy, somewhat easy, somewhat difficult, or very difficult? If you have attempted other exercises in this book, how did the effort required here compare to those?

b. What kind of rating scale blocks did you choose to include? Were you able to use a template at Qualtrics, or did you have to construct the scales from scratch?

c. Take any one of your rating scale blocks and mock up a table or figure. Fill in the figure with a fictive pattern of results that you think makes sense.

   i. Explain exactly what these results will enable management to do. Since this was a brand perceptions study, assume that it will be used either to improve targeting (aiming future marketing at customers who rate the brand a certain way), or in crafting new advertising appeals.

ii. *Extra Credit*: Explain, if you can, how the rating scale block yielded information, or perhaps a quality of information, that could not have been gained from a good set of interviews.

SUGGESTED READINGS

Brace, I. (2008). *Questionnaire design: How to plan, structure and write survey material for effective market research* (2nd ed.). London, UK: Kogan Page. Bradburn, N. S. S., & Wansink, B. (2004). *Asking questions: The definitive guide to questionnaire design* (rev. ed.). San Francisco, CA: Jossey-Bass. Saris, W. E., & Gallhofer, I. N. (2014). *Design, evaluation, and analysis of questionnaires for survey research*. New York, NY: Wiley.	These books focus on the nitty-gritty of crafting and constructing all kinds of questions.
Dillman, D. A., Smyth, J. D., & Christian, L. M. (1999). *Internet, mail and mixed-mode surveys: The tailored design method* (3rd ed.). New York, NY: Wiley.	Just as books on focus groups also contain material on interview design, almost any book on survey research will include material on questionnaire design. This book, mentioned at the end of the Survey Research chapter, has a philosophy of question-phrasing that I think is particularly helpful.

ELEVEN

EXPERIMENTATION

———•◆•———

E xperiments can be conducted in the field or in some kind of laboratory, that is, in an artificial situation constructed by the researcher. The essence of any experiment is the attempt to arrange conditions in such a way that one can infer causality from the outcomes observed. In practice, this means creating conditions or treatments that differ in one precise respect and then measuring some outcome of interest across the different conditions or treatments. The goal is to manipulate conditions such that differences in that outcome (how many people buy, how many people choose) can then be attributed unambiguously to the difference between the treatment conditions. In a word, the experiment is designed to determine whether the treatment difference *caused* the observed outcomes to differ. More properly, we should say that with a well-designed experiment, we can be *confident* that the treatment difference caused the outcomes to differ. (The role of probability in hypothesis testing will be discussed in Chapter 14.)

Experimentation should be considered whenever you want to compare a small number of alternatives in order to select the best. Common examples would include: (1) selecting the best advertisement from among a pool of several, (2) selecting the optimal price point, (3) selecting the best from among several product designs (the latter case is often referred to as a "concept test"), and (4) selecting the best website design. To conduct an experiment in any of these cases, you would arrange for equivalent groups of customers to be exposed to the ads, prices, or designs being tested. The ideal way to do this would be by randomly assigning people to the various conditions. When random assignment is not possible, some kind of matching strategy can be employed. For instance, two sets of cities can provide the test sites, with the cities making up each set selected to be as similar as possible in terms of size of population, age and ethnicity of residents, per capita income, and so on. It has to be emphasized that an experiment is only as good as its degree of control; if the two groups being compared are not really equivalent, or if the treatments differ in several respects, some of them unintended (perhaps due to problems of execution or implementation), then it will no longer be possible to say whether the key treatment difference caused the difference in outcomes or whether one of those other miscellaneous differences was in fact the cause. *Internal validity* is the label given to this kind of issue—how confident can we be that the specified difference in treatments really did cause the observed difference in outcomes?

Because experiments are among the less familiar forms of market research, and because many of the details of implementing an experiment are carried out by specialists, it seems more useful to give extended examples rather than walk you through the procedural details, as has been done in other chapters. The examples address four typical applications for experimentation: selecting among advertisements, price points, product designs, or website designs. Note, however, that there is another entirely different approach to experimentation which I will refer to as conjoint analysis. Although conjoint is in fact an application of the experimental method, the differences that separate conjoint studies from the examples reviewed in this chapter are so extensive as to justify their treatment in a separate chapter.

EXAMPLE 1: CRAFTING DIRECT MARKETING APPEALS

This is one type of experiment that virtually any business that uses direct mail appeals, however large or small the firm, can conduct. (The logic of this example applies equally well to e-mail marketing, banner ads, search key words, and any other form of direct marketing.) All you need is a supply of potential customers that numbers in the hundreds or more. First, recognize that any direct marketing appeal is made up of several components, for each of which you can imagine various alternatives: what you say on the outside of the envelope (or the subject line in the e-mail), what kind of headline opens the letter (or e-mail), details of the discount or other incentive, and so forth. The specifics vary by context; for promotional e-mail offers, you can vary the subject line, the extent to which images are used, which words are in large type, and so forth; for pop-up ads, you can vary the amount of rich media versus still images, size and layout, and the like. To keep things simple, let's imagine that you are torn between using one of two headlines in your next direct marketing effort:

1. "For a limited time, you can steal this CCD chip."
2. "Now get the CCD chip rated #1 in reliability."

These represent, respectively, a low-price come-on versus a claim of superior performance. The remainder of each version of the letter will be identical. Let's further assume that the purpose of the campaign is to promote an inventory clearance sale prior to a model changeover.

To conduct an experiment to determine which of these appeals is going to produce a greater customer response, you might do the following. First, select two samples of, say, 200 or more customers from the mailing lists you intend to use, using formulas similar to those discussed in Chapter 13, the sampling chapter. A statistician can help you compute the exact sample size you need (larger samples allow you to detect even small differences in the relative effectiveness of the two appeals, but larger samples also cost more). Next, you would use a probability sampling technique to draw names for the two samples; for instance, selecting every tenth name from the mailing list you intend to use for the campaign, with the first name selected assigned to treatment 1, the second to treatment 2, the third to treatment 1, and so forth. Note how this procedure is more likely to produce equivalent groups than, say, assigning everyone whose last name begins with A through L to treatment 1 and everyone whose last name begins with M through Z to treatment 2. It's easy to see how differences in the ethnic backgrounds of A to L versus M to Z patronyms might interfere with the comparison of treatments by introducing extraneous differences that have nothing to do with the effectiveness or lack thereof of the two headlines under study.

Next, create and print two alternative versions of the mailing you intend to send out. Make sure that everything about the two mailings is identical except for the different lead-in: same envelope, mailed the same day from the same post office, and so forth. Be sure to provide a code so you can determine the treatment group to which each responding customer had been assigned. This might be a different extension number if response is by telephone, a code number if response is by postcard, different URL if referring to a website, and so forth. Most important, be sure that staff who will process these replies under-stand that an experiment is under way and that these codes must be carefully tracked.

After some reasonable interval, tally the responses to the two versions. Perhaps 18 of 200 customers responded to the superior performance appeal, whereas only 5 of 200 customers responded to the low-price appeal. A statisti-cal test can then determine whether this difference, given the sample size, is big enough to be trustworthy (see Chapter 14). Next, implement the best of the two treatments on a large scale for the campaign itself, secure in the knowl-edge that you are promoting your sale using the most effective headline *from among those considered.*

COMMENTARY ON DIRECT MARKETING EXAMPLE

The example just given represents a field experiment: Real customers, acting in the course of normal business and unaware that they were part of an exper-iment, had the opportunity to give or withhold a real response—to buy or not to buy, visit or not visit a website, and so forth. Note the role of statistical analysis in determining sample size and in assessing whether differences in response were large enough to be meaningful. Note finally the assumption that the world does not change between the time when the experiment was con-ducted and the time when the actual direct mail campaign is implemented. This assumption is necessary if we are to infer that the treatment that worked best in the experiment will also be the treatment that works best in the cam-paign. If, in the meantime, a key competitor has made some noteworthy announcement, then the world has changed and your experiment may or may not be predictive of the world today.

In our example, the experiment, assuming it was successfully conducted, that is, all extraneous differences were controlled for, establishes that the "Rated #1 in reliability" headline was more effective than the "Steal this chip" headline. Does the experiment then show that quality appeals are generally more effective than low-price appeals in this market? No, the experiment only establishes that *this* particular headline did better than this *other* particular headline. Only if you did several such experiments, using carefully structured sets of "low-price" and "quality" headlines, and getting similar results each time, might you tentatively infer that low-price appeals in general are less effective for customers in *this* product market. This one experiment alone cannot establish that generality. You should also recognize that the experiment in no way establishes that the "Rated #1 in reliability" headline is the *best possible* headline to use; it only shows that this headline is better than the one it was tested against. The point here is that experimentation, as a confirmatory technique, logically comes late in the decision process and should be preceded by an earlier, more generative stage in which possible direct mail appeals are identified and explored so that the appeals finally submitted to an experimental test are known to all be credible and viable. Otherwise, you may be expending a great deal of effort merely to identify the lesser of two evils without ever obtaining a really good headline.

The other advantage offered by many experiments, especially field experiments, is that in addition to answering the question "Which one is best?," they also answer the question "How much will we achieve (with the best)?" In the direct mail example, the high-quality appeal was responded to by 18 out of 200, giving a projected response rate of 9 percent. This number, which will have a confidence interval around it, can be taken as a predictor of what the response rate in the market will be. If corporate planning has a hurdle rate of 12 percent for proposed direct mail campaigns, then the direct mail experiment has both selected the best headline and also indicated that it is may not be worth doing a campaign using even the best of the headlines under consideration, as it falls below the hurdle.

Much more elaborate field experiments than the direct mail example can be conducted with magazine and even television advertisements. All that is necessary is the delivery of different advertising treatments to equivalent groups and a means of measuring outcomes. Thus, split-cable and "single-source" data became available in the 1990s (for consumer packaged goods). In split cable, a cable TV system in a geographically isolated market has been wired so that half the viewers can receive one advertisement, while a different advertisement is shown to the other half. Single-source data add to this a panel of several thousand consumers in that market. These people bring a special card when they go shopping for groceries. It is handed to the cashier so that the optical scanner at the checkout records under their name every product that they buy. Because you know which consumers received which version of the advertisement, you can determine empirically which version of the ad was more successful at stimulating purchase. See Lodish et al. (1995) for more on split-cable experiments.

One way to grasp the power of experimentation is to consider what alternative kinds of market research might have been conducted in this case. For instance, suppose you had done a few focus groups. Perhaps you had a larger agenda of understanding the buying process for CCD chips and decided to include a discussion of alternative advertising appeals with a focus on the two headlines being debated. Certainly, at some point in each focus group discussion, you could take a vote between the two headlines. However, from the earlier discussion in the qualitative sampling chapter, it should be apparent that a focus group is a decisively inferior approach to selecting the best appeal among two or three alternatives. The sample is too small to give any precision. The focus groups will almost certainly give some insight into the kinds of responses to each appeal that may exist, but that is not your concern at this point. That kind of focus group discussion might have been useful earlier if your goal was to generate a variety of possible appeals, but at this point, you simply want to learn which of two specified appeals is best.

You could, alternatively, have tried to examine the attractiveness of these appeals using some kind of survey. Presumably, in one section of the survey, you would list these two headlines and ask respondents to rate each one. Perhaps you would anchor the rating scale with phrases such as "high probability I would respond to this offer" and "zero probability I would respond." The problem with this approach is different from that in the case of focus groups—after all, the survey may obtain a sample that is just as large and projectable as the sample used in the experiment. The difficulty here lies with interpreting customer ratings obtained via a survey as a prediction of whether the mass of customers would buy or not buy in response to an in-the-market implementation of these offers. The problem here is one of external validity: First, the headline is not given in the context of the total offer, as it occurs within an artificial context (completing a survey rather than going through one's mail). Second, there is no reason to believe that respondents have any good insight into the factors that determine whether they respond to specific mail offers. (You say you never respond to junk mail? Huh, me neither! Funny, I wonder why there is so much of it out there . . .)

Remember, surveys are a tool for description. When you want prediction—which offer will work best—you seek out an experiment. If it is a field experiment, then the behavior of the sample in the experiment is virtually identical, except for time of occurrence, to the behavior you desire to predict among the mass of customers in the marketplace. Although prediction remains irreducibly fallible, the odds of predictive success are much higher in the case of a field experiment than if a survey, or worse, a focus group were to be used for purposes of predicting some specific subsequent behavior.

EXAMPLE 2: SELECTING THE OPTIMAL PRICE

Pricing is a topic that is virtually impossible to research in a customer visit or other interview. If asked, "How much would you be willing to pay for this?" you should expect the rational customer to lie and give a low-ball answer! Similarly, the absurdity of asking a customer, "Would you prefer to pay $5,000 or $6,000 for this system?" should be readily apparent, whether the context is an interview or a survey. Experimentation offers one solution to this dilemma; conjoint analysis offers another, as described subsequently.

The key to conducting a price experiment is to create different treatment conditions whose *only* difference is a difference in price. Marketers of consumer packaged goods are often able to conduct field experiments to achieve this goal. Thus, a new snack product might be introduced in three sets of two cities, and only in those cities. The three sets are selected to be as equivalent as possible, and the product is introduced at three different prices, say, $2.59, $2.89, and $3.19. All other aspects of the marketing effort (advertisements, coupons, sales calls to distributors) are held constant across the three conditions, and sales are then tracked over time. While you would, of course, expect more snack food to be sold at the lower $2.59 price, the issue is *how much more*. If your cost of goods is $1.99, so that you earn a gross profit of 60 cents per package at the $2.59 price, then the low-price $2.59 package must sell at twice the level of the high-price $3.19 package (where you earn $1.20 per package) in order to yield the same total amount of profit. If the experiment shows that the $2.59 package has sales volume only 50 percent higher than the $3.19 package, then you may be better off with the higher price. Note how in this example, the precision of estimate supplied by experimentation is part of its attraction.

Business-to-business and technology marketers often are not able to conduct a field experiment as just described. Their market may be national or global, or product introductions may be so closely followed by a trade press that regional isolation cannot be obtained. Moreover, because products may be very expensive and hence dependent on personal selling, it may not be possible to set up equivalent treatment conditions. (Who would believe that the 10 sales-people given the product to sell at $59,000 are going to behave in a manner essentially equivalent to the 10 other salespeople given it to sell at $69,000 and the 10 others given it to sell at $79,000?) Plus, product life cycles may be so compressed that an in-the-market test is simply not feasible. As a result, labora-tory experiments, in which the situation is to some extent artificial, have to be constructed in order to run price experiments in the typical business-to-business or technology situation. Here is an example of how you might proceed.

First, write an experimental booklet (or, if you prefer, construct a web survey) in which each page (screen) gives a brief description of a competitive product. The booklet or website should describe all the products that might be considered as alternatives to your product, with one page in the booklet describing your own product. The descriptions should indicate key features, *including price*, in a neutral, factual way. The goal is to provide the kind of information that a real customer making a real purchase decision would gather and use.

Next, select a response measure. For instance, respondents might indicate their degree of buying interest for each alternative, or how they would allocate a fixed sum of money toward purchases among these products. Various meas-ures can be used in this connection; the important thing is that the measure provide some analogue of a real buying decision. This is why you have to provide a good description of each product to make responses on the measure of buying interest as meaningful as possible. Note that an advantage of work-ing with outside vendors on this kind of study is that they will have resolved these issues of what to measure long ago and will have a context and history for interpreting the results.

Now you create different versions of the booklet or web survey by vary-ing the price. In one example, a manufacturer of handheld test meters wished to investigate possible prices of $89, $109, and $139, requiring three different versions of the booklet. Next, recruit a sample of potential customers to par-ticipate in the experiment. This sample must be some kind of probability sample drawn from the population of potential customers. Otherwise the responses are useless for determining the best price. Moreover, members of the sample must be randomly assigned to the treatment groups. If you use a list of mail addresses or e-mail addresses and have some other information about customers appearing on these lists, it also makes sense to see whether the types of individuals who respond to the three treatments remain equivalent.

If one type of buyer has tended to drop out of one treatment condition, for whatever reason, confidence in the results is correspondingly reduced. Finally, administer the experimental booklet. Again, this could be done by mail, on the web, or in person at a central site(s).

In this price example, to analyze the results, you would examine differences in the projected market share for the product at each price (i.e., the percentage of respondents who indicate an interest or who allocate dollars to the product, relative to response to the competitive offerings). To understand the results, extrapolate from the projected market shares for the product at each price point to what unit volume would be at that level of market share. For example, the $89 price might yield a projected market share of 14 percent, corresponding to a unit volume of 76,000 handheld test meters. Next, construct an income statement for each price point. This will indicate the most profitable price. Thus, the $109 price may yield a market share of only 12 percent, but this smaller share, combined with the higher margin per meter, may yield a larger total profit.

What you are doing by means of this experiment is investigating the *price elasticity* of demand, that is, how changes in price affect demand for the product. Of course, demand will probably be lower at the $109 price than the $89 price; the question is, Exactly how much lower? You might find that essentially no one is interested in the product at the highest price tested. In other words, demand is very elastic, so that interest drops off rapidly as the price goes up a little. The experiment in that case has averted disaster. Or (as actually happened in the case of the handheld test meter example) you might find that projected market share was almost as great at the $139 price as at the $89 price, with much higher total profit (which is only to say that demand proved to be quite inelastic). In this case, the experiment would have saved you from leaving a great deal of money on the table through overly timid pricing.

COMMENTARY ON PRICING EXAMPLE

Whereas a direct mail experiment can be conducted by almost any businessperson with a little help from a statistician, you can readily understand why, in a semi-laboratory experiment such as just described, you might want to retain an outside specialist. Finding and recruiting the sample and ensuring as high a return rate as possible are nontrivial skills. Selecting the best response measure takes some expertise as well. In fact, a firm with a long track record may be able to provide the additional service of comparing your test results with norms accumulated over years of experience.

Note that your level of confidence in extrapolating the results of a laboratory experiment will almost always be lower than in the case of a field experiment. In the direct mail example, the experiment provided an exact replica of the intended campaign except that it occurred at a different point in time with a subset of the market. A much larger gulf has to be crossed in the case of inferences from a laboratory experiment. You have to assume that (1) the people in the obtained sample do represent the population of potential customers, (2) their situation of receiving a booklet and perusing it does capture the essentials of what goes on during an actual purchase, and (3) the response given in the booklet does represent what they would actually do in the marketplace if confronted with these products at these prices. By contrast, in the direct mail case, the sample can easily be made representative, inasmuch as the initial sample is the obtained sample; the experimental stimulus is identical with the real ad to be used; and the experimental response is identical to the actual response: purchase. Nonetheless, when field experiments are not possible, laboratory experiments may still be far superior to relying on your gut feeling—particularly when your gut feeling does not agree with the gut feeling of a respected and influential colleague.

Finally, the difficulty and expense of conducting a laboratory-style price experiment has pushed firms toward the use of conjoint analysis when attempting to estimate demand at various price points. This application of conjoint analysis makes use of simulations, as discussed in Chapter 12.

EXAMPLE 3: CONCEPT TESTING— SELECTING A PRODUCT DESIGN

Suppose that you have two or three product concepts that have emerged from a lengthy development process. Each version emphasizes some kinds of functionality over others or delivers better performance in some applications than in others. Each version has its proponents or partisans among development staff, and each version can be characterized as responsive to customer input obtained through earlier qualitative and exploratory research. In such a situation, you would again have two related questions: first, which one is best, and second, what is the sales potential of that best alternative (a forecasting question). The second question is important because you might not want to introduce even the best of the three alternatives unless you were confident of achieving a certain sales level or a certain degree of penetration into a specific competitor's market share.

Generally speaking, the same approach described under the pricing sample can be used to select among these product designs. If you can introduce an actual working product into selected marketplaces, as consumer goods manufacturers can, then this is a field experiment and would be described as a *market test*. If you must make do with a verbal description of a product, then this is a laboratory experiment and would be described as a *concept test*. Whereas in the pricing example, you would hold your product description constant and vary the price across conditions, in this product development example, you would vary your product description across three conditions, while you would *probably* hold price constant. Of course, if your intent was to charge a higher price for one of the product designs to reflect its presumed delivery of greater functionality, then the price would vary along with the description of functionality, and what is tested is several different combinations of function + price.

Note, however, that the experimental results can only address the differences between the complete product descriptions as presented; if these descriptions differ in more than one respect, the experiment in no way tells you *which* respect caused the outcomes observed. Thus, suppose that you find that the high-functionality, high-price product design yields exactly the same level of customer preference as the medium-functionality, medium-price design. At least two explanations, which unfortunately have very different managerial implications, would then be viable: (1) the extra functionality had no perceived value and the price difference was too small to have an effect on preference; or (2) the extra functionality did stimulate greater preference, which was exactly balanced by the preference-retarding effect of the higher price. You would kick yourself for not having included a high-functionality, medium-price alternative, which would have allowed you to disentangle these effects. But then, once you decide it would be desirable to vary price and functionality across multiple levels, you would almost certainly be better off pursuing a conjoint analysis rather than a concept test. In a concept test you can examine only 2–4 combinations; whereas in a conjoint analysis you can examine hundreds of permutations.

When an experiment is planned, the cleanest and most certain inferences can be drawn when the product designs being tested differ in exactly one respect, such as the presence or absence of a specific feature or functionality. If both product design and price are issues, then it may be best to run two successive experiments, one to select a design and a second to determine price, or to run a more complex experiment in which both product design and price are systematically varied—that is, an experiment with six conditions composed of three product designs each at two price levels. At this point, however, many practitioners would again be inclined to design a conjoint study instead of an experiment. In terms of procedure, the product design experiment can be conducted by e-mail invitation, as in the price example, or, at the extreme, and at greater expense, at a central site using actual working prototypes and examples of competitor products.

COMMENTARY ON PRODUCT DESIGN EXAMPLE

There is an important problem with concept testing of the sort just described if we examine the situation faced by most business-to-business (B2B) and technology firms. Market tests, if they can be conducted, are not subject to the following concern, but we agreed earlier that in many cases B2B and technology firms cannot conduct market tests of the sort routinely found among consumer packaged-goods firms. The problem with concept tests, in B2B and technology contexts, lies with the second of the two questions experiments can address (i.e., not Which is best? but How much will we achieve with the best?). We may assume that B2B concept tests are neither more nor less capable than consumer concept tests at differentiating the most preferred concept among the set tested. External validity issues are certainly present, but they are the same as when consumers in a test kitchen read descriptions of three different kinds of yogurt and indicate which is preferred. The problem comes when you attempt to generate a sales forecast from the measure of preference used in the concept test. That is, generalizing the *absolute* level of preference is a different matter than generalizing the *rank order* of preferences for some set of concepts.

Consumer packaged-goods firms have a ready solution to this problem. Over the several decades that modern concept testing procedures have been in place, so many tests have been performed that leading research firms have succeeded in compiling databases that link concept test results to subsequent marketplace results by a mathematical formula. The data have become sufficiently rich that the concept test vendors have been able to develop norms, on a product-by-product basis, for translating responses on the rating scale in the laboratory into market share and revenue figures in the market. The point is that the rating scale results in raw form cannot be extrapolated in any straightforward way into marketplace numbers. Thus, consumers' response to each tested concept may be summed up in a rating scale anchored by "Definitely would buy"/"Definitely would not buy." For the winning concept, 62 percent of consumers might have checked "Definitely would buy." Does this mean that the product will achieve 62 percent trial when introduced? Nope. Only when that 62 percent number is arrayed against past concept tests involving yogurt are we able to determine that, historically, this is actually a below-average preference rating for yogurt concepts (it might have been quite good for potato chips) that will likely only translate into a real trial rate of 29 percent given the database findings.

There is no straightforward algorithm for translating rating scale responses for a never-before-tested category into a sales forecast. As most B2B firms are new to such market research arcana as concept tests, this means that the necessary norms probably do not exist, making concept test results less useful than for consumer goods manufacturers. (By definition, an innovative technology product cannot have accumulated many concept tests, so the point applies in spades to B2B technology firms.) Thus, B2B and technology firms are encouraged to explore the possible uses of concept tests but cautioned to use them mostly for differentiating better from worse concepts. Absent historical norms, one of the most attractive features of experiments, which involves projecting the absolute level of preference for purposes of constructing a market forecast, is simply not feasible in B2B technology markets.

EXAMPLE 4: A–B TESTS FOR WEBSITE DESIGN

For this example, assume your firm has a website, and that this site has an e-commerce aspect—browsers can buy something by proceeding through the site to a shopping cart, or if in a B2B context, can advance down the purchase path, whether by registering for access, requesting literature, signing up for a webinar, and so on. Another name for purchase path is purchase funnel, with the metaphor suggesting that large numbers of prospects take an initial step toward purchase, that a smaller number take the next step, and so forth, with only a small fraction of initial prospects continuing all the way to purchase. There is a drop-off at each step, and the size of the drop-off can be thought of as a measure of the inefficiency of your marketing effort. The better the design of your website—the more effective your web-based marketing effort—the greater the fraction of prospects who continue on to the next step. Although 100 percent is not a feasible goal, in most real-world contexts, pass-through is so far below 100 percent as to leave plenty of room for improvement.

Given this setup, the business goal is to improve the efficiency of your web-based marketing, and one path to this goal is to optimize your website design, as measured by the proportion of prospects, at any step, who continue on to the next step, for some specified purchase funnel. The outcome of any experimental effort, then, is straightforward: an improvement, relative to baseline, in the fraction of prospects who continue to the next step.

The complexity comes in the nature of the experimental design itself. Recall that in the direct mail example, there was the simplest possible experiment: a headline or subject line offered to one group in version A, and to another group in version B. And that's the heart of any A–B test: exposing people to two versions of something, with an opportunity to observe differences in response. But now consider how much more complex an e-commerce website is, relative to a simple direct mail pitch. There will be a home or landing page that will contain text of several kinds, probably one or more images, and a series of links. These links will be part of a purchase funnel, designed to move the casual browser on to the next step, and providing different routes for doing so. Each of these routes makes use of secondary and tertiary landing pages, which again have links designed to move the prospect forward toward purchase or inquiry. If e-commerce is a primary goal of the website, the entire link structure can be thought of as a sort of Venus flytrap, designed to attract the casual browser buzzing around the web ever deeper into the purchase funnel, until he's committed.

Another key difference relative to the direct mail example is that your website is in operation already, and must remain in operation. This fact has a number of implications. First, any experimentation must not be too radical or disruptive. This is not a matter of experimenting offline with an e-mail to a few hundred customers from your vast customer base, where you could try something wild and crazy. This website *is* your marketing effort, and it has to be the best it can be, yesterday, today, and every day. Second, there are literally count-less ways to vary some aspect of your website: the phrasing of this introductory text, the choice of that image, whether to foreground this link, and so forth. Third, it would be cumbersome to test different manipulations offline, and few would believe that browsing behavior in the lab under observation would gen-eralize exactly or tightly enough to casual browsing in a natural setting. Fourth, your current website design is the fruit of a long history of attempts to design the website in the best possible way. This suggests that the most natural struc-ture for an A–B test would be to let the current site design, exactly as it is, constitute the "A" treatment, which will function as a baseline or control group, against which some novel redesign can be compared. In this structure, there is in some sense only one treatment, the novel design element not now present on your website, which you want to test to see if it is an improvement.

Given all of the above, A–B testing in the context of website design con-sists of programming the host computer system to randomly serve up two versions of the website as each browser comes upon it. These can be two ver-sions of the primary landing page, or two versions of any secondary or tertiary landing page. The programming is simple and assignment to the A or B ver-sion truly is random, fulfilling one of the most important conditions of exper-imental design. If the site has any reasonable amount of traffic, you'll have an adequate sample size within a day or two. If the site has a lot of traffic, you can control the risk that the B version is actually worse by serving it up to only a fraction of browsers. Since you automatically have a good probability sam-ple, once the B version has a big enough sample, the comparative statistical analysis can proceed, even if the B version was served up to only hundreds and the A version to tens of thousands (see Chapter 13 on quantitative sampling).

If the B version is found to produce more of the desired outcome, such as a higher percentage of clickthrough to the next step in the purchase funnel, then the next day you tell your website programmers to retire the A version and serve up the B version from now on to all browsers. The new B version then becomes the baseline against which future attempts at optimization are tested.

COMMENTARY ON THE A–B TEST EXAMPLE

Although an A–B test in principle is simply an experiment with two treat-ments, no different in kind from the direct mail example with which I began, its application to website design produces a noteworthy and distinctive twist on conventional experimentation. To some extent it shares elements with Big Data, most notably its scale, it application in real time, and even its potential automaticity. That is, in the example, the website redesign was portrayed as a one-off effort. Someone had a bright idea for improving the current site, and this new B version was approved for a test. But this limitation is not intrinsic. I can equally well imagine that the website has a crew of designers who are constantly thinking up new twists on the current design—as might be the case if the site in question is a major e-commerce site. In that event, one can imagine that there are four candidate images for the primary landing page, each one a really "good" image, so far as one member of the design crew is concerned. For that matter, the design philosophy may be that the key image on the landing page needs to change weekly or monthly, for variety's sake. In that case, A–B, or A–B–C–D tests, may be running every week, as different images are continually vetted. It's not that complex a programming task to set up the website hosting so that experimentation is ongoing—that is, so that B versions of one or another element of the site are constantly being tested on a fraction of browsers.

When experimentation is ongoing, so that large numbers of "experiments" are fielded every week on the website, a genuinely new kind of market research emerges. In the past, most design efforts in marketing were discrete efforts, occurring maybe once a year, or even less often. An example would be the design of a new television advertising campaign back in, say, 1989 (aka, "ancient times"). Even back then, multiple types of appeal, or two or three different ad executions, would typically be generated by the ad agency. The question of which one was best—the experimental question par excellence—was often decided politically, via the HIPPO rule (highest paid person's opinion as to which one is best). If an experiment was done to decide the issue, it would be a laborious and often costly one-off effort, consuming months.

A vast gulf separates this old world from website design via A–B testing. Experiments in this domain are virtually cost-free, except for the salary cost for the designers who continually dream up new tweaks to the site design. Hundreds or thousands of experimental conditions can be run each year, and results can be obtained in a day or two. Opinion plays little role, except for deciding what tweaks are worth testing (assuming a surplus of ingenuity—else, everything gets tested). Experiments are field tests, and the results are unambiguous: the new tweak measurably improved site performance, or it did not. It's a brave new world, in which experimentation becomes a mindset rather than a specialized skill.

GENERAL DISCUSSION

Returning to the product design example, it may be instructive to examine once again the pluses and minuses of a controlled experiment as compared to conjoint analysis. The most important limitation of controlled experiments is that you are restricted to testing a very small number of alternatives. You also are limited to an overall thumbs-up or thumbs-down on the alternative as described. In conjoint studies, you can examine a large number of permutations and combinations. As we will see, conjoint analysis is also more analytic: It estimates the contribution of each product component to overall preference rather than simply rendering an overall judgment as to which concept scored best. Conversely, an advantage of controlled experiments is the somewhat greater realism of seeing product descriptions embedded in a context of descriptions of actual competitive products. Similarly, product descriptions can often be lengthier and more representative of the literature buyers will actually encounter, unlike conjoint analysis, where sparse descriptions are preferred in order to foreground the differences in level and type of product attribute that differentiate the design permutations under study.

FUTURE DIRECTIONS

Direct mail experiments such as the one described have been conducted since at least the 1920s. Experimentation is thus much older than conjoint analysis and on a par with survey research. Single-source data revolutionized the conduct of field experiments, but that was decades ago; the development of norms similarly revolutionized the conduct of concept tests, but that too occurred decades ago. The logic of conducting an experiment with e-mail or search engine key word purchases instead of "snail mail" is identical. Whether to do a concept test or a conjoint analysis remains a fraught question in many practical circumstances, but that's been true for decades. Certainly, by some point in the 2000s, experimental stimuli became more likely to be administered by computer or over the web, but so what?

A reasonable conclusion with respect to experimentation, then, is that outside of website testing, nothing fundamental has changed. Worst of all, the knee-jerk reaction of most managers confronted with an information gap, certainly in B2B and technology markets, remains to do a survey or to interview customers. Hence, the power of experimental logic remains underappreciated. That stasis in mindset is far more important than the switch from paper to web presentation of experimental materials.

However, I do see one emerging trend that consists not so much of a new methodology as of a radical change in the economics and feasibility of experimentation, as described in the A–B testing example. The ability to deliver structured alternatives to a random sample of customers and observe any difference in outcome is the essence of experimentation. It follows that the cost, turnaround time, and feasibility of doing marketing experiments, in e-commerce, has plunged relative to what it costs to test different television ads, price points, or product concepts or any other marketing tool outside of an e-commerce context. This suggests that in the years to come, a mindset favoring experimentation may become a more crucial element in business (and in the career success of individual marketing professionals): In e-commerce, it's cheaper, quicker, and easier to deploy this powerful research tool than ever before.

STRENGTHS AND WEAKNESSES

Experimentation has one crucial advantage that is so simple and straightforward that it can easily be overlooked or underplayed: Experiments promise causal knowledge. Experiments predict what will happen if you provide X functionality and/or price this functionality at Y. Although strictly speaking, even experiments do not offer the kind of proof available in mathematics, experiments provide perhaps the most compelling kind of evidence available from any kind of market research, with field experiments being particularly strong on this count. In short, experiments represent the most straightforward application of the scientific method to marketing decisions.

Experimentation has two subsidiary strengths. First, the structure of an experiment corresponds to one of the knottiest problems faced in business decision making: selecting the best from among several attractive alternatives. This is the kind of decision that, in the absence of experimental evidence, is particularly prone to politicking, to agonizing uncertainty, or to a despairing flip of the coin. In their place, experiments offer empirical evidence for distinguishing among good, better, and best. Second, experiments afford the opportunity to forecast sales, profit, and market share (again, this is most true of field experiments). The direct mail experiment described earlier provides a forecast or prediction of what the return rate, and hence the profitability, will be for the campaign itself. The pricing experiment similarly provides a prediction of what kind of market share and competitive penetration can be achieved at a specific price point, while the product design experiment provides the same kind of forecast for a particular configuration of functionality. These forecasts can be used to construct pro forma income statements for the advertising, pricing, or product decision. These in turn can be compared with corporate standards or expectations to make a go/no-go decision. This is an important advantage, inasmuch as even the best of the product designs tested may produce too little revenue or profit to be worthwhile. Other forecasting methods (e.g., extrapolation from historical data or expert opinion) are much more inferential and subject to greater uncertainty.

It must be emphasized that the predictive advantage of experiments is probably greatest in the case of field experiments. Laboratory experiments, when the goal is to predict the absolute level of response in the marketplace, and not just relative superiority, raise many issues of external validity. By contrast, in academic contexts where theory testing is of primary interest, laboratory experiments may be preferred because of considerations of internal validity. Academics routinely assume that nothing about the lab experiment (use of student subjects, verbose written explanations) interacts with the theory-based treatment difference, so that external validity can be assumed absent explicit evidence to the contrary. Practical-minded businesspeople can't be so sure.

Experimentation is not without weaknesses. These mostly take the form of limits or boundary cases beyond which experimentation simply may not be feasible. For example, suppose there are only 89 "buyers" worldwide for your product category. In this case, you probably cannot construct two experimental groups large enough to provide statistically valid inferences and sufficiently isolated to be free of reactivity (reactivity occurs when buyers in separate groups discover that an experiment is going on and compare notes). In general, experiments work best when there is a large population from which to sample respondents. A second limit concerns products bought by committees or groups. It obviously does you little good if an experiment haphazardly samples fragments of these buying groups. You must either pick one kind of job role and confine the experiment to that kind, with consequent limits on your understanding, or find a way to get groups to participate in the experiment, which dramatically increases the costs and complexity.

More generally, experiments only decide between options that you input. Experiments do not generate fresh options, and they do not indicate the optimal possible alternative; they only select the best alternative from among those specified. This is not a problem when experiments are used correctly as the culmination of a program of research, but it can present difficulties if you rush prematurely into an experiment without adequate preparation. A related problem is that one can only select among a quite small number of alternatives. Conjoint analysis is a better route to go if you want to examine a large number of possibilities. Last, experiments can take a long time to conduct and can potentially tip off competitors, especially when conducted in the field.

DOs AND DON'Ts

Don't be overhasty in arranging to do an experiment. You really have to know quite a lot about customers and the market before an experiment can be valuable. If conducted prematurely, you risk getting wonderfully precise answers to the wrong question.

Don't let fear of costs prevent you from doing an experiment where appropriate. A laboratory experiment such as the price and product design examples described earlier may cost no more than a focus group study and considerably less than traditional survey research with a large national sample. E-mail tests, and concept tests using a website, can be very inexpensive.

Do obsess about getting the details exactly right in your experimental design. The test groups have to be made as equivalent as possible, and the test stimuli have to differ in precisely those respects, and only those respects, under investigation.

Don't be afraid to be a pioneer. Experimentation is one of several areas of market research where business-to-business and technology firms tend to lag far behind consumer goods firms as far as best practice is concerned.

Don't expect brilliant new ideas or stunning insights to emerge from experiments. Experimentation does one narrow thing extremely well: It reduces uncertainty about whether a specific message, price change, or product design is superior to another and whether it surmounts a specified hurdle rate. Experimentation is confirmatory market research par excellence; it is not a discovery tool.

DISCUSSION QUESTIONS

1. As discussed, there has been a great surge in A–B testing applied to website design. It is interesting to note that academic consumer research almost never uses a simple A–B test, except at the most early phases of pretesting for some larger experiment of interest. Instead, most experiments reported in the *Journal of Consumer Research* or the *Journal of Consumer Psychology* take the form of multi-way Analyses of Variance (ANOVA), in which two or more treatments, which may have more than two levels, are crossed.

   a. Why do A–B tests in a website context, when you could do A–B–C tests, or even A–B–C × X–Y tests? Are there really only two versions of the website that can be conceived at any one time?

   b. Might the focus on A–B tests have something to do with the difference between practitioner and academic concerns? Explain.

   c. A count in favor of practitioners is that A–B tests may be run repeatedly, even regularly, with successive tests of new "B" options. Does this change your answer to 1.a?

   d. Many websites get thousands of hits per day. This would allow for hundreds of subjects per cell in even a very complex experimental design. Say there are five versions of the central image, three ways of presenting site navigation links, and four options for the text lead-in on the home page. In a completely crossed design, that equals 60 experimental cells. Many websites could populate those cells with 500–1,000 browsers apiece, per day, more than enough for an acute statistical analysis. Explain why this more sophisticated multi-way ANOVA would or would not be superior to performing multiple A–B tests on successive pairs of cells.

2. Academic experiments in the marketing domain, especially laboratory experiments published in scholarly journals like *Journal of Consumer Research* or *Journal of Consumer Psychology*, are sometimes criticized for being unrealistic and artificial, or even irrelevant to managers. Critics point variously to the use of student subjects, paper and pencil measures of response in place of actual purchase behavior, environments that compel attention, and manipulations that could not be implemented outside of a university environment in which students are trained to read written instructions very, very carefully.

   a. Academics, naturally, defend their methods as appropriate for their purpose, which is to contribute new understanding at the theoretical level. A common defense is that "it's not the data that generalize, but the theory." This means that it doesn't matter that the experimental data come from college sophomores filling out 7-point scales; the relationship between the theoretical concepts embodied in those scales is what will prove general, and provide new knowledge of what works in marketing. Evaluate this defense.

   b. A rebuttal would be that academic *psychologists* can be as theoretical as they wish, with no need to be relevant, but that someone claiming to do *marketing* science has to do experiments whose data will generalize to marketing contexts, that is, to the real circumstances with which marketing practitioners must deal. Otherwise, in what way is he or she a marketing scientist, as opposed to an academic psychologist? Discuss.

      i. *Extra Credit*: Salaries for marketing professors in a business school can be as much as twice as high as those for psychology professors—an extra hundred thousand dollars or more per year. Integrate this factor into your discussion of a and b above.

3. *Exercise*. Design an experiment for a business or in a product category you know well. Decide whether this will be an experimental test of product concepts, advertisements, or something else, and decide whether it will be a field or laboratory experiment. Your write-up needs to include: (1) statement of the decision problem, with background information as necessary; (2) specific research

objectives; (3) research design, including the population from which you will sample, the sampling procedure, and the size of the initial and obtained samples (read the quantitative sampling chapter first); (4) a description of the two (or more) experimental treatments; (5) a description of the key outcome measure that will be used to assess the treatment effect(s); and (6) a description of any other questions that you think should be asked of experimental subjects as part of data collection.

SUGGESTED READINGS

McQuarrie, E. F. (1998). Have laboratory experiments become detached from advertiser goals? *Journal of Advertising Research, 38,* 15–26. McQuarrie, E. F. (2003). Integration of construct and external validity by means of proximal similarity: Implications for laboratory experiments in marketing. *Journal of Business Research, 57,* 142–153. McQuarrie, E., Phillips, B., & Andrews, S. (2012). "How relevant is marketing scholarship? A case history with a prediction," *Proceedings of the Association for Consumer Research.* McQuarrie, E. F. (2014). Threats to the scientific status of experimental consumer and marketing research: A Darwinian perspective. Marketing Theory.	I wrote these articles to outline criteria for determining when a laboratory experiment can (and cannot) be generalized to real-world marketing contexts. The first article is accessible to practitioners, while the third is an update with a bit more philosophy of science brought to bear. The second paper is aimed at instructors who want a supplement to the standard literature on internal and external validity. The fourth is written primarily to stimulate self-reflection among my fellow academics, but may be of use to executives, say senior partners in a market research consultancy, who are supposed to keep up with academic research in marketing and bring new findings to bear in practice. Some of the threats I develop will be chilling in that context.

Almquist, E., & Wyner, G. (2001). *Boost your marketing ROI with experimental design.* HBS #R0109K. Cambridge, MA: HBS Publishing.	A nice illustration of how some procedures more typically associated with conjoint studies can be applied in the context of a field experiment.
Dolan, R. J. (1992). *Concept testing.* HBS #9–590–063. Cambridge, MA: HBS Publishing.	Discusses the major approaches used to test new product concepts.
Lodish, L., et al. (1995). How T.V. advertising works: A meta-analysis of 389 real world split cable T.V. advertising experiments. *Journal of Marketing Research, 32*(May), 125–139.	A fascinating examination of general principles revealed by split-cable advertising experiments. Citations provide a guide to other studies in this vein. Forward citation search (find this article on scholar.google.com, and then click on the list of articles citing it to do a forward citation search) will bring you up to date on more recent developments.
Thomke, S. H. (2003). *Experimentation matters: Unlocking the potential of new technologies for innovation.* Cambridge, MA: Harvard Business Press.	Particularly helpful in getting across what it would mean to adopt an "experimental mindset" across all aspects of business operation, not just market research as narrowly defined.

⊰ TWELVE ⊱

CONJOINT ANALYSIS

---◆·◉·◆---

C onjoint analysis is the best-known example of a larger family of procedures that attempt to model the factors that underlie and drive consumer choice. Any procedure that attempts to analyze how different factors combine to influence the choice of one product over another can be considered a kind of choice modeling. The underlying assumption is that any product or service offering can be conceptualized as a bundle of attributes. Each of these attributes may be more or less important to any particular buyer, and each attribute has multiple levels: It may be delivered to a greater or lesser degree by any particular product offering. Gas mileage, engine horsepower, and warranty length would be familiar examples of automobile attributes. In general, attributes can be thought of as the components that make up the product's performance (e.g., how fast a laptop is, how much memory it has, how much it weighs) and also as points of difference that distinguish the offerings of various competitors (here more abstract attributes such as reliability, availability of support, and brand reputation may come into play). All choice modeling procedures provide an estimate of the importance or the weight of each attribute in a buyer's purchase decision. Many procedures also allow one to simulate in-market results for a specific combination of attributes at a specified price. The fact that price can be incorporated as an attribute has important implications for the actionability of conjoint analysis.

Choice modeling is one of the newest market research procedures, and it is generally the least familiar to a managerial audience. Because it has been a focus of academic research and development (R&D), there are a large number of methods. In keeping with the concise approach of this book, I focus exclusively on a particular approach to choice modeling—conjoint analysis—and on one of the many possible implementations of it.

DESIGNING A CONJOINT ANALYSIS STUDY

Let's suppose you are designing a new 25-inch LCD monitor intended to be purchased as an upgrade to a personal computer. Experience suggests that the following attributes may be influential:

1. Price

2. Intensity of contrast

3. Latency of response in milliseconds

4. Analog or digital inputs

5. Width of the bezel surrounding the actual screen

6. Brand

Note that most of these features are nice to have, and the rest are matters of taste. It won't do you much good to conduct customer visits to see whether these features matter to buyers; you already know that they do matter. In fact, customer visits in combination with secondary research may have been the source of these attributes in the first place. What you don't know is precisely how important each attribute is. You also don't know which of these attributes is worth extra money or how much extra, nor can you discern what the ideal combination of attribute levels at a given price point might be or how consumers make trade-offs between attributes. A conjoint analysis study can potentially address all of these questions.

Given a set of design attributes to be studied, the next step is to decide how many levels of each attribute you will examine. The complexity of the study can quickly become unmanageable if too many levels of too many attributes are investigated. Even seven attributes, each with two levels, allows for 2^7, or 128, permutations of the LCD monitor design. Five attributes each having three levels would be even worse, with 243 permutations. In practice, consumers will not rate all possible permutations of the attribute. A technique known as fractional experimental design is used to reduce the number of permutations to a much more manageable number, perhaps as few as one or two dozen in these examples. Essentially, only the permutations that convey the maximal amount of information about how the attributes and levels contribute to choice are retained. (A statistician should be consulted if a complex fractional design is desired; the specific permutations that are best to use in a given case are not intuitively obvious if you are new to the technique. On the other hand, routine designs may be available in commercial software packages that execute conjoint analyses; see Suggested Readings at the end of this chapter.) Alternatively, you may use software that has been designed to interactively determine the specific permutations that have to be presented to an individual respondent, based on the responses to the first few permutations presented. In either case, the effect is to make the consumer's task much more feasible. At the extreme, the consumer simply makes a short series of pairwise comparisons; he or she is required only to have a preference between any two concrete product designs made visible on screen at that moment, nothing more.

Regardless, it is still imperative that you simplify the design as much as possible. Although the number of permutations presented to the consumer can be kept to a low number, these permutations tacitly include the entire design. Reading 10 pieces of information, each of which may be present at three or four different levels across permutations, and then deciding just how much more one prefers the one permutation to the other is many times more complex a judgment task than reading six pieces of information, each of which has two possible states across permutations. This remains true even if one is only rating a total of 15 permutations in each case. Excessive complexity breeds random responses on the part of participants, which, once submitted to statistical analysis, produce a very precise form of garbage.

Two considerations have to be balanced when setting levels of the attributes. On the one hand, you want to investigate all the relevant levels of an attribute. If response latencies of 2, 4, 6, or 10 milliseconds (ms) would have either very different implications for manufacturing costs or a significant impact on the usability or attractiveness of the monitor (i.e., the shorter the latency, the more effective the reproduction of moving images), then you have to include each of these levels in the design. On the other hand, if a latency of 15 ms is really not an option (perhaps because respected trade magazines are on record that anything slower than 10 ms is unacceptable or because there is no difference in the manufacturing cost between 10 and 15 ms), then it need not be studied. From yet another angle, if the attribute levels are too far apart (i.e., you only study latencies of 2 and 10), then the conjoint analysis will not help you as much as it might have when it comes to selecting the optimal design. That is, you may find that 2 ms is strongly preferred, but you denied yourself the opportunity of discovering that the cheaper-to-manufacture latency of 6 ms would have been almost as strongly preferred. Then again, if you use attribute levels that are too close (i.e., you look at latencies of 2, 3, 7, and 9), consumers may apply a chunking rule, categorizing 2 and 3 as "real fast" and 7 and 9 as "not so fast," proceeding from then on as if your conjoint design only had two levels of latency. In that event, you doubled the complexity of your design for no gain in understanding.

In practice, the number of attributes and levels actually studied is determined partly by your budget and partly by a sorting-out process wherein you determine what's really important to analyze and understand and what can be taken for granted. Thus, you may decide not to study latency at all, reasoning that a latency of 2 ms is objectively superior, not much more expensive to manufacture than slower latencies, and in any case a strategic necessity given your business plan, which requires you to go head to head against competitor X, who has standardized on a latency of 2. If you reason thus, you might choose to simplify your design by dropping this attribute altogether.

Next, you create cards or screen shots that correspond to all the permutations that you want to test; like survey research, conjoint analysis is increasingly computer based in terms of how it is presented to a respondent. Again, a statistician or a specialist in conjoint analysis can help you devise a design that estimates all parameters of interest using the minimum number of permutations. Such a reduced design may include some absurd or unlikely permutations if they serve the purpose of efficient statistical estimation. It may also include a few additional permutations not required for statistical estimation but useful for adding precision to an anticipated simulation (see below). The point here is that the role of the manager paying for the conjoint analysis is limited to deciding what attributes to include and what levels of these attributes are meaningful to customers and managerially actionable. The translation into the actual permutations to be seen by participants is best left to professionals, whether embodied as consultants or virtual in the form of conjoint design software.

To continue our example, we now have perhaps 20 profiles, each of which describes a possible LCD monitor design variant. Next, these cards will be administered to a good-sized sample (200+ people) drawn from the population of interest. Formulas similar to those discussed in Chapter 13 can be used to determine the necessary size. As always in quantitative research, sampling is crucial. The people who participate in the conjoint study must represent the population for whom the LCD monitor is being designed. It is *their* choice process that we want to understand. No amount of powerful mathematics in the analysis stage can overcome the negative effects of a poor sample selection procedure.

Next, you determine what kind of rating or judgment procedure you want subjects to apply to the 20 monitor designs. One approach is to have subjects make pairwise comparisons, so that all they need do is choose. Alternatively, there may be a measure of preference; perhaps a 10-point scale where 10 indicates a very strong positive reaction to the design and a 1 equals a very strong negative reaction. Other measures, such as a probability to purchase, may also be used. The specific measure to be used depends in part on how the conjoint analysis will be used and in part on the software used or statistician consulted.

A notable feature of conjoint analysis is that the response requested of subjects is very simple and straightforward: to make a choice or to assign a number indicating how much one likes some specific product design (compare the amount of cogitation it takes to complete the typical four-page survey). Although the conjoint task itself generally requires only a single judgment of each permutation, it is generally good practice to collect additional data on respondents. The information collected is of the sort used to profile customers (spending level, involvement with the product category, purchase plans) or segment markets (demographic and other descriptors). This information can be used in simulations and other follow-on analyses of the basic conjoint analysis.

Last, statistical analysis will be applied to determine utility weights for each attribute. In essence, the analysis considers the differences in expressed preferences and applies a regression equation to relate these back to variations in specific attributes (see Suggested Readings for more detail). Was preference consistently higher whenever a design specified a faster rather than slower monitor? If so, this attribute will have a high weight: It appears to be an important factor in choosing a monitor. Was there little or no difference in preference stemming from various levels of contrast? If so, the analysis will assign a low weight to this attribute. The analysis will also detect nonlinear preferences, that is, situations where preference is greatest for a middle level of some attribute. Perhaps a middle level of bezel width is preferred to either a very wide border or a very thin border. Part of the power of conjoint analysis is precisely that it allows you to estimate utility weights for each *level* of the attribute and not just the attribute as a whole.

The analysis just described produces weights for each individual customer participating in the study. Because marketing strategies typically target not individuals but either segments or entire markets, the final step in the conjoint study is to determine how the utility weights for individuals should be aggregated. If experience or inspection of the data suggests that preferences are relatively homogeneous, then one can simply lump all respondents together to determine average utility weights for each attribute. Alternatively, there may be reason to believe that there are two, three, or four quite different segments with distinct preferences. A statistical procedure known as cluster analysis can then be applied to the initial conjoint results. Cluster analysis separates respondents into groups based on the similarity of their utility weight profiles. Then you can determine average utility weights for each attribute separately for each segment. This then indicates what the optimal product design would look like on a segment-by-segment basis. Additional data collected from respondents may assist in profiling and identifying these segments. Note that if you anticipate performing such a segmentation analysis, a larger sample size, closer to 500 or even more, will be required.

As a result of the preceding steps, you will have learned which combination of attributes and levels is judged to be optimal by this sample of respondents. If price has been included, you can estimate how much a move from one level of an attribute to the next is worth to consumers in dollars and cents. Similarly, if price is given a low weight or importance by the analysis, then this suggests that demand is relatively inelastic in this category within the price range investigated.

Optionally, analysis can be pushed to the next level, using what is sometimes labeled simulation analysis. Simulations are particularly powerful if brand was among the attributes included in the conjoint analysis and if one or more permutations can be taken to be a replica of a specific competitor's product. Essentially, the simulation extrapolates from the results of the conjoint analysis to estimate market share for a hypothetical product relative to some competitive set (see Joachimsthaler & Green, 1993, for a detailed example). Given an estimate of market share, you can estimate revenues; given an estimate of revenues and knowledge of probable costs, you can apply a hurdle rate to determine if even the "best" new product design is worth doing, and you can make a forecast of income to be expected from the product once introduced. In short, the use of simulation techniques allows conjoint analyses, like experimentation, to answer two questions: not only Which one is best? but also How much will we achieve (with the best)?

FUTURE DIRECTIONS

When the first edition of this book was written, conjoint analysis itself was the answer to "What's new in market research?" That remains true today. I've rarely met an MBA student or executive education participant who wasn't familiar with or had some sense of the use of questionnaires to guide business decisions. But it remains equally rare to find such a student who had a good sense of conjoint analysis before taking the course. In that sense, conjoint analysis remains a secret open only to a few people in marketing, the privileged knowledge of a limited cadre of professionals and experts. This situation seems to be only slowly changing. You will find conjoint analysis given its due in most graduate-level market research textbooks but not necessarily in a textbook focused on undergraduates. As a result, many managers who have questions ideally suited to conjoint analysis but don't know of it still try to get the needed information from surveys or even customer visits—very imperfect tools when the goal is a sophisticated analysis of the trade-offs customers make.

To the extent there is something new in conjoint analysis, it is the increased use of computer presentation to respondents and the diffusion of easy-to-use software for setting up and designing conjoint studies. Today, one can administer a conjoint study over the Internet about as easily as one can administer a survey. Likewise, software has begun to become available that takes statistical knowledge once confined to a few experts and makes it widely available. Hence, continued diffusion of conjoint analysis into everyday management decision making can be expected, although perhaps not as rapid as the unique capabilities of this tool would justify.

If I were to adopt a prescriptive rather than descriptive standpoint, what I would like to see is a movement away from the present, mound-shaped distribution of market research effort, in which both qualitative interviews and experimentation are scarce relative to surveys, which are over-used. Ideally, 10 years hence, this mound-shaped distribution would change to a barbell-shaped distribution of research effort, in which surveys were less common than either interviews on the one hand, or experimentation, including conjoint, on the other. In that future era, there would be no textbooks, undergraduate or practitioner-focused, from which conjoint would be omitted. However, although I think this would be a splendid development for the field, I would not bet money on it transpiring. Surveys are too cheap, easy, and familiar; interviews remain under suspicion as "not truly scientific"; and conjoint remains an esoteric topic in too many treatments. Pity.

STRENGTHS AND WEAKNESSES

The great strength of conjoint analysis is the amount of complexity that these procedures can incorporate. This is most clearly seen if one contrasts conjoint analysis with an attempt to get at the same kind of information through a series of customer visits. Human beings simply aren't that good at thoroughly explicating how they weight various factors in coming to a decision or what sort of combination rule they apply for integrating information. Nor are human beings (the data analysts in this case) all that good at integrating a mass of interview data so as to precisely delineate different choice models across several segments within a market. Customer visits *would* be quite effective at identifying attributes that matter, explaining why they matter, and even explaining how a customer might trade off one attribute rather than in favor of another. Customer visits could also help the data analyst glimpse the possibility that several different segments exist and what some key points of difference might be. But customer visits would be unlikely to provide anything close to the analytic precision that conjoint analysis so readily offers.

A survey would similarly be a weak reed on which to base the analysis of customer preference. Of course, one could ask customers to rate the importance of each of a dozen or two attributes, and use a rating scale that will allow you to estimate average importance to two decimal places. But in many cases, these average ratings will all be in excess of 6.00 on a 7-point scale—in other words, customers judge everything to be "important." Doh! You made sure to only put on the survey attributes you believed to be important. You could ask customers to make specified trade-offs, but you could only ask for a handful of pair-wise trade-offs, from among the total number of possible trade-offs, which will quickly grow large as the count of attributes increases. Surveys are simply ineffective at distinguishing what's more important, from among important attributes, or at examining how customers make trade-offs among important attributes.

Another way to explain this key strength is that conjoint analysis goes beyond the customer's self-report. Rather, the consumer is given the opportunity to *act* toward structured stimuli and then powerful mathematical techniques are applied to the task of understanding those actions by decomposing them into preferences for specific levels of the attributes considered.

Conjoint analysis represents the acme of the application of modern statistical analysis to the solution of enduring business and marketing questions such as how to design winning products and how to improve existing product offerings. It provides one of the clearest instances of the practical payoff of academically driven R&D within the marketing profession. Fifty years ago, it was practically impossible to do what anyone with a personal computer and a reasonable statistical background can readily do today. Although conjoint analysis is hardly a panacea, it is difficult to imagine a substantial new product development effort (absent the caveats and limiting conditions cited below) that would not benefit from some type of choice modeling initiative. A particular advantage of conjoint analysis procedures is the ability to deal with and sort through a large number of product design alternatives. This strength is most evident in contrast to the controlled experiments described in the previous chapter.

Conjoint analysis also offers an interesting mix of confirmatory and exploratory opportunities. Although predominately a confirmatory technique in the sense that findings are constrained by your initial choices concerning what attributes to study, within those constraints, it is possible to explore via simulation the probable outcome of making any number of changes in product design and positioning. A study done at the level of a product platform (i.e., the technological base from which several generations of specific product models will issue) may provide useful simulation opportunities for some time to come.

The most important weaknesses of conjoint analysis can be thought of in terms of limits or constraints. Two are particularly crucial: the sample of customers used and the set of attributes examined. Just as a biased sample in a survey renders suspect or useless any number of precise percentage breakdowns, so also a biased sample in a conjoint analysis study could lead to seriously misleading results, as you precisely describe the choice process of an idiosyncratic (and perhaps small) subsegment of the overall market. An even more fundamental limitation concerns the set of attributes chosen for study. Here, the garbage in–garbage out rule applies: If crucial attributes are omitted, if the wrong levels are set, or if the attributes are poorly stated or are misinterpreted by customers, then the results may be of little value.

Less crucial but important to remember is the fact that conjoint analysis can take a long time and cost a large amount of money—although, as with surveys, cost and time frame are actually highly variable, so a straightforward conjoint analysis on a single segment might not cost any more than a good focus group study.

Last, conjoint analysis can be difficult to implement for products purchased through a group decision process. And it is necessary to assume that buyers process the information presented to them in the conjoint analysis exercise in the same way they process that information in actual buying decisions. This assumption may not hold for buyers who have little experience with a product category, for products where market conditions are in flux or rapidly changing, or in the case of extremely new products whose implications may be difficult to grasp. For instance, just imagine yourself participating in a conjoint analysis aimed at designing a smartphone in, say, 1985: "Would you prefer to make menu choices by tapping the touchscreen or swiping your finger across it?" Customer answer: "Uh, what's a touchscreen?"

Another limit particularly relevant to business-to-business and technology products concerns complexity. To be feasible, most conjoint studies have to be limited to half a dozen attributes with two or three levels. Now imagine an enterprise-planning software package such as those marketed by SAP, IBM, and Oracle. Such a product may have a hundred or more "attributes," all of which can be varied as the design team considers how the next version might be improved over the current version. Conjoint analysis can assist in such a design task only to the extent that you can boil down competing design alternatives to a small number of key design choices ("attributes") that (1) can be readily apprehended by customers (an attribute is probably not suitable for conjoint analysis if it requires a multipage explanation) and (2) can be formulated in terms of levels—at least, as the presence or absence of the attribute.

Conversely, there is one final strength of conjoint that is particular to concentrated B2B markets: A conjoint analysis can be executed at the level of a single individual. In this case, the conjoint quantifies the trade-offs made by this individual decision maker. Rather than asking how many thousands of dollars more he or she would pay for a switch containing some piece of software functionality, the conjoint analysis would estimate the dollar value, for this decision maker, based on choices actually made within the conjoint study, as various permutations with and without that piece of functionality were presented to this customer and choices made. And conjoint can handle group decision making—the bane of B2B market research—by being administered to different members of the buying group, and treating these like segments. Insight is gained not by averaging attribute importances across members of the buying group, but by examining differences across the different job roles of participants.

CHOOSING AMONG OPTIONS FOR EXPERIMENTATION

As mentioned in the overview of Part IV, conjoint is best considered a kind of experimentation, rather than a separate methodology altogether. Whereas in most marketing experiments, particularly field experiments, different treatments are delivered to different groups of customers, conjoint can be thought of as an experiment in which different treatments are given to the same customer, one after another. These are "within-subjects" treatments, in academic lingo. The underlying experimental methodology is the same: You set up a situation in which structured contrasts among treatments allow you to infer that the cause of any difference in response was due to the treatment difference.

Accordingly, a substantial number of research questions, especially in the area of product design, can be addressed by either the experimentation procedures discussed in the previous chapter or the conjoint methodology discussed here. There are two rules of thumb that may help you to decide whether to use mainstream methods of experimentation or a conjoint methodology. The first rule is that experimentation only makes sense if the number of distinct alternatives to be tested is very small. Six is probably a practical maximum, and the bulk of commercially conducted experiments probably examine but two or three alternatives. As the number of alternatives increases beyond three, it becomes more likely that these represent permutations and combinations of some set of elements, and the conjoint methodology is a more powerful means of evaluating all possible permutations of a set of elements.

Conversely, a second rule that may incline you to choose *field* experiments is that conjoint analysis as currently implemented is always a laboratory technique. Consumers respond to abstract representations of products by giving ratings or other kinds of judgment that do not involve the expenditure of limited funds or time. By contrast, in many field experiments, respondents engage in behaviors in the market or in some approximation to real consumption behavior. Those behaviors are closer to what the mass of consumers have to do when you take the results of the experiment to the market, and thus your confidence may be higher that marketplace results will replicate the experimental results.

As always, there are trade-offs in doing laboratory versus field research, and part of research planning is determining how this trade-off plays out in a particular case. Whether in the area of experimentation or elsewhere, you won't always make the same choice of whether to do laboratory versus field research.

DOs AND DON'Ts

Don't try to put together the attributes for use in a choice modeling study by huddling around a white board with your colleagues. Do go out into the field and use customer visits, focus groups, and other exploratory techniques to identify these attributes and ascertain the words customers use to represent different levels of attribute performance.

Don't assume that any convenience sample of potential customers will do. Strive to get the best possible sample in terms of representing the population to which you want to appeal.

Don't be hasty in assuming that choice criteria and preference structures are basically the same for most buyers in the market. Be alert to possible segments.

Do look for opportunities to do conjoint. It is almost certainly an under-used technique in your firm, the more so if you are a B2B or technology firm.

DISCUSSION QUESTIONS

1. Conjoint requires that a product consists of features or attributes, whose "performance" level varies (like a computer screen that can be 12" or 15" or 17" wide, or a car that can get 30, 35, or 40 miles per

gallon). Name some product categories where conjoint might *not* be applicable. Can you derive a general rule that identifies product types that are and are not suitable for conjoint?

2. Conjoint is often used in new product development. In the innovation literature, however, "newness" is differentiated as to degree: Some products may be simply new versions of old products, others may be really, really new. The latter may be referred to as discontinuous or radical innovations. Does newness place a limit on the applicability of conjoint—can there be products so new, so radically different, that an investment in conjoint is unlikely to pay off? Give an example or two, and try to formulate a rule for how innovative is too innovative for conjoint.

3. At this point, conjoint analysis is almost 50 years old (early efforts at Bell Labs date back to the 1960s). That's only half as old, more or less, as surveys and experiments, but it's still pretty old. And yet, in the 30 years I've been teaching market research, base levels of awareness of conjoint among MBA students have scarcely increased. One reviewer of this book even argued that the conjoint was too esoteric and advanced a topic to be included in this guide for beginners. Discuss why conjoint remains such an unfamiliar research technique, given its fitness for two of the toughest questions in market research: setting a price, and configuring a new product for optimum price–performance.

4. Conjoint is almost always executed as a laboratory technique. Consumers make choices, but no money changes hands and no opportunities are foregone. Discuss the strengths and weakness of this particular aspect of executing a conjoint study: The fact that results are always, to some degree, a product of an artificial context.

5. *Exercise.* Design a conjoint study for a product category that you know well. Assume the purpose of the conjoint is to configure the next generation of some product. Your write-up needs to include: (1) statement of the decision problem, with background information as necessary; (2) specific research objectives; (3) research design, including the population from which you will sample, the sampling procedure, and the size of the initial and obtained samples (read the quantitative sampling chapter first); (4) a description of the attributes that will be examined (e.g., will you include price or brand as an attribute);

(5) a statement of the levels to be included for each attribute; (6) whether subjects in the conjoint will make pairwise comparisons, or, if not, a description of the scale on which individual attribute profiles will be rated; and (7) a description of any other questions subjects will be asked, and for what purpose.

SUGGESTED READINGS

Dolan, R. J. (1999). *Analyzing consumer preferences.* HBS #9–599–112. Cambridge, MA: HBS Publishing.	An excellent and accessible introduction to how conjoint analysis can be interpreted to guide marketing decisions.
Green, P. E., & Krieger, A. M. (1991). Segmenting markets with conjoint analysis. *Journal of Marketing, 55*(October), 20–31.	Recommendations illustrated with examples for how to segment markets using conjoint analysis.
Joachimsthaler, E., & Green, P. (1993). *New ways to answer old questions.* HBS #594–003. Cambridge, MA: HBS Publishing.	Gives an extended example of how simulation analyses can be applied to the results of a conjoint study.
www.qualtrics.com www.sawtooth.com www.spss.com	Each of these firms is a major source of conjoint analysis software. White papers providing worked-out examples are also available on these sites.

⊰ THIRTEEN ⊱

SAMPLING FOR QUANTITATIVE RESEARCH

———•◦●◦•———

S ampling to support surveys and other quantitative research is one of those key technical skills that does not form part of a general manager's train- ing but is central to competence in market research. Because it rests on specific, narrow technical skills, in many real-world cases it will be outsourced. The market research vendor, or perhaps even an independent consultant retained by that vendor, will devise the sample plan. Given this book's goal of offering only a concise introduction to market research, this chapter, more than most, only skims the surface of the actual procedures required to select and size a sample in any real-world case. By contrast, the typical market research textbook devotes several chapters to the topic of sampling and begins the treatment with a review of the fundamentals of probability, essentially recapitulating a portion of the statistics courses required of all business students. Although it is almost certainly true that one cannot really understand sampling without a solid grounding in the basics of probability distributions, that traditional approach has been set aside as not appropriate in the context of this book.

The goals of this chapter are limited. The first goal is to prevent or at least minimize bewilderment in connection with the topic of sampling. General managers are going to sit in meetings where terms like *probability sample*, *random sample*, and *systematic sample* get tossed around in a context where the basic question reduces to How much money do we need to spend?—a question that is very much the province of general managers. Interestingly, engineering managers often need help avoiding bewilderment in these same conversations. Although engineers get exposed to plenty of high-level math in most engineering curricula, the math that underlies sampling approaches in the context of social science tends to be quite different from the math that underlies physics and, at least initially, may be unfamiliar to the trained engineer.

The second goal of this chapter is to enable a modicum of critical thinking about samples in the context of both proposed research and completed research. In the case of proposed research, critical thinking about the kind of sample required facilitates a more effective research design. Critical thinking about the samples used in completed studies, such as those found in secondary research, helps you decide which findings deserve the most weight or should have any credibility at all. There really are a lot of bad samples out there in today's world! Awareness of this fact, combined with an understanding of what makes a sample good or bad, fosters a healthy skepticism that will serve a general manager well.

In light of these limited goals, this chapter has two sections: a discussion of probability samples and why they are highly valued, followed by procedures for determining sample size. Determination of sample size is where the rubber hits the road in commercial market research; it is a key cost driver and may determine the feasibility of a given research project.

A final limitation on this chapter's discussion is that I will generally assume that you are seeking to sample human beings. Fascinating problems and challenges of great interest to the professional statistician arise when the goal is to sample something other than humans. For instance, one might need instead to sample from the population of sales calls that occurred in the third fiscal quarter, from retail transactions that occurred at stores in a given region, from highway intersections in the state of California, from truck trips between your warehouse and distributors, and so forth. However, the complexities that would be introduced if the treatment had to be sufficiently general to cover all sorts of sampling tasks would undercut my limited goals. Hence, I assume throughout that you intend to sample individual customers or customer organizations.

TYPES OF SAMPLES

A few definitions may help. A *population* is the total set of people that results obtained from the sample are supposed to reflect. Populations can be of any size or level of generality, for instance, all residents of the United States, all U.S. households with phone service, all persons who own a hydro-widget, all purchasers of *our* brand of hydro-widget, all our own hydro-widget accounts who purchased more than 10 hydro-widgets in the past 24 months, and so forth. Sometimes multiple populations may be involved in the research, such as domestic versus international hydro-widget owners or widget accounts in one sales territory versus those in another.

The *initial* sample refers to the limited number of people within the population who are contacted to participate in the research. If the population is so small and your effort so diligent that you can contact all of them (e.g., all widget accounts that were opened in the first fiscal quarter), then there is no sample—you can refer to this as a census of the population. When a census is feasible and cost-effective, it should be done. Continuing in this vein, the *obtained* sample is the people within the initial sample that actually completed the research. Finally, the *sample frame* is the device you use to access the population to draw a sample. A mailing list is a simple example of a sample frame (e.g., members of the National Association of Widget Operatives). The subset of all 10-digit numbers, where the first three numbers correspond to telephone area codes now in use, would be a more subtle example of a sample frame.

THE TERRIBLE BEAUTY OF PROBABILITY SAMPLES

This is the single most important thing to understand: Some samples are probability samples, and these have special advantages; all other samples are nonprobability samples and lack these advantages. Don't misunderstand—the category of "good" samples, in the sense of being suitable to the task at hand, includes nonprobability samples as well as probability samples; but nonprobability samples are good samples only in circumstances where the inferences you intend to make are strictly limited.

The beautiful thing about probability samples is that simple mathematical formulae can be applied to determine the sample size you need for any given survey, conjoint analysis, or experiment. The second beautiful thing about probability samples is that a host of wonderfully sophisticated mathematical and statistical tools can be applied to the results of surveys and so forth when you draw a probability sample. The terrible truth about probability samples is that large numbers of commercial market research samples aren't probability samples. And another terrible truth is that the formula for sizing a sample is not applicable when the sample is not a probability sample. And the final terrible truth is that none of the wonderfully sophisticated statistical apparatus available to the market researcher is, strictly speaking, applicable when the sample is not a probability sample.

Much quantitative market research rests on a wink and a nod: an agreement to treat the sample in hand as if it were a probability sample when in fact it is not. It is, after all, large, and consultants and staff desperately wish to apply the sophisticated statistical toolkit waiting in the wings; plus, management is demanding precise numbers projectable to the population and only gave a budget when promised those numbers. And so it goes. As long as the sample is as large as it would need to be to be a good probability sample, and as long as the kind of measures associated with the statistical analysis of probability samples, such as rating scales and frequency counts, were used, everyone agrees to look the other way.

This Potemkin village grew up slowly over time, and a little history may help in understanding how the industry reached this parlous state. Long ago in the 1950s, it was relatively easy to get a probability sample of households in a metropolitan area. You consulted a street directory and then sent out a force of clipboard-wielding interviewers to each kth block with instructions to knock on every nth door. Properly done at well-chosen times of day, you had a probability sample of residences, and refusals and not-at-homes were both few in number and essentially random. But nowadays, if I start to describe this kind of in-person survey to a class of Silicon Valley MBAs, they are soon rolling in the aisles. Asked what they would do if a stranger approached their personal residence armed with a clipboard, "Call the police!" was one of the milder responses. The era of in-person survey sampling is over here in 21st century urban America, and with it died a prototypical example of a commercial probability sample.

But wait—as it was slowly becoming unwieldy, expensive, or impossible to sample residences door to door, the technology of random-digit dialing for telephone surveys came into play. In the United States, local phone numbers have seven digits; this means that in any area code, one essentially has a list of 10^7 numbers to call. Once one has a list, a probability sample is easy to draw. And, back in the 1960s and perhaps the 1970s, virtually any household would have a landline; not-at-homes were few, refusals were still relatively low, and both were arguably random. So once again, an initial probability sample could be gotten for a reasonable cost, and the obtained sample, because of the minimal number of not-at-homes and refusals, was also arguably still a probability sample.

Nowadays, of course, fewer and fewer people have a landline, and ordinary consumers are more and more reluctant to participate in phone surveys. So survey work is gradually shifting to the web, as discussed in the chapter on survey research. But here, not even the initial sample is likely to be a probability sample: It is biased in terms of web access, web usage, and a high enough level of comfort with various types of web content to successfully navigate an e-mail invitation to a web survey (my 89-year-old mother helps me keep this kind of thing in perspective). And, of course, now that the novelty has worn off, refusal rates are huge. This led ultimately to the recruitment of web panels, whose members participate regularly in web surveys for an incentive and who are recruited to have a reasonable distribution across age groups and other demographic variables. But the obtained sample from one of these panels, given the layers of self-selection and the quota sampling used to get a reasonable distribution across demographic groups, can't by any stretch of the imagination be called a probability sample.

If we step back from this sorry history for a moment, a few key points about the probability of obtaining a probability sample in commercial market research stand out. First, if you don't have a list, the odds of getting a cost-effective probability sample are very low. This means that getting an initial sample that is a probability sample is much more likely to occur when the goal is to survey existing customers. In almost all B2B cases, a complete list of the population of current customers can be found in some kind of corporate database. Second, if you are surveying only existing accounts, you almost certainly can make your *initial* sample a probability sample. But confidence that the obtained sample is a probability sample decreases as refusal rates increase. When refusals are few, it can be argued with a straight face that these refusals and could-not-be-contacted accounts occurred at random and, hence, are unrelated to any of the population variables of interest (e.g., happy vs. unhappy customers, busy vs. less busy executives, large vs. small accounts). No matter how carefully drawn the initial sample, if refusal rates are high, it is difficult to argue that the obtained sample is a probability sample. As participation drops below 50 percent, you are put in the untenable position of arguing that there was nothing else unusual about people who performed the quite unusual behavior of participating in your survey. Inasmuch as most commercial market research deals either with self-selected volunteers (automatically not a probability sample) or has very low response rates, it follows that most commercial attempts to conduct quantitative research do not succeed in obtaining a probability sample.

I hope you found this brief introduction chastening, and that the terrible demands of probability sampling now loom larger in your mind. I nonetheless predict that in the end, most of you reading this will join the little man behind the curtain and participate in the great sham. Your manager wants precise numbers. He saw them over and over in Harvard cases, stated as exact figures, without any band of imprecision. He expects no less of you, and I predict that you will present him with such numbers, suitably armored in statistics, and hedged about with fine-print qualifications, if he gives you a budget to do so. But perhaps after reading this account, from time to time you'll want to stand over here with me and Dorothy and call for a halt to that show.

You won't find many texts in marketing or social science research that make this critical point. I think the criticism is important, however, and to bolster the point I'd like to introduce a counter-argument: what about Nate Silver? Mr. Silver, late of the *New York Times* and now at fivethirtyeight.com, is famous in certain circles for his spot-on predictions of the 2012 elections. These predictions were based on his weighting of surveys conducted by others—surveys using the same supposedly flawed sampling approaches I just pilloried. If commercially obtained samples fall as far short of being probability samples as I have argued, how could Nate Silver have been so successful in his 2012 election predictions?

The answer, I think, is instructive: Mr. Silver had *a lot* of survey samples to work with: hundreds of polls, each with approximately 1,000 respondents. Probably every single one of these polls fell short of obtaining a true probability sample by the criteria laid out above; but, importantly, these deviations were one part random—this poll over-sampled cell phone owners, this one under-sampled—and one part predictable, so that adjustments could be made within Mr. Silver's model. That is, most polls come from a polling company with a long track record, allowing an analysis of systematic biases in the methods of each—this one over-samples senior citizens, this one over-samples young voters. With hundreds of randomly biased polls to work with, and copious historical data on systematic biases of the pollsters, one ends up with a highly predictive aggregate data set.

And, of course, this is precisely *not* the situation of any individual firm conducting commercial market research. Almost all of your research will consist of one-off efforts, and you will never have the power of an aggregate data set carefully weighted based on historical data. There is one exception: You may assess satisfaction or track brand awareness on a regular basis. When you repeat a sampling procedure over and over, you begin to overcome some of the sampling limitations described. Each particular satisfaction assessment probably uses something less than a true probability sample, but each successive sample is probably biased in a similar way, not counting small random deviations. Hence, cross-time samples are not biased with respect to one another. Each point-in-time estimate is biased, but the trend, if one emerges, is likely to be more reliable.

HOW TO DRAW A PROBABILITY SAMPLE

You are likely to be more familiar with the term *random sample* than with the term *probability sample*, but simple random samples are only one kind of probability sample. The property that distinguishes probability samples and that gives them their peculiar advantage is that every member of the population has a known or calculable probability of ending up in the initial sample. Thus, if you use a random number table to construct seven-digit phone numbers within an area code, you know that there is one chance in 9,999,999 that any given phone number would appear in the sample (assuming that all the possible three-number prefixes are in use). Similarly, if you obtain from the Internal Revenue Service a list of all foundations that filed a tax return in 2003 and contact every 50th name on the list, you would also have a probability sample—of foundations that filed. Note that the second example is not a random sample. You have to use a random number table or its equivalent to claim to have a random sample. The second instance is referred to as a *systematic sample*, and because of the prevalence of lists in market research and the unwieldy nature of random number tables, systematic samples are probably more common than strictly random samples.

The advantage enjoyed by probability samples is that if one additional piece of information is known (the "variance," to be defined later), you can calculate a margin of error for a given sample size for any numerical value that you obtain from the sample. The importance of this property can be grasped if

I permutate the preceding sentence slightly: If you can state your allowable or acceptable margin of error, then you can calculate the exact size needed for your sample. With a probability sample, you can say to a general manager, "If you can tell me how precise the research results need to be, I can tell you exactly what the sample size has to be." Knowing the precise sample size required means you can decide whether the research is feasible from a cost standpoint, and you can proceed in confidence that you have spent not one dollar more than is necessary.

Put another way, if you will be happy with a percentage breakdown that is within 10 percentage points of the true value, you will generally have to pay for only a small sample; if you require that results be within 5 percentage points, you will have to pay quite a bit more; and if you want it to be within 2 points, then you will generally have to pay a very large sum. Of course, many people recognize intuitively that more precision requires a larger sample, all else being equal. The advantage of probability samples is that you can quantify that intuition. This means you can quantify "small, but adequate for our purposes" as precisely 100 respondents (not 50 and not 250) in some given case. And, most important, you can quantify "if we increase the size of the sample by this much, it will be more precise to about this degree." It makes a huge practical difference if "larger" means 400 instead of 100 respondents—or if it means thousands instead of hundreds of respondents, as could be the case if your manager insisted on a high degree of precision.

In short, probability samples allow you to derive the needed sample size with the huge practical advantages that confers. And as noted earlier, technically speaking, virtually all statistical analyses commonly applied to market research data assume that the sample being analyzed is a probability sample of the population of interest. Only with probability samples can you be certain to a known degree that the sample *represents* (is similar to, allows us to project results to) the population. And it is that population that constitutes the market you seek to understand.

ESTIMATING THE REQUIRED SAMPLE SIZE

Given a probability sample, estimating how big a sample to draw is quite straightforward provided that three pieces of information are available:

1. The decision maker's tolerable margin of error, that is, desired degree of precision

2. The confidence level required

3. The variance, in the population, of the quantity being estimated via the research

The first item is the easiest to explain. Decision makers have to be apprised of the fact that market research conducted using samples of human beings yields only approximate values, that these values, which are the research results, can be made more or less approximate, that it costs money to make these approximations tighter, and that very tight approximations can cost orders of magnitude more than looser but still serviceable approximations. As an example of a looser but still serviceable approximation, consider a survey that contains a set of opinion statements with which customers have to agree or disagree. Suppose your goal is to identify which opinions, if any, are held by a majority of customers—especially those held by a large majority. Under these circumstances, a decision maker might be satisfied with a margin of error of ±10 percentage points. Thus, if 61 percent of the customers in the survey agreed with a viewpoint, one could be confident that this view was held by a majority of customers (between 51 percent and 71 percent, specifically); if upward of 77 percent agreed, then one could be confident this view was held by two-thirds or more of customers (specifically, 67 percent to 87 percent); and if a viewpoint was agreed to by 50 percent, then one could be confident that it was probably not held by a strong majority (with the degree of adherence in the population estimated at 40 percent to 60 percent, given the margin of error of ±10 percent).

The desired degree of precision (another name for margin of error) is discretionary to the decision maker and should be matched to the risks and rewards of the decision at hand. Thus, I can envision an alternative scenario where a corporate goal had been set to improve product documentation and design such that fewer than 20 percent of customers would suffer from unscheduled downtime within any given three-month period. Large bonuses will accrue if the goal is met; pay raises will be frozen if it is not. Here, a much higher degree of precision might be sought, perhaps as few as 2 percentage points, along with a higher level of confidence to boot. The sample in this case may have to be 10 or even 100 times as large as in the previous example, given that decision makers, concerned to protect their salary and bonus, might well desire a very tight margin of error in this case.

The next two terms require a brief discussion of statistical theory and usage. *Confidence level*, more properly *confidence interval*, has a specific meaning in statistics. Although it can be any percentage, it is conventional to use the 95 percent confidence interval in social science research, corresponding to a significance level of $p = .05$. (See Chapter 14 for more on significance tests.) You will also encounter 90 percent confidence intervals and 99 percent confidence intervals corresponding to significance levels of $p = .10$ and $p = .01$; however, most other values (any value between about 0 percent and 100 percent can be estimated) do not appear in practical contexts. To return to the examples explaining margin of error, technically speaking, when you estimate that 61 percent of customers, ± 10 percent, agree with a viewpoint, you do this with an assumed confidence interval which, if left unstated, is probably the conventional 95 percent confidence interval. The researcher is stating only that if the survey were repeated an infinite number of times with samples drawn the same way from this same population of customers, then 95 percent of the time the estimate of the proportion of customers agreeing with this viewpoint will be a value that falls between 51 percent and 71 percent. Likewise, on about 1 occasion in 20, the survey will be wildly wrong, with the true value lying more than ± 10 percent away from the survey's estimate of it. Remember, there is almost never any conclusive certainty in market research, only estimates, with a stated imprecision given a specified confidence level. Engineers often have trouble accepting this truth; physical quantities can of course be estimated with much, much greater precision.

Put another way, if I say that a given survey has a precision of ± 10 percentage points (or ± 3 points, the value typically found in newspaper reports describing opinion polls taken during election years), I really mean that I am about this much confident (90 percent, 95 percent, 99 percent) that in this research, I obtained the claimed degree of precision. Precision, in samples, is never absolute but is always precision at the specified confidence level. Readers with the soul of an engineer are again free to frown: Yes, the precision of our estimates, in quantitative market research, is itself only an estimate. Welcome to research with human beings. Remember what I said in the beginning about market research never eliminating uncertainty but only reducing it?

The third piece of information you must supply is the variance in the population of the quantity you seek to estimate in the sample. *Variance* is a statistical term close in meaning to *variability*; what follows is limited to an intuitive explanation of the concept of variance and of its importance in determining sample size. It may be helpful to use stock prices as an example. Consider two stocks, one a young speculative Internet stock, like Baidu, and the other an old, conservative stock like IBM. Let us further suppose that their average price during the year was about the same, maybe $120 a share or so. Now consider the set of all prices that Baidu and IBM may have traded at during this calendar year. I would expect that Baidu would have traded at a wider range of prices over the year, relative to its average price in that year, than IBM. In that case, Baidu's price series would have a higher measured variance. Now suppose your task was to estimate the average price that Baidu or IBM sold for during that year. You are a historian undertaking this task hundreds of years hence long after an EMP pulse destroyed all digital records. The only information available is a scattered selection of old newspapers found in a basement.

   The idea connecting variance to sample size estimation is simply that it would be more difficult to estimate the average price of Baidu using only a few newspaper issues; put another way, you would need to sample a greater number of old newspapers in the case of Baidu than IBM in order to come equally close to estimating the true average price during some time period. In a nutshell, this is why you need to estimate the population variance when computing required sample size—the larger the variance, the larger the sample size required to secure a given margin of error.

FORMULA FOR COMPUTING SAMPLE SIZE

Assuming that the population from which you are sampling is much larger than the sample itself, the formula is as follows:

1. Square the Z value associated with the desired confidence interval.

2. Multiply it by the population variance.

3. Divide by the square of the desired precision.

Precision is the number following the ± sign in the examples that discussed margin of error. Thus, if our margin of error is ±10 percentage points, the quantity that must be squared to obtain the denominator is .10. If you want to know the average amount spent on music downloads per month to ±$5, then 5 is the quantity to be squared. Variance is as just defined; we'll examine how to calculate a numerical value for variance in a minute. The value for the confidence interval, Z, is found in tables showing the area under the curve for normally distributed data ("bell curve"). For our purposes, it is enough to keep the following three Z values in mind:

$$Z \text{ for a } 99\% \text{ confidence interval} = \sim 2.6$$

$$Z \text{ for a } 95\% \text{ confidence interval} = \sim 2.0$$

$$Z \text{ for a } 90\% \text{ confidence interval} = \sim 1.6$$

Here is a simple calculation to anchor the formula. Suppose you are looking at the opinion survey used earlier in this chapter as an example. Let the margin of error be ±10 percent; let the chosen confidence interval be 95 percent; and let the variance for the agree–disagree proportion be .25. The necessary sample size is then computed as follows:

$$2^2 \times .25 \,/\, (.10)^2$$

$$= 4 \times .25 \,/\, .01 = 100 \text{ customers}$$

If you are correct about the variance associated with these opinion items, then a probability sample of 100 customers will yield results with a precision of ±10 percentage points at the 95 percent confidence level. Once the three pieces of necessary information are obtained, calculation of the needed sample size is as simple as that.

To empower you to make actual use of this formula, the crucial next step is to explain how to obtain a numerical variance in specific cases. The other two pieces of the formula are constrained by convention or custom. It is straightforward to standardize on the use of the 95 percent confidence interval, since this is the norm in contemporary social science; departures are some-times appropriate but represent exceptions that should be carefully justified. Similarly, decision makers can generally settle on a needed precision after some reflection and coaching. In the case of percentages, setting the margin of error is often easy, because there are some widely accepted norms or customs. Thus, few decision makers would be comfortable with a margin of error any wider than ±10 percentage points. If you fix the variance at .25 (we'll see why in a minute), then the minimum size of the obtained sample has to be 100.

Another common margin of error, when the focus of the results will be percentage breakdowns, is ±5 percentage points. Here you'd be able to identify with confidence any "majority" view that was held by 55 percent or more of the population instead of just those where the agreement is 60 percent or more, so long as you had a probability sample of 400. Note that doubling the precision quadrupled the needed sample size. That should set off a little "uh-oh"; and indeed, to tighten the precision even a little further, to ±3 percent, is going to drive the needed sample size up over 1,100. That's a number that won't be affordable or cost effective in many commercial market research contexts. Hence, here is a rule of thumb: if simple two-way percentage breakdowns are the focus of the study, then the sample size should be either 100 (for quick and dirty estimates) or 400 (for something more comfortably precise).

When margin of error is not stated in terms of percentages, more thought is required, because there won't be any simple conventions. Consider the music download example again. Perhaps the issue is whether average monthly expenditure is on the order of $10 or a little less or, instead, is something north of $15, perhaps $17 or even $20. A margin of error of ±$5 is probably too loosey-goosey here; if the survey estimates an average expenditure of $12 or $13, we haven't resolved the issue: the confidence interval, or band of imprecision, the margin of error, includes both the opposing hypothesized values. Conversely, if you were interested in whether casual restaurant expenditures of families had dropped from the $50 range, where it had been before the Great Recession, to somewhere in the $30 range, setting the margin of error at $5 might be acceptable, depending on the variance of family restaurant expenditure. And that's another difficulty when margin of error is set in terms of some quantity other than a percentage: variance is more variable, and there is no single value, like .25, that you can start with. Nonetheless, I can conclude with this rule of thumb. In the nonpercentage case, the margin of error should be set at a small fraction of the kind of difference that would be accepted as "evidence of change" or "notable." In the restaurant example, where the two expectations were about $20 apart, many managers would seek a margin of error of no more than ±$5, and perhaps as tight as ±$2. In the download example, most would set the margin somewhere between ±$2 and ±$1.

Let me note in passing that the best way to estimate average restaurant expenditure by families in casual dining establishments would be to get the cooperation of Applebee's or a similar establishment and sample from their cash register receipts; likewise, it would be best to sample from the actual sales database of iTunes or Amazon.com in the download example. Either would be superior to relying on a might-not-be-probability sample of families asked to consult their might-not-be-reliable memories. If this realization had already struck you while reading, then bravo: You have the potential to achieve more than a beginner's level of skill in designing and drawing samples for quantitative market research. No need to construct a sample for primary research if secondary data can answer the question.

In short, confidence interval and margin of error can often be set by convention or by rule of thumb. This leaves finding the value of the variance as the major head scratcher. It is simplest to do in the case of percentage splits, so I begin there.

ESTIMATING THE VARIANCE FOR A PROPORTION

The variance for a proportion is computed as follows:

$$\text{Variance} = \text{proportion \# 1} \times [1 - \text{proportion \#1}]$$

If you are working with agree–disagree items and you expect that opinion may be evenly split, then the variance to plug into the formula is $.50 \times .50$, or $.25$, as in the preceding example. Interestingly enough, this is the largest value you will ever have to plug into the formula for the variance of two proportions. For instance, if you expect that customers are opposed to a viewpoint by 2 to 1, then the variance is $.666 \times .333$, or $.22$; if you expect an 80–20 split, then the variance is $.8 \times .2$, or $.16$. Hence, if you don't have any prior expectations about how customer opinion is split, the conservative thing to do is to estimate the needed sample size assuming a 50–50 split. You may end up spending extra money beyond what was needed (should the actual split turn out to be 65–35), but in that event, you will achieve extra precision as well.

ESTIMATING THE VARIANCE FOR A MEAN VALUE

Suppose that the survey is aimed at examining numerical values rather than proportions. You may be interested in the average expenditure, the average size of a customer's maintenance budget, the average number of man-hours required by some task, and so forth. Although the formula for computing sample size is the same, estimating the variance requires more information than in the case of proportions. The best approach is to obtain an estimate of the actual variance for this question and this population by examining some previous sample gathered by yourself or someone else. Thus, if this question was used in a trade magazine survey or any secondary research report, the standard deviations may be tabled along with the average values, and the variance may be estimated by squaring the reported standard deviation.

Note that if you are interested in the average customer rating on some rating scale, you can use published values to estimate the variance. Thus, the possible variance in numerical terms, for a 5-point satisfaction scale or for a 5-point scale indicating the strength of buying intentions, is in each case mostly a function of the fact that there are only five possible ratings customers can give. This is because variance is computed as the sum of the squared deviations of each value from the population mean divided by the number of population elements. Because the mean of a set of ratings has a limited range—the largest possible deviation from the mean, given a 5-point scale, is ≤ 4—the variance of a rating scale must itself fall within a limited range. The same holds true for any 4-point scale, any 7-point scale, and any 10-point scale, regardless of what is being measured. Table 13.1 gives the range of variances typically encountered for commonly used rating scales.

With rating scales, use the lower value for the variance in Table 13.1 if you have reason to believe that the distribution of customer responses looks like a bell curve, that is, if you expect most customers to give the middle rating, with fewer and fewer customers checking the more and more extreme ratings. If you think the distribution will be lopsided, with the majority of customers giving either extremely high or low ratings, or if you think customers will be all over the map, with the middle rating used about as often as the extremes, then use the high value for the variance. Groundwork laid by customer visits and focus groups can be very helpful in making these decisions. Keep in mind also that a precision of, say, ±0.25 is quite a bit more precise in the case of a 10-point rating scale than in the case of a 4-point scale. A desire for tight precision combined with use of a high variance scale (10 points rather than 4 points) is going to drive sample size—and costs—considerably higher.

Not using a rating scale? No prior research on which to piggyback? A variable like hours per production task for a complicated manufacturing process could be very difficult to pin down in advance. (You might even protest, "This sort of ignorance is why we wanted to do research in the first place!")

Table 13.1   Estimated Variance for Rating Scales

Number of Scale Points	Example	Variance (Normal Distribution)	Variance (Flat or Skewed Distribution)
4	Performance scale: poor, fair, good, excellent	0.7	1.3
5	Likert scale anchored by strongly agree/strongly disagree with a neutral midpoint	1.2	2.0
7	Semantic differential scale with end points anchored by bipolar opposites (e.g., boring/exciting)	2.5	4.0
10	Ratings of preference or attractiveness	3	7

Note: Use the larger variance to obtain a more conservative estimate of needed sample size, especially if there is considerable uncertainty about the distribution of customer responses or if there is reason to believe that the distribution of responses will be relatively flat as opposed to humped in the middle.

Adapted from Churchill & Iacobucci, 2009 (see Suggested Readings in Chapter 2).

The two possible approaches in such cases are simulation and guesstimation. For purposes of simulation, simply open an Excel spreadsheet and create a plausible distribution for the variable in question using an assumed sample size that is very small. Thus, using a small sample of 20, your spreadsheet might look like this:

Production Hours Required	Number of Customers at This Level
20	1
25	2
27.5	4
30	6
32.5	4
35	2
40	1
Mean = 30	$N = 20$

You would compute the variance as the sum of the squared deviations from the mean (= 262.5) divided by the number of population elements (= 20), giving a variance of 13.125. If the decision maker requests a precision of ±1 hour with a confidence level of 95 percent, then the needed sample size is $(2^2 \times 13.125) / 1^2 = 53$ factory customers. If you aren't confident that the distribution looks like a bell curve, then flatten it out and recompute the variance (which will be larger), and consider using the larger sample computed thereby, depending on whether the amount at stake justifies a more expensive study.

The guesstimation approach, which is even simpler, takes advantage of the fact that in a normal distribution, 99+ percent of all values will fall within 3 standard deviations of either side of the mean. Here you simply ask yourself, Do I have a feel for the minimum and maximum values I can reasonably expect to encounter? Qualitative research or plain old industry experience may indicate that the range of production hours required for the task is probably between 20 and 40. If so, and if normally distributed, then the standard deviation would be the range of 20 divided by 6, or 3.66. Because variance is the square of the standard deviation, you would plug 13.34 into the sample size formula (a result not so different from the variance of 13.125 computed in the Excel spreadsheet simulation, reflecting the fact that the simulation values had the same range and roughly mimicked the shape of a normal distribution).

There are doubtless some readers, confronted with these two heuristics, who might reply, "Do I need to spell it out for you: WE HAVEN'T A CLUE! We don't know range, minimum, maximum, or anything else about this value. THAT'S WHY WE WANT TO DO RESEARCH!" Indeed, how *do* you compute sample size if neither of the heuristics just described seem to apply? The answer is that if you can't even guess the range of some quantity of interest, then it really is premature to be doing quantitative research—you need to do some secondary research or qualitative research first. (How could the decision makers even specify the desired precision if they didn't have some sense of the range?) Alternatively, this highly uncertain item may not be central to the research, in which case you can set sample size using information on some other key item and accept whatever precision that sample size yields for the uncertain item. Precision at a given confidence level can always be calculated after the fact using the obtained sample size and the obtained distribution of answers, and this precision can be respected in decision making.

SAMPLING REMINDERS AND CAVEATS

The first caveat is that the preceding discussion has been drastically simplified relative to any standard statistical treatment of the topic. It would literally take more pages than this chapter itself to list all the assumptions, special cases, and exceptions that have been omitted. If there is a lot of money at stake, you owe it to yourself to consult a statistician experienced in drawing samples. Any competent market research vendor will either have such a statistician on staff or know where to find one. The point to take away is that quantitative research succeeds only to the extent that it is based on good probability samples of adequate size. If the sample is bad or simply too small, a result stated as "a small majority of customers, about 55 percent, agreed that . . . " should really be reported as "we won't be too far off if we assume that somewhere between 25 percent and 85 percent of our customers would agree that . . . " Precision is everything in quantitative research, and good samples are required if precision is to be adequate.

The second caveat is that the formula for sample size given assumes comparison of a single estimate to some absolute standard—that is, whether more or less than 50 percent of customers agree with some view. A different formula is required if the task is to determine whether more customers agree with viewpoint A than viewpoint B or whether customers in segment 1 are more likely to hold viewpoint A than customers in segment 2. The basic approach involving an interplay of confidence level, variance, and precision remains the same, but the formulas used are distinct. Such formulas can be found in market research or other statistical texts under headings such as "Computing Power for a Given Sample Size." The details vary depending on what type of comparison is involved, so professional assistance is advisable.

The third caveat is that precision as discussed in this chapter is precision with respect to random sampling error only. The tacit preface was always "assuming that every other part of the research is free of every other kind of error" then and only then would a sample of such and such a size have the calculated precision. Because random sampling error is only one of the many kinds of error, it is futile to keep ramping up sample size in search of a vanishingly small margin of error. Other kinds of error, such as a bad sample due to incompetent interviewers, poorly worded questions, inappropriate statistical techniques, and so on, aren't reduced by increases in sample size and can even be aggravated (as when less competent interviewers are pressed into service to produce a large sample under deadline). Because nonsampling errors are difficult to eliminate or even detect, large increases in sample size can produce a misleading tightening of precision. Total precision, taking all kinds of error into account, becomes markedly more loose than the stated precision, which only reflects random sampling error. And it is total precision that matters as far as real-world decisions are concerned.

As a practical matter, commercial studies of proportions should rarely seek a precision any tighter than ±5 percentage points. Even well-funded pollsters trying to predict closely fought U.S. elections don't generally shoot for any more precision than ±3 percent and associated sample sizes in the low 1,000s. Similarly, commercial studies of quantities (e.g., production hours) should generally be satisfied with a precision not much tighter than 10 percent of whatever difference is expected. If a decision maker expects more precision than that, then I suspect he or she has not really accepted the fact that market research can only reduce uncertainty, not eliminate it.

In terms of reminders, perhaps the most important is that all the calculations in this chapter apply to the final obtained sample and not to the initial sample. Furthermore, regardless of whether the initial sample was a probability sample, the obtained sample should only be considered a probability sample if nonresponse bias can be judged to be minimal or absent. When response levels are very low, it is difficult to believe that responders are not systematically different from the nonresponders. If a survey doesn't ultimately rest on a probability sample of adequate size, then its results are really no more precise and no more projectable than those of any competently conducted piece of *qualitative* research.

The second reminder is that sample size really does relate to precision as a matter of mathematical law. If you have an adequately sized probability sample, you are going to achieve a reasonable degree of precision. A corollary is that a sample size of as little as 100 can give more than satisfactory precision in many practical contexts. This is why it can be so powerful and costeffective to follow up a qualitative research study with a short, focused survey. One hundred phone calls may yield sufficient certainty that a substantial proportion of customers really does hold some negative perception—a perception whose existence went unguessed prior to the discoveries made through qualitative research.

DISCUSSION QUESTIONS

1. In a meeting with a senior manager, you convey this chapter's discussion of the difficulty of obtaining a probability sample in commercial market research. Said manager scoffs: "Not to worry—as long as the number of customers who complete the survey is large, say a thousand or more, the Law of Large Numbers will protect us—results won't be too far off what a probability sample would have given." Evaluate this rebuttal.

   a. *Extra Credit*: Work "Literary Digest poll" into your answer.

   b. *Extra Extra Credit*: Relate the Law of Large Numbers to the discussion of Nate Silver's work in the chapter.

2. The chapter argued that regardless of how good the initial sample frame was, considered as a probability sample of the population of interest, the lower the response rate, the less the likelihood that the *obtained* sample would still be a probability sample of that population. Draw a graph to show numerically the relationship between response rate (x-axis, 100% to 0% on the right) and the likelihood that the obtained sample is a probability sample, given that the sample frame was a probability sample (y-axis, 0 up to 1.0). The first point on the graph will be at 100%, 1.0, and the line will presumably decline thereafter. But what do you think the shape of the line might be? Discuss and defend the shape of your line.

3. A colleague ruefully acknowledges, "We don't have enough time and money to get a good probability sample for this upcoming piece of quantitative research. We can execute the study quickly and cheaply, and on a large sample, but we won't know for sure how that sample relates to the population. It won't be a crappy sample—everybody in it will be a bona fide member of the population of interest—we just won't know how biased the sample is, or even the direction of any bias."

   a. What would you recommend that your colleague do: Execute the study, change it, or do something else? Assume that top management likes to see data-based decisions, and that top management hasn't read this book or any other market research text. Be sure to justify your recommendation.

b. Would it make a difference to your recommendation if the quantitative study was: (1) a descriptive survey, (2) a laboratory experiment, (3) a field experiment, or (4) a conjoint study? Discuss.

c. Would it make a difference to your recommendation if:

   i. The product was in a B2B market and a set of 24 customer visits had been completed, about which your colleague remarked, "We learned a lot in the visits and came out of it with a clear direction. We just don't know how far we can trust a sample of 24 exploratory visits, especially given the freedom we took with the agenda as the visits accumulated."

   ii. The product was in a B2C market and your colleague remarked, "It's been years since we've done any kind of research with this customer population. The quantitative study was conceived as a way of dipping our toe back into the water with these consumers."

4. Here are three problems for you to test your ability to apply the sample size formula given in the chapter. The "discussion" question comes after you have completed your calculations.

   a. A restaurant wants to determine the average amount spent per month on sit-down restaurant dining by households in the area. It is believed that some households spend nothing at all, while others spend as much as $300 per month. Management wants to be 95 percent confident, and wants the margin of error (precision) to be ±$5. What sample size is needed to achieve these goals?

   b. To determine the effectiveness of an ad campaign for a new DVD player, management would like to know what percentage of the market has been made aware of the new product. The ad agency thinks this figure could be as high as 70 percent. In estimating the percent aware, management has specified a 95 percent confidence interval, and a precision of ±2 percent. What sample size is needed?

   c. A firm wishes to track satisfaction on a quarterly basis using a 10-point scale. They'd like a precision of ±0.05—that is, to be able to interpret a change in average satisfaction from 8.90 to 8.95 as a true increase in customer satisfaction (95 percent confidence). What sample size will they need?

d. After you have calculated the sample size in each case, consider whether the choice of precision in each case was reasonable, excessively tight, or too loose. In the world, the desired precision is selected by management judgment, case by case; you will have to use your judgment to assess how reasonable each of the choices was.

SUGGESTED READINGS

Lohr, S. L. (2009). *Sampling: Design and analysis* (2nd ed.). Boston, MA: Duxbury Press.	A more advanced and comprehensive but still accessible treatment.
Scheaffer, R. L., Mendenhall, W., & Ott, L. (2005). *Elementary survey sampling* (6th ed.). Boston, MA: Duxbury Press.	As the title suggests, this text provides an introduction that relies less on advanced mathematics than many other treatments.
Silver, N. (2012). *The signal and the noise.* New York, NY: Penguin Press.	A good primer on forecasting and sampling that goes beyond aggregating multiple polls, as in the chapter's discussion.

FOURTEEN

QUANTITATIVE DATA ANALYSIS

———•◆•———

O n the one hand, data analysis is a core competence of market research professionals. Thus, any graduate-level market research text will devote hundreds of pages to this topic. On the other hand, the material in those chapters is virtually indistinguishable from what might be found in any text on applied statistics or statistics for the social and behavioral sciences. In that sense, there is little that is unique about the data analyses performed for market research. In essence, the same statistical procedures are used across all the social sciences, and many of the practitioners of data analysis in market research will have a PhD in some related discipline like psychology, sociology, or economics. In fact, there are three specific statistical procedures, widely used across the social sciences, that account for the bulk of the data analyses actually performed in day-to-day commercial market research. The limited goal of this chapter is to give the general manager and the engineering manager a handle on these procedures so that you know what to expect.

Given the brevity of this chapter, its goals must be especially limited. Think of it as a briefing. I can't teach you how to do data analysis in this space: that requires at least the hundreds of pages found in the standard market research text or, more properly, the years of practice designing and conducting statistical analyses that form the core of most contemporary social science PhD programs. What I can do is give you the names of things and put these names in a context. If this reduces your bewilderment or increases your composure the next time a market research study is discussed, then you should be able to ask more critical questions and ensure that the proposed study meets your needs as a decision maker. In addition, I hope to make you a more critical reader of secondary research and completed market research reports.

PROCEDURE

First, an overview of how quantitative "data" come into existence and get analyzed and reported.

1. In most cases, somehow, some way, an Excel spreadsheet containing numbers corresponding to respondents' answers gets created. If the procedure was a web-based survey, involved computer-assisted telephone interviewing, or was administered on a computer (as in the case of many conjoint studies), then the Excel spreadsheet is created automatically as part of data collection. If paper forms were used, then someone entered the responses, represented numerically, into Excel. The Excel data are generally in matrix form ("flat file," in computerese) where the rows correspond to individual respondents and the columns contain a numerical representation of each respondent's answer to each of the questions administered. For example, if a 5-point scale was used to measure purchase intentions, and that respondent indicated he would definitely purchase the new product when available, a "5" might be entered in the corresponding cell of the spreadsheet.

2. From Excel, the data are typically imported to a specialized statistical analysis program. SPSS (www.spss.com) and SAS (www.sas.com) are two comprehensive packages used by many academics; numerous other such packages exist, including free versions available over the web. Within the statistical package, raw data can be recorded, transformed, aggregated, or disaggregated at will, and virtually any statistical analysis can be performed simply by pulling down a menu and selecting a few options.

3. The data analyst often has a PhD, but routinized analyses on standardized instruments, such as a satisfaction questionnaire, may be performed by MBAs or other people who have accumulated hands-on experience. If the study is a one-off affair, then the analyst will probably generate a variety of tentative analyses never seen by the client as the analyst assimilates the data and decides on a reporting approach. If the study is more routinized, then analysis may be as simple as pushing a button to trigger a canned series of tests. In this case, the analyst sees roughly the same output as the client.

4. The results of the analyses are formatted as tables and embedded into a narrative (which, in routinized cases, such as the nth satisfaction study done within the banking category, may be largely boilerplate).

5. Results are presented to the client and discussed. Depending on the contract and what was paid for, the research firm may attempt to add quite a bit of interpretation to the data, to the point of recommending specific courses of action based on the data. Alternatively, the research firm may confine itself to explaining, clarifying, and defending the validity of the results and the procedures used, leaving substantive interpretation to client management.

TYPES OF DATA ANALYSIS IN MARKET RESEARCH

Most data analysis in market research consists of one of the following:

1. Tabulating and cross-tabulating proportions; an example would be agreement with an opinion item cross-tabulated with some other factor such as brand owned or education, in the consumer case, or size of business in the B2B case.

2. Comparing means (averages) across items, groups of customers, or time periods; an example would be total annual expenditure on the product category for males versus females, in summer vs. winter, on the West Coast vs. the East Coast, or by homeowners versus renters.

3. Predicting an outcome as a function of antecedent variables, as when level of satisfaction is shown to covary with expenditure, length of relationship with the vendor, number of changes in account team personnel, size of customer, and type of service contract.

Many more esoteric kinds of analyses, such as multidimensional scaling or structural equations models with latent variables (to convey the flavor of the jargon), also play a role in market research, but these three types of analyses are the workhorses employed every day. In the case of each of these procedures, individual numbers are compared in an attempt to detect meaningful or real differences. How do customers of Brand A differ from customers of Brand B? Which attributes are worth a lot of money to customers, and which attributes are not worth any money? Which factors serve to increase customer satisfaction, and which have no effect?

Sometimes the reality of the difference between two numbers is deemed to be obvious, as in the following cross-tabulation:

	Brand A	Brand B
Agree	80%	20%
Disagree	20%	80%

If the sample is large, further statistical analysis of this comparison only confirms what we see at a glance—owners of Brands A and B hold very different opinions. On the other hand, much of the time the data looks more like this breakdown of the customer base for each of three brands:

Income	Brand A	Brand B	Brand C
< $50,000	15%	12%	10%
$50,000–$100,000	34	31	28
$100,000–$250,000	43	43	49
> $250,000	8	14	13

Or maybe like this:

Perceived Importance (10 = max)	Segment 1	Segment 2	Segment 3
Feature 1	8.6	7.6	8.3
Feature 2	7.0	8.2	8.8
Feature 3	6.2	7.5	7.9
Feature 4	5.9	4.0	5.8
Feature 5	3.8	5.6	5.7

As we move from 2 × 2 cross-tabulations to 3 × 5 cross-tabulations, and as the different results move closer and as the numbers become more abstract, as in the preference ratings, it becomes more and more difficult to say, with confidence, that customers of Brand A tend to have lower incomes

than customers of Brand B, or that different segments place different importance weights on key features.

If you recall the sampling chapter, you know that all these numbers
obtained on the sample are only fallible estimates of the true population values
in any case. The question becomes, When does a difference between two numbers obtained in the sample represent a reliable, actionable difference, and
when is the difference only apparent and dismissible as an artifact of the random variation inherent in all sample data? (Sometimes the question is more
naturally thought of as whether two items have a real *association*; but this
reduces to the question of whether the degree of association is different from
zero. Hence, I shall refer to "difference" throughout this discussion.)

Modern statistical data analysis arose to address precisely this question:
Which apparent differences in data are real, and which are not? It is important
to understand that statistical analysis gives us no direct access to the truth; it
simply indicates whether the apparent difference is probably real or, alternatively, how probable it is that the apparent difference in the sample reflects a
real difference in the population, so that it is signal rather than noise.

By convention, an apparent difference is accepted as a real difference if,
when the appropriate test statistic is applied, it indicates that the difference in
question would arise by chance in fewer than 5 of 100 cases. Now, let us
unpack that unwieldy sentence. Every kind of data difference has associated
with it one or more statistical procedures, and each such statistical procedure
allows a computation of a number known as a test statistic. These test statistics
are computed using the same sorts of assumptions about probability and probability distributions as underlie the discussion of sample size.

Suffice to say that when you calculate a test statistic, you acknowledge
that if the study were repeated with a new probability sample, you would not
get exactly the same results each time. This variability follows from the fact
that you are drawing a limited sample from a very large population. The mathematics underlying the test statistic then envisions repeating the study an
infinite number of times and uses the data in the present sample to estimate
how often, in that infinite series of repetitions, you would get a difference this
big *by chance alone*. If the answer is fewer than 5 in 100, such results are
generally given an asterisk and a footnote that reads something like "$p < .05$."

The important thing to retain from this discussion is that statistical analysis
is simply a set of mathematically based conventions for determining when you
can accept an apparent difference as a real difference. More pointedly, if no

statistical analysis has been applied, and the difference is not of the order 80–20 versus 20–80, you ought not to assume that the apparent difference is a real one. If you are reading a report that makes much of certain apparent differences— say, the 52 percent agreement in segment 1 versus the 43 percent agreement in segment 2—but that includes no statistical analysis, then you should become very suspicious. Worse, if there is a plethora of such statistical analyses, but the sample is not a probability sample, then you should question how much weight can be placed on the results; strictly speaking, in the absence of a probability sample, the results of the significance tests are not correct. More exactly, the results of conducting a statistical test on a nonprobability sample are of unknown validity. You simply don't know whether to accept them or not.

MANAGERIAL PERSPECTIVE ON DATA ANALYSIS

As a general manager receiving the results of data analyses, your primary responsibility is to understand that apparent differences need not be real differences. It behooves a general manager to have a deep humility concerning the ability of any research endeavor to produce a picture of the world as it truly is. Given this stance, you know to be skeptical as soon as you are intrigued. That is, when you see a difference that seems actionable or would resolve an uncertainty, your next response should always be, Is it real? Your second responsibility, then, is to understand the role played by statistical analysis in vetting apparent differences. You must have the discipline not to accept reported differences at face value, absent an appropriate test. Your final responsibility is to accept that even statistical analysis only provides an estimate of the odds that a difference is real rather than apparent. It takes quite a bit of tough-mindedness to accept that some proportion of statistical judgments indicating that a difference is real will be wrong—about 5 in 100, actually. Because general managers may encounter hundreds of data comparisons in a year, they can be virtually certain that some differences vetted as real are not. As I said at the outset, market research reduces uncertainty but cannot eliminate it.

Put in more positive terms, if a good sample was obtained—that is, a correctly sized probability sample—and if two key numbers appear to be really different ($p < .05$), and you have no countervailing data or experience, then you should feel comfortable acting on these results. More than 95 times out of 100, the data will be vindicated. But remember: It is never 100 percent certain.

DOs AND DON'Ts

Don't be intimidated by statistical tests, no matter how scanty your education in this area. From a managerial standpoint, every test, no matter how esoteric, is just an effort to mark out certain findings as real and noteworthy.

Do be suspicious of any quantitative research report that doesn't include statistical tests. Without a test, how are you to know which nominal differences can support a decision?

Don't accept a statistical test at face value in the absence of information about the sampling procedure and a judgment as to whether it was a probability sample.

Do acquire a habit of skepticism when presented with table after table of numbers, and slide after slide of full-color charts and graphs. Which differences are real, and which are just random variation?

DISCUSSION QUESTIONS

1. Although many market research efforts use only some combination of (1) comparison of means, (2) cross-tabulations, and (3) regression, there are many other statistical tools available to be applied when specialized circumstances demand.

   a. Test your skills as a web searcher: Identify half a dozen other statistical tools that are applied with some frequency in market research. For each one, explain what it does for the manager that tests of means, cross-tabulations, or regressions cannot do. Pinpoint the unique insight available through this tool, and the kinds of marketing decisions it might support.

   b. How many of these tools are applicable to: (1) mostly B2C, (2) mostly B2B, or (3) equally applicable? Discuss.

2. In the prior chapter the claim was made that all statistical tests presume a probability sample. Explain why this is so. (You will need to recall your instruction in prior statistics classes.)

3. You read in a report, or hear in a presentation, a test result. For instance, a cross-tabulation is tested and men and women are shown to hold different

opinions "at $p < .05$." You determine that the research did not use a probability sample. It appears to be a bona fide sample from the population of interest, but it is certainly not a probability sample.

a. What stance would you take toward the finding that "men and women hold different opinions"? Your answer could be anything from "the truth value of this finding is unknown" to "men and women probably do differ, but maybe not by quite as much as the cross-tabulation shows." Explain and defend your answer.

b. How does your answer change, if at all, if I change the example in each of the following ways:

   i. The finding was instead that men and women do *not* hold different opinions, as seen by the test result, which was "$p > .20$."

   ii. The original finding of a difference was actually "$p < .01$."

   iii. The sample was twice as large as you initially thought, say, 800 versus 400.

   iv. The difference between men and women was lopsided: 2:1 versus 1:2 in terms of the ratio of agreement to disagreement in men versus women.

   v. *Extra Credit*: Find the reverse split, men versus women, in a sample of 400, that would produce a chi-square value of exactly 3.84 (corresponding to an alpha of exactly .05).

   vi. *More Extra Credit*: How big would the sample have to be for a reverse 2:1 split across men and women to produce a chi-square of exactly 3.84?

   vii. If you do the extra credit, does this change your initial answer to (a)? Discuss.

4. A senior colleague, apprised that a probability sample was imperative if statistical tests were to be performed, shrugs and says "too bad—we've always included statistical tests in these reports and management expects to see them. I'm not going to drop the tests and I'm certainly not going to include some mealy-mouthed footnote about probability samples—I don't need the grief." Discuss how much weight should be placed on the tests in this report in terms of guiding real world decisions.

a. You express your qualms more forcefully in a second conversation, and your colleague says, "Look—I understand the technical issue. This test of means I'm flagging as 'significant at $p < .05$' is probably not significant at exactly that level. If I collected a real probability sample over and over, sometimes I'd discover the probability to be only .09 (borderline significant, as some would say), and others it would be even better, maybe .01, strongly significant. The fact remains that the results are going to be roughly the same as in a probability sample, meaning that those differences that are significant at .05 are worth more attention than those differences where the odds of a chance result are .50. You see, the significance tests are just a way to flag certain differences and direct the attention of management to those. This is a business, not a classroom."

b. Now what would you say?

SUGGESTED READINGS

Any standard market research text, such as those listed at the end of Chapter 2	If more than one is available, pick up the thickest—it will have hundreds of pages on the topic of this chapter.
SAGE Publications	If a particular kind of statistical analysis procedure is of interest, SAGE Publications offers dozens of books devoted to specific procedures, and their website (sagepub.com) can be searched using the name of the technique.
Journal of Market Research *Marketing Science*	For coverage of new and emerging statistical techniques, the key academic journals are the *Journal of Marketing Research* and *Marketing Science*. These outlets are where you would expect to see a new technique for analyzing the effectiveness of key word search advertising, a new procedure for testing the effectiveness of a social media campaign, or a new way to do conjoint analysis, and so forth.

SUGGESTED CASE: XEROX #1 (HARVARD 9-591-055)

Synopsis

[This case has two foci: a set of satisfaction surveys, and a small experiment to test guarantees. This synopsis only applies to the satisfaction surveys; see below for a synopsis of the portion of the case that presents an experiment.] [1]

In the late 1980s, Xerox pioneered the development of ongoing surveys of customer satisfaction. At the time of the case, management had put in place four different surveys, and the questions below ask you to assess the value of these efforts.

Questions

1. These surveys were justified in part by a commitment to Total Quality Management. Explain why it is important to survey customers as part of such an effort. Why not just count defects and complaints, which would be arguably simpler and cheaper, and might pinpoint more exactly any manufacturing quality problems?

2. What is the business rationale for investments to achieve higher levels of customer satisfaction? What sort of financial payoff can a firm like Xerox reasonably expect?

3. At the time of the case, a quite massive survey effort is described. In any such instance, now or then, we may suppose that sooner or later, budgets will tighten. If you had to jettison one of the four survey efforts as least important, which one and why? Conversely, which one is so valuable that you would hold on to it until the very last?

4. Evaluate the sample size used in the Periodic Survey—is it too small, too big, or about right? How can you tell?

---

[1] I use both parts of this case and order it under the number given; if you are only going to use one part, Harvard provides a split A and B version, allowing you to order only the part you need.

5. Consider the example survey instrument included as an exhibit. Critique this from the standpoint of good questionnaire design. Are any important types of questions missing? Are there questions that don't really belong?

6. A lot has changed in both survey research and the business of measuring customer satisfaction in the decades since the Xerox effort described in this case. What, exactly, do you suppose a firm like Xerox does differently in 2015? What elements remain more or less the same?

   (a) Hint: Answer separately in terms of what has changed in survey implementation, versus what has changed in the nature of the questionnaire used. Change may (or may not) be much greater in one versus the other.

   (b) The easy answer here is "now they do it over the Web instead of with paper." So what? Does that difference in administration make a difference to anything else?

       i. Is the change to Web administration the biggest change, or are there any more fundamental changes?

   (c) Regardless of changes in how satisfaction surveys are done or in the content of satisfaction questionnaires, has there been any change in the basic rationale for surveying customers about their satisfaction?

       ii. Equivalently, would your answers to questions #1 and #2 above have been any different in 1990 than today? Why, or why not?

SUGGESTED CASE: XEROX #2 (HARVARD 9-591-055)

Synopsis

[This case has two foci: a set of satisfaction surveys, and a small experiment to test guarantees. This synopsis only applies to the experiment; see above for a synopsis of the satisfaction survey portion, and see footnote to Xerox #1 re ordering information.]

Having improved its measured customer satisfaction, Xerox seeks competitive advantage based on the superior quality of its copiers. The suggestion under discussion at the top levels of management is whether to offer some kind of guarantee. This proves not to be a simple yes or no decision—there are multiple ways of constructing a guarantee, and no consensus as to the best approach. Management proceeds to conduct some focus groups along with a small experimental test, delivered by phone and supplemented with a brief questionnaire. Your task is to interpret the findings of this quantitative research to make a recommendation about guarantees.

Questions

1. Were the focus groups' money well spent? What role did they play in supporting the experimental test?

2. Based on the results, which is the best guarantee to offer? What evidence supports your judgment?

   (a) Your instructor may supply you with a mock-up of the underlying data. If so, select the crucial result(s), and apply the appropriate statistical test(s).

   (b) Are the statistical results sufficiently stark to drive the decision, or will a judgment call be involved as well? Explain.

3. Could Xerox have just as well done a conjoint study rather than the simple laboratory experiment described? Why, or why not?

SUGGESTED CASE: STAR DIGITAL (HARVARD #M-347)

Synopsis

Star Digital is described as a video rental company that advertises through banner or display ads on the Web. They have run an experiment in an attempt to quantify the ROI of their Web advertising. The experiment had a test and a control group, and a sample of the data is in hand for analysis of the results.

[Note: You must download the spreadsheet with the results of the experiment from the Harvard site, and load it into a statistics program of your choosing. (The Excel data pack does not contain the necessary statistical procedures.)]

Questions

1. Evaluate the strengths and weaknesses of the experimental design. If your charge had been to determine whether there was a positive ROI for this firm's Web advertising, what, if anything, would you have done differently?

    (a) It's all right to ratify the design exactly as implemented; but you have to give reasons why there is no better or more optimal design.

2. Select an appropriate statistical procedure for this sort of data, and conduct the analyses needed to answer the key question: Did the Web advertising produce revenue in excess of its costs?

    (a) Were the two advertising networks both effective?

    (b) If so, were these equally effective?

3. You may find it helpful to return to the Europet case at the end of Part II. Star Digital exemplifies the difference between online and offline advertising: Unlike Europet, here there is a direct connection between ad exposure and purchase.

    (a) But, there is the same need for a two-step calculation to calculate ROI: (1) quantifying the statistical association between ad exposure and purchase and (2) combining that information with the cost of the ads and the lifetime profit contribution of converting a prospect into a customer.

4. In most ad campaigns, online or offline, some prospects will be exposed to the advertising multiple times; there is a general sense that up to a certain point, multiple exposures are helpful in converting prospects, and a necessary investment. Put another way, effective frequency is generally greater than one; few ads are so powerful as to make the sale after a single exposure. Frequency information was collected in this case; devise a statistical test to determine whether more frequent exposure was in fact associated with higher rates of conversion for the Star Digital ad campaign.

5. As with Europet, only a sample of the total results is provided. Discuss the gains and losses of running analyses on the sample, rather than the

(huge) total dataset, and the implications of your answer for the hullabaloo surrounding Big Data.

SUGGESTED CASE: PORTLAND TRAILBLAZERS (HARVARD #UV2971)

Synopsis

A major league sports team, suffering from an attendance slump and multiple other ills, considers whether to redesign its ticket package. A conjoint study that includes price is conducted to assess the appeal of different possible ticket packages, and key results are available for interpretation.

[Note: This is a much more straightforward case than MSA, and suitable as the first case in a conjoint module].

Questions

1. Do any of the seats appear to be mispriced? What does "mispriced" mean in this context, and what operation could you perform on the conjoint results to answer this question?

2. Assuming there is an opportunity to increase (or decrease) the price of at least one seat type, use the conjoint results to calculate the exact price change to make the seat fairly priced relative to its value as perceived by customers.

3. Are any of the promotional offers cost-effective? By cost-effective, I mean that the value delivered to the customer exceeds the cost to provide it.

4. An alternative to re-pricing a seat that appears over-priced is to add promotional offers that bring additional value. This only makes sense, of course, if the promotional offer itself is "under-priced," in terms of its cost to implement, versus the value it contributes in the eyes of customers.

    (a) Is there a seat where this would make sense? If so, which promotional offer would you add?

SUGGESTED CASE: MSA, PLANNING
THE AMAPS PRODUCT LINE (HARVARD #9-590-069)

Synopsis

This is an enterprise software case, a hard-core, heavy-duty B2B technology case. It will be most successful in an MBA class consisting of working professionals, and where many students have experience with B2B markets.

At the time of the case, MSA has a problematic product offering within the defense contracting market, which itself has been in turmoil. The product consists of software to help defense manufacturers do resource planning. To help decide what to do about the problematic software offering, market research, including focus groups and a conjoint study, has been commissioned. The results of the research are given, and the task is to interpret these results.

Questions

1. State the decision problem that led to the market research reported.

2. If no market research had been done, could you predict management's decision? Explain your answer with respect to what you know about organizational behavior, post-merger and acquisition, and anything you might know about the management of large-scale software projects.

3. Is there a big enough market to justify investing funds in resuscitating the AMAPS/g product? Provide a financial calculation based on the conjoint results.

4. How about the various enhancements to the AMAPS/g—do the conjoint results support investing in any of the enhancements to the core product? Again, provide a financial calculation based on the conjoint results.

5. How confident are you in the market size estimates derived from the conjoint? More exactly, drawing on all the research, including the focus groups and the survey questions that accompanied the conjoint, would you argue that the size estimates are biased upward, or probably conservative, or not obviously biased either way?

6. Why was it important (or was it not) to do focus groups before the conjoint? The focus groups probably added several tens of thousands of dollars, and a month or two, to an already expensive and time-consuming effort. If you think the groups were worthwhile, be specific about the value added, relative to just proceeding directly to the conjoint.

7. Could a survey, or an experiment, have replaced the conjoint? If not, what is it about the MSA situation that mandates a conjoint analysis?

8. This sort of B2B technology product category is sometimes presented as the kind of situation where only customer visits really make sense. If MSA had done only customer visits, with results directionally or impressionistically consistent with the actual conjoint results, what do you suppose management's decision with respect to the AMAPS/g product would have been? Explain.

PART V

THE BIG PICTURE

OVERVIEW

The chapters in this final part fit a "good news, bad news" structure. The good news comes in Chapter 15, which explains how different research techniques can be combined in a way that shores up the weaknesses of each to produce a research strategy that is stronger than any of its component techniques. The goal is to give concrete examples of how research strategies can be assembled, using business situations where managers commonly expect some amount of market research to be helpful—for example, new product development, or repositioning an existing brand.

The bad news comes in Chapter 16. Here I point to business situations where no individual market research technique can contribute much, and no effective research strategy can be devised by dint of combining techniques. Such business situations, unfortunately, are not at all rare or unusual.

It is, of course, highly unusual for a textbook to be so explicit about the limits and shortcomings of its subject matter as occurs in Chapter 16. Most textbooks, especially in business, are relentlessly upbeat. A marketing text-book will go on and on about the importance of marketing to the firm; a finance textbook will use the same sort of laudatory language but substitute "finance" for "marketing." Market research textbooks, in turn, hammer the point of how important market research is, and how valuable it can be to the knowledgeable manager, and so on. Enough already!

I said in the beginning that market research, skillfully conducted over a lengthy period, can generally produce a positive return on investment for a firm large enough to afford high-quality research. But I also said that the judgment of whether market research was worthwhile had to be made on a case-by-case basis, and that there were cases where the answer would be "no." The purpose of Chapter 16 is to drive home the point about the limited utility of market research. As will emerge, there are many situations where market research is not only not cost-effective, but not effective at all.

FIFTEEN

COMBINING RESEARCH TECHNIQUES INTO RESEARCH STRATEGIES

───◆•◆───

I t is rarely the case that a business problem can be addressed by the application of a single research technique in isolation. More commonly, multiple complementary research techniques, conducted in sequence, are required. This chapter describes the kind of complete research strategy that might be developed to address seven common business problems. The examples given are "pure" cases, showing what you might do when the magnitude of the problem justifies a sustained effort and your budget permits it. In actual cases, one or more of the techniques described might be omitted, for the very good reason that the payback for the research expenditure would be too small, in accordance with the calculations described in the appendix to Chapter 2. Other combinations of techniques could also be used; these sequences are intended to be illustrative and not rigid prescriptions.

First, Table 15.1 gives a high-level overview of the typical or canonical research sequence.

Essentially, you start by consulting archival data, continue to some kind of qualitative research, and conclude with a definitive quantitative research project. In an optional final step, you will sometimes return to secondary data to assess what was accomplished, or to qualitative research to refine and unpack quantitative findings. Here are some fleshed-out examples of how this sequence might play out in the context of specific marketing decisions.

Table 15.1   Sequencing Research Techniques Over Time

Type:	Archival Data →	Qualitative →	Quantitative →	[Optional follow-up]
Examples:	• Consult secondary data to assess current situation • Analyze Big Data to identify characteristics of the most brand loyal customers	• Do customer visits to explore customer perceptions • Do focus groups to get a handle on brand perceptions relative to competitors	• Conduct a survey to identify how many customers hold particular views • Conduct a conjoint analysis to determine optimum price–performance point • Conduct an experiment to select the best of three prototypes for further development	• Consult secondary data for market share obtained by new product • Interview customers from the segment identified in a survey as most/least satisfied
Who does:	Product manager Market analyst	Cross-functional team appropriate for research objective	In many cases, an outside research firm	Market analyst Product manager

DEVELOPING NEW PRODUCTS

- Use *secondary research* to assess existing product offerings from competitors and to estimate market size and growth rates in this category. Secondary data can also be used to build a financial justification for any proposed product.

- Conduct *customer visits* among potential buyers for the new product. These visits identify unmet needs and areas of dissatisfaction with existing offerings. Participation in the visits by engineering staff will assist them throughout the project in visualizing how customers might respond to various design trade-offs.
- Execute a *conjoint analysis* study to identify the optimal combination of features and functionality from among several design alternatives produced in response to the secondary research and customer visits, and to test for the trade-off between price and functionality.

REDESIGN A WEBSITE

- Use *secondary research* in the particular form of web analytics: Examine where browsers come from, and how they navigate the site, to determine how the website is currently being used.
- Conduct *focus groups* with current and prospective users of the website to explore perceptions of your own and competitor's websites and to identify user requirements for websites of this type.
- Develop alternative new designs and conduct an *experiment* to determine which of the new designs is best. This experiment can take place in the field by serving up alternative designs to some fraction of daily users, as described in Chapter 11 on experimentation. Depending on how thorough the redesign is, these experiments might be conducted iteratively to pin down various elements of the redesign.
- Monitor the performance of the new design again using *secondary data* in the form of web analytics.

ASSESSING CUSTOMER SATISFACTION

- Use *secondary research* to find any public information on competitors' level of customer satisfaction, plus any internal data on past assessments of your own customers' satisfaction. In addition to these quantitative data, search the literature for more qualitative data: What are the key dissatisfiers or common complaints? What are crucial needs that must be addressed by any satisfactory solution?

- Use Big Data to analyze your own internal records to identify themes running through complaints, calls to the service department, and the like.
- Conduct *customer visits* to identify and explore how customers evaluate their satisfaction with this product category, what standards they use to assess product quality, and how intangibles such as vendor reputation come into play. The goal here is to learn *what* to measure.
- Conduct a *survey* of customers at regular intervals to numerically measure and track customer satisfaction. This survey needs to draw a representative sample, and it needs to be executed consistently over time. Here, you precisely and accurately measure the qualities you earlier identified and explored via secondary research and customer visits.
- Optionally, follow up the survey with interviews of customers from segments known to be satisfied or dissatisfied to probe further the causes in each case.
- If the steps just described are already ongoing or recently conducted, consider whether to move away from a periodic sampling of customers to an ongoing sample of key events, as described under "Future Directions" in Chapter 9, on survey research.

SEGMENTING A MARKET

- Use *secondary research* to identify possible segmentation schemes proposed by industry analysts or actually in use by competitors. Pay close attention to internal secondary data in the form of sales records and customer databases.
- Use Big Data to explore internal data that may suggest significant differences in buying patterns among existing customers.
- Use *focus groups* to explore psychological differences among customers. These might concern values, benefits desired, or intangible cultural or lifestyle differences. Focus groups are helpful in this application because participants often polarize around discussion of certain issues, thus highlighting possible segment differences. The goal here is to discover new ways to segment the market.
- Conduct a *survey* to accurately measure the size and characteristics of each segment in the tentative scheme. Although your earlier research

has generated possible segments, it cannot confirm that any particular segment is large enough to be worthwhile, nor whether the tentative segments actually differ in the marketplace to the degree suggested by your research studies. Because segmentation analyses are typically a prelude to a decision to target one or a small number of segments, it is important to do survey research to accurately assess how attractive each individual segment might be.

- Conduct a *conjoint* study to understand how brand perceptions and product preferences differ across segments of interest. Given two or more targeted segments whose attractiveness has been demonstrated through survey research, the question now becomes how to develop differentiated messages and actual products that precisely address the distinctive wants and needs of each targeted segment. The conjoint study can show how the value placed on your brand differs across segments, thus providing a focus for future advertising efforts, and also how importance weights differ, thus directing product development efforts.

EXPANDING INTO NEW MARKETS

Here, the notion is that you might be able to sell current or modified products to new types of customers.

- Use *secondary research* to identify attractive markets not currently served. A comparison of industry data to your own sales records and customer databases helps to identify underserved or neglected markets and submarkets. Profiles of competitors might reveal to you unsuspected market niches or areas where, despite good sales volume, you have barely penetrated. Discussions with your own sales force may be used to identify patterns among lost leads—people who took a bid or proposal but didn't buy.
- Conduct *focus groups* to gain initial insights into the thought world and point of view of members of untapped markets. Focus groups tend to be a time-efficient means of grasping the basic outline of an unfamiliar worldview.
- Conduct *customer visits* to more thoroughly describe applications, usage environments, and organizational decision processes in the most

interesting subset(s) of these untapped markets. The observational component and the in-depth nature of the interaction make visits a useful supplement to focus groups.

- Conduct a *survey* to more thoroughly describe the size, characteristics, and potential of the one or more new markets under study. (Note that the same logic applies to markets as to segments within markets.)
- Conduct an *experiment* to test different appeals and positionings for the one or two markets identified as most promising.

REPOSITIONING A BRAND

- Use *Big Data* in the form of analyses of masses of web text to determine what people are saying about the brand.
- Conduct *focus groups* to explore perceptions of own versus competitor brands in the category and identify key descriptors that define different brand positions now on offer or potentially available in the product category.
- Conduct a large *survey* to describe more exactly the current position of your own brand and competitor brands, to prioritize different benefits, and to examine customer characteristics associated with favorable evaluations of each brand and position.
- Optionally, conduct an *experiment* or a *conjoint* study to identify the best among several attractive possibilities for a re-positioning. The conjoint study might be used if you are positioning on relatively tangible brand traits and if brand positions in this category can be decomposed into specific traits that vary in level and that can be combined in various ways. Use an experiment if brand positions are relatively intangible or not decomposable into traits with multiple levels.
- Follow up by reanalyzing Big Data in terms of web comments to monitor whether the new positioning is diffusing into the market and beginning to alter perceptions of the brand in the desired direction.

DEVELOPING AN ADVERTISING CAMPAIGN

- Use *secondary research* to identify competitors' level of spending, relative emphasis on various media, and choice of particular vehicles. Gather as well examples of competitors' actual ads so as to identify themes and appeals. (These can be obtained for a fee from competitrack.com.)

- Conduct *focus groups* to gain insight into customers' thinking and to understand the kinds of issues that are important and unimportant to them. It will be important to have both vendor marketing staff and advertising agency personnel be involved with these focus groups.
- Conduct a *survey* to describe brand image of self and competitors, current levels of awareness, and specific beliefs or perceptions about your brand. The goal here is partly to verify findings from the focus groups and partly to measure baseline levels of factors, such as awareness, that the advertising campaign is supposed to influence.
- Conduct an *experiment* to compare the relative effectiveness of several alternative executions, each of which is on strategy, in the sense of addressing issues uncovered in the earlier research, but each of which takes a somewhat different creative approach. Sometimes the goal here will be to pick the strongest execution, and at other times it will be to rank order the effectiveness of a larger group so that the more effective executions receive a larger media budget.
- Conduct a *survey* to track the effectiveness of the campaign. This survey repeats measurements made during the baseline survey.

COMMENTARY

The common theme across most of these research strategies should be apparent. The canonical sequence of techniques in devising a research strategy, as noted earlier, is: first, secondary research; second, customer visits or focus groups for exploratory purposes; and third, surveys or conjoint analysis or experiments for confirmatory purposes. An optional follow-up is to return to archival data to estimate the impact of your decision, or to return to qualitative data to probe more deeply the results of some confirmatory technique. Again, your specific application may differ, so other sequences or more extended sequences may also be valid. Moreover, much depends on the unique circumstances of your case as to whether a particular technique needs to be executed at all. But the canonical sequence, stated more generally, serves as a useful summary for the marketing research advice given in this book:

First, look around.

Second, explore in depth.

Third, identify the best option.

Fourth, measure the results of your decision.

That's a fair summary of how to proceed when market research appears to be possible and pertinent. The final chapter switches perspective and attempts to identify circumstances where this advice isn't going to work, because your particular situation is outside the boundary of where market research is possible or pertinent.

DISCUSSION QUESTIONS

1. Discuss the circumstances where you might follow up a quantitative research project with a set of interviews—an optional procedure, according to the roadmap in Table15.1. As always, give examples in specific product categories.

   a. Is this more likely to occur in the B2B or B2C spheres?

   b. Would you suppose that interview follow-up is more likely to occur in the case of: (1) a survey, (2) a lab experiment, (3) a field experiment, or (4) a conjoint study?

2. Most of the third-stage strategies—survey, experimentation, conjoint—presume a mass market from which to sample. This mass market will often be lacking in B2B contexts. In very concentrated markets, a census can be taken during the qualitative phase, and the third stage need not occur, so the lack of a mass population from which to sample is not a problem. The difficult case is the less concentrated B2B market that may have some hundreds or a thousand buying units. Here the choice is: (1) skip third-stage research and wing it; (2) attempt a large sample that will probably be biased (for instance, you'll have much better access to your accounts than competitors'); or (3) maybe conduct a second semi-qualitative study, perhaps structured phone interviews with a

judgment sample of 50 customers. Discuss the pros and cons of each as a substitute for classic third-stage quantitative research.

3. Although this chapter covers many of the marketing decisions where market research techniques are commonly applied in series, there are of course many other marketing decisions not mentioned. Identify 2–3 more, and devise an appropriate market research strategy for each.

   a. Hint: Flip through a textbook on marketing strategy (e.g., Aaker [2014], in Suggested Readings for Chapter 1) to refresh your memory about the range of decisions that managers face.

   b. Use Table 15.1 to help in sequencing research techniques.

4. Word comes down from the executive suite that the key marketing strategy in the coming year is to grow revenue through the acquisition of new customers. Implementation, of course, will be left to lower-level managers. Your boss translates this mandate into a market research agenda as follows: "Let's start by visiting a broad range of current accounts. We'll follow up with a survey of our customer base that will profile them on the key purchase criteria identified through those customer visits. From there, we'll generate leads for our sales force, and meet our customer acquisition goals."

   a. What's wrong with this plan?

   b. Suggest a better sequence of research activity. Assume a B2B technology market with some thousands of buying units, among which you currently have about a 28 percent market share.

⊰ SIXTEEN ⊱

THE LIMITS OF MARKET RESEARCH

———◆•◉•◆———

It's tough to make predictions, especially about the future.

—Yogi Berra

I s market research always helpful? Is it everywhere possible? As suggested in Appendix 2A on budgeting for market research, the answer must be a firm "no." The purpose of this final chapter is to be frank about the limits of market research. It lays out some conditions under which effective market research is either not possible or not pertinent.

Most textbooks, in market research as elsewhere, tend to be imperialist. Authors have a natural tendency to play up the importance of their chosen topic. Boundless enthusiasm segues into unlimited possibilities for application. This chapter is intended as a corrective. Beginners are too easily bamboozled. The fact of the matter is that market research is a specialized business tool, powerful within its sphere but strictly bounded in its usefulness.

IDENTIFYING BOUNDARY CONDITIONS

The focus of this chapter, as with most of the book, is corporate enterprises held to a profit-and-loss standard. It is here that I want to look for boundary conditions beyond which market research is either not possible or not pertinent and, hence, not an ideal toward which firms—or beginners—are to be universally exhorted. I specify a corporate enterprise to rule out trivial boundary conditions, such as when a small business simply lacks the funds to systematically collect data from or about customers.

Market research is possible, and arguably the optimal decision support, in *many* corporate circumstances. But it is a bounded solution, and beyond the boundary lie numerous business decisions that are neither trivial nor easy.

Initial Case Examples—Inside the Boundary

I begin with two within-boundary cases. Suppose a B2C manufacturer like Procter & Gamble has commissioned a new TV advertising campaign for a laundry detergent. The ad agency presents two different creative strategies, embodied in two different example executions, for P&G to choose between. The media budget will run into the millions; it is imperative to select the better of the two approaches to leverage this investment. It seems to me that market research is clearly applicable here. A lab or field experiment can be set up in which a probability sample of detergent users is exposed to the two ads administered as alternative experimental treatments, and valid measures of response can be used to test which ad is better. In fact, it would be silly not to spend $20,000 on market research to leverage what may be an $8–12 million media buy.

Next, I want to drastically change surface features of this first example while still keeping it within the boundary. Suppose a B2B manufacturer like Hewlett-Packard wishes to develop the next generation of a networked laser printer used by workgroups. HP commissions a conjoint analysis in which a large sample of current users of networked printers make trade-offs between different new feature combinations at different price points. The conjoint analysis establishes that a particular feature–performance–price combination is optimal with respect to taking market share from a specified competitor. Here, the $50,000 expenditure on the conjoint would appear to be a reasonable investment relative to the payoff associated with gaining one or two points of market share in a billion-dollar market.

Note that in this second example, I changed the decision context from advertising to new product development; switched from an inexpensive, frequently purchased packaged good to a more expensive, infrequently purchased capital good; changed the buying decision from B2C to B2B; and moved from a minimally differentiated, not particularly technological product to a differentiated computer product resting on rapidly evolving opto-electronic and networking technologies.

Clearly then, neither new products nor B2B nor capital goods nor advanced technology represents a boundary beyond which market research ceases to be feasible. This is important; more superficial accounts of the limits of market research have gravitated toward simple, broad-brush distinctions of this kind: "Market research works best for consumer packaged goods; B2B is different, technology is yet more different, and new technology products are just beyond the pale." Not true; the actual boundary conditions are more abstract and fundamental than any of these ready-to-hand labels.

Additional Case Examples—Testing the Boundary[*]

In these next examples, I try to go outside the boundary of where market research is feasible. If "new product development" doesn't mark a boundary and "technology" is not a boundary and "B2B" is not a boundary, what could provide a meaningful boundary condition? It will be convenient to start with an example akin to the Hewlett-Packard one, but different in one crucial respect. Here is a second instance of new product development in a B2B context.

Case #1: Cisco

Suppose Cisco is developing a new network switch to carry Internet traffic at key hubs. It will be the first of a new generation using optical components and quantum tunneling, with the expected introduction date several years in the future. Each switch costs tens of millions of dollars with all services included. There are somewhere between 10 and 20 potential customers worldwide for the product, mostly major telecommunication firms, with each customer having the potential to buy 1 to N of these switches, where N is likely to be a single-digit number. As might be expected, purchase of this expensive and complex product is a group decision involving from 6 to M individuals, where M is estimated to be on the order of a dozen but varies by customer. Last, Cisco has access to only about two-thirds of the potential customers, based on its existing installed base plus a few customers relatively unhappy with current switch products obtained from competitors. The rest won't give them the time of day.

---

[*] *Note:* All of the "cases" in this chapter are fictional and should be read as "a company *like* Cisco," etc.

The decision for which the Cisco VP of Product Development would like some support runs as follows. There are substantial R&D and capital costs associated with bringing the new switch to market in a three-year versus a five-year time frame; but a three-year time frame virtually guarantees first-mover advantage, which experience in the switch category shows will be associated with a lifetime sales multiplier of 1.5X to 2.5X. The new switch will not be profitable unless the product sells to enough customers and/or enough units per customer and/or at a high enough price; these thresholds are much more likely to be reached if the product is introduced in three rather than five years and some competitors' customers also adopt it.

Furthermore, an alternative allocation of the R&D and capital budgets beckons within the low end of the switch category. In the low end, the product situation corresponds more to that of the Hewlett-Packard example, and market research has already been conducted. It indicates that investing in the low-end switch instead of accelerating introduction of the new optical switch has an 80 percent chance of producing more profit than a marginally successful new optical switch; a 20 percent chance of matching the estimated profit from a moderately successful new optical switch; and a 90 percent chance of producing less than a third the profit produced by a truly successful new switch. In short, if the new high-end network switch succeeds after an early introduction, it will be much more lucrative for Cisco; if it proves marginal, from the standpoint of profit, Cisco would have been better off if it had gone with the low-end switch and postponed the new switch.

The Cisco executive's decision is straightforward but momentous: Will the new optical switch be successful enough that R&D and capital investment should go to it rather than the low-end extension? There are not sufficient R&D resources or capital to invest in both.

Can market research contribute meaningfully to this decision? It seems to me not, and it is useful to detail specifically why not. The first problem is time frame: Here, customer behavior must be predicted years in the future. The second and related problem is access: Not all competitor customers can be reached. It also seems unlikely that all M members of the buying center could be reached in each customer firm that can be contacted; and even if they could, normal job turnover would mean that many of the individuals questioned today would not be among those making the decision in three to five years. Thus, there can be no question of sampling from or taking a census of the (future) customer population. One can administer an individual conjoint to anyone who can be reached, but it would primarily describe the utilities of the people interviewed as opposed to predicting the behavior of the market in the future, when competitor offerings will have changed, and the customer's own data on Internet traffic—and hence the demand for network switches—will also have changed.

One could, of course, visit a few individuals at the larger firms and have an extended conversation about perceived trends in both network switch technology and growth in Internet traffic. This might even be informative, perhaps more informative than if the executive stayed tethered to his desk, reading only public material and talking only to fellow employees. But such visits would have occurred in the course of normal business, so any learning to be gotten has already taken place.

Generalization. The factors that distinguish the Cisco case include the following: (1) prediction of a relative distant time, (2) a highly concentrated market, (3) multiple customer decision makers, (4) limited access to the total customer population, and (5) need for an exact prediction rather than an approximate sense of direction. Neither Cisco nor telecommunications equipment providers are uniquely subject to these conditions. Most technology component industries (e.g., semiconductors) will face long time frames, concentrated markets, limited access to the total market, uncertainty about decision makers, and the need for a relatively specific dollar estimate. Subsequently, I'll develop in more depth the factors that make such circumstances hostile to market research. First, let's examine another case falling outside the boundary where market research can be successfully conducted.

Case 2: Charging Stations for Electric Vehicles

Suppose a venture capitalist seeks investments in the alternative fuel sector of the automobile market. Charging stations for electric cars are identified as a possible focus. Two start-up ventures then make pitches to the venture capitalist. The business model of Venture A focuses on installing banks of charging stations at shopping malls. Venture B, in its business model, proposes to sell to individual homeowners for installation in a garage. Both business plans use "market studies" authored by consulting firms, which make varying predictions about the adoption rate for electric cars, and for miles-between-charge capabilities of the installed base of these cars over time and by region. The studies themselves, of course, are only estimates, each based nonetheless on a rigorously derived mathematical diffusion model, but, unfortunately, not the same model, and not making the same predictions. Unsurprisingly, Venture A found a model that indicated that a business based on off-site charging stations in Region 1 would achieve profitability faster than homeowner charge stations; Venture B found a model that indicated the reverse, albeit in Region 2.

Can the venture capitalist conduct market research to facilitate the choice of which venture to back? She could certainly commission a survey of consumers' buying intentions with respect to electric cars. Unfortunately, it's highly likely that one or more such surveys has already been done, probably several; in fact, that may be why the two different "market studies" produced two different results. One can easily imagine that answers to such a survey are highly sensitive to both sample quality (innovators and early adopters are likely to be scarce and spottily distributed) and question phrasing (many contingencies have to be specified, in any of several ways, to elicit buying intentions for an expensive durable good a year or more in the future). Can the venture capitalist be confident of drawing a better sample, using a better questioning framework, than any of the existing surveys? How would she know whether she had, in fact, done this, as opposed to commissioning a third flawed survey characterized by a different sampling problem? Worse, the consumer answering any such survey or any such conjoint analysis is either tacitly assuming or being explicitly told how many miles-between-charges that electric car, about whose adoption they are being queried, will get and when. But this is precisely what neither venture capitalist nor consumer knows!

One could survey shopping mall owners about their willingness to adopt charging stations, but doubtless, the response would be, "tell me how many consumers will need mid-trip charging in my region as of the specified year, and I'll tell you whether I'm interested." One could take a census of automobile manufacturers as to when cars with specified miles-between-charge will be introduced to the market, but the answer will be, "why, as soon as consumer demand for electric cars, generally speaking, reaches X level," which, again, is exactly what we don't know.

Not even game theory can help the venture capitalist much. Every player in the game (start-up, consumer, mall owner, automobile manufacturer) is dependent on the unknown future moves and timing of moves of one or more other players. We can model the game and specify what will happen "if X" for all possible values of X; but we cannot know when or whether a given value of X will occur, and that is what the venture capitalist needs to know to make the funding decision today. The market research that would make the game predictive rather than descriptive is not possible to do. Of course, the venture capitalist can vet the two management teams and find one to be more experienced, or take apart the business model and find untenable cost assumptions in the other; but neither of these due-diligence investigations is market research as defined in this book.

The second example usefully differs from the first on several dimensions. First, it is (in part) B2C rather than B2B. Second, it isn't a high-technology case; there isn't any more electronic technology in a glorified electric plug-and-socket (aka charging station) than there is chemical technology in a typical laundry detergent. Third, the market in question is a mass market and not a concentrated market, as in the Cisco case. Fourth, although the futurity of the adoption decision was again part of the problem, there was a crucial second difficulty: its recursive nature, or chicken-and-egg character.

Generalization. The problem with the charging station example will apply to any recursive system where the decisions of one party depend on the decisions of another, which, in turn, themselves ultimately depend on the decision of the first party. Most products that depend on an infrastructure for their usability will have difficulty conducting effective market research because of this chicken–egg problem.

Case 3: Life Insurance Product

Consider now a third example. Suppose MetLife is considering whether to add to its offerings a new kind of whole-life insurance policy in which the cash value buildup is stated in ounces of gold rather than units of currency, and the death benefit is also payable in ounces of gold. The target market is younger, wealthy individuals attracted to permanent life insurance as part of their wealth allocation but concerned about the long-term effects of inflation on policy values, given their relative youth.

Suppose further that MetLife already offers a wide variety of life insurance policies and has a team of people in place who generate policy language and documents (the equivalent of manufacturing a financial service of this kind). They also have an indexed annuity product and to support it, a sophisticated hedging process in place that could manage the long-term price risk of a promise of gold payouts. As a consequence, the direct marginal cost of launching the new policy is estimated at $100,000 or so. Net present value of lifetime profit from a given policy sale is estimated to be on the order of $12,000. All marketing of this kind of insurance product takes place through insurance agents, who have to be regularly briefed about policies and changes anyway, so there are no material incremental promotion costs, either.

I don't think this insurance firm can benefit from market research. It is not feasible and also not pertinent to test whether the new policy should be launched or quashed. Product introduction is the best and only form of concept testing that makes sense here. To see why, consider the cost of either surveying or conducting a conjoint study with the young wealthy; by definition, these people are hard to find, surrounded by barriers designed to shut out market researchers and other pests, and difficult to incentivize to participate. They are also likely to be extremely heterogeneous in the nature of their demand for life insurance, making bias due to shortfalls in sample size a particular concern. In short, the cost of accurately sampling and effectively reaching enough potential customers to determine if the product should be launched converges with the cost of just launching the product and seeing if anyone actually buys it.

This third case doesn't involve any kind of concentrated market or any technological innovation at all, and it can hardly be called a radical or discontinuous innovation. It's a tweak. It doesn't involve a great deal of futurity, and there is no chicken-and-egg problem with recursiveness. It's simply that the cost of the data that could be collected, relative to its pertinence and necessary imprecision, is out of line with the benefits that could be gained from better information. Here, data collection from customers might be possible but isn't really pertinent.

Generalization. Many new services, especially financial products, fit this profile. It also applies to support services, documentation, programs, and other product add-ons that either have no identifiable impact on profit or loss or only a very small one. Unlike capital goods, in which a large investment must be made up front and forfeited if the product is not successful, service concepts and support programs may cost very little to produce and make available. There are opportunity costs, of course, so it is still important to know if a candidate new service has as high or higher potential than any of its rivals or alternatives; but direct costs may be few. So market research would still be desirable if it were feasible. The problem here is a combination of limited payoff and necessary imprecision. It would be expensive to do any research that could even promise precision; yet no matter how much is spent, precision is likely to remain low. It is more cost-effective, and far more precise, to introduce the new service in good faith and see if it catches on.

Case 4: The Inventor–Entrepreneur

Bob is an MIT graduate who went into banking, got bored with it, and quit his job, fortuitously in late 2007, just after bonuses were credited. His wife went back to work, and Bob is responsible for meal preparation, school lunches for their three kids, food shopping, and the like. He's always spent a lot of time in the kitchen, and resealable plastic bags have increasingly come to bother him to the point of active dismay. Some are so hard to open that the bag tears instead of the seal opening, while others are impossible to align and press close except after multiple attempts. Bob minimizes some problems by avoiding certain brands, but many of the resealable packages he has to deal with come from the manufacturer of the enclosed food item and are not his to choose. And he's too much of an environmentalist to always replace the food manufacturer's bag with a new one of his own—that just seems a waste.

A tinkerer by nature, Bob has identified two possible solutions. One would repurpose empty inkjet cartridges and add a tiny reversible pump. Set in a double stapler arrangement, it would use tiny bursts of air through the openings that had once expelled ink to press the bag close; equally important, when the pump is set in reverse, a suction action would unseal the bag without the need to worm a fingernail in or the risk of tearing the bag by attempting to pull the seal open. Bob had fun putting one together in the garage, and it works very well. Unfortunately, the garage version was so ugly his wife forbade him to keep it in the kitchen.

The second solution involves mixing one of the metals used to coat low-E windows into the ethylene compound out of which plastic baggies are manufactured. The same double stapler would now hold a powerful magnet that would seal the bag (at any point, not just the opening—the better to minimize the amount of air trapped with the food). In reverse, the bag would be unsealed by a second pass with reverse magnetism. Back of the envelope, Bob estimates that in bulk, bags manufactured this way, with no sealable strip but with the low-E compound, would cost about the same, assuming enough were sold for economies of scale to kick in. Bob hadn't been able to build one of these, but he'd painted some of the metal on a few old bags, rigged up a magnet, and found it a surprising good seal, certainly able to keep a sandwich from falling out when the bag was inverted.

Bob has plenty of money remaining from his 2007 bonus that could be spent on any reasonable amount of customer research. His question is, which technology should he attempt to commercialize—if either?

Can market research help here? Probably not. The problem in this case is the number of unknowns. It would be challenging to determine, for either technology, whether enough demand could be generated at any of a range of price points to encourage commercialization. There might be enough demand at one price, not enough at another, with these prices falling within the boundary of uncertainty about what the selling price would have to be once the device is manufactured at scale. This is the problem of recursion we saw in the charging station problem. Alternatively, although difficult to do, demand might be estimable and come in at a feasible price, in both cases, more or less; but the odds that the estimates will both be precise enough and reliable enough to identify which of the two technologies has the best prospects seem vanishingly small. This is the problem of imprecision of estimates. It is compounded in this case because the solutions aren't really commensurable: one is an add-on that the consumer can use on any baggie; the other is a whole new type of bag, forming a system with the magnet and involving extensive changes in both the manufacturing and distribution infrastructure and changes in consumer food storage behavior. We can ask the consumer to choose, but his judgment is not equally apt in the two cases, because he faces two different kinds of unknown.

There are still further problems. Bob might be able to do research that shows that either technology will be successful, but only if it can be patented, since if there's competition, volume and profits split among all competitors will be inadequate for each. This is the problem of path dependency: The choice between the two options depends on the uncontrollable decision of a patent examiner.

Another problem is that there are essentially too many options to test: recycled ink cartridges for a green positioning or new ones for reliability; magnet and new bags packaged separately or as a system; and on and on. We can't test them all directly, because we couldn't trust the judgment of a consumer inundated with choices. If we engage in a brute-force larger research effort, the cost will begin to approximate the cost of a trial launch that would obviate the need to do the market research. In any case, while it may be rational for Bob to spend half his savings to optimize a known good solution so he can sell the rights to the invention for the best possible price, it is arguably not rational to spend half his savings to find out that neither option is any good. He shouldn't invest money vetting ideas unless he knows one will pass the test—which is precisely what he doesn't know. Bob can't do (pertinent) market research; he has to bet.

Generalization. The kinds of unknowns with which Bob is struggling will be characteristic of the situation faced by many inventors and entrepreneurs. There are too many incommensurable uncertainties. The market research is unlikely to reduce uncertainty sufficiently for it to pay for itself. Action—introducing the product and letting the market decide—will be more informative than any research.

Case 5: Viral Advertising

A difficulty with the four preceding examples, despite their diversity, is that they all involve new product development. To avoid any misleading impression, I conclude with an advertising example. Suppose Evian decides to incorporate social media into its promotional planning for bottled water. Specifically, archival research finds that when a 30-second TV commercial goes viral, this enormously leverages the advertiser's investment in ad production and conventional media spending. To "go viral" means to be buzzed about on blogs and forwarded via social media so that millions and millions of ad views are generated without the advertiser having to pay. Evian instructs its ad agency to produce two or three rough TV commercials designed for this purpose and then to conduct market research to determine which one will go viral. Once identified, the agency is to put that ad into final production and disseminate it to likely viral progenitors.

Is this a feasible request? Arguably it is not. One could, of course, draw a probability sample from the population of past ads that have gone viral and draw a second probability sample of ads for the same product categories released in the same period that did not go viral. One could then code the ads in each sample for a variety of properties and conduct an analysis to determine which coded property best discriminates between the viral and nonviral sets. The agency would then incorporate that property into newly constructed TV ads, *et voilà*: virality would be the expected result.

Or maybe not. The problem here is an instance of the *post hoc, ergo propter hoc* fallacy in logic; or, put another way, "post-diction" doesn't entail prediction. The underlying conceptual error can be illustrated with an example. Suppose we put an ice cube of known volume and temperature on the corner of a metal table where the room temperature is 72°, and we know the surface properties of both table and floor. We can predict with a high degree of precision how long it will take the ice cube to melt, the maximum extent of the resulting puddle on the floor, the time for the puddle to reach that maximum extent, and so on. But if we come into a room and see a puddle on the floor by a table, we have no way of knowing whether an ice cube was placed on the corner of the table or a glass spilled there, whether the floor was recently mopped and still drying, the roof leaked last night during the rain, and so forth. Prediction forward doesn't guarantee prediction backward, and vice versa; some processes are retraceable, others not.

Generalization. The viral advertising example is typical of fashion, movies, pop songs, and other cultural goods categories for which it really is impossible to know why one movie takes the country by storm while another quickly sinks into obscurity. These are chaotic processes, which provide a pure example of business situations in which everything depends on the creativity and brilliance of the individual designer or auteur who, in the end, must simply take his best shot.

FORMULATING BOUNDARY CONDITIONS

> *"Buy some good stock and hold it till it goes*
> *up, then sell it. If it don't go up, don't buy it."*
>
> —Will Rogers

Suppose this were a book on investments rather than market research and I claimed: "With a few exceptions, ensuing 12-month returns for the stock market, and for individual sectors, can be predicted to within ±1 percent." Such a paper would be tossed aside with something between a snort and a guffaw. No business academic believes that future financial asset returns are predictable with that degree of precision. The simplest gloss on this chapter, then, is that *some* product and service markets are like *most* financial markets: not predictable with an acceptable degree of precision, confidence, or time lag.

Why is future stock market performance generally regarded as not meaningfully predictable? Because there, past is not considered to be prologue: Future returns have not yet been determined. In some sense, these returns can't be known because they don't (yet) exist. Hence, the first fundamental boundary condition on market research may be formulated as: Market research is not effective in situations where the decision maker has to predict the future with some precision; the more precise the needed prediction, and the more distant the future, the less the effectiveness. Prediction can only be reasonably precise in the case of what might be termed "the extended present."

An example: MBA classes turn rapt when I assure them I can predict the future. There is some disappointment in their eyes when, after a pause, I announce: "I predict . . . that I will die!" Since I am living, and all things that are born die, this is not really a prediction of the *future*. There is further disappointment when I name at random a second-year student in the class and announce: "and I also foretell that Sally will graduate from this MBA program!" Most second-year students in this MBA program do graduate; I am simply predicting that an event already well under way will continue to completion. This prediction is fallible but has excellent prospects of being correct— because it is not an attempt to predict *the future*.

Thus, in the first within-boundary example, P&G *can* use market research to predict which of two ad executions is superior, because consumers are already exposed to ads for detergent and are regularly engaged in buying detergent and, hence, are experienced in this domain. The field experiment samples a piece of the present in order to project results to a larger temporal portion of present-day ongoing activity. Likewise, Hewlett-Packard can use market research, because IT managers are making choices about what networked printers to buy today, so the conjoint exercise again simply samples from the present-day domain of printer choice decisions. Conversely, Cisco has difficulty doing market research because it has to predict the future: No one is buying quantum tunneling switches today, and no one today is managing future Internet traffic. The future can't be sampled; it doesn't exist.

Most of the beyond-the-boundary examples had some degree of futurity. But we can drive the formulation of this boundary to a more abstract level. The problem with the charging station example was the degree and nature of uncertainty present. Every player's move depended on the unknown moves of other players. From this perspective, futurity is just a prominent instance of what might be termed true uncertainty: unknown unknowns. So the more abstract boundary condition might be stated as: market research is not effective when there is bona fide uncertainty; the greater the degree of uncertainty, the less effective market research can be. The charging station, resealable bag, and viral advertising examples all involved this kind of uncertainty.

The second boundary condition is different: It occurs when the cost of information, in dollars or time, outweighs the benefit received or when the precision of the information that can be gained for reasonable cost is inadequate. The insurance example and the resealable bag examples are cases in point. Here, market research was possible but not pertinent because it was not cost-effective or insufficiently precise.

In summary, the two boundary conditions that limit the utility of market research are possibility and pertinence. It is not possible to predict the future. And information that is too costly or insufficiently precise is not pertinent. To conceive the boundary conditions for market research in terms of surface characteristics such as B2B markets, technology categories, or development of new products is insufficiently analytic. New product development is rich in instances of futurity; technology products often involve high amounts of uncertainty; and in B2B markets, cost and imprecision often produce lack of pertinence. But, as we saw in the initial within-boundary examples, there is nothing about any of these domains that is, per se, hostile to market research.

There has been one glaring omission in the discussion thus far. All of the case scenarios involved research questions that required quantitative market research, with the research objective of selecting, evaluating, or prioritizing. What about *qualitative* market research? Do the same boundaries apply? Or might qualitative research have broader applicability and/ or a different set of boundaries? Perhaps so, but since qualitative research generally can't support the same kinds of inference as quantitative market research, the question remains: When quantitative market research would be desirable but appears not to be possible or pertinent, how should a manager proceed?

WHEN QUANTITATIVE MARKET
RESEARCH CAN'T BE DONE

Again, the context is corporate decision makers seeking to maximize the success of their enterprises. These are fallible human beings, socially and organizationally situated, having imperfect information and limited cognitive capacity, and facing demanding time constraints. How should a manager proceed when a decision of some magnitude must be made, but quantitative market research—applied management science, if you will—cannot point to the optimal choice?

The first and most crucial response is intellectual honesty: When applied management science is not available to underwrite a decision, managers must regard themselves as gamblers and as game players and act accordingly. As gamblers, managers make bets. Although decisions remain gambles, nonetheless, better and worse bets, with more or less favorable odds, can still be distinguished. To use a casino metaphor, in games like blackjack it is sometimes possible to count cards; and although this is no guarantee of winning, it markedly improves the odds of a successful outcome (which is why casinos throw any card counters they detect out on the street). By analogy, managers as gamblers should prefer games where an activity analogous to counting cards is possible. I'll give some concrete applications of this insight in a moment.

As game players, managers are responsible for knowing the rules of the game being played and for becoming ever more knowledgeable about the game; the greater the knowledge, the better the quality of play. Higher quality of play is far from a guarantee of winning on any given round; but *ceteris paribus* ("all other things being equal"), it makes winning more likely and more lucrative. For instance, every poker player knows that a flush beats a straight. But how many can instantly identify which four-card hand has the better odds of successfully drawing the needed fifth card—the partial flush or the partial straight? If one doesn't understand the game of poker at least at this level of detail, it is difficult to compete successfully.

In summary, gambler managers must continually develop knowledge of the game and should always be seeking an edge. And this is where focus groups and other forms of qualitative market research *may* be able to make a contribution. However, the actual contribution of qualitative market research in these circumstances is not what most people think.

WHAT QUALITATIVE RESEARCH CAN DO

Two assertions will serve to anchor the discussion: (1) qualitative research could have been done in every one of the out-of-bounds cases described above and (2) qualitative research is never able to substitute for quantitative market research in that it never yields the precision that quantitative research, considered as applied management science, can offer in those instances where it is possible. In other words, qualitative research is almost always possible, much more widely so than applied management science; the question is, When is it pertinent? It can't predict the future or resolve true uncertainty when conducted outside the boundary conditions for quantitative market research, and it isn't free or even all that cheap; so, why spend money on it?

This question never comes up in the conventional, within-boundary cases with which most discussions of market research are concerned. Qualitative research is entirely unproblematic within boundary because there it is treated as a preliminary, exploratory effort, able to be confirmed by subsequent quantitative market research. The question to be resolved is whether it can ever make sense to do qualitative research alone, in place of the desired quantitative research, under conditions where quantitative market research does not avail, so that it will not be possible to confirm qualitative results.

The answer, I think, is a qualified "yes": Qualitative research may be pertinent if it promises to the gambling manager either: (1) better knowledge of the game or (2) a means of "counting cards." Decisions supported only by qualitative research remain gambles; but qualitative research may make the manager a better player because he becomes more knowledgeable, or it may give him an edge. In these circumstances, it is pertinent.

A within-boundary example of what focus groups can sometimes contribute will help. Some years ago, P&G did exploratory focus groups with individual consumers of air fresheners (see wsjclassroom.com, January 2005). Participants commented that a problem with air fresheners was a kind of wear-out or habituation: The human nose adapts to any constant smell, so that smell soon becomes imperceptible. A P&G employee observing the groups came up with the idea for a new packaging and delivery system modeled on a CD player. The package contained multiple scents ("discs"), and the dispenser allowed the consumer to change scents the same way a CD player allows one to switch between music albums, without the "disc" being used up. The ability to switch back and forth between scents, it was hoped, might then solve the consumer problem of olfactory habituation. In fact, the new air freshener product proved a big hit and sold extremely well.

What, exactly, was the role of the focus group research in this successful innovation? The product idea did not come from the focus group; it came from the employee, purportedly as a result of listening to the focus group. The mention of habituation by a single participant does not warrant much of an inference about the frequency of that experience in the marketplace or whether any consumer would pay money to address the problem or choose a brand on this basis. Absent a follow-up with quantitative market research, introduction of the new air freshener was simply a gamble, no different than if Bob had gone ahead and introduced his plastic bag sealer–resealer immediately after dreaming up the idea.

Let me suggest that for P&G, the focus group was the equivalent of counting cards. Qualitative research revealed that there was at least one consumer on the planet who experienced olfactory habituation as a problem with existing air freshener products. The rule again, per Chapter 8, is that a single occurrence during the research establishes existence in the marketplace. It doesn't establish incidence; that is the kind of sample inference focus groups cannot support (review the discussion of qualitative sampling in Chapter 8). There may be as few as one customer in the whole world, the one who spoke up in the group; but it is now certain that there is at least one customer with that problem. It is parallel to realizing during the game of blackjack that half the deck has been played, but only three face cards have turned up thus far.

The focus group also improves P&G's knowledge of the game. Doubtless any perceptual psychologist working in the air freshener category is familiar with olfactory habituation; but the focus group makes this knowledge salient and vivid so it can be mentally appropriated as a customer problem rather than just a piece of textbook learning. Everything else had its source in the mind of the employee: that is where the new product originated and was defined. The product itself, the innovation that proved to be a lucrative addition to P&G's portfolio of offerings, cannot be located in anything said or mentioned in the group; it is not, strictly speaking, a user-generated product concept.

With this example in hand, I return to what qualitative research can and cannot do for each of the out-of-bounds examples. Cisco can't do focus groups, but on-site customer visits would serve the same purpose. These visits can't drive the decision about when to bring the network switch to market, but they may give the executive an opportunity to learn something. He's seen the projections for

Internet traffic growth and the analysis showing that the telecomm customers will need to add either rafts of low-end switches or a much smaller number of high-end optical switches. He wonders, Do customers believe these Internet growth projections? Are customers indifferent between buying rafts of low-end versus a few high-end switches? Or does one of these approaches sometimes conflict with a customer's fundamental business model? The Cisco executive will still have to place a bet no matter how many customers he visits or how their "vote" breaks down (it will generally be a split decision in any case). But he has a chance to see some cards turned over. The face-to-face on-site visit brings his entire sensorium to bear on which bet to make. He gets a gut check.

It is the same for the venture capitalist. She can visit shopping mall owners and discuss why they would or would not install charging stations, what their motive might be, what cost structure they expect. She can observe focus groups of homeowners: does Venture B's business model click with them; do consumers get it? Or are consumers focused on some other problem, some other usage or cost model? Are they aware of electrical permits and other obstacles that may inhibit installation? No matter how much qualitative research she does, she will still be placing a bet; but she gets to turn over some cards first. She may wake up one morning with a realization that one of the two business models is going to fail in a whole class of cases. She can't prove it but knows it in her gut, and having a smart gut is what venture capitalists get paid for.

MetLife can certainly do individual interviews with the young wealthy, and an executive can satisfy himself that combining gold with a life insurance product is of interest to at least someone. Likewise, he can gain a better understanding of how the new product might be positioned and promoted. But on balance, it's still questionable whether the $10,000 to $15,000 of travel and lodging expenses required to do those interviews makes sense. Launch of gold-value life insurance will still be a bet, and the caliber of information from a launch will be far superior to anything heard in an interview. Likewise, feedback from the sales channel on how to promote the product, once they actually try to sell it, arguably will give at least as much insight. Hence, the pertinence of qualitative research remains questionable here, which is another way of saying that the ratio of cost to payoff may be a more fundamental bound on market research of any kind than the futurity and uncertainty bounds. A jaundiced observer might expect that if qualitative research does get done here, it stems more from bureaucratic CYA behavior than any genuine quest to improve the quality of marketing decisions.

Turning to Bob, the pertinence of qualitative research is again questionable. In a sense, Bob was his own focus group: he's already established to his satisfaction that at least one consumer has a problem with resealable plastic bags. He may be able to educate his gut by seeing if anyone else in a set of groups spontaneously voices the same dissatisfaction with resealable bags; if no one does, or no one seems to care, he may decide that investing any further effort is a bad bet and more comfortably drop the whole idea (but with only qualitative research to go on, this remains a bet). Conversely, no amount of enthusiasm in the focus group really changes his fundamental conundrum or that of anyone who would try to put a valuation on this innovation: Will it sell enough, and in what configuration, to be worthwhile? Given the asymmetric information gain, why spend even the $15,000 that a good set of focus groups might require?

Finally, focus groups make excellent sense for the ad agency charged by Evian with coming up with a TV ad that could go viral. The situation is exactly parallel to the P&G air freshener example. If we can convene some groups with bloggers and other individuals who have actively forwarded videos, we can have a wide-ranging discussion, with numerous examples of ads that did go viral, of why people forward some ads to their friends and not others, and so forth. If we have ad agency creatives watch the focus groups, as P&G had its engineers view the air freshener groups, we set up conditions where a light bulb may go off in a creative's head. An idea for a video that might go viral or that the creative at least believes could go viral may occur. The qualitative research serves to enrich the creative's understanding of how the "game" of forwarding videos is played. The Evian client manager is still betting, but it's a better bet now.

In summary, although qualitative market research of some kind is always possible, sometimes not even qualitative is really pertinent. Ultimately, to be successful when applied management science does not avail, a manager has to be able to make good bets. If the manager feels that qualitative research can improve his understanding of the game or turn over a few cards not otherwise visible, it will often be time and cost effective to conduct qualitative research. But no matter how much qualitative research he does, he remains a gambler placing bets. And he needs to be tough minded enough to realize that the qualitative research may not actually have improved his knowledge of the game but only produced the illusion of being better informed. When applied management science is not possible, everything hinges on the perspicacity of the decision maker.

Under these circumstances, the function of qualitative research is the education of decision makers and not the prediction of the future or the resolution of uncertainty. Since a manager has many opportunities to be educated, qualitative market research remains optional even when possible and pertinent. Visits to trade shows, ongoing customer contact in the course of everyday business, reading widely, dialogue with colleagues, and many other experiences can provide the same platform for an *Aha!* experience as the air freshener focus groups provided to the P&G employee.

SUMMARY AND CONCLUSION

The goal of this chapter was to formulate boundary conditions beyond which market research is either not possible or not pertinent. The first boundary condition was conceptualized as true uncertainty. Predicting the future provides the type case of this sort of uncertainty. One can't sample from the future, which makes scientific sample inference highly problematic. Recursive systems provided another example of uncertainty. The second boundary involved the ratio of research costs to business payoff. Here, market research might be possible, but the costs of doing it outweigh the benefit or the value of the information obtained. Finally, qualitative market research was found to be almost always possible but not always pertinent. I argued that when quantitative market research is not possible, managers are gamblers who must place bets; but that it would sometimes be possible to become more knowledgeable about the rules of the game being played or to gain an edge, and qualitative research provides one means of doing so.

The five specific cases discussed were used to explode easy certainties about the limits of market research in terms of surface features such as B2B markets, technology categories, or new product development. These happen to be sectors where uncertainty and uncertain payoffs are common, but these fundamental factors can occur in any sector. I presented each of the examples not as a one-off special case but as an instance of a larger category or industry where uncertainty and uncertain payoffs were rife. There are, in the end, quite a few instances in which market research is neither possible nor pertinent.

It isn't always and everywhere possible to do scientific market research in practical business circumstances. As a marketing scholar, I would do my readers, students, and clients a disservice were I to fail to acknowledge this fact.

The purpose of concluding the book with this chapter is to emphasize that market research is an option, not a necessity. Market research is a specialized procedure that is extremely illuminating in some cases, substantially informative in others, and neither possible nor pertinent in still others. You have to decide whether to do market research at all, case by case, as well as what kind of market research to do. Market research is not like tabulating profit and loss. Every business has to be unendingly focused on cost structure and sources of revenue, but not every business and not every business decision can benefit from market research.

In my opinion, the popular press, the business press, and the typical academic presentation of marketing ideas give an overly rosy and upbeat account of the benefits to be expected from market research. (I guess that's probably the best way to market a book on market research . . .). By contrast, I see the applicability of the tools discussed in this book as much more limited. To educate the beginner new to market research I must give you a sober assessment of these limits; hence, the need for this chapter. The need for this sober assessment is more pressing for my key target audience of B2B and technology managers. Sometimes your situation is going to be no different from that of Procter & Gamble, Kimberly-Clark, or General Mills, and you can benefit from market research in the same way as these pioneers of the technique. At other times, you might as well be conducting your business on another planet. Simply ask yourself, Can I get the information I want with the precision I need? And at what cost? Those are always the fundamental questions in deciding whether to do market research.

DISCUSSION QUESTIONS

1. The goal of the chapter was to mark out the boundaries of market research in terms of fundamental factors. Can all the several factors mentioned in the chapter be derived from a single unifying factor? How would you describe that single, underlying ground? Or do you think it is necessary to retain a short list of distinct factors, each of which sets a different kind of boundary condition? If so, is the list in this chapter complete, or could you point to additional factors?

2. The chapter noted that B2B products, technology products, and new product development generally were all domains in which boundary conditions on market research are likely to be encountered. Can you think of any other broad product categories, or specific types of market decisions, where the boundary conditions on market research are likely to limit market research activity? Explain.

3. It might be argued that consumer packaged goods are the product category where boundary conditions are *least* likely to be encountered. This is reasonable because most existing market research techniques were pioneered on that category. Likewise, *selecting customers to target* may be the marketing decision in which boundary conditions are least likely to be encountered, again because this was one of the very first applications for market research: finding the sweet spot in terms of the customers most likely to respond to a marketing effort.

   a. Taking consumer packaged goods as the anchor, array other broad categories of goods along the dimension of "goods where market research is less and less likely to be possible or pertinent." For instance, where would you put financial services on this dimension, relative to, say, luxury or prestige goods, capital equipment sold in a concentrated B2B market, and so forth? Explain your choices.

   b. Taking the decision of *which consumers to target* as an anchor point of that same dimension, where would you place other common marketing decisions, such as repositioning a brand, selecting a price point, devising an advertising appeal, and so forth? For what kind of decisions is market research more or less likely to be possible or pertinent? Explain your placements.

SUGGESTED READINGS

Arthur, W. B. (1996). Increasing returns and the new world of business. *Harvard Business Review,* July–August.	This article grounds the thesis that managers are "gamblers and game players" in economic theory, with numerous examples from technology industries.
Taleb, N. N. (2007). *The black swan.* New York, NY: Random House.	Taleb provides a useful corrective to unthinking faith in statistics and forecast models. If Yogi Berra provided the gloss for this final chapter, perhaps Mark Twain provides the gloss for Taleb's book: "There are three kinds of lies: lies, damned lies, and statistics."

CASE FOR PART V

SUGGESTED CASE: MONTREAUX CHOCOLATES (HARVARD #9-914-501)

Synopsis

A diversified packaged-goods manufacturer seeks to introduce a new gourmet chocolate product to the United States market. A variety of research projects have been undertaken to support the new product launch, and management is uncertain whether additional research, including a market test, may be needed.

Questions

1. Evaluate the sequence of research activities undertaken. Have the correct techniques been used? Have they been conducted in the right sequence? Any notable omissions?

   (a) Please speak to each of the particular techniques employed (e.g., the focus groups) in your answer.

   (b) Would you describe the overall research approach as: (1) exemplary, a good role model; (2) journeyman work, as expected, neither brilliant nor obtuse; or (3) flawed, problematic, partial?

2. No conjoint study was done nor is one contemplated. Evaluate this decision.

3. Conversely, more than one BASES study was done. Evaluate the different contributions of the BASES methodology versus the conjoint methodology, and evaluate whether they are substitutes in this context, complements, or unrelated alternatives focused on different issues entirely.

4. Would you undertake a market test at this point? Commission some other kind of additional research? Go ahead and launch the product? Or bite the bullet and kill it now?

5. In a large firm, market research takes place in an organizational context with multiple participants playing such roles as user of research

results, lead researcher, budget holder or funder, executive to be held responsible for success or failure, and other more miscellaneous roles such as internal consultant, constituent, implementer, and so on.

(a) Whether you found the Montreaux research effort exemplary or problematic, speculate about how the organizational arrangements in place at this firm may have shaped the nature of the market research effort described.

SUGGESTED CASE: ZENITH HD-TV (HARVARD #9-591-025)

Synopsis

At the time the case was written, high-definition television loomed as a new-to-the-world, radical, discontinuous innovation. This Zenith case thus provides a means to consider the role that market research can play in facilitating the successful commercialization of true innovations.

Zenith management wants some guidance on how to approach HD-TV at this juncture. However, what management actually wants to learn (or should want to know) isn't exactly clear, which adds to the organizational realism of the case. There is also one specific research proposal on the table, a large and fairly elaborate conjoint study. But there remains the broader question of what kind of market research, if any, can help when facing such a radical innovation.

Questions

1. Several possible recommendations to management can be envisioned:

    (a) Do not do market research here—the innovation is too discontinuous (explain).

    (b) Do some kind of market research, but not conjoint (be specific).

    (c) Do the Aspect Ratio conjoint study pretty much as proposed (justify).

    (d) Do some kind of conjoint, but not that one (be specific and justify).

2. If you rejected the conjoint analysis, what exactly is the problem that makes conjoint less than helpful here?

3. At times, it appears that what Zenith management really wants you to do is predict the future: that is, trace out on a graph the probable rate of diffusion of HD-TV from 1990 to 2005, say. What market research technique is best suited to predicting the future?

    (a) A colleague suggests that prior to predicting the future, it is always a good idea to summarize the past. Specifically, if the task is to predict the future of HD-TV, in terms of the rate at which it will diffuse, it might be helpful to find previous instances of consumer electronics, and capture their diffusion curves, to serve as analogues.

        i. Which consumer electronic products, relatively widely diffused as of 1990, would you recommend be considered as analogues?

            1. Defend your choices. HD-TV was far from a tweak at the time, so you need innovations that were also somewhat radical and discontinuous.

        ii. *Extra Credit*: Obtain the actual diffusion curves for each of the analogues you selected, and construct a predicted diffusion curve for HD-TV.

        iii. Now compare the actual diffusion curve for HD-TV as of 2015, say. How good was your prediction?

            1. If your prediction was relatively good, explain how that prediction would have helped Zenith management in 1990.

            2. If your prediction was not so good, how badly would Zenith management have been hurt had they relied on it?

SUPPLEMENTAL CASE: SOUTHGATE MALL

Synopsis

A large shopping mall, established 15–20 years ago, appears to be losing ground to competitor malls, with a long-term erosion evident in terms of revenue and profitability. There is no established market research function, and not even much of a marketing group. The issue is whether market research would be a good investment, and if so, what sequence of research activities would be appropriate.

Questions

1. Is market research possible and pertinent here? Of course, individual retail chains will engage in a variety of market research activities, but does market research make sense for the shopping mall owners, who are a kind of landlord?

   (a) Assume 4–6 anchor stores and 100+ specialty stores. What scale of revenues would be realistic to assume?

   (b) A special budget request will be required to the board. Once you have a rough estimate of revenue and profit for a mall of this scale, circa 2015, in a city like Phoenix, Arizona, use the calculations in Appendix 2A to rough out the maximum budget request you think would be feasible.

2. Assuming some kind of market research will be done, the first issue is how to allocate resources between: (a) research on the needs and expectations and perceptions of retail tenants versus (b) research directed at patrons who shop at the mall.

   (a) Take a stand on a rough allocation of research effort between retail tenants and patrons. It could be 0 percent, 100 percent versus 100 percent, 0 percent; or 20 percent, 80 percent versus 80 percent, 20 percent; or something on the order of 50 percent, 50 percent. Don't obsess about the percentages—take a position among the five splits given, and defend.

3. Rough out a program of market research, given your allocation of effort. Use the table and examples in Chapter 15 to get ideas. Be specific about which research techniques you would use, and the sequence in which you would use them.

4. Get rough cost estimates for each proposed research technique. Make sure that Southgate can afford your recommended research, based on your calculations in #1 above.

* * *

(Continued)

(Continued)

John Rastor, CEO of Southgate Mall, winced as he looked over the sales charts. The trend lines were not good. Something had to be done to improve the long-term prospects of Southgate; but what?

BACKGROUND

Southgate Mall was located in Bigtown, Westernstate. Bigtown, population about 3 million, was a fairly typical Sunbelt urban area sprawled over approximately 80 square miles. Southgate was one of six major shopping centers, in addition to a host of strip malls and stand-alone big-box stores (Bigtown had no true downtown shopping area). Southgate wasn't the largest mall, or the most upscale, but it had numerous major national chains as anchor tenants, and a wide range of specialty shops.

The location of Southgate had both pluses and minuses. On the one hand, it was relatively centrally located, and near two major freeway intersections. This meant that a substantial fraction of Bigtown's population was within a reasonable driving distance of Southgate Mall. On the other hand, unlike Northgate, which was located just beyond the outermost freeway ring, such that it was the only reasonably close mall for several hundred thousand residents in the northern reaches of Bigtown, Southgate was situated not too far from three other major malls. This meant that except for those living in its immediate vicinity, almost any customer who was within a reasonable distance of Southgate was also located close to one, two, or even three other malls.

Its location meant that Southgate had to compete hard for both customers and retail tenants. Getting and keeping good retail tenants was one of the keys to attracting individual customers (referred to as "patrons"). But in turn a high, steady traffic volume of patrons from attractive demographics was the key to signing up new retail tenants.

All the major malls in Bigtown endured steady turnover in their crop of small specialty stores. And there was rarely a year that didn't see the lease held by some large anchor store expire, or become available for some other reason (consolidation, bankruptcy, etc.). As a result, the malls competed for new and replacement tenants and generally had ample capacity that needed to be filled. A few empty storefronts and "opening soon" signs were expected in any mall. But there was a tipping point, in John's view. Too many unoccupied storefronts tended to make individual patrons uneasy—no one wanted to be the regular patron of a "loser" shopping area with limited selection, and on the way to going down the tubes. That did not make for an enjoyable shopping experience.

Because of the extent of retailer turnover, and the need to keep the mall populated with stores, a primary task of the senior management of Southgate Mall was signing up new and replacement retailers. The major malls all had good locations, and all were competitive in the eyes of potential retail tenants. In making a selection, the negotiators for the national retail chains tried to balance rent and other fees charged by a mall against the tangible and intangible advantages particular malls offered in terms of facilities, ambience, volume of traffic, and the particular demographics of each mall's patron mix.

Individual patrons were attracted to a specific mall by some mix of location, the particular stores present, general ambience, and perhaps a host of other factors; John wasn't entirely sure. In turn, while all retailers valued traffic volume, some retailers in addition sought out specific demographics, looking for large populations of teenage shoppers, or affluent female heads of household, and so forth.

SOUTHGATE BUSINESS MODEL

Southgate followed a model common in commercial real estate. The land and facilities were financed by a large mortgage; internal operational costs consisted largely of maintenance and upkeep. "External" operations such as marketing were handled by the small management group reporting to Mr. Rastor, so this part of the operational budget consisted of a few salaries plus advertising and promotional expenditures.

On the revenue side, the bulk consisted of rental and lease payments by retail tenants. These were fixed for a period of years. Most retail tenants opted for a somewhat lower monthly rent in return for obligating themselves to pay in addition a small percentage of gross

(Continued)

(Continued)

sales to Southgate, if and when their sales exceeded a certain baseline. Essentially, if times were tough for the retailer, with sales stuck at a modest level, they would owe only the base rent and nothing more to Southgate. If traffic was heavy, or customer purchases were substantial, then the retailer made real money, and also paid some of it as bonus payments to Southgate. In short, both Southgate and its tenants shared a desire to attract high levels of traffic and free-spending patrons.

From Southgate's perspective, when slack capacity was kept under control (i.e., 85%+ of space was occupied by a functioning retail tenant), and all retailers had so-so years, then the mortgage would get paid and essential expenditures covered, but there would be little left to declare as profit. For Southgate to actually make money, and achieve its target return on equity capital, the mall had to be particularly full (93–96% was the practical maximum) and/or a good number of retailers had to be having a good year. The most profitable years in recent Southgate history had been those where the mall was reasonably close to maximum occupancy and large numbers of retailers had high traffic volume, hence made bonus payments to Southgate. These fat years had to cover the inevitable lean years to be expected when the national economy turned down.

THE PROBLEM

John Rastor looked again at the sales charts, which showed total receipts for each of the major malls in Bigtown. They all trended up, including Southgate, over the 10-year span. But it was clear that Southgate was slowly falling behind the three malls located closest to it. Where Southgate sales had generally ranked #1 or #2 within this set five years ago, in the last two years Southgate had been #1 only once or twice, was regularly #3, and once or twice had been dead last. The changes were small (all the malls were closely matched in terms of revenue), but John knew that if he could notice, so would his equity investors. Those guys watched every basis point of ROE like a hawk!

And that was another problem: Although return on equity had remained above the minimum required (i.e., the level below which he would be hauled in front of the board to explain), it too showed a downward slope when plotted quarterly over the past five years. Something had to be done—but what?

THE PROPOSAL

His thoughts wandered back to a family dinner last month and the conversation he'd had with his nephew Tim, a college student in the political science department at the local state university. With the confidence of youth Tim had told him, "Uncle, you need to take a poll of your customers. Find out who they are and what it would take to make them visit your mall more often. Look, it's not that hard. Just go to one of the sites that offer free web surveys."

But did Southgate need a survey of customers? Was that the solution, or even part of the solution? Southgate hadn't done much market research since the initial studies that had led to the selection years ago of Bigtown as an attractive market to enter, and the follow-on studies that had determined its location within Bigtown. (Several of the investors owned multiple malls across the country; retail commercial real estate was their primary business, and they put a lot of effort into selecting new mall locations.) So there certainly was an opportunity to learn more about Southgate's actual and potential patrons.

But what problem was he trying to solve anyway? The board had hiked the minimum base rent for new store tenants 18 months ago, which hadn't made it any easier to attract new stores. Bigtown itself wasn't growing as rapidly as before, so maybe it was unrealistic to expect the same kind of ROE as years ago. Along with the rent hike, the board had cut back on remodeling and refurbishment expenditures. Maybe the premises were looking a little outdated, even though spic-and-span clean? ("Keep the janitors, lose the carpenters" had been heard at the board meeting. "Design and merchandising is the responsibility of individual retailers—our job is to keep the mall scrubbed clean and keep the hidden infrastructure, like wiring, in good working order.") Advertising had been cut back too; maybe Southgate needed to get the word out. Or was that the retailers' job?

He saw it was 6:15 p.m. and began to pack his briefcase for the drive home. "Time to sleep on it," he thought.

INDEX

———•◆•———

ABOUT THE AUTHOR

—•◆•—

Edward F. McQuarrie is a professor in the Department of Marketing, Leavey School of Business, Santa Clara University, in California's Silicon Valley. He received his PhD in social psychology from the University of Cincinnati in 1985 and a BA in psychology and literature from The Evergreen State College in 1976.

His research interests include market research appropriate to technology products, on the one hand, and advertising strategies that call on rhetoric, narrative, and semiotic resources on the other. He has also written the book *Customer Visits: Building a Better Market Focus*, co-edited the volume *Go Figure! New Directions in Advertising Rhetoric*, and published articles in the *Journal of Consumer Research, Journal of Advertising, Marketing Theory, Journal of Consumer Psychology, Journal of the Market Research Society, Journal of Advertising Research*, and the *Journal of Product Innovation Management*, among others. For a current list of publications, you can access his profile on scholar.google.com or researchgate.net.

He was associate dean for Assessment at the Leavey School of Business, 2001–2010, responsible for the assessment of learning outcomes and the evaluation of teaching. He was associate dean for Graduate Studies, 1996–2000, responsible for the MBA and Executive MBA programs.

Professor McQuarrie began moderating focus groups in 1980 for Burke Marketing Research. He has consulted for a variety of technology firms and has taught seminars on effective customer visits, managing focus group research, marketing research methods, and similar topics for the Management Roundtable, Hewlett-Packard, Sun Microsystems, Microsoft, Apple Computer, Tektronix, Varian Associates, Cadence Design, and other clients, in England, Germany, and New Zealand as well as the United States.

⑤SAGE video

We are delighted to announce the launch of a streaming video program at SAGE!

SAGE Video online collections are developed in partnership with leading academics, societies and practitioners, including many of SAGE's own authors and academic partners, to deliver cutting-edge pedagogical collections mapped to curricular needs.

Available alongside our book and reference collections on the *SAGE Knowledge* platform, content is delivered with critical online functionality designed to support scholarly use.

SAGE Video combines originally commissioned and produced material with licensed videos to provide a complete resource for students, faculty, and researchers.

NEW IN 2015!

Counseling and Psychotherapy
Education

• Media and Communication

**sagepub.com/video
sagevideo**

⑤.SAGE | **50** YEARS